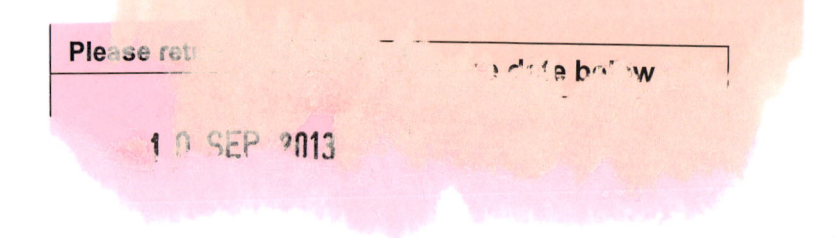

for Eleanor

Popular Music And Television In Britain

Edited by

IAN INGLIS
University of Northumbria, UK

ASHGATE

Published by
Ashgate Publishing Limited
Wey Court East
Union Road
Farnham
Surrey, GU9 7PT
England

Ashgate Publishing Company
Suite 420
101 Cherry Street
Burlington
VT 05401-4405
USA

www.ashgate.com

British Library Cataloguing in Publication Data
Popular music and television in Britain. – (Ashgate popular and folk music series)
  1. Television and popular music – Great Britain – History.
  2. Television broadcasting of music – Great Britain – History.
  3. Television music – Great Britain – History and criticism.
  I. Series II. Inglis, Ian, 1948–
  302.2'345–dc22

Library of Congress Cataloging-in-Publication Data
Popular music and television in Britain / [edited by] Ian Inglis.
    p. cm.—(Ashgate popular and folk music series)
  Includes bibliographical references and index.
  ISBN 978-0-7546-6864-0 (hardcover : alk. paper) — ISBN 978-1-4094-1958-7 (ebook)
  1. Television and music—Great Britain. 2. Popular music—Great Britain—History and criticism. 3. Television music—Great Britain—History and criticism. I. Inglis, Ian, 1948–

  ML68.P66 2010
  781.640941—dc22

                                                                    2010025098

ISBN 9780754668640 (hbk)
ISBN 9781409419587 (ebk)

Bach musicological font developed by © Yo Tomita.

Mixed Sources
Product group from well-managed forests and other controlled sources
www.fsc.org Cert no. SA-COC-1565
© 1996 Forest Stewardship Council
FSC

Printed and bound in Great Britain by
MPG Books Group, UK

Contents

List of Tables   vii
Notes on Contributors   ix
General Editor's Preface   xiii

Introduction   1
Ian Inglis

PART I   HISTORY AND HERITAGE

1   Constructing The Histories Of Popular Music:
    The *Britannia* Series   11
    Paul Long and Tim Wall

2   Television Documentary, Pop Stardom And Auto/Biographical
    Narratives   27
    Ian Goode

3   *Classic Albums*: The Re-Presentation Of The Rock Album On
    British Television   41
    Andy Bennett and Sarah Baker

4   Stone Fox Chase: *The Old Grey Whistle Test* And The Rise Of
    High Pop Television   55
    Peter Mills

PART II   PERFORMERS AND PERFORMANCES

5   *Ready Steady Go!* Televisual Pop Style And The Careers Of
    Dusty Springfield, Cilla Black, Sandie Shaw And Lulu   71
    Adrienne Lowy

6   Sworn In: *Today*, Bill Grundy And The Sex Pistols   85
    Mark Duffett

7   Indie On The Box: The Contribution Of Television To UK
    Independent Music From *C86* To Britpop   105
    Rupa Huq

PART III   COMEDY AND DRAMA

8   *Dad's Army*: Musical Images Of A Nation At War   123
        Sheila Whiteley

9   Little Ladies: *Rock Follies* And British Television's Dramatisation
        Of Rock Music   137
        Peter Hutchings

10   Pop Half-Cocked: A History Of *Revolver*   149
        Richard Mills

11   A Sunken Dream: Music And The Gendering Of Nostalgia In
        Life On Mars   161
        Estella Tincknell

PART IV   AUDIENCES AND TERRITORIES

12   Here, There And Everywhere: Introducing The Beatles   179
        Ian Inglis

13   Granada TV, Johnny Hamp, And *The Blues And Gospel Train*:
        Masters Of Reality   197
        Mike Brocken

14   A Postman Mans Up: The Changing Musical Identities Of
        Postman Pat   213
        Nicholas Reyland

Bibliography   231
Index   243

List of Tables

12.1   The Beatles' UK Television Appearances 1962–63   185

14.1   Tagg's Hypothesised Dualities Of Male And Female Scoring
       Clichés   219

14.2   *Postman Pat* Main Title Shots And Sound Effects Density   220

Notes on Contributors

Sarah Baker is Lecturer in Cultural Sociology at Griffith University in Queensland, Australia. She has previously held research positions at the University of Leeds and the Open University, and was an ARC Research Fellow at the University of South Australia. She is the author of *Creative Labour* (with David Hesmondhalgh) and an editor of the *Journal Of Sociology*.

Andy Bennett is Professor of Cultural Sociology and Director of the Centre for Public Culture & Ideas at Griffith University in Queensland, Australia. He has authored and edited numerous books including *Popular Music And Youth Culture*, *Remembering Woodstock* and *Music Scenes: Local, Trans-Local And Virtual* (with Richard A. Peterson). He is Editor-in-Chief of the *Journal Of Sociology* and a Faculty Associate of the Center for Cultural Sociology at Yale University.

Mike Brocken is Senior Lecturer in Popular Music Studies at Liverpool Hope University. His books include *The British Folk Revival 1944–2002, Bacharach: Maestro! The Life Of A Pop Genius* and *Other Voices: Hidden Histories Of Liverpool's Popular Music Scenes 1930s–1970s*. He hosted his own series – *Brock'n'Roll* – for nine years on BBC Radio Merseyside, and he is the director of Liverpool Hope's MA in The Beatles, Popular Music & Society, the first postgraduate degree devoted to the music and career of the Beatles.

Mark Duffett is Senior Lecturer in Media and Cultural Studies at the University of Chester. After completing an MA on the Canadian music industry, he worked briefly for Sony Music. His doctoral research explored the relationship between Elvis Presley and his fans, and his published research, in journals such as *Popular Music, Information Communication & Society, Convergence* and *Popular Music And Society*, includes articles on webcasting, heckling, fandom, and gender.

Ian Goode teaches Film and Television Studies at the University of Glasgow. His current research interests and publications focus on non-fiction and documentary television, and he is also developing a project on the history of rural cinema in Scotland.

Rupa Huq is Senior Lecturer in Sociology at Kingston University, having previously practised DJing at various live music venues. She is the author of *Beyond Subculture: Pop, Youth And Identity In A Postcolonial World*, and is currently preparing a book on socio-political shifts in contemporary suburbia. Her research interests include youth culture, ethnicity, and Islamic identities.

Peter Hutchings is Professor of Film Studies at the University of Northumbria. His books include *Hammer And Beyond: The British Horror Film*; *Terence Fisher*; *The British Film Guide To Dracula*; *The Horror Film*; and *The Historical Dictionary Of Horror Cinema*. He has also published widely on topics relating to British cinema, and genre theory and criticism.

Ian Inglis is Reader in Popular Music Studies at the University of Northumbria. His books include *The Beatles, Popular Music And Society: A Thousand Voices*; *Popular Music And Film*; *Performance And Popular Music: History, Place And Time*; and *The Words And Music Of George Harrison*.

Paul Long is Senior Lecturer in Media and Cultural Theory at Birmingham City University. His research interests encompass the creative and cultural industries, popular music culture, media histories, and archiving. He is the author of *Only In The Common People: The Aesthetics Of Class In Post-War Britain* and the co-author (with Tim Wall) of *Media Studies: Texts, Production And Context*. He is currently overseeing the development of the archive of the BBC documentarist Philip Donnellan, and co-editing his autobiography.

Adrienne Lowy is a researcher and writer whose doctoral thesis explored the inter-relations between pop music, television and fashion, through the television work of Dusty Springfield, Cilla Black, Sandie Shaw and Lulu. During her lengthy academic career in the School of Art & Design at Liverpool John Moores University, she also worked extensively as a freelance fashion journalist for consumer and trade publications, and as a marketing and public relations consultant to the fashion industry.

Peter Mills is Senior Lecturer in Media and Popular Culture at Leeds Metropolitan University. He was the singer and lyricist for the band Innocents Abroad, who made two albums, *Quaker City* and *Eleven*. He is the author of *Hymns To The Silence: Inside The Music And Lyrics Of Van Morrison*, and was a substantial contributor to the various editions of *The Rough Guide To Rock*. He has published work on Samuel Beckett, Olaf Stapledon, Hungarian folk music, Pink Floyd, national anthems, and The KLF, and has taught music, literature and philosophy at universities in the UK, Hungary, Romania and Croatia.

Richard Mills is Programme Director in Cultural Studies at St Mary's University College, London. He has taught at the University of Ulster, the University of Lodz, Liverpool John Moores University, and Goldsmiths College, London. His research interests are in Irish literature and popular culture, and his work has appeared in *Irish Studies Review*, *Writing Ulster* and *New Voices In Irish Criticism*.

Nicholas Reyland is Lecturer in Music at Keele University. His primary research interests are Witold Lutosławski and Polish music, musical narrativity, film/ television music, music theory and analysis. His articles have been published in *Music & Letters* and *Witold Lutoslawski Studies*, and he contributed several entries to *New Makers Of Modern Culture*. He is currently writing *Zbigniew Preisner's Three Colours Trilogy: A Film Score Guide*, and is the co-author (with Alexandra Lamont) of a study of sound and vision in modern children's television.

Estella Tincknell is Reader in Media and Cultural Studies at the University of the West of England. She has published widely in the area of popular culture and film, and is the author of *Mediating The Family: Gender, Culture And Representation*, co-editor (with Ian Conrich) of *Film's Musical Moments*, and joint author (with Deborah Chambers, Richard Johnson and Parvati Raghuram) of *The Practice Of Cultural Studies*. She is currently writing a book about the films of Jane Campion, and preparing an edited collection of essays about *Ageing Femininities*.

Tim Wall is Professor of Radio and Popular Music Studies, and Director of Media and Cultural Research, at Birmingham City University. His research ranges across popular music culture, the record industry, music radio, and the implications of new technology. He is author of *Studying Popular Music Culture* and the co-author of *Media Studies: Texts, Production And Context*. He has published work on a wide range of topics including jazz, northern soul, 1950s dance fads, music programming, internet radio, the significance of the transistor radio, and is currently working (with Paul Long) on a major project about television's representation of popular music's past.

Sheila Whiteley is Emeritus Professor of Popular Music at the University of Salford. As a feminist musicologist with strong research interests in issues of identity and subjectivity, she is known for her work on gender and sexuality, as well as for longstanding interests in popular culture. She is the author of *The Space Between The Notes: Rock And The Counter Culture*; *Women And Popular Music: Popular Music And Gender*; and *Too Much Too Young: Popular Music, Age And Identity*. She is the editor of *Sexing The Groove: Popular Music And Gender* and *Christmas, Ideology And Popular Culture*, and co-editor (with Andy Bennett and Stan Hawkins) of *Music Space And Place: Popular Music And Cultural Identity* and (with Jennifer Rycenga) of *Queering the Popular Pitch*.

General Editor's Preface

The upheaval that occurred in musicology during the last two decades of the twentieth century has created a new urgency for the study of popular music alongside the development of new critical and theoretical models. A relativistic outlook has replaced the universal perspective of modernism (the international ambitions of the 12-note style); the grand narrative of the evolution and dissolution of tonality has been challenged, and emphasis has shifted to cultural context, reception and subject position. Together, these have conspired to eat away at the status of canonical composers and categories of high and low in music. A need has arisen, also, to recognize and address the emergence of crossovers, mixed and new genres, to engage in debates concerning the vexed problem of what constitutes authenticity in music and to offer a critique of musical practice as the product of free, individual expression.

Popular musicology is now a vital and exciting area of scholarship, and the *Ashgate Popular and Folk Music Series* presents some of the best research in the field. Authors are concerned with locating musical practices, values and meanings in cultural context, and draw upon methodologies and theories developed in cultural studies, semiotics, poststructuralism, psychology and sociology. The series focuses on popular musics of the twentieth and twenty-first centuries. It is designed to embrace the world's popular musics from Acid Jazz to Zydeco, whether high tech or low tech, commercial or non-commercial, contemporary or traditional.

Professor Derek B. Scott
Professor of Critical Musicology
University of Leeds

Introduction

Ian Inglis

When, in 1981, MTV's president Tom Preston explained the success of the newly-formed channel by commenting that it had merely brought together two of the world's favourite leisure pursuits (watching television and listening to music) it was, for many people, a statement of the obvious. But, while the immediate impact and enduring popularity of MTV (and the many similar channels that followed) have made explicit the dynamic nature of the connections between the two forms, music television is, in truth, only a small part of a much broader historical trajectory that stretches back to the birth of television itself.

Indeed, whatever the range of its transmission or the size of its audience, British television has, from its outset, recognised and used the popular music of the day – most obviously in its performative functions. BBC-TV's first public broadcast, from London's Alexandra Palace on 26 August 1936, began with the music of Duke Ellington, accompanied onscreen by a caption card that announced 'BBC Demonstration to Radiolympia by the Baird System'. In the half-hour variety show that followed, the first performer to appear was vocalist Helen McKay, singing 'Here's Looking At You'; the transmission was watched by several hundred viewers, mainly in the London area. The launch of ITV, two decades later, followed a similar pattern. After coverage of the opening ceremony from London's Guildhall on 22 September 1955, the channel's first programme was simply called *Variety*: introduced by singer, bandleader and radio-DJ Jack Jackson, it featured singers Shirley Abicair and Sheila Matthews, and the Billy Cotton Orchestra. It was watched in around 100,000 homes in the South East of England. Thirty years after that, a total audience of more than of 1.5 billion in 160 countries across 24 time-zones tuned in, at some point, during the 16-hour *Live Aid* concerts, broadcast jointly from Wembley Stadium, London and JFK Stadium, Philadelphia, on 13 July 1985. And on 24 August 2008, 778 million viewers watched together as Jimmy Page and Leona Lewis (the winner of ITV's *The X Factor* in 2006) performed Led Zeppelin's 'Whole Lotta Love' during the closing ceremony of the 2008 Olympic Games in Beijing. In theory and in practice, pop and rock have contributed much to, and benefited greatly from, the historical development of television in the UK. And, as popular music and popular musicians enter non-performance based areas of TV production and programming from which they have previously been largely absent,[1] it seems logical to predict that the relationship between the two mediums will continue to expand in future years.

---

[1]   See, for example, Bethany Klein, *As Heard On TV: Popular Music In Advertising* (Aldershot, 2009).

Commenting on the persistent interplay between music, audience and media technology, Wikstrom has noted that:

> Music is an integral part of most media. Movies, radio, videogames and television all depend on music as the core or the enhancement of their products [and] the music industry is completely dependent on the media, as a promoter, user and distributor of its products.[2]

And although there has been an expanding interest in the associations between popular music and film, which has led to a substantial number of important contributions by British researchers in recent years,[3] there have been relatively few concentrated investigations of the relationship between music and TV.[4]

This is, to say the least, surprising. Given the rapid, and parallel, evolution of television and popular music in the UK through the 1950s and early 1960s (as cultural forms and domestic industries), the number and variety of television outputs that consistently make use of popular music (entertainment, drama, documentary, advertisements), the commercial value of TV exposure (as shown by the impetus to new careers and the resurrection of old careers that frequently follow television appearances), and the importance of television as a principal source of contact between audiences and performers (especially since the advent of music video and the explosion of music channels on satellite and digital TV), an analysis of the opportunities and reciprocities that exist between the two mediums is, clearly, long overdue.

The chapters in this book attempt to supply an initial version of such an analysis. They reflect current research, provide indicative contributions to what remains a somewhat sparse academic literature, and may stimulate further investigations. The focus throughout is on British television and, for the most part, British popular music. Although the form and content of both have been heavily influenced by American models (notably in their formative stages) the intention here is to demonstrate the particular routes along which television in the UK has actively sought to incorporate, organise and distribute information about, and images of, popular music – often in unique and groundbreaking ways – rather than

---

[2]   Patrik Wikstrom, *The Music Industry* (Cambridge, 2009), p. 85.

[3]   See, for example, John Mundy, *Popular Music On Screen* (Manchester, 1999); Kay Dickinson (ed.), *Movie Music: The Film Reader* (London, 2003); Ian Inglis (ed.), *Popular Music And Film* (London, 2003); K.J. Donnelly, *The Spectre Of Sound* (London, 2005); Steve Lannin and Matthew Caley (eds), *Pop Fiction: The Song In Cinema* (Bristol, 2005); Ian Conrich and Estella Tincknell (eds), *Film's Musical Moments* (Edinburgh, 2006); Kay Dickinson, *Off Key: When Film And Music Won't Work Together* (Oxford, 2008).

[4]   *Popular Music* 21/3 (2002) contained discussions of music (of all kinds) and (international) television; *Music, Sound And The Moving Image* (published since 2007) takes a similarly broad approach, considering music and sound in television, film, computer games, mixed-media installations, digital art, etc.

merely imitate transatlantic tastes and styles. While the 'international' dimensions attached to assessments of television and popular music are rightly seen as key facets of their production and consumption – indeed, they have consistently been depicted as important elements in the process of globalisation[5] – their status as domestic cultural products and practices is too often overlooked, and the book aims, in part, to redress that balance.

The book is organised into four broad sections, each of which illustrates a familiar area of TV programming. *History And Heritage* examines various facets of British television's documentation and representation of popular music history. In the first chapter, Paul Long and Tim Wall present a critical analysis of BBC's prestigious *Britannia* series which, since 2005, has endeavoured to tell the definitive story of the evolution of specific musical genres and related cultural activities. Their assessment concludes that although there is much to admire in the programmes, television's desire to produce a single, authoritative version of history often results in a 'closed narrative' in which complexities are avoided, contradictions are conveniently negotiated, and alternative interpretations are unheard. To the extent that *Britannia*'s historical accounts are shaped more by the policies and practices of television than by musical experience and insights, the stories they relate are not inaccurate, but they are incomplete. Ian Goode examines the current popularity of (auto)biographical TV documentaries about individual pop/rock stars. Growing out of the emergence of reality television, the cult of celebrity, and the demands of a highly competitive industrial arena, such programmes purport to offer exclusive insights into the 'real' or 'true' story of the stars they feature. However, he suggests that one of the key determinants in the presentation of their stories is the degree of control exerted by the star subject upon the film makers. As a result, the articulations of self are often centred around self-presentation, self-narration and self-promotion. They reflect, and contribute to, levels and stages of stardom in popular music, and pose important questions about the increasingly dispersed functions of documentary and non-fiction television. Andy Bennett and Sarah Baker consider the contribution made by BBC's *Classic Albums* series to the concept of 'heritage' (and the growth of a heritage industry) that underpins a considerable part of television's approach to popular music. They argue that, in the context of the series, the appellation 'classic' has emotional and cultural repercussions that go far beyond the mere evaluation of a collection of songs; it invites an investment in, and identification with, musical artefacts that may become as important for the producers and consumers of given albums as it is for the critical discourse that surrounds the historical development of rock. Finally, in this section, Peter Mills provides an assessment of the importance of BBC's *The Old Grey Whistle Test*. By choosing to ignore the commercial vagaries

[5]   See, for example, Serge Latouche, *The Westernization Of The World* (Cambridge, 1996); Daya Kishan Thussu, *International Communication: Continuity And Change* (London, 2000); Terry Flew, *Understanding Global Media* (London, 2007); Thomas L. McPhail, *Global Communication* (Chichester: Wiley-Blackwell, 2010).

of chart success, and pursuing a musical agenda derived from notions of 'cultural connoisseurship', the programme succeeded unequivocally in establishing itself as the 'serious' face of popular music on television in Britain. Its historical importance is twofold: musically, it reflected the sense of 'maturity' increasingly attributed to popular music (and the division between 'pop' and 'rock') in the late 1960s and early 1970s; televisually, it created a continuing legacy for subsequent programmes, built around understandings of 'liveness' and 'authenticity'.

The second section, *Performers And Performances*, presents a series of illuminating case studies that explore the importance of specific programmes in the careers of particular musicians. Adrienne Lowy's account of ITV's *Ready Steady Go!* focuses on the contours of music, dance, design and fashion that provided the site from which Dusty Springfield, Cilla Black, Sandie Shaw and Lulu constructed their iconic TV images and launched their musical careers. Its innovative studio environment, active audience involvement and informal mode of presentation helped to create an immediate, and unique, correspondence of televisual and musical styles, that not only informed the personae of the four performers throughout their careers, but provided a template that many other TV music shows have sought to emulate. Mark Duffett's investigation of the origins and repercussions of the Sex Pistols' appearance on ITV's *Today* news magazine programme demonstrates that the significance of television in determining the careers of popular musicians is not limited to their participation in music shows. While their interview with Bill Grundy (and the media response to it) created an exaggerated and sensationalised wave of national outrage, it also introduced the group to many millions of viewers and defined the (sub)cultural and behavioural dimensions of punk in succinct and simplistic ways. But rather than merely relate the events, Duffett disentangles the 'meanings' inherent in the (non-musical) performance – as a historical narrative of the 1970s, as a piece of television footage, and as an encounter to which we, as contemporary viewers, can return. In Chapter 7, Rupa Huq traces television's portrayal of indie music in the 1980s through to the emergence of Britpop in the 1990s. Against a background of broadcasting deregulation, political change, technological innovation and a rebirth of cultural regionalism, much of the public's perception of the transition from the perceived austerity of indie bands to the unashamed ostentation of Britpop's star performers was coloured by the presentations, and re-presentations, provided by television. Within this complex musical-historical context, her discussion of the Smiths offers a compelling assessment of a band whose conscious refusal to adopt the conventional vehicle of music television (the music video) in favour of live, studio-based performance allowed them to occupy a distinctive, if uneasy, position as visual and musical stylists.

The chapters in *Comedy And Drama* explore the ways in which popular music has become an integral, almost indispensable, feature of TV entertainment, either as soundtrack or as subject. Sheila Whiteley documents the importance of the musical content in what is perhaps Britain's best-loved comedy series, BBC's long-running *Dad's Army*. Produced and broadcast in the 1960s and 1970s (and frequently repeated in subsequent decades) the series employed the popular music of the 1930s and 1940s in its evocation of day-to-day life in wartime Britain. She shows that in addition to providing appropriate incidental links, the music also performs powerful ideological functions. Blending humour, nostalgia and optimism in its re-creation of an era beyond the memory of many of its viewers, *Dad's Army* used songs from that period to effectively communicate an impression of national identity that had equal resonance within the fictitious world of the Home Guard in Walmington-on-Sea and in the emotional responses of its contemporary audiences. Peter Hutchings examines one of the few British television drama series set within the world of contemporary rock. ITV's *Rock Follies*, which related the fictional story of the Little Ladies over twelve episodes in 1976–77, remains one of the most distinctive programmes of its type. Not only were its downbeat realism and televisual style in sharp contrast with the glamorous escapism that characterised much of cinema's conventional exploitation of popular music, but its emphasis on female performers and their friendships produced a more complex treatment of notions of authenticity, talent and ambition than was apparent in many male-centred movies. Although its apparent engagement with politics may have been stylised, understated and ambiguous, it identified rock music as a dramatic setting from which to comment on broader social and cultural trends, and justified it as an agent of personal and political resistance. Furthermore, its reliance on original songs composed especially for the series allowed those tracks to be integrated into the narrative in an unusually evocative manner. In Chapter 10, Richard Mills offers an evaluation of the relatively unknown and defiantly individual *Revolver*, which ran for just eight programmes on ITV in 1978. Starring the satirical comedian Peter Cook as the manager of a decaying and disreputable club, the show presented live bands who performed to an audience inside the fictitious venue, while Cook made racist and sexist jokes about the musicians, delivered a string of abusive comments about their music, and maintained a sarcastic and insensitive contempt for his customers. Mills suggests that *Revolver*'s unorthodox blend of postmodern irony, political satire, contemporary music and commercial cynicism was unfamiliar to the producers and consumers of television comedy, and led directly to its failure. It provides a telling example of the difficulties faced by programme-makers who wish to present popular music in innovative ways. Moreover, in its combination of parody, self-parody and pastiche, it can be seen to offer a less polished, unglamorous version of the storytelling devices used in such films as *The Rutles: All You Need Is Cash* (Eric Idle and Gary Weis, 1978) and *This Is Spinal Tap* (Rob Reiner, 1984). Estella Tincknell provides a concentrated assessment of the musical components of the hugely successful *Life On Mars*, whose innovative portrayal of a contemporary policeman propelled back in time from the first decade of the twenty-first century to the alien surroundings of Britain in the early 1970s provided the narrative context for a series that explored the cultural and political tensions between 'tradition' and 'modernity'. The series effectively used the popular music of the day for the exposition of dramatic tension and as an ironic commentary on the central character's emotions as he struggled to come to terms with the personal and professional dynamics of his new surroundings. However, she suggests that in pursuit of its 'realist' intentions, the show's radical possibilities were potentially disrupted by an underlying nostalgia for a 'lost' form of working-class masculinity and male solidarity that was significantly reinforced by a soundtrack which was predominantly white, male, and genre-specific.

The book's final section, *Audiences And Territories*, investigates the provision of popular music for specific target audiences and within discrete geographical and cultural boundaries. Ian Inglis re-assesses the importance of their early TV appearances in the career of the Beatles. The common version of the group's history emphasises the significance of a small number of prime-time, nationally-transmitted entertainment and variety shows towards the end of 1963 that suddenly alerted the country to the Beatles and their music, and created the conditions for their spectacular breakthrough and the onset of Beatlemania. However, he argues that they had, in fact, achieved a substantial popularity long before those appearances, largely as a result of their willingness to participate in a steady round of regional television appearances through 1962 and 1963 (often very brief, and in off-peak viewing hours) that included slots on children's shows and news magazine programmes – neither of which were aimed at audiences obviously associated with the consumption of popular music.

In Chapter 13, Mike Brocken considers the production in 1964 by Granada (one of ITV's original regional companies) of *The Blues And Gospel Train*. He contends that the Manchester-based company was particularly well-equipped to present the pioneering, 40-minute special, which showcased many of North America's leading blues musicians, at such a time because of its political commitment, its creative ethic, its strong regional identity, and the singular presence of the influential producer Johnny Hamp whose knowledge of musical cultures and tastes was evidenced by the number of jazz, blues, gospel, pop, and rock'n'roll TV specials he produced for Granada in the 1960s. In addition, the visual imagery employed in the programme challenged (stereo)typical patterns of music and race, and contributed to a broader social debate about regional community, cultural geography and the role of television. Finally, Nick Reyland provides a fascinating, and detailed, analysis of the manner in which plot and character developments in the children's stop-motion animation series *Postman Pat* have been paralleled by changes to its musical score. From its first appearance on BBC in 1981, the programme's central character has undergone four distinct incarnations, moving gradually from a placid, good-natured, village postman to an all-action hero. The musical changes have been no less startling: the gentle, folk-pop ballad of the earlier episodes has been replaced by an approach which mixes elements of hard rock with Britpop sensibilities, and there have been significant increases in the density of sound effects. Overall, Reyland demonstrates how *Postman Pat*'s associations between musical identity and televisual identity work to supply its young viewers with musically-mediated stories that introduce them to a set of ideological roles and stances.

As a child, I sat cross-legged on the floor, surrounded by members of my extended family, watching black-and-white pictures (that were likely to disappear completely if any other electrical appliances in the home were in use) on a small, square screen, contained within a bulky wooden cabinet in the corner of the living-room. Today, I watch high-definition, colour images (often pre-recorded or remotely-programmed) on a large, flat, wide screen from the comfort of an armchair, while my own children watch online or streamed programmes in their own bedrooms. Television-viewing as a domestic activity has been re-modelled in recent decades; how, when, and where we watch TV has changed significantly. At the same time, the way in which we listen to music has overcome the restrictions of time and space imposed by the transistor radio, the jukebox and the record player. The variety, availability and accessibility of popular music have been transformed by a string of new technologies that store and deliver music in alternative ways (the audio-cassette recorder in 1963, the Sony Walkman in 1979, the compact disc in 1982, Napster in 1999, the iPod in 2001). Despite these developments, the role of television as a vehicle through which exposure to popular music is facilitated, and ideas about it are generated and circulated has never been more vibrant, as the success of shows like *The X Factor* (ITV, 2004–) and *Britain's Got Talent* (ITV, 2007–), both of which reach end-of-series audiences of nearly 20 million (63 per cent of the viewing public), clearly demonstrates. Furthermore, its influence has extended into the routine aesthetics of live performance, as increasingly flamboyant stage presentations attempt to satisfy expectations of visual (as well as musical) entertainment from audiences accustomed to the extravagant imagery of much music video. The significance of popular music's proven ability to embellish programmes, provide new topics for documentary investigation, and attract and retain audiences has become a central component of television production, and the chapters that follow supply a wide-ranging assessment of those reciprocal patterns of interest, involvement and interaction.

PART I
History And Heritage

Chapter 1

Constructing The Histories Of Popular Music: The *Britannia* Series

Paul Long and Tim Wall

Since the broadcast of *Jazz Britannia* in 2005, BBC-TV has produced several documentary series and one-off programmes about the history of musical genres and related cultural activities in the UK under the 'Britannia' label. These programmes include *Folk Britannia* (2006), *Soul Britannia* (2007), *Dance Britannia* (2007), *Pop Britannia* (2008), *Prog Rock Britannia* (2009), *Synth Britannia* (2009), *Blues Britannia* (2009) and *Heavy Metal Britannia* (2010). In the same stylistic vein, *Classic Britannia* (2008) ventured outside popular music forms and *Comics Britannia* (2007) extended the idea to print culture.

In this chapter, we explore the significance of these programmes within the context of the place of music on television. Notable for the manner in which they treat their subject matter, we suggest that as a whole the *Britannia* series represents a remarkable commitment of resources to music television under the guise of 'quality TV'. We explore this characteristic for what it tells us about the institutional context of production and the cultural politics of such programming. A key concern is with the approach to music taken in the series, and the way in which the various projects are worked through as historiography. Our examination reveals much that is original and innovative about the series, but also some continuing limitations attendant upon the relationship between popular music and television. This raises some questions about the project of the BBC as a public service broadcaster, and the expectations generated amongst the intended audiences for these series.

Quality Television And Music Programming

The issue of 'quality' has engendered much discussion among academics in television studies. Questions arising relate to problems of judgement and critical evaluation (or its avoidance); hierarchies of taste, consumption and power; conflicts between ideas of culture and commerce and the way in which ideas of quality inform broadcasting policy and regulation.[1] For television producers, markers of 'quality' are important aspects of brand identity and in market differentiation. This

---

[1]   See Charlotte Brunsdon, *Screen Tastes : Soap Opera To Satellite Dishes* (London, 1997); Mark Jancovich and James Lyons (eds), *Quality Popular Television: Cult*

sometimes results in a distancing from the traditional dismissal of TV as a mass-produced, culturally ephemeral medium. As one US channel's publicity claims, 'It's not television. It's HBO'.[2] In a similar vein, the BBC has a well-established (if contested) reputation for culturally valuable public service output, expressed most explicitly in the aim of its digital TV channel BBC4: 'to offer an intelligent alternative to programmes on the mainstream TV channels'.[3]

Launched in March 2002, BBC4 was the first of the Corporation's forays into the digital delivery of TV, 'establishing a reputation as an originator of high-quality, distinctive programming, proving it was possible to be both unashamedly intelligent yet stimulatingly pleasurable'.[4] In particular, the channel has been lauded for its strength in music programming. Peter Maniura, BBC's Head of Classical Music, and one of the people charged with formulating the channel's music policy, has said that his intention for BBC4 was to give airtime to music such as folk and jazz, genres not usually covered on 'mainstream' channels, in order to 'broaden the mix and give more depth and volume'.[5] Furthermore, Janice Hadlow, BBC4's original controller (2004–2008), has said that the channel aimed to challenge viewers: its goals in music programming are to 'allow people to enjoy what they know and love already, but also about introducing an intelligent and discerning audience to new and challenging music'.[6] Thus, the channel offers music-themed nights or extended seasons of music programming, 'acting as a testing ground for new approaches to music broadcasting'.[7]

Even within such a context, the various *Britannia* series offer a distinctive approach to music addressed to the intelligence and discernment of BBC4's intended audience. *Jazz Britannia* created a template for further series, with its three-part history of jazz in Britain narrated by actor Terence Stamp. Formally, the series draws upon an impressive wealth of archival research and uncovered material: clips from television, film and radio, still images, press cuttings, and original interviews with British jazz players from the post-war period. In addition, critics and chroniclers of the genre such as Val Wilmer and John Fordham are also employed to lend weight and perspective to the narrative focus and interpretation.

To date, a generous range of appreciative previews has heralded each series. These have served to highlight the programmes as instances of 'must-see' TV,

---

TV, The Industry And Fans (London, 2003); Jane McCabe and Kim Akass, *Quality TV: Contemporary American Television And Beyond* (London, 2007).

[2]   For a discussion, see Jane Feuer, 'HBO And The Concept Of Quality TV', in McCabe and Akass, *Quality TV*, pp. 145–57.

[3]   www.bbc.co.uk/bbcfour/faq/.

[4]   www.bbc.co.uk/pressoffice/biographies/biogs/controllers/janicehadlow.shtml.

[5]   Peter Maniura, quoted in 'The Insider: BBC4', *Music Week*, 13 August 2005: p. 16.

[6]   www.bbc.co.uk/pressoffice/biographies/biogs/controllers/janicehadlow.shtml.

[7]   Maniura, quoted in 'The Insider'.

aimed at both genre aficionados and other interested viewers. The care for the material and aesthetic flair in its treatment have been noted in each case: *The Times* trailed the *Classic Britannia* series in this way:

> It helps that for once a production team has really thought about how to illustrate orchestral music, as well as which items to choose. The result is the evocative blending of the post-war avant garde with other linking genres (particularly architecture and film), as well as a canny, deliberately over-exposed finish for the filming of orchestras themselves: bleached in black and white, the look is tremendously effective.[8]

Each series has been underlined as a significant event in the BBC schedule by a programme of synergistic live concerts at the Barbican, organised under each generic title. *Jazz Britannia* again established a precedent and format, featuring many of the artists who contributed to the series, including Michael Garrick, Soweto Kinch, Bobby Wellins, Stan Tracey, Courtney Pine, and DJ and label owner Gilles Peterson. Each of these live events was broadcast on BBC4 (and echoed in radio scheduling on Radio 2 or the digital Radio 6 Music) alongside repeats from the BBC TV vaults such as complete episodes from *Jazz 625* (1964–65) or compilations of available performances from series such as *Monitor* (1958–65), *Colour Me Pop* (1968–69) or *The Old Grey Whistle Test* (1971–87). The one-off *Synth Britannia* was followed in the following week's schedules by the documentary *Krautrock* (2009), a footnote on German electronica that was deemed to be an influence on the UK scene. Such programmes demonstrate some of the originating sources and contexts for material used in each *Britannia* series, thus offering an appendix of sorts in the wider BBC4 schedule for viewers.

Opportunities presented by new media have enhanced the wider dissemination and understanding of the *Britannia* series, underlining the intention to create 'event TV'. Matt Harvey, who oversees music posts on the BBC website, has claimed portentously that 'We don't just make programmes at the BBC, we make social objects – and social media is enhancing their power to affect people'. Blogs and forums generate widespread conversations around the content of the programmes, 'increasing their resonance as a social object'.[9] Harvey points to the conversations taking place through social media forms such as Twitter, where participants exchange memories, and suggestions for music playlists on other platforms like Spotify. Such activity extends the scope of each series to contributions from those who consume the music and who originally participated in the cultural events depicted.

---

[8]   Neil Fisher, 'Orchestral Manoeuvres', *The Times: Features*, 15 June 2007 p. 21.

[9]   Matt Harvey, 'Synth Britannia: Stuff About Stuff' (www.bbc.co.uk/blogs/bbcmusic/2009/10/synth_britannia_-stuff_about_st.html)

Television History And Popular Music

It has been noted that since the 1990s there has been an efflorescence of history programming on TV, which in turn has generated an equally prodigious corpus of academic analysis in response.[10] This television genre reflects the broader narrative styles and concerns of historiography, both popular and academic, from the traditional in tone and focus to innovative hybrids. Thus, the genre as it is made in the UK encompasses both Simon Schama's aim of telling stories in *History Of Britain* (BBC, 2000), Michael Wood's more exploratory style in *Conquistadors* (BBC, 2000) and *In Search Of Myths And Heroes* (BBC, 2005), as well as the jocular entertainment of *The Worst Jobs In History* (Channel 4, 2005–) and 'reality-history' programmes such as *1940s House* (Discovery, 2001).[11] We suggest that the BBC's *Britannia* series presents a significant extension of this genre in its project to treat popular music seriously, placing its practices, meanings, and attendant cultures as integral to contemporary social history.

There are some important precursors and contemporaries of the kinds of history offered in the *Britannia* series and its particular approach and positioning as 'quality TV'. The defining series in presenting the history of popular music on UK television is *All You Need Is Love* (ITV, 1976) written and directed by Tony Palmer. Palmer had previously directed theatrical opera performances, written about popular music for *The Observer*, and made numerous television documentaries about European art music. Produced for London Weekend Television, and running for nearly 15 hours over 17 episodes, the series used archive footage and original filmed material (including colour pieces), expert and musician interviews, to survey the origins and development of jazz and blues, vaudeville and Tin Pan Alley, American folk and country, rock and pop. To prepare for the series, Palmer commissioned essays from a wide range of knowledgeable commentators – including George Melly, Leonard Feather, Rudi Blesh, Paul Oliver, Jack Good, Humphrey Lyttelton, Derek Taylor, Stephen Sondheim, Nik Cohn and Charlie Gillett – but he formed and set the storyline himself, providing the key narration along with a range of experts on popular music.[12] He gave a particular emphasis to the importance of African-American and white folk forms,

---

[10]   For a summary of this growth see: Erin Bell, 'Televising History: The Past(s) On The Small Screen', *European Journal Of Cultural Studies*, 10/1 (2007), pp. 5–12. See also: Vivian Sobchak (ed.), *The Persistence Of History: Cinema, Television And The Modern Event* (London, 1996); Graham Roberts and Philip M Taylor (eds), *The Historian, Television And Television History* (Luton, 2001); David Cannadine (ed.), *History And The Media* (London, 2004).

[11]   On narrative styles in TV history, see: Erin Bell and Ann Gray, 'History On Television: Charisma, Narrative And Knowledge', *European Journal Of Cultural Studies* 10/1 (2007), pp. 113–33.

[12]   The essays are collected in Tony Palmer (ed.), *All You Need Is Love: The Story Of Popular Music* (New York, 1976).

and their exploitation by a capitalist music industry. Its style, narrative form and thesis remain an under-acknowledged and unexplored benchmark for the televised histories of pop that came after.

More recent programming includes a range of programmes made for the US Public Broadcast Service (PBS). These include the Martin Scorsese-produced *The Blues* (2003) and his treatise on Bob Dylan, *No Direction Home* (2005). Most important here is Ken Burns's series *Jazz* (2001) that, alongside his approach in other historical epics for PBS such as *The Civil War* (1990) and *Baseball* (1994), is an implicit reference point for the BBC series. Closer to home, it is appropriate to mention UK landmark series such as the Beatles' *Anthology* (ITV, 1995) and BBC's collaboration with VH-1 to produce *The Seven Ages Of Rock* (2007), which was first broadcast on the terrestrial BBC2. Outside television, we would situate this programming in relation to some notable successes in contemporary popular publishing, including Greil Marcus's *Like A Rolling Stone: Bob Dylan At The Crossroads* (2005), Jon Savage's work on punk rock in *England's Dreaming* (1991), his *Teenage: The Creation Of Youth* (2007), Ian MacDonald's *Revolution In The Head: The Beatles' Records And The Sixties* (1994) and Simon Reynolds' *Rip It Up And Start Again* (2005).

The television programmes cited above pay serious attention to popular culture, and are distinguished from the familiar ways in which popular music has generally featured in the medium. In a consideration of the relationship of these forms, Simon Frith has suggested that 'music is omnipresent on television, in short, but the television experience is rarely just about music'.[13] This sense is conveyed in Paul Morley's exasperation with the popular UK series *The X Factor* (ITV, 2004–):

> Many people point out to me ... that I am making the big mistake of approaching the show as if it has something to do with music. It may use music, songs, and guest musical acts, and fabricate the process of talent development, and cleverly conjure up grotesque caricatures of a great pop song, and produce hygienically packaged pop-style winners like Leona Lewis whom the show's PR machinery instantly talks of as a living legend, but it is not a music show.[14]

For our purposes, particular illustrations that extend this frustration to the experience of music history on TV would include 'list' shows such as *100 Greatest Albums* (Channel 4, 2001), *I Love The 1970s* (BBC, 2000) or the long-running *The Rock And Roll Years* (BBC, 1985–94). Ostensibly, such programmes make music their central feature, inasmuch as they facilitate the delivery of a series of standard gags and anecdotal asides about celebrity. Rarely dealt with for itself, music then

---

[13]   Simon Frith, 'Look! Hear! The Uneasy Relationship Of Music And Television', *Popular Music* 21/3 (2002), p. 280.

[14]   Paul Morley, 'Showing Off', *The Observer Music Monthly* 74, November 2009, p. 49.

becomes a secondary feature of 'music' television, relegated to the soundtrack, which is often quickly faded in the mix.

In the *Britannia* series, music is a central object of each history. Avoiding the habitual approach of television that treats popular music as ephemeral, as background, or as nostalgic mnemonic, the sounds are foregrounded in the rhetorical organisation of each programme. Music is sometimes presented in filmed performance (where available) and often heard on soundtracks derived from original recordings. It is sometimes attended by montage sequences of record covers integrated with still photographs from performances or publicity shoots. These sounds are framed in relation to the testimony of interviewees that is generally concerned with the inspiration for the music, its production, reception and, indeed, its meanings.

Britannia series producer Mark Cooper has highlighted the nature of the investment represented by the programmes he commissioned. Relative to BBC4's niche audience, each programme represents a considerable financial outlay: 'the archive budget is often a quarter of the cost of making the programme. If we want to put something out on DVD it's the same cost of making the programme all over again, just to clear the archive ... which is why things don't come out on DVD and, sometimes, why programmes only get shown once'.[15] This investment also represents a considerable cultural commitment, an issue that is signalled by the politics of the TV archive, and the nature and extent of the material available to the various *Britannia* series. Historically, while certain productions were deemed to be of obvious merit and were recorded, and continue to be preserved (epochal news reports and dramatic literary adaptations, for example) numerous instances of pop culture covered on TV were dismissed as ephemera. Individual programmes, whole series, and other appearances by a range of popular musicians – across different genres and of varying degrees of popularity – were dismissed as unworthy to be recorded for repeat viewing. And when they were recorded, such documents were often the first to be discarded when tapes were wiped to be re-used.[16] This treatment is noted by one viewer of *Folk Britannia* who suggests that footage of performances recalled and sought out by fans can be found in 'the bin with most of the other BBC musical archives'.[17]

It is worth noting that Cooper's background includes some years as a music journalist, and time spent in the music industry. He identifies his ethos as that of the committed fan, and gives a very personal perspective on his attachment to pop culture:

---

[15]   David Hepworth, 'The Difficult Business Of Putting Music On The TV: A Conversation With The BBC's Mark Cooper', *The Word*, 16 May 2008.

[16]   On the TV archive see: Dick Fiddy, *Missing, Believed Wiped: Searching For The Lost Treasures Of British Television* (London, 2001), and Helen Wheatley (ed.), *Re-viewing Television History: Critical Issues In Television Historiography* (London, 2007).

[17]   Jonny Bee, 8 March 2006 (www.bbc.co.uk/dna/mbradio2/F2142825?thread=243 2265).

because that's what our parents said to us, when we were growing up: 'What a load of rubbish ... it'll all be gone tomorrow. What are you going to do then?' ... For those of us who have ended up cherishing this culture, I think they were so wrong ... we all still care about it.[18]

Thus, with the original *Jazz Britannia*, the wealth and variety of material gathered together and the nature of the story presented evince Cooper's celebratory care for popular culture, and represent a considerable act of historical retrieval. The opening sequences of the first episode emphasise this project at the outset, stating in bold white-on-black type that this is 'An untold story'. Furthermore, the series is offered as a 'story of firsts', of 'Britain's first love affair with black music' and 'Britain's first youth culture'. Echoing this, *Soul Britannia* finds the 1970s scene in particular as one that is 'unique and often overlooked', and *Prog Rock Britannia* opens with the claim that the genre represents a 'lost continent' of activity.

This act of retrieval and project to validate aspects of popular music as important to social history informs the rhetorical strategies of each programme. Still and moving images, with and without contextual sound, or with the addition of a new soundtrack, are the viewers' way into each context, evoking the events explored that are nonetheless and inevitably unrecoverable. This last fact is true of all histories, of whatever medium, but it presents a particular problem for television that is perforce forever in the present tense. As Gary Edgerton argues in an assessment of Ken Burns's historical work for PBS, film and television lack precision in the rendering of time, because they lack 'grammatical analogues for the past and future tenses of written languages. Instead, the visual media amplify the present sense of immediacy out of all proportion'.[19] Like Burns's work, and much TV history in a medium which deals in the immediacy of presence and the present tense, the major televisual problem that the *Britannia* programmes have, in spite of the source material that is available, is that there is, in fact, a dearth of empirical audio-visual evidence concerning the key events of each narrative of when and how music was originated. An aspect of Burns's work which seeks to compensate for a similar lack is that 'he treats old photographs as if they were moving pictures, panning and zooming within the frame, shifting back and forth between long shots, medium shots and close-ups; while correspondingly handling live shots as if they were still photographs'.[20] Most noticeable is Burns's motif of approaching contemporary portraits of individuals through rostrum camera work, as if offering access to their interiority: his camera zooms in close to facial features – the eyes and brow – of Duke Ellington or Louis Armstrong, as witnesses recall

---

[18]   Hepworth, 'Difficult'.

[19]   Gary Edgerton, 'Mystic Chords Of Memory: The Cultural Voice Of Ken Burns', in Gary R. Edgerton, Michael T. Marsden and Jack Nachbar (eds), *In The Eye Of The Beholder: Critical Perspectives In Popular Film And Television* (Bowling Green, Ohio, 1997), p. 24.

[20]   Ibid., p. 14.

their actions and critics ponder their artistic motives, indexed by the ever-present sound of their music.

This strategy is echoed throughout the *Britannia* series, and a lyrical example of the arrangement is illustrated in the second episode of *Folk Britannia*. One sequence concerns the emergence in the 1960s of the reclusive singer Anne Briggs, encouraged onto camera for an interview, in order to discuss her approach to singing. Her recording of 'Blackwater Side' commences, as a rostrum camera tracks up a black-and-white photograph from the same period of Briggs in performance. Musician Martin Carthy and critic Karl Dallas opine on Briggs's style, the latter praising her visceral engagement with traditional music. There is a cut to a close-up of the record label to her release of the sea shanty 'Lowlands Away', the sound of which is used as a further reference point for her style that is deemed to be innovative and pure. This natural purity is indexed by nature itself, as her on-camera interview segues into sepia footage of waves crashing on rocks and then a sequence of still images of her younger self in performance, focused on her face, as if in touch with Briggs's interiority and creativity in the historical moment.

What then, do such instances and this rhetorical strategy tell us of the overall project of the various series? What is the folk of *Folk Britannia*, the soul of *Soul Britannia* and so on? What is the nature of the historical story constructed or 'retrieved' in treating music seriously, and with what result? Cooper emphasises the value of the impassioned nature of the witnesses in each series, arguing that the programmes were conceived as a means to 'explore the conditions that made them make their music, what the values were, what they cared about, not in a nostalgic way ... to be critical in the true meaning of critical ... because ... to me, too much pop music programming is sloppily nostalgic or judgmental'.[21] The key question he has sought to ask of musicians in pursuit of insight is 'what did *they* think?'

The stories of *Britannia* then are told from the 'inside'. In taking this approach, the various series are structured around, and reproduce, the discursive repertoires upon which popular music culture and its practices are constructed. To illustrate this idea, it is worth citing Jim McGuigan's description of the discursive formations of contemporary cultural debate, policy and demand. He suggests that these discourses are productive in that 'they all function in some sense to define "the real world" of culture and to position agents and subjects, producers, consumers, citizens and mediators, within the discursive space of the cultural field'.[22] Discourses of popular music that structure the stories of jazz, folk, soul et al. include a teleology of 'rupture' and discovery in the origination of music.[23] This is underwritten by romantic motifs celebrating the individual genius and of creativity *ex nihilo*. This romanticism is allied to constructions of 'mainstream' and 'margins' in relation to the music business and the aesthetics of music practice. In construction of this last idea, a distinction is drawn between ideas of the commercial, apparently

21   Hepworth, 'Difficult'.

22   Jim McGuigan, *Rethinking Cultural Policy* (Maidenhead, 2004), p. 35.

23   See, for example, Tim Wall, *Studying Popular Music Culture* (London, 2003).

undemanding and easily consumed sounds, and 'difficult' or innovative sounds and artists.

These discourses are all evident across the tropes of the various series. The romantic genius or innovative group is writ large in the stories of a series of figures who are both 'ahead of their time' (the 1970s soul group Cymande) or tragic and/or largely ignored (jazz player Joe Harriott, folk guitarist Davey Graham, singer Sandy Denny). Instances of rupture tie interpretations of musical dissonance to wider social occurrences such as the student protests and uprisings of 1968 (presented as the moment of a boom in rock and jazz), or the election of the Thatcher government in the late 1970s (contemporary with punk, a rebirth for a moribund jazz scene, and a prompt for the invigoration of the oppositional attack of folk in the 1980s). Concepts of mainstream and margins are worked through in each generic case, a theme signalled overtly in *Pop Britannia*, where the narrative is ordered by an idea that 'for the last 30 years, British pop has been locked in a constant struggle between the forces of art and commerce. That struggle has both fuelled and crippled our pop artists'.

A further aspect of the way in which popular music discourse is indulged is apparent in the conjunction of each programme title. Each one signals an overall project which is not only to explore jazz, or folk, or synthesised music in Britain, but to underline an argument in each case about the 'Britishness' of each genre in its home-grown form. In *Jazz Britannia*, Gilles Peterson spells out the basis for the thesis of a national genius in a statement that is used as punctuation at the beginning and end of the series:

> I think it is really important that people realise that there was this amazing body
> of music that was made in this country, and if you look back to it, and listen back
> to it, it's got this little edge, it's got its own little sound which is a British sound
> … there has always been a strong jazz heritage to this country.

This idea is conveyed in the resonance of the series name, and also in the series titles as we see two figures in outline: stereotypical English gentlemen in bowler hats and with umbrellas. The theme tune (by Soweto Kinch) begins with a quotation of 'Rule Britannia', while figures and sequences from the series are marshalled in a collage of images within the segments of a Union flag design. This design is utilised as a feature of the titles of each of the various series, and the project is signalled in the programme summaries set out on the BBC website: *Pop Britannia* is announced as a series which 'explores our flair for pop, our fascination with finding our own pop voice, and our obsession with style and the imagery of empire and nationhood.[24]

These various discourses are complexly interwoven in the narrative of each programme. For example, the moment identified as key to the origination of a specifically British jazz is located in the recording of *Jazz Suite Inspired By Dylan*

---

[24]   www.bbc.co.uk/musictv/popbritannia/episodes/

Thomas' 'Under Milk Wood' (1965) by the Stan Tracey Quartet. Pianist Tracey's recollection of the sessions is told over images of the original album cover, stills and footage of him and saxophonist Bobby Wellins in the studio (we infer that these are the sessions for the album), and shots of generous contemporary reviews. Critic John Fordham is enlisted to describe a moment of great improvisation, of how Wellins's sparse phrasing echoes nothing less than the pipes of his youth in Scotland. The sequence is arranged to the sounds of 'Starless And Bible Black', a key track from the album, which segues into an extract from the 1954 BBC radio version of *Under Milk Wood*, and its famous opening lines: 'To begin at the beginning'. Series narrator Terence Stamp announces in triumphant and portentous tones that:

> The most celebrated British jazz record of the first half of the 1960s was inspired by the nation's best known poet. Stan Tracey and Bobby Wellins had stumbled upon the future of British jazz. It lay not in slavishly imitating the Americans, but in developing its own voice.

Note the idea that this innovation has the sense of a Platonic ideal: it is unbidden, 'stumbled upon'. This is an idea supported by the testimony of the players that they came to the studio, made their contribution, were paid, and went their separate ways. Tracey and Wellins appear nonplussed by the success of their album and the regard in which it is held. This is not a job, it is what they *are*, their playing and creativity integral to their identity.

The subsequent episode reiterates these points by rehearsing the sequence and wryly pursues the idea of a specifically British jazz. A series of images of the musicians deemed important to the emergence of a native sound pass by. This gallery is underlined by Soft Machine's 'A Concise British Alphabet': the unmistakably English tones of Robert Wyatt recite the alphabet in song, conveying a sense that here is the raw material from which an indigenous creative language was formed.

Such sequences are skilfully organised and lyrical in their arrangement. Nonetheless, the repeated and uncritical reproduction of the discourses of popular music culture present potential problems in the aspirations of these series to be properly critical and to offer convincing historical insights.

Critiquing The History Of *Britannia*

Jeremy Black has evaluated some of the issues that arise when history is dealt with by cinema and television. Whether in the form of documentary or dramatic 're-creation', these forms draw repeated criticism, and often engender negative reactions from scholars. Defending the approach of TV and film makers however, Black writes that 'the perspective of academic critics is to miss the point, as however much film-makers might draw attention to their academic advisers …

the market that is sought is not that of scholars. Nor, much more seriously, are the values the same'.[25] It is certainly the case that despite considerable appreciation and public plaudits, each *Britannia* has engendered insightful criticism – not from scholars or professional historians, but from aficionados of the genre and the wider intelligent and informed audience at whom each series was aimed.

Unsurprisingly, repeated comments from viewers have concerned the historical reach and inclusiveness of each history, and reflected the partisan tastes of specific sets of fans. One viewer's comment about *Jazz Britannia* illustrates this point, representing the nature of discontent with the series, and the terms upon which it is sometimes expressed:

> Very dull, very predictable. In no way a true reflection of British jazz in the 1950s and 1960s. I suppose some of the problem is the paucity of filmed material and the dreary black-and-white (mostly grey) filming … So many great modernists were not even mentioned – Jimmy Deuchar, Harold McNair – plus our many exports to the US. Even George Shearing was ignored. Disgraceful. Just another excuse for the BBC to re-use archive film.[26]

It would be unproductive to simply quantify those instances where each *Britannia* strays from, or upsets, the personal preferences of fans. Such reactions are to be expected as an aspect of the culture of fandom with its own canons and prescriptions. Ultimately, the issue here is the overall way in which the histories of the *Britannia* series are presented *as* history.

Our critical perspective is structural in nature, expressing dissatisfaction with a feature again pinpointed by Black. He suggests that 'film and television present history as answers, necessarily so, as the amount of time available for verbal elucidation is limited. Film and television also present history as narrative, preferably with a beginning, a middle, and an end, rather than as social process'.[27] In the *Britannia* series, narrative answers are pre-ordained by the reliance on the familiar structures of the discourses of pop music. The issue is not one of distinguishing between truth and falsehood here, but in noting the manner in which these discourses are productive of meaning in popular music practice. They constitute the truths, feelings, dispositions and actions of players, industry personnel and consumers. Yet, they are also reductive, and tend to obscure an exploration of aspects of the wider terrain of the story related. On one hand, for example, romantic constructions of musicians often work to elide their relationship with the music business *qua* business that, across these series, is deemed to be a monolithic organisation at odds with the production of popular music; from another perspective, commerce is the very reason for innovation, as well as supporting continuity and undermining the idea of disjuncture. Likewise, potential problems are also signalled in claiming

---

25   Jeremy Black, *Using History* (London, 2005), pp. 32–3.
26   (www.bbc.co.uk/bbcfour/yoursay/jazz.shtml).
27   Black, *Using History*, p. 33.

that such things as specifically British forms of music exist, which here relies on a nationalist, essentialist and idealised set of connotations. That these are asserted, rather than explored, makes such ideas hard to accept.

More troubling is the fact that in repeated instances across the various series, statements and insights from a plurality of interviewees are assembled, sometimes apparently contradicting each other, only to be qualified and reassuringly explained by the narration. Sequences and statements that invite questions are left unanswered: for viewers, these are striking and tantalising dead ends. In *Jazz Britannia*, for example, guitarist John McLaughlin observes that it is important to recognise the interaction of players and the multiplicity of their reference points in the context of the 1960s. He reflects that he was 're-educated' in his tastes by paying attention to the pop of the Beatles, Jimi Hendrix and the funk of James Brown: 'There's a story there' he comments. Obligingly, the narration makes this clear for us, insisting that 'The story *was* that British musicians … saw the connection between the psychedelic movement in rock and the sonic experiments of Miles Davis and John Coltrane: British jazz rock was born'. Subsequently, pianist Keith Tippett states that the 1960s was 'a period where, I think, young English musicians were trying to get out of the shadow of the great Americans, they really wanted to find their own voice'. Yet such a comment does not automatically entail the conclusion that an essentially British 'sound' was born, which is the overall thesis of the series. Indeed, bassist Dave Holland comments (on the idea of a native jazz sound) that 'we should not obsess about this', and composer Mike Westbrook recalls that although critics have spoken of a British jazz, he would not wish to be part of such a grouping. The potential problems and complexities offered by such a plurality of positions are passed over with a turn to the work of Michael Garrick, and the explanation that 'and yet there were composers giving natural expression to their roots in British music and song that drew on folk and liturgical sources'. It is not perhaps that such ideas might sit alongside each other, irreconcilable and undoubtedly complex in their implications, but that the narrative cannot allow for such equivocation.

Producer Ben Whalley gives a pragmatic insight into how this impulse for focus originates. In an outline of the production of *Pop Britannia*, he has written that the challenge lay in the fact that the subject matter was broadly defined ('"pop" is a word that can describe pretty much anything'), and that the material was likely to be familiar to audiences. Furthermore,

> The whole series was made in 34 weeks, loosely divided into three parts: research, filming and editing. The series began with the team sifting through a huge mass of viewing material and literature, and talking to hundreds of potential contributors. Once treatments for each of the three films had been written, we started shooting around the ideas and subjects – the fun phase of any project! In late spring we began putting the films together in the edit – often the most challenging, but ultimately the most rewarding part of any production.[28]

---

28   Ben Whalley (www.bbc.co.uk/musictv/popbritannia/sleevenotes/).

He explains that the various series are concept-driven, where no sole contributor is the main protagonist: 'The challenge is to fit a host of interesting characters and subjects into an over-arching narrative.'[29] The problem, in spite of this, is that the experiences of the figures featured are translated into general statements about the fortunes of British music and thus, everyone else involved.

One label for the result of these narrative decisions is 'totalising'. Linda Hutcheon has suggested that the function of this term is to indicate the process by which historians, social theorists, creative writers, and perhaps, even television producers, 'render their materials coherent, continuous, unified – but always with an eye to the control and mastery of those materials, even at the risk of doing violence to them'.[30] In the *Britannia* programmes, this 'violence' is noticeable in its supply of answers to the many questions raised, despite the allusions and contradictions of the sources deployed.

In relation to the idea of a totalising project, we might also ponder the nature of the narrative voice of the series. Once more, we can draw a profitable comparison with Ken Burns's PBS histories. Edgerton defines Burns's approach as a form of 'bricolage' that serves to counter those who complain about his lack of historical rigour.[31] Edgerton uses the term to refer to the practice of bringing together an array of materials, and in relation to Claude Levi-Strauss's employment of it to describe a mode of mythmaking. In this sympathetic analysis, Burns's various series work through poetic analogy, producing histories that are not reducible to a question of accuracy, of a 'right' or 'wrong' historical rectitude. Burns's stated objective has been to address a question about American identity, its origins and direction.[32] For Edgerton, whatever answers Burns arrives at are framed by his liberal pluralist perspective:

> where social and cultural differences between Americans are kept in a comparatively stable and negotiated consensus within the body politic. A celebration of the nation, and a highlighting of its ideals and achievements, are fundamental aspects of both consensus thinking and Burns's body of work.[33]

Burns's approach is paralleled in the authorial perspective of each *Britannia* series, which can be understood as the voice of the BBC itself. One way of interpreting the

---

[29]   Ibid.

[30]   Linda Hutcheon, *The Politics Of Postmodernism, Second Edition* (London, 2002) p. 58.

[31]   For a critique of Burns's work on *Jazz*, see, for example, Alan Stanbridge, 'Burns, Baby, Burns: Jazz History As A Contested Cultural Site', *The Source: Challenging Jazz Criticism*, 1/04 (2004) pp. 82–99.

[32]   Ken Burns, 'Four O'Clock In The Morning Courage', in Robert Brent Toplin (ed.), *Ken Burns's The Civil War: Historians Respond* (Oxford, 1996), pp. 153–84.

[33]   Edgerton, 'Mystic Chords Of Memory', p. 16. See also Gary R. Edgerton, *Ken Burns's America* (New York, 2001).

totalising approach then is to see that the various series offer a Whiggish form of cultural history, whose motifs and practices speak to a celebratory story of native genius – that there is, for example, such a thing as 'Soul Britannia'. In this way, each story continues a tradition established in relation to classical and folk forms noted by Raphael Samuel: that the history of the BBC can be understood as one 'responding to a powerful, if diffuse, cultural nationalism' and playing 'its part in the renaissance of English music'.[34] Extending a cultural nationalism to the diffuse popular forms of post-war Britain constructs a benign version of modernity, in which *Britannia*'s stories amount to a tale of the acceptance, assimilation, and reconciliation of difference in the sphere of popular culture.

The benign interpretation of cultural reconciliation is brought home in each *Britannia* series, wherein the totalising aspect of the narrative often comes to the fore. The final episode of *Folk Britannia* is emphatic in underlining the way in which the 'voice' of the genre in post-war Britain has been oppositional in tone. Throughout the programme, the enmities between traditionalists and innovators, which have marked folk practice, are explored: its closing scenes explore the collaboration between Beth Orton and Bert Jansch, representatives of the new and old in the genre respectively. Through the performance of a hybrid song written and sung (with echoes of Anne Briggs) by Orton, and featuring Jansch on guitar, the emphasis is upon how she embodies a continuing spirit, an essence common to all aspects of the genre. The narrator sagely concludes: 'So, no matter which route you take back through the annals of British folk, you will still arrive at the same source.'

A similar reconciliation is conveyed in *Soul Britannia,* delivered by series producer Jeremy Marre:

> At the dawn of the millennium, UK soul-inspired sounds exploded into a thousand different shapes: from Ms Dynamite to Corinne Bailey Rae, Joss Stone to Amy Winehouse, Lemar to Lethal Bizzle. Currently in a rude state of health, British 21st century soul is a result of our unique multicultural society. Over 40 years, we've moved from a nation of fans and imitators to one of black and white musicians creating original, cutting-edge music. We've travelled from segregation to integration, as black American and Jamaican cultures have been embraced and become entwined with English life, changing our society forever.

Whether in terms of race, class, politics, taste, or artistic practice and difference, the tale told by *Britannia* is one of overcoming adversity, resulting in a pluralist settlement. Here, one can again consider the resonances of the series title and its moment of production, which echoes the advent of the Blair administration and the ascription of the label 'Cool Britannia' in expressing an overcoming of narratives of national decline, in favour of a cultural confidence and confidence in

---

[34]   Raphael Samuel, *Island Stories: Unravelling Britain* (London, 1999), p. 182.

culture. While there are complex contradictions within this label, Alexei Monroe summarises the nature of the project to which it refers as an 'ongoing attempt to "rebrand" Britain as a multi-ethnic, youth-culture dominated, globalisation-friendly country, in which ideological divisions have been erased'.[35]

Conclusions: Popular Music And Good And Bad TV History

The *Britannia* programmes represent a significant commitment to the presentation of popular music on TV, the investigation of its history, and its location within a wider social understanding. The treatment of each genre in each series would merit attention for itself, for the material generated, and the particular nuances of particular insights. Whalley's verdict on the overall achievement of the series is that 'given the high level of access, collaboration and permissions required to make a project of this ambition, the BBC, due to its unique position, is perhaps one of the few places in the world that can attempt to create content of this scope'.[36] Such grand claims merit critical scrutiny of the project, especially one offered by a public service broadcaster that seeks to engender high expectations amongst the intelligent, informed and demanding audience to which it seeks to speak.

John Corner has questioned the 'integrity' of television history and the different systems of historical value we might bring to bear upon it.[37] We may, for instance, respond as critics, 'general' audience members, genre buffs or scholars – we might inhabit all of these positions. Corner cites the work of Tobias Ebbrecht on German and British docudrama, and the tendency of television to offer the 'clear and definite' rather than the 'controversial and inconsistent'; thus, television offers a 'closed narration', and a tendency to reduce complexity to the simple and single viewpoint. All of these facets are visible in the *Britannia* series, as are tantalising glimpses of what it might have been, had it allowed the suggestiveness, complexities and (often) uncertainties of the material to escape from the drive to present 'answers'.

> Can we point confidently to examples of 'bad television history' and identify with some precision the causes of its bad-ness? Are we confident in the criteria by which we want to acclaim 'good television history' and to encourage its further development?[38]

---

[35]   Alexei Monroe, 'Bread And (Rock) Circuses: Sites Of Sonic Conflict In London', in Pamela K. Gilbert (ed.), *Imagined Londons* (Albany, NY, 2002), p. 138. See also: Stephen Bayley, *Labour Camp: The Failure Of Style Over Substance* (London, 1998).

[36]   Whalley, (www.bbc.co.uk/musictv/popbritannia/sleevenotes/).

[37]   John Corner, 'Epilogue: Sense And Perspective', *European Journal Of Cultural Studies,* 2007; 10/1, pp. 135–40.

[38]   Ibid, p. 136.

The criteria that we might bring to bear are our understandings as members of the audience addressed by such programmes and their originators. We have sought to pitch our critique in response to the claims of the series and its producers, and in recognition of the way in which it calls upon our expectations for something different from the habitual manner in which popular music and popular culture have been treated by the medium. The sum total of the *Britannia* programmes is not 'bad television history' *per se*. Rather, given the ambition and material on offer, *Britannia* allows us to consider what television histories of popular music might look like if a genuinely critical and exploratory approach were to replace a policy of shoehorning plurality into a single, assertive organisation. With its high production values and genuine commitment, *Britannia* at least suggests that pop can be taken seriously, and that music *qua* music can be presented in innovative ways by television, offering a positive addition to our shared history.

Chapter 2

Television Documentary, Pop Stardom And Auto/Biographical Narratives

Ian Goode

One of the recent trends in the relationship between popular music and an increasingly serially produced television is the preponderance of one-off biographical and autobiographical documentaries centred on the individual lives of pop stars. The titles of these programmes offer the promise of a privileged insight into the life of the single star subjects concerned and an answer to the question of their identities. Examples include *Being Mick* (Channel 4, 2001); *Being Victoria Beckham* (ITV, 2002); *Being Brian Harvey* (BBC, 2005); *Who The Fuck Is Pete Doherty?* (BBC, 2006); *Elton John: Me, Myself And I* (ITV, 2007); and *Amy Winehouse: What Really Happened* (Channel 4, 2008). This chapter examines the evolution of the practice, and aims to identify possible reasons for its emergence, including the growth of reality television formats, an intensified culture of celebrity, and the effect of narrowcasting and multi-channel television.

In each case (apart from *Amy Winehouse: What Really Happened*) the exposition of the self-disclosure is predicated on television's ability to deliver a rare degree of access to the lives of the stars. This access involves a variable mixture of private and public footage, or what might be more appropriately described as the private disclosed in the public. Such documentaries belong to the media culture of a perpetual quest for the essential life narratives of stardom that precedes this recent trend in television non-fiction. In fact, the cultural popularity of the celebrity auto/biography is most concentrated in book publishing where, as Ira B. Nadel suggests:

> the reasons for the popularity of biography are multiple – from the interests of human nature in people rather than events, to our fascination with the habits and personal details of 'eminent men and women' – or with what our age confuses with celebrity.[1]

However, the visual media history of the auto/biographical narrative in popular music can be linked back to the direct cinema movement that emerged in North America during the 1960s. *Don't Look Back* (D.A. Pennebaker, 1967) exploited

---

[1]   Ira B. Nadel, 'Narrative And The Popularity Of Biography', *Mosaic* 20/4 (1987), p. 131.

the behind-the-scenes access granted to the director during Bob Dylan's tour of the United Kingdom in 1965; this early example of direct cinema came out of the growth in photojournalism and the availability of lighter and more portable cameras. The continuation of the concert film was demonstrated by *Gimme Shelter* (Albert and David Maysles, 1970); currently termed the 'rockumentary', it is epitomised by *Shine A Light* (Martin Scorsese, 2008). In addition, the film genre of the biopic also finds productive subject matter in popular music.[2] This continuity of the relationship between pop music and documentary has become established through the cinema, and demonstrates a symbiotic relationship between auteur film directors and pop stars.

What is less apparent and less researched is the manifestation of the connection between popular music and television documentary. John Hill has traced the presence of popular music on British television during the 1950s and 1960s through live performance shows such as *Oh Boy!* (ITV, 1958–59) and *Ready Steady Go!* (ITV, 1963–66) – programmes that sought to address younger viewers rather than a family audience.[3] One of the first examples of TV's investigation of the singular life of the pop star was provided by a distinctive episode of the current affairs series *World In Action* (ITV, 1963–98) in 1967, in which a panel of representatives of the English establishment questioned the moral probity of Mick Jagger after his arrest for drug use. More recently, the growth of MTV (and similar music video television outlets) and the contraction in live music performance programmes such as the long-running *Top Of The Pops* (BBC, 1964–2006) has created opportunities for different kinds of popular music programming. The reality television formats of *Pop Idol* (ITV, 2001–2003), *Fame Academy* (BBC, 2002–2003) and *The X Factor* (ITV, 2004–) have expanded significantly, following the shift in the late-1980s to a more visible concern with the improvement and welfare of the self, and an attendant increase in what Jon Dovey terms 'first person media'.[4] It is within the space created by this shift in production priorities, underlined by the proliferation in cable and digital channels and changes in communication technology, that the auto/biographical documentary has also grown. The discursive pressure of the media and popular music industry to identify and promote the raft of emerging pop stars is intimately bound up with these cultural and political developments.

These developments can also be situated in John Corner's summary of changes in British documentary and non-fiction television:

> British television documentary has passed from being a genre of inquiry and argument, of observation and illustration and, particularly in the last few years,

---

[2]   Ian Inglis, 'Popular Music History On Screen: The Pop/Rock Biopic', *Popular Music History* 2/1 (2007), pp. 77–93.

[3]   John Hill, 'Television And Pop: The Case Of The 1950s', in John Corner (ed.), *Popular Television In Britain: Studies In Cultural History* (London, 1991).

[4]   Jon Dovey, *Freakshow: First Person Media And Factual Television* (London, 2000).

of diversion and amusement. Within British television, a strong journalistic dimension to documentary emerged quite rapidly in the early 1950s, as the medium became a primary source of national news and public knowledge.[5]

What is important here are the terms of the movement away from inquiry and argument, and towards diversion and amusement. The recent biographical focus of pop star documentaries on television offers less of a report, and more of an individualised mode of self-articulation that is symptomatic of the status of current non-fiction television culture.

The Location Of Auto/Biographical Criticism

Ownership of the critical discourse of autobiography and biography is traditionally located in literary criticism. However, the increased presence of this form of biographical/autobiographical cultural production outside the literary field has prompted the question of how appropriate existing literary criticism is for these more mediated texts; indeed, there have been several significant contributions exploring the ways in which visual autobiography can draw upon and extend the work of its literary equivalent.[6]

However, Elizabeth Bruss has questioned the validity of autobiographical expression that is not written:

> the unity of subjectivity and subject matter – the implied identity of author, narrator, and protagonist on which classical autobiography depends – seems to be shattered by film; the autobiographical self decomposes, schisms, into almost mutually exclusive elements of the person filmed (entirely visible; recorded and projected) and the person filming (entirely hidden; behind the camera eye).[7]

Suzanne Egan raised related questions 'about the subjectivity-in-representation of that life (because that which is manifest is the object of the camera eye, and often of a photographer, other than the apparently originating subject)'.[8] However, she also believes that 'the use of film may enable autobiographers to define and

---

[5]   John Corner, 'Sounds Real: Music And Documentary', *Popular Music* 21/3 (2002), pp. 357–8.

[6]   See, for example, Suzanne Egan, 'Encounters In Camera: Autobiography As Interaction', *Modern Fiction Studies* 40/3 (1994), pp. 593–618; Jim Lane, *The Autobiographical Documentary In America* (Madison, 2002); Michael Renov, *The Subject Of Documentary* (Minneapolis, 2004).

[7]   Elizabeth Bruss, 'Eye For I: Making And Unmaking Autobiography In Film', in James Olney (ed.), *Autobiography: Essays Theoretical And Critical* (Princeton, 1980), p. 297.

[8]   Egan, 'Encounters', p. 593.

present subjectivity not as singular or solipsistic but as multiple and as revealed in relationship'.[9] One of the relationships where autobiographical subjectivity is located is that with the camera itself, and the proliferation of video-diary formats throughout non-fiction television support an increase in autobiographical expression captured by the increasingly intimate technologies of the camera. Jim Lane's discussion of (mostly) independent film also suggests that the autobiographical documentary 'presents an extraordinary site of subjective narration'.[10] The self-narratives and relational subjectivities that occur within television documentary do not offer as much formal complexity as independent cinema. These relational subjectivities of television are much more significantly mediated than the texts which constitute the critical objects within this body of criticism.

My focus here is on a populist mode of British television non-fiction programming that involves already intertextual subjectivities. One of the characteristics shared by these documentaries is not their relationship to literary antecedents or to the radical possibilities of independent film-making, but that together they demonstrate the connection between television and mainstream book publishing. This supports an understanding of television as a parasitic medium, through the often dependent, transmitting relationship it has with other media and forms of culture.[11] This takes place against a background of a wider discussion around the diminishing role of 'the serious' within cultural production. Valerie Grove argues that the culture of celebrity is harming the serious biography: 'Hilary Spurling's *Life Of Matisse*, which won the Costa Prize, sold 12,000 copies, while *Being Jordan*, the ghost-written memoirs of the glamour model Katie Price, shifted 335,000. Not really surprising: what's bought and read in quantity reflects the state of the nation. It's like comparing audiences for MTV and Radio 3.'[12] In fact, several years earlier, Hugh Look had noted that book publishing, like other areas of popular culture, was beginning to develop a dependence on the star system:

> The rise of the 'star' author and the cult of celebrity overwhelms publishing in the same way that it has movies and professional sports. Television creates the star system, agents nurture it. Publishers must find ways of surviving it. The Internet provides a means for star authors to reach their public without the intermediation of their publisher, but it is not yet a medium in which stars are born.[13]

---

[9]   Ibid.

[10] Lane, *The Autobiographical Documentary*, p. 25.

[11] Stuart Hall, 'Technics Of The Medium', in John Corner and Sylvia Harvey (eds), *Television Times: A Reader*, (London, 1996), pp. 3–10.

[12] Valerie Grove, 'Celebrity Culture Is Killing The Serious Biography', *The Times*, 5 September 2008.

[13] Hugh Look, 'The Author As Star', *Publishing Research Quarterly* 15/3 (1999), p. 12.

In the same way, the willingness of TV channels such as BBC3 and Channel 4 to engage in the production of (pop) star documentaries seems to confirm that public service broadcasting is no longer synonymous with the promotion of cultural distinction.[14]

The Auto/Biographical Television Documentary

The programmes I want to examine include a range of pop stars at different stages in the process of stardom. On this basis, I have identified the following typology to structure my discussion of the documentaries: *the pop star as rebel* (Amy Winehouse, Pete Doherty, Brian Harvey); *the pop star as global icon* (Victoria Beckham); and *the canonised rock star* (Elton John, Mick Jagger).[15] The difference between the pop star as global icon and the canonised rock star lies in the relationship between critical acclaim for musical achievement and a stardom that is more dependent on the commercial and promotional activity of celebrity. These categories are clearly overlapping (as well as gendered) but I hope to demonstrate that they are borne out by the documentaries.

The Pop Star As Rebel

In *Amy Winehouse: What Really Happened*, Jacques Peretti narrates the current life-as-story of the relatively new but troubled pop star:

> Amy and Blake are the most compelling, self-destructive and publicly hounded couple of our time. But what is the truth about their relationship? Is Amy really fatally in thrall to Blake's control? Did it really all go wrong for her when she met him? Called the poster girl for drug abuse, her life appears to be in freefall. My name is Jacques Peretti and I want to find out the truth about Amy. Who really pulls the strings in this modern day soap opera of sex, drugs and obsessive love?

The celebrity exposé promised by Peretti's voice-over accompanies assembled footage of Winehouse and partner Blake Fielder-Civil in public space being pursued by the media. There is no input from Winehouse herself to this expositional documentary. Peretti's claim is not exceptional but it underlines the extent to which this degree of salacious curiosity about life stories has become a journalistic orthodoxy of contemporary culture that now includes British television's fourth

---

[14]   See Pierre Bourdieu, *Distinction: A Social Critique Of The Judgement Of Taste* (London, 1984).

[15]   The concept of the canonised rock star is introduced in Robert Strachan, 'Where Do I Begin The Story? Collective Memory, Biographical Authority And The Rock Biography', *Popular Music History* 3/1 (2008), p. 68.

channel. The narrative of the public rise and fall of the subject is not explained by Winehouse, but is instead approximated through the assembled sources of Peretti's commentary, testimony from family, and musical selections such as Johnny Cash's poignant recording of 'Hurt':

> What's fascinating to us, compelling to us, is that Amy and Blake seem to loathe the attention, and crave it, simultaneously … willing or not they have turned themselves into a horror movie.

Peretti willingly assumes the role of the public enquirer into the personal history of the star, and this is justified and rendered free of any guilt or ethical ambiguity by the well established and legitimised desire of the public to know. The intermediary/ narrator has no access to the subject of the programme. What is offered instead is an attempted biographical explanation, and a promised truth of the life narrative summarised by the opening questions. The rhetoric of the narration seeks to convince the viewer that the speaker is in a position to discover the answers to the question contained in the title without the input and agreed self-exposure of the star herself. Winehouse's status as rebel is assumed by the co-existence of her distinctive confessional song-writing style and the accompanying tabloid headlines for drug and alcohol consumption. Peretti's reference to her life as a soap opera is a testament to the biographical story of Winehouse as an ongoing and open narrative, and also to a familiar part of the mythology of pop.[16]

Who The Fuck Is Pete Doherty? adopts a more serious stance towards a star subject who occupies a similar position in the process of fame. The programme was shaped by the investigative endeavours of the television and video promo director Roger Pomphrey, who spent ten months following his subject; the result is an attempt to demystify the notorious and controversial performer.

The exposition of the documentary combines voice-over by Pomphrey, self-disclosure direct to camera by Doherty, witness testimony from fellow band members, friends and pop critic Paul Morley, tabloid headlines and concert footage. Pomphrey's opening description of his subject states that:

> Peter Doherty is the product of a comfortable middle-class couple, the son of an army major and a public school matron. From a very early age he showed a talent for rhyme, verse and a love of literature. He gained four A-levels and a place at Oxford University to read English.

This introduction is delivered over footage of Doherty's band performing on *Later…With Jools Holland* (BBC, 1992–) and the documentary proceeds through recursive attempts to find sources of autobiographical exposition and biographical explanation that are appreciative of the creativity of the pop songwriter.

---

[16]   See Roland Barthes, *Mythologies* (London: Cape, 1972).

A fellow member of Babyshambles states, 'He's been responsible for bringing a lot of soul back into music … he's the most real person out there at the moment, musically'. And the band's agent, Matt Bates, claims that '[his] lyrics generally have got the strength to hold him in the high category of the greatest – Dylan, Lennon & McCartney, Joe Strummer … he's probably the nearest thing we've got to a genius at the moment'. Such eulogising and mythologising declarations of Doherty's creative status are juxtaposed with a montage of tabloid headlines detailing his drug-taking exploits, against a background of his songs. Here, music is not used as a means to secure and guarantee the continuity of a pop persona, but as part of the hermeneutic of the pop rebel that is prompted by the programme's title.

Pomphrey is sympathetic to Doherty's need to be able to maintain the balance between the input of drugs and the creative expression required to maintain the written output of regular pop songs. The fragility of this balance and the impossibility of its long-term security are fundamental to the prospect of answering the documentary's central question. The reporting of this narrative of non-conformity, and its evaluation, is summarised by Paul Morley in the programme:

> The problem with Pete Doherty is that it all happens too quickly now, because we're all so self-conscious about it. So even before the Dohertys of the world have had a chance to develop their art, if you want to call it that, their entertainment, their personality, their history, make a few albums, a few songs in the margins, that create a kind of solid myth, they're plucked now, too quick almost, out of the *NME* world, if you like, into the tabloid world, and the glare of the *News Of The World*. And the *News Of The World* has found its victim, found its target, and it starts to hound and persecute. We don't really know the truth, we don't really know what he's like, we're only told when he's gone into a George Best moment or an Oliver Reed moment. We're not told anything else, we're only told the sordid bits of the story, so we're losing our real sense of judgment on it and therefore, from an intelligent point of view, you're slightly mistrusting him.

The status of Morley and what Bill Nichols describes as 'the voice of documentary' are thus deployed to supplement and counter the tabloid account of the Doherty persona.[17] Significantly, the contributions are all made by men; Doherty's then partner, Kate Moss, is mentioned, but offers no view herself. When asked about his dependency on drugs, Doherty is candid and admits to a relational self: 'It depends who it is that I'm being. If it's Peter someone who takes drugs, then, yes, I need drugs. If I'm being Peter who doesn't take drugs, then, no, I don't.' This scene takes place in a small room whose walls are covered by enlarged copies of handwritten notes. As such, the discourse of the pop star-as-writer is frequently interwoven with the problems and possibilities of drug dependency that have resulted in an addiction to heroin.

---

[17] Bill Nichols, 'The Voice Of Documentary', *Film Quarterly* 36/3 (1983), pp. 17–30.

The identity of the subject as constructed by the programme is a discursively interwoven combination of rebellious, drug dependent, white, male, pop songwriter, who is admired by those close to him, and incompletely represented by the constant attention of the tabloid press. While there is a mythical dimension of the necessarily rebellious pop writer within its narrative, it is a more thorough investigation than that presented in *Amy Winehouse: What Really Happened.*

Being Brian Harvey offers an account of the current life of the former member of successful boy band East 17. In contrast to Winehouse and Doherty, Harvey is at a more advanced stage of declining pop stardom. The documentary is formed out of the recorded interaction between the subject, his partner Emma B, and the director Clio David. This observational combination strives to provide an explanation for Harvey's dismissal from the band and, like the other documentaries, assumes an interstitial relationship with the subsequent 'chain of tabloid stories involving decline through drugs and depression'. In contrast to the opportunistic approach and tone of Peretti, David's documentary, which was part of BBC's *One Life* strand, carries a rhetoric of feminine concern for a troubled star searching for the means to revive his career. Unlike Winehouse and Doherty, who are able to draw upon the legitimacy of fame to explain the course of their lives and the actions through which they are made by the media, the version of the self articulated here involves a physical struggle to recover from serious injuries and a psychological struggle for self-expression that reflects a condition of rapidly diminishing fame.

Diane Negra argues that:

> the recent saturation coverage of female stars in crisis contrasts dramatically with the journalistic restraint often exhibited in relation to male stars. Current media invite us to root against such toxic celebrities as Jade Goody and Amy Winehouse, but it is taken for granted that we root for their troubled male counterparts.[18]

Thus, in *Who The Fuck Is Pete Doherty?* the subject's drug-fuelled antics are justified as both symptom of, and support for, his creativity and a status that combines the figures of the rebel and the pop poet; the assembled associates and critics collectively value Doherty as a figure of errant genius, against a background of tabloid notoriety. Conversely, Winehouse is positioned as a vulnerable, but apparently willing, victim of drugs: rather than complementing or enabling her musical talent, her dependency (and her partnership with Fielder-Civil) threaten to disrupt her musical career while she undergoes rehabilitation. This contrasting treatment 'reminds us that fame is still understood to use up women, while it energises men'.[19] However, the example of Harvey demonstrates that the self as 'commodified self' that was 'used up' post-East 17, has an attendant economic life

---

[18] Diane Negra, 'The Feminisation Of Crisis Celebrity', *The Guardian*, 9 July 2008.
[19] Ibid.

cycle which does not necessarily follow the patterns of gender; and the history of popular music includes numerous figures who underline this parable of stardom.

The Pop Star As Global Icon

There are exceptions to the cycle of fame that consumes stars, and there are many examples of stars who are careful to ensure that their fame endures beyond the phase of rebellion. This can be achieved through an unapologetically commercial strategy and the cultivation of an image that conforms to social norms in order to maximise media exposure. It is here that the figure of Victoria Beckham serves as a useful example.

The continuity announcer for ITV repeats the promise that the next programme will offer viewers the opportunity to 'discover what it's like, *Being Victoria Beckham*'. Produced after six months with its subject, the programme promises an inside view of a star (at a time which was also commercially advantageous to the Victoria Beckham brand). Its audience of 8.83 million followed on from the earlier success of *Victoria's Secrets* (Channel 4, 2000) which involved Beckham in dialogue with other British celebrities. Both programmes demonstrate how the post-Spice Girls Beckham is aware of the need to actively negotiate her relationship with the media.

Victoria Beckham represents an unusual kind of star subject, since she is as (or more) famous for her marriage to footballer David Beckham, as she is for her membership (as Victoria Adams) of the Spice Girls in the 1990s. It is indicative that Beckham chooses to grant the film's producer (Caroline Mendall) greater access to her life at a moment when her future career is relatively uncertain, following Geri Halliwell's departure from the Spice Girls in 1998, and the group's collective decision to pursue solo careers in 2001.

The opening of the documentary gives an indication of the directness of its voice: a head and shoulders shot shows Beckham declaring to the camera that 'when I was a little girl I always wanted to be famous, but I had no idea what it would be like being Victoria Beckham'. The relationship between her life narrative and her career in music is much more clearly influenced by the management and exploitation of fame than is evident in the documentaries discussed above. Furthermore, her announcement also reveals that she considers the desire for fame to be a legitimate pursuit in itself.

The opening sequence continues with an assembly of sources, including comments from her husband and members of her immediate family, and the song 'Not Such An Innocent Girl' from her recently released, first solo album *Victoria Beckham*. This is combined with footage of domestic life, in which the couple discuss the popularity of stars such as Tom Cruise and Angelina Jolie. Their evident self-consciousness in the presence of the cameras and the carefully selected view of Beckham family life attracted press derision,[20] but it also serves as evidence of

---

[20]   Kathryn Flett, 'Nights With The Laydeez', *The Observer*, 10 March 2002.

the extent to which Beckham seeks control over the parameters of the image that she wishes to disclose to the audience. This exercise of power is in stark contrast to *Geri* (Channel 4, 1999) in which film-maker Molly Dineen was able to explore the life of the more vulnerable, and single, Geri Halliwell.

Despite this clearly measured disclosure, Beckham does intimate a supposed naivety in respect of her image, demonstrated by a talk-show extract in which she states, 'I think it's actually quite unbelievable, you don't actually realise until you actually stop and take a look at yourself, how everybody else sees you'. The comment is juxtaposed with her mother's observation that 'if you don't like her as a person, I'd say, how well do you know her?' Beckham's awareness of, and sensitivity to, negative press commentary is further illuminated through her husband's discussion of her public image of his wife: 'there are two personalities – one in the media, and the one at home where she is laughing and joking, the best side of what no one sees'. The strategy of using the television production as an opportunity to launch a public corrective to the negative portrayal of the star by certain sections of the media is articulated as a necessary and ongoing part of *being* a global star.

Through the programme's biographical and autobiographical story of Victoria's rise to stardom, it offers the audience a perspective on the pursuit and exploitation of fame itself (the role of pop music is peripheral, as music in the wake of the Spice Girls is only one of the vehicles through which Victoria Beckham maintains her public profile). Beckham recounts how her early career motivation was provided by *Fame* (Alan Parker, 1980), a narrative fiction forerunner of formats that have recently proliferated on non-fiction television. But primarily, the acquisition of fame is articulated from inside the Beckham/Adams family in largely domestic terms, ensuring that the audience is granted a view of the star in the roles of wife, mother and daughter. As Jo Littler has noted, 'seeing celebrities outside of the traditional places and spaces in which it is acceptable to inhabit celebrityhood – in either ordinary or extraordinary contexts – has been a key part of the appeal of the spate of many recent celebrity reality TV programmes'.[21] Beckham has not surrendered herself to the producers of reality television, but she has consented to a documentary production that is informed by the developments identified by Littler. There are clearly agreed limits to the private exposure and disclosure but, in comparison to the other documentaries examined here, it does mean that *Being Victoria Beckham* provides a more comprehensive, if conventional, autobiographical narrative.

David Furnish (friend of the Beckhams and partner of Elton John) summarises the life story on display: 'she is living a dream, living a fantasy for other people, it is what a lot of young women, young girls I think, in today's society, aspire to'. His belief supports many contemporary observations about the extent to which the pursuit of fame has increased, and the desire to 'want to be a celebrity' has

---

[21] Jo Littler, 'Making Fame Ordinary: Intimacy, Reflexivity, And "Keeping It Real"', *Mediactive* 2 (2004), p. 19.

been naturalised under an intensification of individualism.[22] A corollary of these developments is a celebrity press that exists to both legitimate celebrity figures and subject them to irreverent commentary and salacious imagery. Her admission that 'most people have a price, which is a bit sad really' suggests a knowledge of, and vulnerability to, the process of fame that has impacted upon Brian Harvey more severely than it has upon Victoria Beckham. Here is a subject who is happy to announce that 'I love being famous'; after the Spice Girls' debut single had embodied the desire of the 'Wannabe', she has abandoned their exclusive focus on pop music, and subsequently retained (and expanded) her fame.

The Canonised Rock Star

Elton John typifies the performer who, after a long career built upon huge record sales and public acclaim, can be plausibly described as a 'canonised rock star'. The difference between the nature of his stardom and that of Victoria Beckham is indicated by the greater emphasis given to the role and process of making popular music in *Me, Myself And I*. The documentary is also given a more distinctive televisual form through the use of the studio as the setting for the subject's narration and the general use of visual effects which combine to affirm the pop star's status and investment in elaborate spectacle.

The opening sequence depicts an animated rocket superimposed over concert footage of John performing 'Rocket Man' in Las Vegas. As he is revealed to be the pilot of the rocket, this marks the literal beginning of a journey into and through his past, represented by specific images and figures, and the simulated interior of his own body. The visual excess and attention to artifice are supplemented by a voice-over, asserting that 'this space contains 60 years of treasured memories of a real rock legend'. The title of the documentary and its lavish opening signal an awareness of the process and grammar of self-narration. The visual element is maintained as John emerges from the rocket into the all-white studio environment from where he will present his autobiographical account; the stark, empty location is digitally filled by additional footage from the past. His account is delivered through his responses to unheard questions from an unseen questioner. This device – a 'prompted journey' where the star 'meets himself in the past' – creates the space in which he recounts, without interruption, major events from his life. The framework for the narration is the requirement to explain his route to pop stardom, and a key contributor to his status is songwriting partner Bernie Taupin, whose contribution as a lyricist is acknowledged, without ever threatening the focus on John himself. The combination of the blank studio setting and the digital manipulation of imagery break up the verisimilitude and sobriety of the documentary space. Alongside this, the flaunting of artifice is counterbalanced by the musical referents of Elton John's vast catalogue of songs and the voice-over of television actress Sian Reeves.

---

[22]   See Nick Couldry, *Media Rituals: A Critical Approach* (London, 2003).

Elaboration of the stages of emergence as a single artist and the process of making and producing pop songs is key to the presentation of self that is offered in *Me, Myself And I*. The emphasis on songwriting in conjunction with the multiple selves suggested by visual surface and the private life of the pop star determine the voice of this documentary, and the impersonal, if not estranging, studio setting and the degree of visual manipulation undermine a reading of this programme as simply another celebrity exposé.

The documentary makes extensive use of newspaper and magazine extracts that confirm the status of the star at different parts of his career. A review in *The Los Angeles Times* from 1970 declaring 'Elton John New Rock Talent' is mounted in an ornate picture frame for the rostrum camera and, typically, these sources of evidence are cut into the narration; the pace of his rise to stardom is confirmed when the voice-over states that 'in the early seventies, Elton John was the biggest selling pop superstar in the world, with a record seven Number One albums in a row'. The acquisition of pop stardom through critical and commercial success is constructed as unproblematic and inevitable. In a typical manipulation of the image, the older Elton John looks back at footage of his younger self and retrospectively states, 'I always knew I'd be famous'. The effects-driven manipulation of space and time disrupts the televisual convention of a talking head in the studio, and positions the programme as an (auto)biographical celebration, made in the flamboyant style that is typical of the subject.

The problems that accompany fame are considered in the narrative: 'being onstage was very comfortable, being offstage was very uncomfortable'. Although he speaks of a dependency on drugs that he was able to overcome and also gives a frank account of his marriage and sexuality, the form of the documentary withholds any intimacy and the potential transition to a confessional register. There is no indication that revisiting these events is unsettling, and the consistency of tone and chronologically directed narrative support the maintenance of control that is representative of the canonic male pop star.

In *Being Mick*, the intimate observational style of director Kevin MacDonald is directed at the life of its rock star subject Mick Jagger. The camera follows the performer around numerous public and domestic locations, including the recording sessions for his solo album *Goddess In The Doorway*. The documentary supplies no biographical past and includes little self narration; instead, it serves as a clear testament to the comfortable relationship that Jagger enjoys with his wealth and fame. There is no attempt to interrogate past events, nor to challenge the evident control that Jagger exercises over the entire project (which extends to the production company – Jagged Films). The degree of control exercised within *Me, Myself And I* and *Being Mick* is a direct consequence of the performers' canonical reputations which, accordingly, are further strengthened by the terms and conditions of the completed programmes.

These six documentaries offer differing versions of biographical and/or autobiographical registers. The presence of interlocutors, while varied, remains evident in all of them, suggesting that these 'guiding figures' and their production colleagues have some understanding of the areas of biographical narrative that such programmes should include. However, the realisation of these investigative directions is influenced by the degree of control that the star is able to wield over the production and also the intertexts connected to the star subjects that precede the documentaries.

The constitution of the self that is represented in these documentaries confirms the scepticism of the literary critics of autobiography. For Bruss, the unity of subjectivity and subject matter is problematised by film; for Egan, there is uncertainty over the apparently originating subject.[23] But it is less a subjectivity articulated by the genre than a document of the subject in dialogue with an interlocutor (and, to varying degrees, their preceding intertexts). This produces a relational and partial self that is also symptomatic of the proliferating production of biography and autobiography, annexed by competing television channels and demonstrated by the effects of reality formats on the amended co-ordinates of documentary production, all within what Christopher Lasch has labelled 'the culture of narcissism'.[24]

David Marshall observes that 'the celebrity is an embodiment of a discursive battleground on the norms of individuality and personality within a culture'.[25] These documentaries reveal that the integrity of the means through which the media set out this battleground and its attendant norms, is by no means straightforward. The role of popular music is at the heart of this. For Paul Morley, the non-conformity of Pete Doherty is essential to the creative potential of his songwriting, but for the tabloid press this is more than outweighed by the consequences of his often excessive drug taking. In comparison with Doherty, Amy Winehouse is perceived to be at a more advanced stage of self-destruction, where the self expression that fed her songwriting has been curtailed and displaced by drug addiction; the media continue to narrate her life story in these revised terms. Victoria Beckham appears to use music (and the documentary) to attempt to reinforce her embodiment of feminine norms, while the tabloid media's assessment of her celebrity is characterised by a fluctuation between admiration and derision that is much less to do with her music than it is pathological. Brian Harvey is attempting to recapture the popularity he attained through music in order to occupy the position that Doherty and Beckham have not yet surrendered. And the canonical male stars whose stardom has lasted for four or five decades occupy this normative ground most comfortably. What the form and content of these programmes indicate is that the relationship between popular music and television documentary is able to reveal and illustrate the culturally contested parameters of stardom and the cycle of fame.

---

[23] Bruss, 'Eye For I'; Egan, 'Encounters'.

[24] Christopher Lasch, *The Culture Of Narcissism: American Life In An Age Of Diminishing Expectations* (New York, 1978).

[25] Marshall, P. David, *Celebrity And Power: Fame In Contemporary Culture* (Minnesota, 1997), p. 65.

Chapter 3

Classic Albums: The Re-Presentation Of The Rock Album On British Television

Andy Bennett and Sarah Baker

The creation and reproduction of heritage discourses has long been an aspect of the cultural work performed by television. The heritage industry around rock music has been gathering momentum for a number of years with regular contributions from television networks. In the UK, one of the more innovative television forays into rock heritage is BBC's *Classic Albums* series. Beginning in the early 2000s, the appeal of the series continues to increase with new episodes continually being produced – recent additions to the series include the Doors' eponymously titled debut album and John Lennon's first post-Beatles solo album, *Plastic Ono Band*. The success of the *Classic Albums* format can be attributed to two main qualities. First, the series adheres to some extent, though not exclusively, to what Hayes has referred to as the *Rolling Stone* version of rock history in its choice of featured albums.[1] Secondly, each show features a mixture of archive and new footage – in the case of the latter, this comprises tightly focused interviews with key musicians, producers, engineers, and critics – that works to situate each album in the socio-historical and technological context in which it was made. This second point is significant in that what often emerges from such vignettes is the very 'human' story of how an album was produced, often under conditions of extreme personal upheaval and turmoil. As this chapter will thus argue, through the *Classic Albums* documentary series, the 'classic' album is significantly re-presented. Although emphasis continues to be placed upon the importance of the classic album as an artefact – an aural document of a band's or artist's stage of musical development at a particular period in their career and its significance for a specific socio-historical milieu – equally important to the *Classic Albums* format is the emotional dimension that is brought to bear on the production and subsequent evaluation of the album as artistic.

Classic Albums And Rock As Heritage Discourse

The alignment of rock music with discourses of culture and heritage can be located within a series of critical trends in late modernity, namely, the dissolution

---

[1] David Hayes, 'Take Those Old Records Off The Shelf: Youth And Music Consumption In The Postmodern Age', *Popular Music And Society* 29/1 (2006), pp. 51–68.

of boundaries between high and low/popular culture, the emergence of digital technologies and their impact on music production, and finally, the increasing significance of what is now referred to as cultural memory as a means through which generations forge a collective sense of identity and situate themselves in socio-cultural contexts. In relation to the first trend, key institutions such as *Rolling Stone* and the *Rock And Roll Hall Of Fame* have played a significant part in the repositioning of rock music as a cultural form worthy of the same prestige bestowed upon 'high art' forms such as classical music, opera, and literature.[2] Such institutions are in no small way responsible for the coining of the term 'classic rock', a descriptor now routinely applied to those critically acclaimed rock artists who emerged during the period 1968–79. From the early 1980s onwards, the digitisation of popular music, punctuated by the CD reissue market and subsequent introduction of the DVD, has functioned to corner a highly lucrative market in the form of middle-aged baby boomers and post-boomers with the necessary economic capital to renew and expand their personal music collections.[3] This market has been significantly boosted through its offering of previously unreleased studio and live material from key artists associated with the 'classic rock' label.

Such repositioning of rock, discursively and technologically, has in its turn forged new understandings about the cultural meaning of rock in the collective consciousness of the rock audience. At the level of everyday consciousness, the term 'classic rock' fuels a series of memories through which audiences understand how their initial investment in rock as teenagers was orientated as much around the cultural aspects of music's production and consumption as the musical characteristics of the rock genre. From the point of view of many, their ongoing investment in classic rock – as what they perceive to be a pure and 'authentic' form – also connotes a reflexive understanding of rock as underpinning and informing the biographical trajectories of ageing baby boomers.

The Album As 'Artefact'

The notion of the rock album as a cultural artefact and musical statement is also tied into a history of critical discourse and technological development spanning back to the mid-1960s. Prior to this time, little importance was placed upon the album at all. This began to change with the release of the Beach Boys' *Pet Sounds* (1966) and the Beatles' *Sgt. Pepper's Lonely Hearts Club Band* (1967). Both albums relied heavily on studio technology for their production (in 1966 the Beatles had retired from live performance and announced their intention to focus exclusively on studio music). *Pet Sounds* and *Sgt. Pepper* each showcased the creative potential of the recording studio, and critically contributed to the aesthetic

---

[2]   Vaughn Schmutz, 'Retrospective Cultural Consecration In Popular Music', *American Behavioral Scientist* 48/11 (2005), pp. 1510–23.

[3]   Andy Bennett, *Cultures Of Popular Music* (Buckingham, 2001).

separation of studio and live performance as distinct events. As studio technology advanced, bands and artists became increasingly ambitious in their use of the studio to produce work that went well beyond the limits of the live performance context – culminating in the lavishly produced concept albums of British progressive rock groups such as Yes, Genesis and Pink Floyd.[4]

The sanctity of the album as an artistic statement was further assured through the emergence of the 'new' journalism of music critics such as Greil Marcus and Lester Bangs, whose writing centred on a discursive positioning of rock music as distinct from pop and chart material.[5] Important in forging such an aesthetic separation was a focus on the album, as opposed to the single, as a key medium for the rock artist. The single was regarded as the purview of the chart-orientated artist, targeting the teen audience with accessible, radio-friendly music. The album, on the other hand, was considered the mainstay of the rock artist – a sonic tapestry on which the latter's more invested interest in music as a form of creative expression could be fully exercised.

The notion of the 'classic album' takes this representation of the rock album as artefact a critical stage further. Considering the ready application of heritage discourse to popular cultural artefacts which, in addition to music, also include film, television drama and popular literature, Schmutz argues that what can be observed here is a process of what he refers to as retrospective cultural consecration.[6] Thus, following decades of exposure to critical discourse and the selective benchmarking of readers' and writers' polls in magazines such as *Rolling Stone*, *Billboard* and *Mojo*, albums such as Cream's *Disraeli Gears* (1967) and Pink Floyd's *Dark Side Of The Moon* (1973) begin to take on a new canonical importance as works that have stood the test of time, and are thus deserving of attention as authentic documents of critical periods in both the musical and broader cultural history of the late twentieth century. Such sentiments are clearly conveyed in both rock journalism and related mediums, notably the special liner notes that often accompany CD re-issues and special anniversary editions of particular albums.

The *Classic Albums* Series

The *Classic Albums* series was initially conceived as a radio show in the late 1980s, when it was jointly presented by John Pidgeon and Roger Scott on BBC Radio 1 (with later episodes presented by Richard Skinner). Albums featured on the show, which was first broadcast in May 1989, included Dire Straits' *Brothers In Arms*, the Rolling Stones' *Beggars Banquet*, Genesis' *Invisible Touch*, Pink Floyd's *Dark Side Of The Moon*, The Who's *Who's Next*, Fleetwood Mac's *Rumours*, the

---

4   See Andy Bennett, 'Heritage Rock: Rock Music, Re-Presentation And Heritage Discourse', *Poetics* 37/5–6 (2009), pp. 474–89.

5   Roy Shuker, *Understanding Popular Music, Second Edition* (London, 2001).

6   Schmutz, 'Retrospective'.

Beach Boys' *Pet Sounds*, Police's *Synchronicity*, the Eagles' *Hotel California* and U2's *The Joshua Tree*. The migration of the *Classic Albums* concept to television came in the late 1990s. Several of the albums included on the *Classic Albums* radio show (*Dark Side Of The Moon*, *Rumours*, *Who's Next*) have also featured in the TV series which, at the time of writing, runs to 31 episodes, the most recent addition being Duran Duran's *Rio* (broadcast in October 2008). The television episodes are 50 minutes in length; the DVD versions contain additional footage (which, in the case of Queen's *A Night At The Opera*, extends to an additional special thirtieth anniversary CD, containing a mixture of original and specially commissioned videos for each of the songs that appeared on the original album released in 1975).

The general format of *Classic Albums* is standard throughout each episode. This includes interviews with the featured group or artist, session musicians who played on the album (where relevant), and the producer and/or engineer who worked on the album. These are often presented together with observations from music critics and/or music industry employees. Such new material is generally intercut with concert, rehearsal or studio footage recorded at the time the album was being produced and released.

Classic Albums offers the audience an in-depth and often highly personal account of how the songs for each of the featured albums were written (including the underlying inspiration), arranged, and recorded in the studio. Detailed, section-by-section analyses of particular songs are presented. This is achieved by isolating specific instrumental and vocal tracks in the mix and/or adjusting volume levels in order to demonstrate the importance of particular elements, sounds and effects integral to the overall aural effect of the song. Similarly, many episodes also feature live, unplugged versions of songs featured on the album, as a means of illustrating the essential quality of a song through performing it in its most basic context (typically guitar and voice).

As noted earlier, however, the *Classic Albums* format does not merely orientate around the music, its composition and technical orchestration. Equally important are the personal accounts – of featured artists, studio musicians, producers and engineers – that weave in and out of the music-centred narratives presented in individual episodes. To some extent, the centrality of such personal narratives to the series may have a bearing on the deviation evident in *Classic Albums* from more conventional renderings of the classic album as most often seen in print journalism. We consider the emotional elements present in the *Classic Albums* series shortly, but will first outline some important deviations of the series from the conventional rock canon.

Departures From The Rock Canon

As noted earlier, to some extent the *Classic Albums* series does adhere to conventional notions of the classic album as represented in the music press. That said, however, there are significant gaps in the repertoire of critically acclaimed albums that the series has featured in its 11-year history. For example, no Beatles or Led Zeppelin albums have yet been included, despite the albums of both of these groups regularly featuring in classic albums live shows.[7] Similarly, while the Beach Boys' *Pet Sounds* and the Eagles' *Hotel California* were both featured in the preceding *Classic Albums* radio programmes, they have thus far failed to appear in the television series. Furthermore, and perhaps to some extent a facet of the more arbitrary selection of albums for the series, there is also something of an imbalance in selection towards particular genres: while five albums by heavy metal artists have featured in the series, only one rap album has been included, and there has been no representation from electronic and dance music artists.

The series also deviates from the more conventional definition of the classic album in other important ways. For example, to consider two albums featured in the *Classic Albums* series, Phil Collins's *Face Value* and Duran Duran's *Rio*, neither album could be considered a classic album in the conventional sense. Certainly, neither has attracted the level of critical kudos attached to albums such as *Dark Side Of The Moon* or *Who's Next*. On the strength of more conventional definitions of the classic album, *Face Value* would appear to be an unlikely addition to the series. Certainly, it is highly probable that the album's commercial impact would have been far less than it ultimately was, had it not been for the inclusion of the track 'In The Air Tonight', Collins's debut single and a major worldwide hit for him. That so much attention is focused on this particular track in the episode dedicated to *Face Value* is clear evidence of this. Much is made of the qualities that combined to make the song a worldwide hit, to the extent that at times it seems set to overshadow other featured songs. For such an album to be included in the series, it would appear that a link is being made by the series producers between an album's significant commercial success and the subsequent branding of the album as 'classic'. This is a less frequent attribution in the rock press.

The *Classic Albums* television series is thus neither an accurate reflection of the dominant canon of classic albums material, as this is understood by critics and, by definition, audiences of magazines such as *Rolling Stone* and *Mojo*, nor, in its departure from established standards for the definition of a classic album, does the series necessarily serve up a consistent repertoire of alternative titles to be included within the canon. We would argue that the series' departure from established definitions of a classic album rests with the medium. The way in which music heritage comes to be (re-)presented in television documentary is necessarily very different to its presentation in print media. This is partly to do with the nature of the television audience. Unlike a magazine article on the rock canon in, for example, *Mojo*, which would have a narrow and arguably specialised readership, a television documentary has the potential to garner a much larger and more diverse audience on whom it needs to press the importance of an album. The potential diversity of the audience means that a sole genre canon must be broadened out

---

[7]   Bennett, 'Heritage'.

to include genres, albums, or artists that may not conventionally be considered 'classic'. And, of course, a television documentary is also dependent on the availability of compelling archival footage, access to the album's contributors and, importantly, an engaging story that will draw an audience.

Building Human Interest Through Emotional Narratives

In order to capture a wider audience it is imperative for the *Classic Albums* series to be genre-inclusive (not rock-centric) and for the discussion of the selected albums to go beyond just the technical aspects of production. Thus, the stories being told in each episode about what makes the album 'classic' need to be expanded beyond those narratives that dominate in the music press. This is because the series is commissioned as a television documentary and so it is expected it will meet some of the basic rules of documentary production relating to 'human interest' – something which is perhaps more tangential in classic albums print journalism. Psychological characterisation is presented in documentary manuals as a way to invest the available materials to be assembled in the telling of a story

> with dramatic and emotional values and so build up 'human interest'. In general, one is advised to focus on the psychological experience of individuals and, frequently, to draw out a sense of conflict within or between these individuals as 'characters' in the program.[8]

In order for this to occur in *Classic Albums*, it is not sufficient to focus only on the technical or musical aspects of the album that make it worthy of being considered part of the popular music canon. Something more is needed to entice an audience to invest their time in watching the documentary. What we see occurring in *Classic Albums*, then, is a shift, in varying degrees, away from the musical product (the album) towards the workers – the socio-cultural-psychological conditions under which the album was produced.

Contemporary culture is currently experiencing something of a '(post)emotional turn', most widely evident in television's reality and talk show genres.[9] Kristyn Gorton suggests that people often watch television programmes 'in order to experience a "journey": one that provides an emotional and intellectual engagement

---

[8] Dugald Williamson, 'Television Documentary', in John Tulloch and Graeme Turner (eds), *Australian Television: Programs, Pleasures And Politics* (Sydney, 1989), pp. 88–102.

[9] See, for example, Stjepan G. Mestrovic, *Postemotional Society* (London, 1997); Laura Grindstaff, *The Money Shot: Trash, Class, And The Making Of TV Talk Shows* (Chicago, 2002); Minna Aslama and Mervi Pantti, 'Talking Alone: Reality TV, Emotions And Authenticity', *European Journal Of Cultural Studies* 9/2 (2006), pp. 167–84.

with the story that unfolds'.[10] The extent to which a programme can be judged to be 'good' depends on the depth of the emotional journey it provides.[11] She argues that 'the value of emotion in a text can be understood as something that creates good television and constructs a sense of connectedness and belonging' for the audience.[12] However, although television can 'construct intimate moments' through its use of emotion and psychological characterisation, the extent to which this will resonate with a viewer's emotional journey cannot be certain as audience members do not necessarily '*catch* emotion in the same ways' – emotional connection for one viewer might register as boredom for another.[13]

The story that comes to be told in many of the *Classic Albums* episodes concerns the emotional labour involved in album production. Emotional labour is defined by Hochschild as the inducement or suppression of 'feeling in order to sustain the outward countenance that produces the proper state of mind in others';[14] with the management of the emotions of self and others being integral to the carrying out of 'good' work. Though this concept is most often applied to service workers, it has recently been utilised in discussions of cultural industries workers in terms of their engagement with audience members, television programme contributors, and the emotional work that goes into maintaining a cohesive production unit.[15] The *Classic Albums* series picks up on that last point, with an attempt to include in most episodes a narrative based on the emotional relationships between the musicians, and sometimes also the other key creators involved in the album's production.

To get across the emotional struggles of the labour of music making – the human interest material so important in the documentary form – *Classic Albums* relies on the self-disclosure that comes from first-person interviews. The resulting 'confessional monologues'[16] provide the 'inner story' of the creation of the album, with the documentary foregrounding 'a highly defined narrative of localized feelings and experiences'[17] presented against the background of the album's technical production. What this means for *Classic Albums* is that 'the viewing invitation slides from the dynamics of understanding', in terms of the musical

----

[10]   Kristyn Gorton, 'A Sentimental Journey: Television, Meaning And Emotion', *Journal Of British Cinema And Television* 3 (2006), p. 72.

[11]   Ibid.

[12]   Kristyn Gorton, 'There's No Place Like Home: Emotional Exposure, Excess And Empathy On TV', *Critical Studies In Television* 3/1 (2008), p. 12.

[13]   Ibid., p. 5.

[14]   Arlie Russell Hochschild, *The Managed Heart: Commercialization Of Human Feeling* (Berkeley, 1983), p. 7.

[15]   See, for example Grindstaff, *The Money Shot*; David Hesmondhalgh and Sarah Baker, 'Creative Work And Emotional Labour In The Television Industry', *Theory, Culture and Society*, 25/7–8 (2008), pp. 97–118.

[16]   Aslama and Pantti, 'Talking', p. 168.

[17]   John Corner, 'Performing The Real: Documentary Diversions', *Television & New Media*, 3/3 (2002), p. 256.

reasons which make the album worthy of being considered a classic, 'to the involving, but at the same time more passive, transaction of vicarious witness and empathy' regarding the emotional labour or investment that goes into producing a work that would take its place in the popular music canon.[18]

Phil Collins's *Face Value*

Two specific examples are illustrative of this shift in the way that the classic album is re-presented in the series. The first is the episode devoted to *Face Value*, the debut solo album by Genesis lead singer and drummer Phil Collins. *Face Value* begins with a voiceover provided by Collins, accompanied by the opening bars of 'In The Air Tonight' and the album image featuring a black-and-white close-up of the singer's face:

> This record is definitely autobiographical, but not just focusing on a sadness. That's the thing that's a misconception I think. It's triggered by an event. It chronicles, you know, a life in motion.

As stated above, this episode of *Classic Albums* is significantly orientated around one track on the album, Collins's debut hit single 'In The Air Tonight'. An interesting narrative trick is employed by the series producers, as Collins and other interviewees suggest a critical link between that track and the other songs included on *Face Value*. Thus, it is argued, what connects each song on the album is their cathartic resonance with Collins's personal life around the time. The album was produced and released in 1981, as the artist confronted the breakup of his first marriage. In an interview recorded for the episode, Collins explains:

> I had a wife and two children and two dogs and the next day I didn't have anything. So I really had a lot of time on my hands. That sounds terrible. I don't want it to sound like I had the carpet ripped out from underneath me. I played my part in this mistake too. So a lot of these songs were written because at the time I was going through all these emotional changes. But to me it was just the sound of the words. I didn't know what I was singing about, but obviously when you're going through a divorce, all kinds of things run through your mind. There's anger, there's bitterness, there's hurt, and all that stuff is in 'In The Air Tonight'. Menace: finally losing your temper in the end where the drums come in ... the songs were just songs based on my emotions at the time.

Later, behind a piano and talking about another of these songs ('Please Don't Ask'), Collins's continued emotional connection to the lyrics can be heard in his voice and observed in his facial expressions in the close-ups. And close-ups are

---

[18] Ibid.

recognised by Collins himself as integral to conveying the emotion of his music. He says of the album cover, 'You wouldn't put a face like this on the cover really if you wanted to sell a record, would you? The idea of putting it on the cover was to try and get as close as you could – to almost see inside the person's head – because this is what was going on inside my head'.

From this perspective, the classic album discourse takes on a new dimension – the emotional investment surrounding the album's production. At this point, it becomes necessary to go beyond the conventional reading of the classic album as an artistic statement or creative work. Rather, what has been stamped on the album is the artist's ability to work under difficult personal circumstances, which are then conveyed to the audience as key elements of the classic album. Indeed, viewed from this angle, there are clear parallels between albums such as *Face Value* and those that would more conventionally fall under the categorisation of a classic album. An example here is Paul Simon's *Graceland*. Although offering a richer platform for critical appraisal of its individual tracks and in-studio dissection of the individual instruments and sonic layers that make up its songs, a surprising amount of time in the *Graceland* episode is given over to Simon's confessional account of how personal upheaval, feelings of insecurity and other details of a highly idiosyncratic nature provided creative inspiration for his songwriting.

Fleetwood Mac's *Rumours*

The second example of emotional narratives in the *Classic Albums* series is the episode about Fleetwood Mac's album *Rumours*, which essentially centres on the emotional work undertaken by band members during the album's production. As the DVD sleeve for the episode dramatically states:

> By 1977, when *Rumours* was recorded, John and Christine McVie were separating, and Stevie Nicks and Lindsey Buckingham's relationship was also breaking up. This was the album that almost never made it!

The impact of these break-ups on the making of the album is a story that is thread purposefully throughout the episode. Mick Fleetwood begins this narrative by talking about the two challenges faced in the recording of *Rumours*: the musical challenge – a narrative addressed in the documentary using the section-by-section analyses of the songs – and the personal challenge which, in the overarching story being told in the documentary, comes to be connected to the musical challenge. Christine McVie, in particular, talks expansively about the impact of the tensions between various members of the group on the songwriting process:

> We were all writing songs about each other basically, although we were unaware of it at the time. All the songs were about our own private relationships and our own troubled relationships and I think it was John who suggested the name

Rumours because we were writing diaries and journals about one another which we hadn't realised until we heard all the songs all strung together.

McVie's confessional monologue intensifies, as she goes on to describe the very real problems faced by the group in the recording studio because of the disintegration of their personal relationships:

> One of the hard things was to see John so sad. We actually did not talk at all. John and I did not talk. Stevie and Lindsey didn't get on very well either, but they used to fight, whereas John and I used to avoid each other. They used to fight, although not all the time, they could in actual fact get on quite well, especially when they were writing songs together. John and I did not write songs together, and we did not talk, period, except for the civilities in life, like 'what key is this song in?' That would be more or less it, and so we spent six months in that studio more or less avoiding each other.

The ways in which Stevie Nicks and Lindsey Buckingham's break-up could potentially have compromised the music is also raised in the documentary with Nicks awkwardly articulating, 'Lindsey had an amazing way of taking my songs and making them wonderful, um, when he was, ah, when he was happy with me'. This thread is then taken up in the interview with Buckingham, where he confesses:

> Whatever Stevie's music was, somehow I was this soulmate that just knew exactly what to do with it. And that never went away; it just became a little bittersweet in terms of wanting to do it. There were times when I had the urge not to want to help her. And that's a weird thing to admit, but these were the challenging things.

However, as John McVie states when explaining his feelings at the time of his separation from Christine, 'at the bottom of all of that stuff [the break-ups] was, we have something musically that we could achieve ... the bottom line is, this is what we do, we make music, and this is an unfortunate situation'. The culmination of the narrative then is that through emotional labour, with the band members working to maintain a productive relationship with each other despite personal turmoil, something musically valuable, and which is also based on each songwriter's emotional situation, was ultimately produced. What the documentary seems to be saying is that it is the interplay of emotion, in the music and between the band members during the album's production, that makes *Rumours* a classic album.

Classic Albums **And Memorial Discourse**

Another means through which the emotional work of musicians, producers and others involved in the production of albums is registered is through their accounts of creative partners who have since passed away. Given the retrospective nature of *Classic Albums* and the relative newness of the concept, archive interview footage of deceased artists is rarely adequate to integrate their views and opinions of particular songs within the broader framework of the classic album discourse. As such, it typically falls to fellow band members to supply an authoritative voice for the audience. A clear case in point is the *Classic Albums* episode dedicated to Queen's *A Night At The Opera*. In itself a rare foray into the highly complex, studio-crafted music of Queen in an era where the technology could barely keep up with the group's creative vision, there are poignant moments in which guitarist Brian May offers his own, often highly personal, account of the late Freddie Mercury's musical contributions to the album, and to Queen as a whole. In doing so, May is at pains to concentrate on the musical achievements of Mercury – a point made purposefully when May offers an acoustic rendition of Mercury's 'Love Of My Life', a song which, as May explains, he continues to perform in latter-day live appearances as a tribute to his dead friend and colleague. Prior to the acoustic performance, May is pictured in the studio, holding his guitar and, speaking gently, offers the following account:

> There's some lovely backing harmonies from Freddie on this as well. Freddie had the ability to sing multi-track so accurately that it would actually phase, one take would phase with another, 'cos he would sing it so similarly each time. His beautiful backing harmonies … I just remember him doing it in the studio. He had a wonderful touch on the piano, Freddie. Really, he didn't think he did, he was very deprecating about his piano playing, and in later years really didn't do any of it. He played less and less piano on stage because he wanted to run around and deliver to the audience, as he did so magnificently. He didn't have the classical range, but he could play what came from inside him like nobody else – incredible rhythm, incredible passion and feeling. But I love this song ['Love Of My Life'] and pretty much every concert we play I sing this song now for Freddie, and I find it much more satisfying than singing one of my own songs, because it seems to bring back so much of Freddie for me and with the audience.

Another highly effective example of such memorial discourse is seen in the *Classic Albums* account of Nirvana's *Nevermind* album. Interestingly, in this case, the widely accepted status of Kurt Cobain as the creative driving force in Nirvana is accentuated in a quite different way. Neither of the surviving members of Nirvana – bass player Krist Novoselic and drummer Dave Grohl – are featured in the studio dissections of the album's tracks, nor do they attempt to demonstrate technical aspects of the music through close-up performances of particular riffs and hooks. Instead, such technical and musical analyses are provided by *Nevermind*'s producer Butch Vig. Novoselic and Grohl are thus left with the task of supplying the cultural backdrop against which the album was made, an account which often suggests that both Novoselic and Grohl were as drawn in and captivated by the creative and performative charisma of Cobain, as were his legions of fans, admirers and copyists. Equally evocative is the way in which both Novoselic and Grohl work, in separate interviews, to make sense of the turmoil that engulfed Nirvana, and Cobain in particular, following the worldwide success of *Nevermind* after its release in 1991. Without revisiting the specific context and moment of Cobain's demise – a story that was in any case well documented by the global media following Cobain's suicide in 1994 – the detail of Novoselic and Grohl's experience as sidemen to a rock tragedy is vividly brought home as the pressures upon the classic rock icon 'vocalist-guitarist-front man' are revisited as a means of explicating the degrees of separation between death and survival in the surreal world of overnight success.

A final means through which memorial discourse is played out in *Classic Albums* is via tribute. As has been variously noted,[19] tribute bands and classic album recitals offer an important means through which the music of deceased rock icons can be consumed and enjoyed as a live spectacle. In the episode featuring the late Frank Zappa's albums *Apostrophe (')* and *Over-nite Sensation*, the tribute concept is moved a step closer to the tributed artist in the form of Zappa Plays Zappa, a Frank Zappa tribute band led by Frank's son Dweezil. While working through and demonstrating with apparent ease some of the highly complex, *avant-garde* arrangements of his dead father, Dweezil Zappa's approach is one of extreme reverence for the professed genius of Zappa – a figure who is addressed as an artist of high critical acclaim, as much as the interviewee's father. Thus, in one scene, holding a guitar with which he illustrates Zappa's licks, Dweezil observes: 'He had an ability to write a song filled with so much information, he really looked at using a rock band in the same way he would use an orchestra.' In another scene, Dweezil is seated at a sound console, isolating music effects, to provide an appropriate illustration:

> Another great texture idea that Frank was so brilliant at in his arrangements … When you sit down to learn this stuff, you are just constantly amazed, with 'wow, I didn't even know that was in there' and if you take it out, that's the thing that really made it have that special thing he would call 'the eyebrows'.

Finally, towards the end of the episode, he says emphatically of his father: 'He just really was very creative, and he enjoyed the process of being creative. And he didn't feel like there were any boundaries that should constrict what he was able to do.'

---

[19] See, for example, Shane Homan (ed.), *Access All Eras: Tribute Bands And Global Pop Culture* (Buckingham, 2006); Bennett, 'Heritage'.

Conclusion

This chapter has sought to illustrate that because of its reliance on the medium of television the *Classic Albums* series has employed a series of creative strategies to tell the story of the classic album in a way that will appeal to a wide audience. In doing so, the series has to some extent moved away from the accepted canon of classic albums, something that may offend rock 'purists', but has nevertheless been necessary in exploiting the broader tastes of the general public. To what extent then does the *Classic Albums* series complicate the acknowledged definition of the classic album and its relationship to the heritage rock discourse as outlined in the earlier part of this chapter? Clearly, there is no straightforward answer to this and much depends, at one level, on the nature of the investment by audiences in the rock album as artefact. This said, scholarship in the sociology of music has increasingly focused on the everyday meanings of popular music – a focus that prises open canonical readings of music as mapping accurately onto the ways in which individuals understand music as meaningful in their everyday lives.[20] To this end, such contributions have investigated in depth the emotional work invested by listeners in popular music texts – with the implicit suggestion that artefacts such as albums engender deep personal meanings for listeners that may, in some cases, surpass the overarching canonical discourses of critics and other taste makers. Setting this more firmly in the context of this chapter, there may well be acute resonances between the emotional discourse of musicians and artists featured in the *Classic Albums* series and those of individual viewers/listeners. *Classic Albums* may take the concept of rock music and heritage beyond the canonical trope of the taste maker and into the sphere of cultural memory, where understandings of rock as tied to culture and heritage acquire a new level of locally acquired personal experience.

---

[20] See, for example, Simon Frith, *Performing Rites: On The Value Of Popular Music* (Oxford, 1996); Tia DeNora, *Music In Everyday Life* (Cambridge, 2000).

Chapter 4

Stone Fox Chase: *The Old Grey Whistle Test* And The Rise Of High Pop Television

Peter Mills

The Old Grey Whistle Test was televised on BBC2 from 1971 to 1987; for most of that time, it was the only programme where viewers could see and hear non-chart music on British television. However, its fate turned out to be not unlike that of its brightly-coloured cousin, BBC1's *Top Of The Pops* (1964–2006). Both were eventually cancelled after suffering a slow decline, and are now very rarely seen as whole programmes with an internal logic: the intermittent, compilation-based *TOTP2* (1994–) dices the original, weekly chart show into various thematic blocks (Christmas, single artist specials) and although performance clips from *The Old Grey Whistle Test* are the backbone of BBC4's music documentary output, complete editions of the show (with its magazine/information network contexts) are almost never seen. The memory of the show's fuller identity has therefore been somewhat eviscerated, and yet the story of the programme is close to the pulsebeat of British popular music, and to its representation on British television.

In his autobiography, the programme's most celebrated host, Bob Harris, connects the accelerated spread of pop music in the UK to TV's cultural impact after the coronation of Queen Elizabeth II in 1952.[1] While this might appear initially incongruous, he is not incorrect: there is certainly an association between the domestic integration of television and the rise of the new music, whether rock'n'roll (from America) or skiffle (the musical dandelion born out of British post-war austerity). Skiffle, in particular, had its own telegenic frontman and embodiment of the music of the post-war generation – those whom Van Morrison (in the lyrics of 'Wild Children') called 'the war children, 1945' – in Lonnie Donegan, a man whose combination of energy and personal charm drew in the young, without alarming the adults. These new musics found a natural fit with the visual medium. Suddenly, the weeks of touring and performing, night after night, could be eclipsed as millions of potential buyers were reached simultaneously, a phenomenon most famously illustrated in the US by the appearances of Elvis Presley and, later, the Beatles on CBS-TV's *The Ed Sullivan Show*. On both occasions, the images flashed across America, confirming the new realities of music and the moving image in a single mercurial moment.

---

[1]   Bob Harris, *The Whispering Years* (London, 2001).

This new dynamic was felt even more acutely in the UK, where a single market existed, and ideas and trends could spread rapidly without needing to negotiate the time-zone delays and cultural chasms between American states. British television displayed a quick and ever-developing response, with dedicated shows flowing from the mid-1950s, many from the frantic imagination of Jack Good, who created *Six-Five Special* (BBC, 1957–58) and *Oh Boy!* (ITV, 1958–59). The daring, wild format of *Oh Boy!* and its emphasis on high-wire, live performance threw down a challenge to music and television which, arguably, still remains only partially met. When Good moved from BBC to the new, commercial network of ITV, he left behind not only a methodology, but also a young, commercially powerful audience who demanded more of the same. It took the arrival of Merseybeat and Beatlemania to really force the broadcasters' hand; from 1964, popular music programming was foregrounded by both channels, via *Top Of The Pops* and a sequence of commercial competitors, including *Ready Steady Go!* (ITV, 1963–66) which, despite capturing the musical excitement of the period more successfully, never quite toppled *Top Of The Pops*.

It was the success of the Beatles which, as in so many other aspects of popular culture, re-routed the nature of popular music programming in the UK, and changed the rules that determined how pop was shown and understood. *Top Of The Pops* was completely dependent upon the new market, in the shape of the charts – who was hot that week, today, *right now* – and laid bare the competitive dimension within the production and consumption of pop. Music became a race: Beatles vs. Stones; EMI vs. Decca; BBC vs. ITV. When the Beatles retired from live performance in 1966, television became even more central to the promotion and marketing of pop; the subsequent arrival of the Monkees cemented this connection. As a consequence, there came a kind of schism: 'rock' for adults and 'pop' for kids. The 'serious' music listener was served by *Blonde On Blonde* and Jefferson Airplane, while the pop fan had *More Of The Monkees*. In terms of both production and consumption, the two strands of popular music were suddenly separated. In some ways, this can be related to the distinction made by Adorno in 1941 between 'serious' and 'popular' music.[2] 'Serious' referred to the music of Europe that he had left behind when fleeing from Nazi Germany – the leider of Schubert, the fugues of Bach, the late quartets of Beethoven; 'popular' described the jazz, swing and big band styles he found in the US in the early 1940s. The shock of the new and the divergence of interpretive vocabularies noted by Adorno found an unexpected resonance in the split between rock and pop. Television, for its part, needed to record and respond to this schism.

In the UK, part of the more localised response to this changing cultural scene was the formation of BBC2 – launched in 1964, after the 1962 Pilkington Report had awarded Britain's third television channel to the BBC, partly as a reproach to the perceived populism of ITV's broadcasting output. It was in this spirit that

---

[2]   Theodor Adorno, 'On Popular Music' (1941), in Richard Leppert (ed.), *Essays On Music* (Berkeley CA, 2002), pp. 437–69.

the channel was programmed, and the content reflected its refreshed Reithian sensibility; early successes included its 26-part adaptation of John Galsworthy's *The Forsyte Saga* (1967) and Sir Kenneth Clark's groundbreaking series *Civilisation* (1969) The channel was specifically charged to expand TV coverage of the arts and culture, an obligation it has always endeavoured to continue.

In the early 1990s, this was partly accomplished by *The Late Show* (1989–95) a nightly arts and entertainment programme, from which came the long-running musical spin-off *Later … With Jools Holland* (1992–) whose title acknowledged its original location. In the early days of BBC2, its equivalent was *Late Night Line Up* (1964–72) a Monday–Friday late night arts discussion programme whose chief characteristic was the undivided nature of its representation: a single edition might include Ivor Cutler, Leo McKern, Jimi Hendrix and Pierre Schoendoerffer. This was programming which, if not quite in pursuit of the Wagnerian totality of art, was certainly ready to explore the connections between cultural activities, as well as the distinctions. The post-*Sgt. Pepper* recognition of popular music as something worthy of extended scrutiny led part of its schedule to be re-christened as *Colour Me Pop* (1968–69), a weekly half-hour showcase for a single artist, which ran for 53 editions. The show presented musicians who typified the new conditions, poised between the established pop terminologies of the first part of the decade, and the development into more self-consciously artistic composition and performance. Directed by Steve Turner, the series opened with Manfred Mann, and went on to feature an unlikely assortment of artists: Honeybus, the Fortunes, and Clodagh Rodgers, alongside the Small Faces, Family, and Robert Fripp's first TV exposure as part of Giles, Giles & Fripp. Such musical eclecticism was healthy enough, but also illustrated how the contemporary scene was beginning to cleave apart down a substantial cultural faultline which, of course, represented a considerable problem for programmers: to characterise the difficulty at its extreme, could Harmony Grass and Spooky Tooth be presented side by side?

Late Night Line Up and *Colour Me Pop* were both produced by Michael Appleton, whose musical enthusiasm was the motor for both shows. After *Colour Me Pop* ended, Appleton returned to his original concept, and in 1970 produced *Disco 2* (the generic connotations of 'disco' as a musical form were still several years away) which differed from its predecessor in adopting a magazine-like approach.

> In the early 1970s the album market was very strong – possibly even stronger than the singles market – so there was a disparity in coverage that needed to be addressed, as there was an enormous wastage of good music going on. *Disco 2* was album music, but presented in such a way that it was a little bit more hip to the time.[3]

---

[3]   Michael Appleton, *The Old Grey Whistle Test 30th Anniversary DVD* (BBC, 2001).

Disco 2 initiated a form of popular music programming which both responded, and actively contributed, to these changed conditions. In its magazine format it created the template for 'adult' or 'rock' television for years to come. Yet in itself it was a relative failure, running for less than a year. This, it should be noted, is the fate of most pop music programming, and although the exceptions tend to dominate the field, sometimes surviving for many years, it is often the short-lived shows which offer real discoveries and breakthroughs. In this regard, *Disco 2*, *Supersonic* (ITV, 1975–77), *So It Goes* (ITV, 1976–77) and *Revolver* (ITV, 1978) are all in their own ways as important as *Top Of The Pops*, *Later … With Jools Holland* and *The Old Grey Whistle Test*. The show was not completely forgotten, however: in a typically knowing gesture, the Pet Shop Boys called their 1994 remix album *Disco 2*.

The magazine component of the show was in response to, and shadowed by, the development of a new journalism that addressed this music. Beginning in the US with *Rolling Stone* (1967), *Creem* (1969) and *Who Put The Bomp* (1970) a high seriousness was directed upon the way in which music was understood and the spirit in which it was being made. *Disco 2* had combined these assumptions of value and significance in its presentation of news, new releases, interviews and performance footage in a structure significantly removed from the *Top Of The Pops* model, and the traditional fan-based journalism of teen magazines like *Fab 208*. Yet the format had not quite found its shape; the preference for non-chart music was still a challenge to the accepted criteria for TV appearances. When planning his successor to *Disco 2*, Appleton was acutely aware of the new and critical criteria emerging in print and on screen:

> *The Old Grey Whistle Test* was a spawning ground where we experimented with various ideas. I'd had the idea of doing *New Musical Express* or *Melody Maker* on television, a kind of magazine programme that had never really existed before, and it seemed that there was a place on TV at that time for something that looked at rock music, in particular, in a slightly more serious way. One of my first thoughts became one of the rules of the programme: the people who were going to present it were going to be journalists, who knew their subject matter, and who were going to be doing presentation on TV as a hobby rather than as a career, so they never became bigger than the programme.[4]

Those early experiments also included on-screen text which, although commonplace today, at the time was technically difficult, and was abandoned. Most importantly, the presenter was permitted to do more than simply present. Unlike the hosts of *Top Of The Pops* or *Ready Steady Go!* whose enthusiasm for each and every disc spun was equal and equable and who were expected to leave their opinions in the dressing room, those who presented the 'serious' music of the late 1960s and early 1970s were required to be critical and knowledgeable,

---

[4]   Ibid.

as befitting the distance that now separated 'rock' from 'pop'; this was music that warranted scrutiny and contextualisation, rather than mere introduction. In this, it attempted to flatter, direct and reflect the interests of its intended audience. The programme's first presenter was Richard Williams, then deputy editor of the top music weekly *Melody Maker*:

> *Disco 2* was a part of *Late Night Line Up*. Tommy Vance was the original presenter of *Disco 2*, I think, but they wanted someone with a journalistic background to present special features. The first one I did was an interview with Frank Zappa. Michael Appleton was the producer. When it mutated into *The Old Grey Whistle Test*, he asked me to present it, with, as I recall, Ian Whitcomb, who lasted only a couple of programmes in that role.[5]

In fact, Appleton described Williams's appearances on *Disco 2* as 'on-air auditions for *The Whistle Test*'.[6] His subsequent appointment provided evidence of the perceived correspondence between the music and the new writing that surrounded it, as the still-young visual medium poached a little of the cultural authority of the older print medium; moreover, he also fitted Appleton's 'hobby' criteria, as he maintained his full time post on *Melody Maker* during his tenure on the show: 'I'd arrive at Television Centre at eight o'clock on Tuesday morning, write the script, then go on to work at the newspaper. For writing the script and presenting the programme, I was paid £20.00 a week. I think it went up to £30.00 halfway through the season.'[7] A devotion to the subject was clearly essential. As the new show was designed with a deliberate emphasis on its *not* being *Top Of The Pops* (that is, not solely driven by what was commercially successful at that particular moment), there was room for the archival or vintage clips which had occasionally featured in *Disco 2*, and for music unreleased or unavailable in the UK. This was a deliberate form of connoisseur programming – just as conscious of its market as *Top Of The Pops*, but concerned to develop a new way of presenting music on television.

It was christened *The Old Grey Whistle Test*, a name which had its roots in what might seem to be the musical antithesis to a show that flourished in the singer-songwriter boom of the early 1970s – the songwriting factory based around the Brill Building in New York:

> The Brill Building had its own designated doormen, cleaners and ancillary workers, known as the 'old greys'. At the end of the working week, all were invited into a playback room to listen to a selection of the new songs ... the mantra was 'the hook'. If the 'old greys' could hum or whistle along to the chorus of a song having heard it only once, it proved the song was catchy, had

5   Richard Williams, personal interview, 17 June 2009.
6   Appleton, *The Old Grey Whistle Test*.
7   Williams, personal interview.

a good hook, and was likely to be a hit. In other words it passed the 'old grey whistle test'. That's how the programme got its name.[8]

An alternative name also considered was *The Florence Foster Jenkins Music Emporium*; the final title was the decision of Gloria Wood, who had worked on *Late Night Line Up*. Its purpose, as revealed by Appleton, was to provoke puzzlement, 'so people would always wonder what the hell it meant'.[9] Given the historical irony that some of the most successful musicians of the period were themselves products of the Brill Building (notably Carole King) the title too was a part of the new conditions. In contrast to the bright, direct, marketplace certainties of *Top Of The Pops* and *Ready Steady Go!* it utilised an in-joke, a hipster reference, to what seemed like an outdated mode of creativity. The whole purpose of the new show was to foreground music which would fox the 'old greys' – how would that notional doorman like to whistle along to Captain Beefheart or Caravan? Somewhat giddy with the spirit of the time, the nomenclature was geared up to confuse the straights.

The Old Grey Whistle Test's claims to the new authenticity were, to a large extent, tied into issues of liveness. *Top Of The Pops* was widely considered to be a show on which miming to records (or pre-records) was the standard, although this was not entirely true (witness the Jackson Five's stunning 'Rockin' Robin' in December 1972, or New Order's deliciously capricious and completely 'live' performance of their new machine music for 'Blue Monday' in March 1983). Nevertheless, live performance was core to the theory, if not always the practice of *The Old Grey Whistle Test*, and generally distinguished its acts from those appearing on *Top Of The Pops*. Moreover, while there would often be one-off *Top Of The Pops* versions of current hits (where the original performance would be supplemented by additional vocal backing from the Ladybirds or an orchestral arrangement by Johnny Pearson), no such intrusions upon artistic sanctity were permitted on *The Old Grey Whistle Test*, demonstrating how, in at least one way, the show's reification of its music was far more pronounced than its supposedly populist competitor. In passing, it is interesting to note that this is another of the many ways in which *Later … With Jools Holland* has combined elements of both shows, through Holland's frequent keyboard additions to performances of familiar songs by a variety of guests.

The programme's structure was determined almost from the start. In an early edition from October 1971, introduced by Williams as 'the show with the funny name' (as one reviewer had called it), it is clear that it can be as market-led as *Top Of The Pops*: new releases from Fanny and Isaac Hayes are joined by plugs for the Mamas and Papas reunion album *People Like Us*, movie screenings, two songs from Elton John, and an interview with John and his songwriting collaborator Bernie Taupin, in which it is revealed that 'Tiny Dancer' was written about Taupin's wife

---

8 Harris, *Whispering*, p. 60.

9 Appleton, *The Old Grey Whistle Test*.

Maxine. It also contains what would become one of the programme's signifiers – a clip of vintage black and white film, here accompanying a song by Andy Pratt. These came at first from the film library of Philip Jenkinson (the presenter of *Late Night Line Up*'s movie strand) and were used in the absence of any artist-specific footage. They became celebrated, even iconic, in themselves: the film of a downhill skier shot by Leni Reifenstahl in the 1930s which illustrated the opening three minutes of Mike Oldfield's *Tubular Bells* in 1973, and the newsreel footage of Parisian dancing girls that accompanied Led Zeppelin's 'Trampled Underfoot' in 1975 are among the best remembered. In passing, it is interesting to note that, somewhat surprisingly, the first widely-seen use of this technique was in the Monkees' movie *Head* (Bob Rafelson, 1968). The magazine element of the show is especially pronounced: Williams is torn between admiration and amusement by the elaborate packaging of Isaac Hayes' *Black Moses*, enthuses about Andy Pratt's album, and eagerly recommends an upcoming BFI screening of the Rolling Stones' *Gimme Shelter* (Albert and David Maysles, 1970): 'go and see it!' However, as the series progressed, the requirement to present music for which he had little or no enthusiasm, soon became onerous:

> Pretty soon I realised that I hated having to present music I really disliked (David Crosby, Focus, Fanny, David Bowie). I found it impossible, actually, to set aside my own feelings. Having to act as a salesman for such stuff was what in the end persuaded me to tell them I wasn't interested in doing a second series.[10]

He left the show in the summer of 1972, to be replaced by the man who came to embody the programme's values, tone, rules, and its relationship with the audience. Bob Harris was – and perhaps still is – wholly synonymous with the show, as much as the 'starkicker' graphics of Roger Ferrin, and the unmistakable theme-tune, 'Stone Fox Chase' by Nashville country-rock outfit Area Code 615. A policeman's son from Northampton, he was the representative figure of the new conditions *par excellence* – the hippie who was also a savvy businessman, the radical who was also a middle-class entrepreneur. In addition, he was closely involved with the creation of *Time Out* (the innovative and influential London 'what's on' magazine). As someone used to selecting his own content, he initially found the shift from producer/compiler to frontman tricky: 'This was very different from radio, where I built my shows, drove my own equipment.'[11] Through a slow process of attrition, the show effectively evolved into a reflection of his own interests and tastes, in which occasional breaches of his gatekeeping role were met with on-screen disapproval. Three decades later, his fans' enthusiasm continues to drive his radio broadcasts which reflect his devotion to the musical vocabularies that characterised his period of tenure on *The Old Grey Whistle Test* – broadly, but not exclusively, American music, notably country-rock, the James Taylor singer-

---

[10] Williams, personal interview.
[11] Harris, *Whispering*, p. 63.

songwriter model, or anything on the Warner/Asylum/Reprise labels. Furthermore, his enthusiasm for the music (much of it now reborn as 'Americana') has survived numerous sackings and low periods. Yet from the start, *The Old Grey Whistle Test* proved a great success under his stewardship. It was widely perceived as being completely in tune with the times, and regularly won the music weeklies' 'Best TV Show' awards through the next half-decade. The industry soon realised that, for the right act, an appearance on the show was as much of a boost as a visit to the *Top Of The Pops* studio.

In the light of this, it is important to consider how the music industry sought to satisfy new market demands, and absorb them into a product that could be successfully and appropriately marketed. The greatest difference between the audiences for *Top Of The Pops* and *The Old Grey Whistle Test* was simple: one was interested in the single, the other was interested in the album. Where *Top Of The Pops* was about the now, the three-minute rush of the current chart hit, *The Old Grey Whistle Test* asserted the gravity and significance of the album as a cultural document which would linger longer than its last note. Hence, it contributed to the birth of the 'album artist': the popular musician(s) who could be substantially successful, and yet never get near the Top 40 singles chart. This became its natural constituency. Very few acts were equally comfortable on both shows, and when a performer did slip from one domain to the other it appeared as something akin to a coup: Focus and the Sensational Alex Harvey Band (both favourites of *The Old Grey Whistle Test*) experienced pop chart successes which led to appearances on *Top Of The Pops*, but this kind of crossover was rare. Intriguingly, the road was blocked more completely from the centre to the margins. Rory Gallagher or Richard and Linda Thompson on *Top Of The Pops*? If they had a hit single, maybe. Slade or Donny and Marie Osmond on *The Old Grey Whistle Test*? Never. There was thus a kind of defiance around the show's admissions policy, predicated as it was on something other than the pure lines of commercial success, and concentrated on the ur-text of the album: '*Top Of The Pops* was Edison Lighthouse. *The Old Grey Whistle Test* was "heavy", as we used to say.'[12] Because bands like Led Zeppelin and Pink Floyd refused to issue singles in the UK in the early 1970s (although they were happy to do so in the US), the problematic relationship between the charts and credibility, a success of a certain *estime*, was a particularly British phenomenon. At the same time, the absence of rock's most prestigious performers from the singles charts allowed bands such as Queen, Sparks, Mott the Hoople and Roxy Music, all *Top Of The Pops* regulars, to become genuinely popular while injecting fresh ideas into pop's bloodstream.

The 'serious purpose' that ran through *The Old Grey Whistle Test* was emphasised by the very look of the show: what made it visually different from previous pop programmes was its physical environment. Instead of the music being performed to an enthusiastic studio audience, dancing, singing and applauding (as was the norm for music television of the 1950s and 1960s) the show presented

---

[12]   Williams, personal interview.

the music direct to camera, delivered 'authentically' to the viewer at home. This certainly added to the show's impact, but was less of a conscious decision than a virtue born of necessity. The 10 metres by 7 metres studio allotted to the show, 'Pres B', was usually home to weathermen and continuity announcers: 'it was a tiny cubicle meant for one person and a bunch of flowers ... The mixing desk was laughable – there were only eight faders, and if you had echo on one, you had to have it on them all. Some bands took it as a challenge, others as a nightmare'.[13] In fact, Williams has admitted that because of the difficulties created by the lack of facilities, the 'liveness' of the show was not always total: 'What most people don't remember is that quite a few of the studio "performances" were mimed. Just like *Top Of The Pops*.'[14] However, Appleton maintains that the vocals were live on '99 per cent' of performances, even if the backing tracks were pre-recorded.[15] The 1973 appearance of Brinsley Schwarz heralded a change in policy, as the band insisted on bringing in its own equipment in order to perform live: 'It was so successful that they [the programme's production team] managed to persuade the powers to get a proper mixer so they could do it themselves.'[16]

With space limited and equipment basic, the decision not to have a set encouraged performers to regard the studio as a rehearsal room, in which one guest would be filmed in the afternoon, and one would appear live in the evening. While solo singer-songwriters understandably found the environment more welcoming than did super-amplified rock bands, the show did deliver some major technical innovations, including the world's first TV/FM radio simulcast of Van Morrison's concert at London's Rainbow Theatre in 1973.

In terms of its legacy for the presentation of popular music on television, the show was revolutionary in that it set out to show what '*authentic* musicians' looked like, positioned in the reality of a genuine musical performance. Significantly, the dominant trend in British pop at the time was the deliberately *inauthentic* glam rock, which flaunted its fakery and actively pursued the cheap, the transient and the novel. The size of the studio was key to the televisualisation – three cameras kept motionless because they had no space to move around. This necessary minimalism unintentionally fed into the way the music was presented, and thereby understood. Later series enjoyed bigger studios, but the signature elements remained: a black, bare space; mediating technologies on full display; wires and amplification systems in camera; the presenter as cultural gatekeeper; an essential 'liveness'; and the undeniable musical status that resulted from an appearance.

One of the programme's defining moments, which illustrated Harris's sensitivity over any infringements of his gatekeeping role, was his encounter with the New York Dolls in 1973. In reality it delivers less than legend suggests – the band had pre-recorded its contribution and was not present in the studio. Harris

[13] Appleton, *The Old Grey Whistle Test*.
[14] Williams, personal interview.
[15] Appleton, *The Old Grey Whistle Test*.
[16] Brinsley Schwarz, *Shindig* 2/11 (2009), p. 52.

introduces them as being 'to the Stones what the Monkees were to the Beatles: a pale and amusing derivative' and back-announces 'Jet Boy' by describing it as 'mock rock there from the New York Dolls' – all, it should be noted, with good humour. Following their segment, his pleasure as he begins to talk about The Band's *Moondog Matinee* is evident: 'It's great!' he comments and, after presenting their recording of 'Promised Land' (accompanied by a 1930 *Felix The Cat* cartoon) he concludes, 'Nice!' He reports back on two movies: *Gas* (Roger Corman, 1971) starring Country Joe McDonald, and the documentary *Red White And Bluegrass* (Elliott Erwitt, 1973). The anonymous elderly couple who sing in the extract from Erwitt's film are echoes of a world that had all but vanished by the early 1970s, and their presence on the same show as the New York Dolls illustrates how broad the musical palate of the show could be. In addition, Michael Chapman performs two songs, to the obvious approval of the host, who sits by him as he plays. A clip of B.B. King provides the musical highlight of the show, which closes on a second song from the New York Dolls, squeezed in under the credits.

Harris's comments about the New York Dolls betrays his irritated amusement rather than brow-furrowed rage. Nevertheless, they reveal a central facet of the programme in the early 1970s: there are very definite rules to this club, and those who fail to observe them are not welcome. While this may have been commendable, it also implied a reluctance to acknowledge and admit change. And so it was: while the derided *Top Of The Pops* was, paradoxically, able to accept, reflect and display change, *The Old Grey Whistle Test* began to seem out of touch with music that fell outside Harris's playlist, despite Appleton's stated wish that the presenter should always serve the programme.

From the mid-1970s, Harris's personal distaste for punk made his departure from the programme inevitable and he left in 1978, to be replaced by Radio 1's Annie Nightingale. Shortly after she took over, the show featured its first punk performance. It was by the Adverts, whose lead vocalist – the appropriately named TV Smith – prefaced their opening song by declaring 'At last, the 1978 show!' However, the change also signalled the beginning of a slow unravelling of *The Old Grey Whistle Test* as an enduring television brand. It quickly updated its booking policy – 'the show missed punk, but energetically pursued the next wave of acts'[17] – so that despite the absence of the Sex Pistols, the Clash or The Jam, it did present XTC, Talking Heads and Police in their first, energetic surges. The appearance of Public Image Ltd in their *Metal Box* finery in late 1979 sealed the reputation of the programme as the place to see and hear this new, forward-looking, and *British* music.

But the problem of how to respond to the new re-appeared in the 1980s, when the programme's position began to be threatened by an increase in the availability of visual material and television outlets for it. Trevor Dann was drafted in from BBC Radio, where he had created the documentary series *Twenty Five Years Of Rock* (1980) which led to the subsequent BBC-TV series *The Rock And Roll*

---

[17]   Mark Ellen, personal correspondence, 5 May 2009.

Years (1985). His appointment reflected a widespread assumption that the show was in trouble. During the early and mid-1980s, the series was being created by two separate teams, which often resulted in an uneven fit between one show and the next that destabilised its overall identity. Although Harris's easy charm could sometimes tip over into a complacent banality, the show in his time had undoubtedly possessed a clear and strong identity, both musically and visually. Particular competition came from *The Tube* (1982–87), the success story of the newly launched Channel 4, which was hosted by Jools Holland and Paula Yates, and broadcast live from the Tyne Tees TV Studios in Newcastle upon Tyne. Its fresh, unforced style and audience impact were decisive:

> BBC2 was under a lot of pressure because it didn't have *The Tube*, so Graeme McDonald, then BBC2 controller, decided that *Whistle Test* had to be brought 'up to date'. So he gave us an earlier time slot, initially 7.30 on a Tuesday. The first few shows did really well, and then in the autumn of 1986, BBC1 launched *EastEnders* and as soon as we were placed against that, we were finished. They then moved it to an even earlier slot of 6.00 pm, but it was no use. It was completely the wrong place for it.[18]

Further efforts were made to reinvigorate the show; the title was changed simply to *Whistle Test* (which had always been the title used informally by its audience) but this too backfired:

> There was a press release for the name change which began 'No longer old, no longer grey'. Of course, all this did was give the music weeklies the chance to say 'well, yes it is!' So it was all a half-hearted rebranding, alas. As a producer on it all those years, I felt I was managing decline. It was a late night brand that would probably still be running now, had the BBC had the courage to stick with it but, once you muck about with those things, you ruin them. There are, of course, totally different audiences at 10.45 and 7.30 or 6.00 pm – exactly at the time when nobody could watch it. It was very much the same as what they did years later to *Top Of The Pops*, when they moved it to Fridays. It was a misplaced reinvention, and the skids were under us from the minute we did it.[19]

The sense of decline outlined by Dann was demonstrated by the decision to present the final series of (the newly re-christened) *Whistle Test* live on the road, as an *ad hoc* combination of *Rock Goes To College* (BBC, 1978–81) and *The Tube*. Yet this only came about because there were no studios available for the show at BBC Television Centre in London; instead, it was forced to use BBC facilities in Manchester, Glasgow and Belfast, which was the venue for the final edition of *Whistle Test* in 1987, and which featured a live set by U2. The band's appearance

---

[18] Trevor Dann, personal interview, 21 September 2009.

[19] Ibid.

was seen by Dann as 'a coup for the show although, as now, U2 like and understand the promotional power of TV'.[20] Nevertheless, the show disappeared down the road to irrelevance and its demise was barely noted or lamented, even amongst its own audience.

In the period following its disappearance, pop music on BBC (with the exception of *Top Of The Pops*) became subsumed as a 'strand' within a wider, aspirational, youth-oriented programming policy, rather than a discrete subject fit for presentation in its own right. This was partly because of natural progressions in the ways in which music is understood, but also because of changes in the way that television felt it necessary to present music. Shows on BBC2 such as *DEF II* (1988–94) or *The O-Zone* (1989–2000) were not without precedent; the same channel's *Something Else* (1978–82) and *The Oxford Road Show* (1981–82) had previously, and similarly, placed music within a wider field of youth culture and programming to good effect. But the repercussions of the power shifts in the music and television industries initially signalled by the arrival of the CD and MTV, coupled with the British contemporary taste for electronic dance music which de-emphasised the persona of the performer, were challenging many traditional assumptions about pop, its uses, and its audiences. Perhaps it proved that *The Old Grey Whistle Test* was, and always had been, a television exception, through its dedication to performance, that was entirely, and uniquely, of its time.

Between 1987 and the advent of *The Late Show*, there was a significant gap in the BBC's music archive, which stretched roughly from the final *Whistle Test* to the Stone Roses' stinging rebuke of 'Amateurs!' to the crew of *The Late Show* when the power supply went down during their 1989 performance. Not until *Later … With Jools Holland* (which grew out of *The Late Show* in the way that *The Old Grey Whistle Test* had grown out of *Late Night Line Up*) did the BBC find a new model through which to present popular music in a weekly format. Surprisingly, Dann's judgement on the extent of *The Old Grey Whistle Test*'s influence on subsequent music programming is rather limited: 'To be honest – not much, although in its mix of what's good, rather than what's fashionable, *Later* sometimes feels like it has the ghost of *The Whistle Test* at its best hovering around it.'[21] His perception is shared by Williams: 'When *Later* appeared, I realised that this was the show I'd wanted *The Old Grey Whistle Test* to be. I wanted more energy, not to be so laid back … but of course it didn't have the resources or the space.'[22]

In TV terms, the availability of 'resources' and 'space' indicates the value that the broadcaster (in this case, BBC) puts on the show, its content and its remit. It is instructive to note that many of the creative personnel who struggled with the latter stages of *Whistle Test* – Trevor Dann, Mark Ellen, David Hepworth – are now key figures in music, television, radio, Internet, and magazine publishing in the UK. Indeed, in 1996, Dann was appointed as BBC's Head of Music Entertainment, a

---

[20]   Ibid.

[21]   Ibid.

[22]   Williams, personal interview.

newly-formed department that promised a renewed commitment to present music on its own terms rather than as part of a notional 'lifestyle'. It is this department which oversaw the hotly disputed closure of one brand (*Top Of The Pops*) in 2006, and the enduring success of another (*Later … With Jools Holland*).

The success of *Later … With Jools Holland* (longer than *The Old Grey Whistle Test* itself) supplies evidence of the cultural shifts which have brought the formerly distinct markets for 'rock' and 'pop' into a musical space that accommodates the musical vocabularies (and more) of both. Its strengths lie in its equivalence and even-handed presentation (the circular studio gathers together established acts and new faces, all of whom are obliged to participate in the jam at the opening of the show), and in the persona of Holland himself – a well-connected musician, rather than the informed journalist of Appleton's original vision. While he too functions as a cultural gatekeeper, his knowledge and experience qualify him as an audience spokesperson who can ask the kind of questions that Bob Harris would have never been able to. It is in the pure musicality of the space that *Later … With Jools Holland* provides on British television – via the link between what is deemed 'good' and what has proven popular – that the lasting influence of 'the ghost of *The Whistle Test* at its best' may be most clearly sensed.

PART II
Performers And Performances

Chapter 5

Ready Steady Go! Televisual Pop Style And The Careers Of Dusty Springfield, Cilla Black, Sandie Shaw And Lulu

Adrienne Lowy

Dusty Springfield, Cilla Black, Sandie Shaw and Lulu established their iconic images with British television audiences through the equally iconic 1960s television pop music programme *Ready Steady Go!* (ITV, 1963–66). This innovative show, with its fusion of the newest fashion, graphics and dance, was, and still is, acknowledged as the definitive television site for British visual pop music style of the period.[1] Dusty launched her solo career, and Cilla, Sandie and Lulu began their recording careers and gained their first chart singles in the first two years of the programme's three-year run. This chapter explores the way in which they, and the show, were centrally involved in creating and representing the connection between the look and the sound of British pop, in both musical and fashion terms, at a key moment for British popular culture, nationally and internationally.

I begin with an overview of the programme's lifespan, contextualising its position within contemporary British pop music television programming. The reciprocal importance of Dusty, Cilla, Sandie and Lulu to the programme, and the programme to the establishment of their significance as musical and style icons of the period, are then considered. A discussion of the televisual style of *Ready Steady Go!* leads to an exploration of fashion as a key component, focusing not only on the four singers, but also on presenter Cathy McGowan, who became one of the most influential fashion role models of 1960s British pop television. I conclude by considering the lasting impact that their association with *Ready Steady Go!* had on the pop music and television careers of Dusty, Cilla, Sandie and Lulu.

Ready Steady Go! And Its Television Pop Context

Ready Steady Go! was an Associated Rediffusion network production, broadcast live on Friday evenings in London and the South East – initially from Television

---

[1]   Important sections of this chapter were informed and refined through personal correspondence (Summer 2009) with Nicholas Ferguson, the set designer for *Ready Steady Go!*

House, Kingsway, and subsequently from Studio 1, Wembley, both in London. The first programme was shown on 9 August 1963, and the last, the 'special farewell programme' *Ready Steady Goes!*, on 7 December 1966. It is the most retrospectively documented British television pop music programme of its time.[2] Television ownership was increasing rapidly, although transmission remained monochrome, and there was a common recognition of the medium's ability to perform a significant visual showcasing function for pop music[3] and particularly for solo performers.[4]

The London start time of 6.08 p.m. made *Ready Steady Go!* a key component of the Friday evening viewing ritual. Programme length varied: the majority of the shows ran for 50 minutes, although later editions were cut to 30 minutes. Dusty appeared in some of the early programmes while still a member of the Springfields; Cilla appeared in the month of her first single release; the teenage Sandie and Lulu watched the show in its first year, and were performing on it a year later.

'The weekend starts here' – the widely-remembered *Ready Steady Go!* subtitle, subsequently became its 'cherished slogan'[5] and has been described by Green as 'the rallying cry of a generation'.[6] It implied that the teenage audience, similar to the programme's on-camera studio audience, would watch this as part of their preparation for going out for the evening. The phrase appeared on screen immediately after the show's title (and in the *TV Times* listings) from its August 1963 launch through to April 1965 when the title, and the programme format, changed to *Ready Steady Goes Live!*, and the location switched from Kingsway to Wembley. Performers had mimed up to that point, but pressure from the Musicians Union brought this to an end. Elkan Allan, the show's Executive Producer, saw the ban on miming as an opportunity to publicise the revamping of the programme.[7] Allan was Associated Rediffusion's Head of Entertainment in 1963, and is expressly

---

[2]   See, for example, Richard Mabey, *The Pop Process* (London, 1969), pp. 105–6; Nik Cohn, *Awopbopaloobop Alopbamboom: The Golden Age of Rock* (London, 1969), pp. 184–5; George Melly, *Revolt Into Style* (London, 1970), pp. 187–9; Iain Chambers, *Urban Rhythms: Pop Music And Popular Culture* (Basingstoke, 1985), pp. 75–6; Iain Chambers, *Popular Culture: The Metropolitan Experience* (London, 1986), p. 159; Jonathon Green, *All Dressed Up: The Sixties and the Counterculture* (London,1998), p. 93; John Mundy, *Popular Music On Screen* (Manchester, 1999), pp. 203–4; Shawn Levy, *Ready Steady Go! Swinging London And The Invention Of Cool* (London, 2002), pp. 127–9; Dominic Sandbrook, *White Heat: A History of Britain In The Swinging Sixties* (London, 2006), pp. 101–2.

[3]   Jane Reid, 'Triumph Of R&B', in Robert H. Hill (ed.), *The Year Book 1965: A Record Of The Events, Developments, And Personalities Of 1964* (London, 1965), pp. 200–204.

[4]   Philip Abrams, 'Radio and Television', in Denys Thompson (ed.), *Discrimination And Popular Culture* (Harmondsworth, 1964), pp. 50–73.

[5]   Richard Williams, 'The Birth Of Cool', *The Guardian*, 13 February 2006.

[6]   Green, *All Dressed Up*, p. 93.

[7]   Dave Lanning, 'Ready Steady Goes Live!' *TV Times*, 25 March 1965, pp. 4–5.

credited as the programme's inventor; when he died in 2006, his obituaries in *The Guardian* and *The Times* highlighted *Ready Steady Go!* as a major achievement in a long career of print and broadcasting innovation, while *The Independent* referred to 'this seminal pop show ... which caught the buzz of sixties Britain, and became an icon of its time, while the BBC was still relying on *Juke Box Jury*'.[8] It was Allan who appointed McGowan, was responsible for the show going 'live', and ultimately for bringing the programme to a close.[9]

In addition to its audience in London and the South East, the programme was nationally networked, although viewers in other ITV areas saw it at different times and, in the later part of its run, on different days. Granada broadcast it much later on Friday evenings, prioritising its own *Scene At 6.30* which also featured pop music, in the earlier, prime-time slot. Ironically, it was another regional ITV programme that is thought to have inspired *Ready, Steady, Go!*: TWW's *Discs A Gogo* (1961–67) on which Cilla made her television debut in August 1963.[10] In particular, its use of a selected dancing studio audience was seen as a central element of the template:[11]

> The combination of elements that made *Discs A Gogo* a success in the regions have now found their apotheosis in Associated-Rediffusion's Friday programme *Ready Steady Go!* Its original brief was 'to let teenagers into the studio to dance with the stars'. They don't, in fact, come straight in from the streets ... the teenagers must have an informal audition to see 'that they can dance and that they look all right'.[12]

The idea that a television pop programme could feature an active, on-screen studio audience was not entirely new: in Britain, it was the legacy of *Six-Five Special* (BBC, 1957–58) which was itself modelled on the US popularity of ABC-TV's *American Bandstand*.[13] However, *Ready Steady Go!* launched at a propitious moment for British pop music and fashion, announced by the impact of the Beatles. Not only did the group have four Number One singles in 1963, but went on to have eight more chart-topping singles during the programme's lifetime. In this first year of Beatlemania, it is worth noting *TV Times* journalist Dave Lanning's description of the planned activities for the programme's fans who came to Television House:

---

[8]   Roy Addison, 'Elkan Allan', *The Independent* 29 June 2006 .

[9]   See Melly, *Revolt*, p. 189: 'Not only was *RSG* in advance of its time. It knew when its moment was over. It was true to pop even in this.'

[10]   Cilla Black, *Through The Years: My Life In Pictures* (London, 1993), p. 14.

[11]   Although networked, *Discs A Gogo* was never shown in the London area because of its perceived similarity to *Ready Steady Go!*

[12]   Pat Williams, 'Getting Together', *The Observer*, 5 January 1964.

[13]   John Hill, 'Television And Pop: The Case Of The 1950s', in John Corner (ed.), *Popular Television In Britain: Studies In Cultural History* (London, 1991) pp. 90–107.

> In the lobby, David Gell will introduce youngsters who will be dancing to the music of the show, relayed on monitor sets. And outside Television House, scores of fans will watch proceedings in the lobby, and perhaps catch a glimpse of their idols arriving and leaving.[14]

Significantly, *Ready Steady Go!* was the only nationally networked Friday night pop music TV programme. Its main national competitors in August 1963 were *Juke Box Jury* (BBC, 1959–67) and *Thank Your Lucky Stars* (ITV, 1961–66) both of which were broadcast during the family-oriented, early evening Saturday schedules: Dusty, Cilla, Sandie and Lulu all appeared as panellists on the former, and guest performers on the latter. *Ready Steady Go!*'s Friday slot captured a greater slice of the youth audience, and stole a march on its two Saturday rivals by beating them to 'the start of the weekend'.[15] In January 1964, BBC's introduction of *Top Of The Pops* – which also featured a dancing studio audience, and was broadcast on Thursday evenings – clearly demonstrated its recognition of the impact made by *Ready Steady Go!*.[16]

While McGowan remains the most celebrated of the *Ready Steady Go!* presenters, she did not become the programme's sole host until April 1965, having originally been employed as its 'teenage adviser'.[17] Keith Fordyce and David Gell were the presenters for the first five transmissions, before a brief spell in which Fordyce presented alone. McGowan and Michael Aldred joined him from January to June 1964; from then on, McGowan and Fordyce were the joint presenters until April 1965. Fordyce, like *Juke Box Jury*'s David Jacobs and *Thank Your Lucky Stars*' Brian Matthew, came from a radio disc-jockeying background, and all were seen as 'avuncular figures who were meant to act as go-betweens, trusted by the adult establishment but benign and sympathetic enough to be accepted by teenage listeners'.[18] The programme itself was introduced in *TV Times* – under

---

[14]   Dave Lanning, 'Stand By For Take-Off', *TV Times*, 2 August 1963, p. 32.

[15]   Hill, 'Television And Pop', p. 103.

[16]   That *New Musical Express* introduced a 'TV Show' category to its NME Pop Poll in 1964 could be considered further acknowledgement of the impact of *Ready Steady Go!*, the first winner in this category.

[17]   Accounts of her employment pre-*Ready Steady Go!* vary. In *Television Show Book* (London, 1964), she is described as 'born in Woking, started her career on the show after previously doing model work and writing articles for teenage readers' (pp. 27–8). On the website of her partner Michael Ball, a 1991 biography gives her career start as a fashion department junior on *Womans Own* (www.justball.net/home/cathymcgowan/home.php). Another account has her 'working in an office at the television company' (http://televisionheaven.co.uk/rsg.htm). However, accounts agree that her *Ready Steady Go!* career began when she provided the winning response to an Associated Rediffusion advertisement for a 'typical teenager', and impressed Allan by citing fashion as the key teenage priority (ahead of sex and music); see Williams, 'The Birth Of Cool'.

[18]   Stephen Barnard, *On The Radio: Music Radio In Britain* (Milton Keynes, 1989), p. 15.

the 'Light Entertainment' heading – as 'a new show for the young at heart'.[19] So, while it is remembered historically as a major television youth programme, it set out initially to attract a wider viewing audience, as its original promotion in *TV Times* indicates:

STAND BY FOR TAKEOFF: READY, STEADY, GO!

A Royal occasion? An assassination scare? A visit from an astronaut? No, the cause is a new series starting today called *Ready Steady Go!* which will bring pop and film stars to Television House, Kingsway, London … *Ready Steady Go!* is a pot-pourri of records and films, packed with exciting, unconventional ideas. An audience of 200 young people will kick off their weekend watching, by listening to and appearing *with* their favourite stars.[20]

The show ensured that it continued to draw attention to itself by staging 'specials' and marking landmarks in its own history, including its New Year's Eve shows. The December 1963 'New Year Starts Here' featured Cilla; the 1964 New Year's Eve programme included Dusty and Sandie; the 1965 show presented Dusty and Lulu. Cilla also starred in the April 1964 *Ready Steady Go! Mod Ball* in which '8,000 Mods, the smartest fashion-conscious teenagers, get together in aid of children's charity in The Empire Pool, Wembley'.[21] She also performed on the programme's first birthday show on 7 August 1964 when *TV Times* asked 'Can you remember a time when there was no *Ready Steady Go!*? Yet it hit the air only a year ago this week. It changed pop, teenagers, and television, and will be celebrating in style tonight'.[22]

Ready Steady Go! And Dusty, Cilla, Sandie And Lulu

In addition to the 'specials', all four singers appeared regularly on the programme. Their association with the *Ready Steady Go!* brand, and its synthesis of music and visual style at a historic moment for British pop music, British pop art and British fashion design, was critical for each in establishing her own brand, television image and persona. This association helped to make them the interlinked four key female singers of the period, and provided a longevity to their names that extended well beyond pop single success.

Dusty's informal co-hosting of some of the programme's earliest editions, while still with the Springfields, helped to prepare viewers for her solo debut later in 1963 with the release of 'I Only Want To Be With You'. Her love of US

[19]   *TV Times*, 2 August 1963, p. 2.
[20]   Lanning, 'Stand By For Takeoff'.
[21]   *TV Times*, 3 April 1964, p. 3.
[22]   *TV Times*, 7 August 7 1964, p. 33.

black music and her friendship with Vicki Wickham, the programme's assistant editor and subsequent editor, influenced the Tamla Motown content of the show, leading to the April 1965 spin-off 'Tamla Motown Special' which Dusty hosted. Her opposition to racial segregation, epitomised by her effective deportation from South Africa in 1964 for refusing to play to a segregated audience, concurred with Allan's insistence on the presence of black dancers in the studio audience.[23] She was the oldest and most experienced of the four women, in both recording and television terms; she had begun her TV career in 1959, as 'Shan' in the Lana Sisters, before reinventing herself as 'Dusty' in the Springfields. The group had considerable success (including its own TV series) and going solo was her third career reinvention. *Ready Steady Go!* supplied the nationally networked platform for this transition.

Cilla's debut on the programme, as part of the Beatles-led Merseybeat phenomenon, was arranged by Brian Epstein. The programme's designer, Nicholas Ferguson, generally insisted that decisions on guest selection should be made without agent/manager influence, by Wickham and her immediate team: assistant Rosemary Simon (changing, after marriage, to Samwell-Smith, and subsequently Keane), McGowan, and himself. However, Epstein was the one manager whose power allowed him to exert a personal influence.[24] Cilla established a close friendship with McGowan and, through the programme's policy of informal on-air interviews, began to develop the television personality which grew alongside, and out of, her singing career. For her too, the timing of the show's launch was fortuitous, the debut of *Ready Steady Go!* coinciding with the release of her first single, 'Love Of The Loved'. The determination of Bobby Willis, Cilla's husband (and long-time manager after Epstein's death in 1967) that each of her TV appearances should be an 'event'[25] was underlined by her frequent appearances on so many of the *Ready Steady Go!* specials.

When Dusty and Cilla appeared on the show in its first year, the slightly younger Sandie and Lulu were still unknown. Within a year, however, both were *Ready Steady Go!* performers with Top Ten singles. Like Cilla, they had both been 'discovered' singing in front of male groups to local audiences. They quickly became the 'Fab Girl Four': the token girl singer for each of the major record labels: Dusty on Phillips, Cilla on EMI (Parlophone), Sandie on Pye, Lulu on Decca.[26] British pop star Adam Faith had recommended Sandie to his manager Eve Taylor, who teamed her with Chris Andrews, the composer of many of Faith's hit singles. On her first appearance on the programme, in July 1964, she performed Andrews's 'As Long As You're Happy Baby'. The song was not a hit, but the TV debut helped her second single, Burt Bacharach and Hal David's 'Always Something There To

[23]   See Pat Williams, 'Mixing The Colours', *The Observer*, 12 January 1964.

[24]   Nicholas Ferguson, personal correspondence.

[25]   *BritGirls: Cilla.* Channel 4, 22 November, 1997.

[26]   Lucy O'Brien, *She Bop II: The Definitive History Of Women In Rock, Pop And Soul* (London, 2002), p. 95.

Remind Me', to reach Number One in the UK charts later that year; she was, in fact, the first of the four singers to top the charts. Sandie's appearance – glossy black hair similar to McGowan's, a photogenic bone structure, trademark bare feet, and a minimalist performance style that was 'true to the mod code'[27] – helped to establish her fashion model look, as photographed by David Bailey for *Vogue*.

Lulu was the youngest of the four; her first hit single 'Shout' was made with the Luvvers, the band with whom she had been a regular performer in Scotland. John Lennon's praise for the song on *Ready Steady Go!* in the week of its release (15 April 1964) was an invaluable endorsement, and she appeared on the show to perform the song on 1 May. Two weeks later, it entered the charts and climbed to the Top Ten. Her appearances on *Ready Steady Go!* definitively established her television persona, built around a startling vocal power and youthful energy, within a diminutive physical frame. Her recollection of going out to dinner with Wickham after her debut on the show and being approached in the restaurant by a congratulatory Bobby Darin[28] illustrates the social informality of the programme, as was often emphasised by Wickham.[29]

During the lifespan of *Ready Steady Go!*, Lulu had a second Top Ten single, 'Leave A Little Love'; Sandie had six, including a second Number One, 'Long Live Love'; Cilla topped the charts with 'Anyone Who Had A Heart' and 'You're My World', in addition to securing five more Top Ten singles; Dusty achieved seven Top Ten singles, including the chart-topping 'You Don't Have To Say You Love Me'. Their successes confirmed the importance of television within popular music's commercial strategy:

> A record promotion campaign in Britain in the sixties was short and simple. It consisted of sending single records to television's *Juke Box Jury*, *Thank Your Lucky Stars* and *Ready Steady Go!*, and to radio programmes *Housewives Choice*, *Junior Choice*, *Saturday Club*, *Easy Beat*, *Two-Way Family Favourites*, and Radio Luxembourg. If any three of that combination played the record, it virtually resulted in a hit.[30]

[27] Charlotte Greig, *Will You Still Love Me Tomorrow? Girl Groups From The 50s On* (London, 1989), p. 6.

[28] Lulu, *I Don't Want To Fight* (London, 2002), p. 66.

[29] Williams, 'The Birth Of Cool'.

[30] Ray Coleman, *Brian Epstein: The Man Who Made The Beatles* (London, 1989), p. 265.

Ready Steady Go! **And Televisual Pop Style**

Ferguson's success in bringing Pop Art to pop television through his set designs[31] manifested Allan's intention that *Ready Steady Go!* should 'reflect the growing power of the new pop culture through a programme that had a feeling of pop art'.[32] Working within a severely limited budget, Ferguson created his collages and paintings individually each Thursday night for the forthcoming Friday programme. These works were used as backdrops for the guest musicians, and thus provided the immediate visual environment for both performers (photographs of whom often appeared in the collages) and the dancing studio audience, whose members were selected for their own televisual style. His original 10 inches x 8 inches colour artwork was blown up to 30 feet x 20 feet, its colour meticulously translated into highest quality monochrome by the programme's rack engineers, and displayed to complement the performers:

> Each week we would look at the positions of rostra. I would sit with the director at the start of the week and suggest where to put the artists, in which part of the studio. Each rostrum was 6 feet by 8 feet, or circular. Each show was different: for example, having Dusty standing in the middle of people. Artists were positioned so that you knew that the space round the artist was part of the design, such as Dusty in the foreground with one of my collages in the background. The planning was in 3D. It was tremendously atmospheric, like being in a nightclub. There was always a planned background for the artists.[33]

After discussions with Epstein, Ferguson framed Cilla's performance of 'Anyone Who Had A Heart', by using 'blowups of Cilla as part of a collage and a huge cut-out in a Surrealist way'; furthermore Epstein's personal interest in the aesthetic presentation of his artists on *Ready Steady Go!* led him to employ Ferguson as the designer for his hosted contributions to NBC-TV's US television pop show *Hullabaloo*.[34]

Ready Steady Go!'s signature look was firmly established in the period from late 1963 to early 1965, when it was broadcast from Television House (considered by many fans to have been a better venue than the later, and larger, Wembley studio) where the confined space helped to produce a dynamic atmosphere. Its convention of cameras and technicians on view was a calculated reference to the on-screen television apparatus of the equally innovative BBC satirical programme *That Was The Week That Was*, which was in its successful second (and final) year in 1963.[35] On *Ready Steady Go!*, performers, presenters, sets, cameras, microphones,

---

[31]   See Melly, *Revolt*, p. 190; Chambers, *Urban Rhythms*, p. 82.

[32]   Penny Valentine and Vicki Wickham, *Dancing With Demons: The Authorised Biography Of Dusty Springfield* (London, 2000) p. 19.

[33]   Ferguson, personal correspondence.

[34]   Ibid.

[35]   Melly, *Revolt*, p. 188.

technicians and dancing on-screen audience were all shown against the backdrop of a sparse studio. Ferguson used the limited design budget (relative to that of the other nationally networked pop shows) to his advantage, and drew on his experience of Brecht and theatre workshop to provide a stylistically groundbreaking visual setting for television pop music performance. It was 'a visual goldmine: cameras swooping back and forth like robot jivers, tangled black leads from the guitars, and pop art décor'.[36]

The opening graphics, which accompanied the programme titles and title tracks,[37] were the viewers' crucial first experience of the programme each Friday. They featured montages of photographs, including dancing figures, close-ups of the faces of McGowan (and co-host Gay Singleton, who appeared in early editions) coupled with now-familiar pop art emblems such as hearts, arrows and targets.[38] They were created by photographer Clive Arrowsmith and graphic artist Arnold Schwartzman, and formed a key component of the show's visual style. As if to further emphasise this pop art/pop music connection, fashionable young painters Derek Boshier and Pauline Boty were among the dancers selected to appear on the programme; Boty went on to exhibit her portrait of McGowan alongside those of movie stars Marilyn Monroe and Monica Vitti.[39]

The dances and the dancers were integral to 'the successful creation of an informal party atmosphere in which the audience were as much the stars as the musicians'.[40] For the programme's first seven months, *TV Times* exhorted viewers to 'dance with the teenagers in the studio'; choreographer Patrick Kerr regularly created and promoted new dances, performed by dancers selected from London clubs for their ability to look good and to move well; and there was a clear assumption that the fashions (in both dance and dress) might spread from *Ready Steady Go!* across the UK.[41] Kerr, McGowan and (during his time on the programme) Aldred invited Sandie to join them on the informal selection panel for the studio audience: 'We all went out together to dance halls, talent spotting for trendy dressers and good movers to give audience tickets to.'[42] In order to effectively capture and convey the atmosphere and immediacy of a style-setting, weekly club venue, director Michael Lindsay-Hogg employed cameramen with

---

[36]   Mabey, *Pop Process*, p. 106.

[37]   In chronological order, these were: the Surfaris' 'Wipeout'; Manfred Mann's '5-4-3-2-1'; Them's 'Baby Please Don't Go'.

[38]   'a flurry of animated pop art': see Mabey, *Pop Process*, p. 84.

[39]   Alice Rawsthorn, 'Tomorrow's Girl', *The Guardian*, 19 June 2004.

[40]   Hill, 'Television And Pop', p. 103.

[41]   'The programme also encourages viewers who may have some crazy dance ideas to write in for auditions and then, if successful, be able to demonstrate them on the show': see *Television Show Book* (London, 1964), p. 27.

[42]   Sandie Shaw, *The World At My Feet: A Personal Adventure* (London, 1991), p. 91.

TV experience in outside broadcast and sports programmes for their ability to react spontaneously to events in the studio.[43]

This deliberate mix of specifically created sets (which changed on a weekly basis) and a studio populated by dancers carefully chosen for their fashion and dance flair was, in the hands of Allan and his visually and musically expert team of young professionals, the ideal stylistic showcase for its guest performers. Guests and presenters were shown *with* the studio audience and *in* the highly stylised environment. All formed part of the most immediate visual/musical production on British television, at a point in the 1960s when pop music, pop art and fashion were undergoing an unprecedented convergence. Dusty, Cilla, Sandie and Lulu each made her performance style (whether sung, spoken or worn) complementary to, yet distinctive within, this creative and created environment. McGowan, the teenage adviser hired by Allan at the outset of the programme because of her explicit emphasis on the importance of fashion to viewers who were her contemporaries, quickly became the literal 'face' of *Ready Steady Go!* In April 1965, at the age of 22, she became its sole presenter and the most recognised woman in British pop television.

Ready Steady Go!, Cathy McGowan And Fashion

McGowan was the ultimate pop fan, breathlessly introducing and interviewing the programme's guest stars, and often shown dancing with her idols in the midst of the studio audience. Hers was a knowing innocence linked to an innate camera-awareness, an inherent fashion sensibility, and a fashion model image that was perfect for the time.[44] She enhanced the visual proximity of guest stars to the stylish studio audience, and thus the relationship with the nationwide viewing audience, by creating and performing the role of the fashion-conscious fan, who became a presenter, who went on to become a star; contemporary critics noted her ability to transcend class barriers of speech and fashion.[45] Furthermore, Dusty's co-hosting duties, and interviews with Cilla from Liverpool, Sandie from Dagenham, and Lulu from Glasgow familiarised the audience around the country with stars as speakers (as well as singers) whose accents were very different both from each other, and from the 'received' English or pseudo-American previously used by TV personalities and British pop performers.

---

[43]   Ferguson, personal correspondence.

[44]   Cohn, *Awopbopaloobop Alopbamboom,* p. 185; Sue Steward and Sheryl Garratt, *Signed, Sealed And Delivered: True Life Stories Of Women In Pop* (London, 1984), p. 85; Ferguson, personal correspondence.

[45]   See, for example, Melly, *Revolt*, p. 189; Kenneth Allsopp, 'Pop Goes Young Woodley', in Richard Mabey (ed.), *Class: A Symposium* (London,1967), pp. 127–43; Christopher Booker, *The Neophiliacs: A Study Of The Revolution In English life In the Fifties And Sixties* (London, 1970), p. 131.

McGowan's on-screen style made an enormous contribution to the programme's explicit emphasis on fashion, and reflected the increasingly evident associations between the music, media, and fashion industries[46] as displayed by 'a new crop of young, fashion-conscious, British singers such as Lulu, Cilla Black, Dusty Springfield, Marianne Faithfull, and the famously barefooted Sandie Shaw'.[47] Youthful creativity in pop music and fashion attracted worldwide media attention, thereby creating the mythology of 'Swinging London' and the 'Swinging Sixties'. British fashion designed by young British designers established a national and international prominence. Photographic publicity for pop singers, produced both by their publicists and television companies, appeared in British listings publications, the music press,[48] the news media (including the new Sunday supplements), and in teenage magazines and annuals.[49]

McGowan, pop presenter rather than pop performer, personified this synergy. Described as 'Queen of the Mods', she considered it her duty to look the part. While still the show's 'teenage adviser', she asserted: 'I've got to be continually with-it on the dress bit. It would be death if I appeared in anything square. Actually I'm crazy about fashions – mod fashions, not Paris clothes.'[50] Viewers paid close attention to her weekly wardrobe; designers hoped she would wear their creations; manufacturers believed that an outfit (or a near approximation) worn by her on a Friday night could sell out on the following Saturday afternoon.[51] The national networking of *Ready Steady Go!* spread her influence UK-wide, and the programme's own spin-off publications further promoted this: the cover of the *Ready Steady Go! 1965 Annual* featured a trouser-suited McGowan, at a time when women were still unable to wear trousers to work.[52] Steward and Garratt's discussion of the stage's influence on street fashion notes that 'the lucrative marriage between the rag trade and the pop industry was celebrated on *Ready Steady Go!*'[53] McGowan, Dusty, Cilla, Sandie and Lulu all led this street fashion, by wearing on-screen the British-designed, informal, youthful daywear originally pioneered by

---

[46] See, for example, Barbara Hulanicki, *From A To Biba* (London, 1983), p. 74; Valerie Steele, *Fifty Years Of Fashion: New Look To Now* (New York, 1997), p. 59; Christopher Breward, David Gilbert and Jenny Lister (eds), *Swinging Sixties: Fashion In London And Beyond 1955–70* (London, 2006) p. 92; Adrienne Lowy, *DustyCillaSandieLulu As Seen On TV: A Study Of Interrelations Between Pop Music, Television And Fashion* (Ph.D. thesis. Institute of Popular Music, University of Liverpool, 2008), p. 62.

[47] Breward, Gilbert and Lister, *Swinging Sixties*, p. 92.

[48] McGowan was the 1965 winner of *Melody Maker*'s poll for Top Female TV Star.

[49] Lowy, *DustyCillaSandieLulu As Seen On TV*, p. 3.

[50] *Television Show Book*, 1964, p. 28.

[51] See Hulanicki, *From A To Biba*, p. 81; Steele, *Fifty Years Of Fashion*, p. 59; Breward, Gilbert and Lister, *Swinging Sixties*, p. 92.

[52] Another spin-off publication was the *Ready Steady Go!* magazine; the third edition, published in August 1964, featured cover pictures of Dusty and Cilla.

[53] Steward and Garratt, *Signed, Sealed And Delivered*, p. 26.

Mary Quant, who cited 'the girls in the street' as her principal inspiration.[54] This was a radical departure from the formal 'evening' or 'party' costumes previously worn by even young, female pop music performers. In an early programme, McGowan appeared in the Quant dress modelled by Jean Shrimpton on the first *Sunday Times* supplement cover; Wickham shopped at Quant for Dusty; Cilla was photographed (when meeting Dionne Warwick) wearing a Quant Ginger Group dress;[55] Sandie performed at a Quant US press party; Lulu wore a Quant skinny rib jumper in her debut year, 1964.

As the oldest and most experienced (in television terms) of the four, Dusty was sufficiently fashion-conscious to implement the change from her appearance with the Springfields. Now wearing blonde wigs and false eyelashes (both key fashion additions at the time) and the new high-fashion daywear, she reinvented herself on-screen as a stylish 1960s solo female pop performer. Cilla's informal friendships with a number of prominent young British fashion designers (and with McGowan) influenced her *Ready Steady Go!* dressing to the extent that she was widely regarded as an important trendsetter.[56] Sandie and Lulu, before their debuts on the programme, had paid close attention to the show's fashion as well as its music content, and had also derived ideas and inspiration from the contemporary teenage audiences to whom they had performed; both their careers went on to involve high profile fashion industry alliances.

While McGowan's fashion influence undoubtedly promoted the work of the designers whose clothes she wore on-screen, this influence also extended to the creation of new young ranges by established clothing manufacturers, and the increasing opening of 'boutiques', the fashion retailing phenomenon of the 1960s, to sell these designs. Alongside McGowan's championing of new designers, the studio audience surrounding her showed their *avant-garde* mod fashion credentials by making their own outfits in designs not (yet) commercially available. Viewers who wanted to emulate the *Ready Steady Go!* style, but who lacked the financial or geographic access to designer labels or to boutiques selling them, were equally likely to make their own versions.

Biba, however, was the fashion name with which McGowan most frequently associated herself on *Ready Steady Go!* She astutely confirmed her 'street credibility' through this connection, from the label's 1964 launch. Biba offered the most affordable, as well as the most directional, fashion, inventively merchandised in the most innovatively-designed London environment. Its designer, Barbara Hulanicki, has recalled making clothes for both McGowan and Cilla, as part of a typically hectic working week in the mid-1960s, well aware of the benefits of their

---

[54]   Quant quoted in Valerie Steele, *Fifty Years of Fashion*, p. 52.

[55]   Quant launched Ginger Group, what would now be called a 'diffusion' (cheaper) range in 1963.

[56]   'Cilla Black, with her "Anyone Who Had A Heart" disc, caused a sensation when she starred on the show wearing that now familiar long dress. It was to be the start of a new fashion amongst girls.' See *Television Show Book*, p. 30.

television celebrity endorsement, both for her London boutique and her nationwide mail order operation.[57] McGowan and Cilla in turn recognised the reciprocal value of their connection with Biba, by appearing in press photographs that showed them 'helping' with the move in 1966 to the boutique's second, and much larger, premises in Kensington Church Street.

McGowan's importance as a fashion arbiter also brought a range of commercial tie-ins. In this she set an important precedent at the time for her immediate British fashion and pop music contemporaries, Twiggy, Sandie and Lulu, and since then for succeeding generations of British fashion models and pop singers. She possessed the perfect combination of fashion model looks and a weekly nationally-viewed pop music television platform but, in addition, her authority as a style expert emanated from her insistence that all products (non-fashion as well as fashion) which bore her name should accurately and completely reflect her personal taste:[58] 'Fortunately, Cathy McGowan's taste seems to epitomize that of the majority of her generation.'[59] Through Cathy McGowan Enterprises, she worked with clothing companies including Lee Cooper, Dannimac rainwear, and the G.U.S. mail order catalogue[60] (in later years, Lulu became the 'face' of the young fashion section of Freemans mail order catalogue). There was also a range of Cathy McGowan cosmetics, and a Dansette record player and Silentnight teenagers' beds which bore the McGowan name.[61] Such was the perceived power of her endorsement that a number of these commercial enterprises either began or continued after the December 1966 ending of *Ready Steady Go!*[62]

Conclusion: *Ready Steady Go!* And Its Impact On The Careers Of Dusty, Cilla, Sandie And Lulu

Ready Steady Go! was the shortest-lived of the three major British television pop music programmes running concurrently in the 1960s, yet more footage has survived than that of its two chief competitors. Dave Clark (drummer and leader of the Dave Clark Five) bought the rights to the programmes some years later, from which he produced two compilation videos (released in 1983 and 1985)

---

[57] Hulanicki, *From A To Biba*, p. 83.

[58] See Suzy Menkes, 'Fashion Extra', *The Times*, 31 January 1967; Prudence Glynn, 'The Medium Is A Missed Opportunity', *The Times*, 20 February 1968.

[59] Menkes, 'Fashion Extra'.

[60] Cynthia Rose, 'Worn Out: Career Chic', in Tony Stewart (ed.), *Cool Cats: 25 Years Of Rock'n'Roll Style* (London, 1981), pp. 66–7.

[61] Glynn, 'The Medium Is A Missed Opportunity'.

[62] While McGowan is described (on the justball website) as continuing to work in television (and to have been involved in the launch of London's Capital Radio), she has never published memoirs or discussed her *Ready Steady Go!* work: 'Cathy McGowan is a grandmother, and prefers not to talk about the past', Williams, 'The Birth Of Cool'.

and a Channel 4 television series (broadcast in 1993); however, all three intercut extracts from the programme with performances of the Dave Clark Five taken from other sources.[63] After the conclusion of *Thank Your Lucky Stars* in 1966 and *Juke Box Jury* in 1967, the chart-based *Top Of The Pops* was left as the only regular, national, long-running British weekly pop music programme. Relatively little original footage remains of *Thank Your Lucky Stars* and *Juke Box Jury*, because of the nature of their recording technologies and of contemporary attitudes to the archiving of popular culture programmes.[64] Yet the legacy of *Ready Steady Go!* was visible for many years in *Top Of The Pops* via its on-screen audience interaction, studio space apparatus and equipment, and similarly in Channel 4's *The Tube* (1982–87)[65] and BBC2's *Later … With Jools Holland* (1992–).

Dusty, Cilla, Sandie and Lulu all went on to have further hit singles and, importantly, each was given her own BBC TV series. Their *Ready Steady Go!* appearances played a major part in their achievements, and gave them a durability unusual (then and now) for female pop music performers reliant on singles success. While the four singers appeared on many other British television shows, children's programmes and variety series, it was undoubtedly their association with *Ready Steady Go!* – the acknowledged pop music television phenomenon of the 1960s – that gave each of them the opportunity to create a lasting relationship with British TV audiences.

Dusty's role as occasional presenter on *Ready Steady Go!* and its 'Tamla Motown Special' led directly to her *Dusty* series in 1966, over which she continued to exert a strong musical influence. Cilla established her television persona through her *Ready Steady Go!* interviews, and fashioned her Merseybeat roots into a lifelong career, starting with the first of her numerous *Cilla* series in 1968. Sandie's interest in fashion led (like McGowan) to her own design labels and boutique. In 1968, *The Sandie Shaw Supplement* mixed location with studio performance to create a television version of the Sunday newspaper supplement; its on-screen cameras and microphones, blown-up Sandie portraits and sculptured studio sets drew directly from *Ready Steady Go!* Like Cilla, Lulu went on to have numerous eponymous TV series (beginning with *Lulu's Back In Town* in 1968) as well as hosting a number of pop shows and starring in two comedy series; all showcased the image of youthful energy and vitality, and powerful singing voice first demonstrated on-screen in *Ready Steady Go!* In each case, the distinctive televisual styles and screen personalities of all four singers were conclusively shaped by the innovative fusion of music, fashion and art that characterised *Ready Steady Go!*

---

[63]   Sandie Shaw described her reaction to discovering Clark's unauthorised use of her performance on these programmes in her autobiography, Shaw, *The World At My Feet*, p. 193.

[64]   Lowy, *DustyCillaSandieLulu As Seen On TV*, pp. 37–47.

[65]   Hill, 'Television And Pop', p. 103.

Chapter 6

Sworn In: *Today*, Bill Grundy And The Sex Pistols

Mark Duffett

At around 6.15 p.m. on 1 December 1976, guitarist Steve Jones caused a national outcry when he called interviewer Bill Grundy a 'fucking rotter' live on Thames Television's *Today* show. Whilst the shock of vulgar language is what made the moment famous, what makes it interesting is, as repeat viewing confirms, that its organiser took a deliberately confrontational approach to his quarry from the start. For those who have seen the footage, the scene in the studio is familiar: the Sex Pistols seated, a small clutch of punk fans behind them, Grundy to one side in his comfortable chair. After goading the band about their materialist values, Grundy changed the angle of his attack to the musical field: 'I want to know one thing. Are you serious or are you trying to just make me laugh? Really? About what you are doing? Beethoven, Brahms, Bach have all died –.' At this point Johnny Rotten interrupted and said sarcastically, 'They're all heroes of ours. They're all wonderful people. They really turn us on.' Grundy replied, 'Well, suppose that they turn other people on?' Under his breath, Rotten responded, 'That's just their tough shit.' The exchange continued:

> Grundy: It's what?
> Rotten: Nothing – a rude word – next question!
> Grundy: No, no. What was the rude word?
> Rotten (looking down): Shit.
> Grundy: Good heavens, you frighten me to death.

In this brief moment, Rotten shifted from a mood of defiant cynicism to one of adolescent embarrassment. He began rocking shamefully on his chair, knowing that he had just broken a taboo live on television. Grundy, who appeared to be winning, turned to the fans standing and asked, 'What about you girls behind?'[1] Bemused, bass player Glen Matlock cut in, 'He's like your dad, ain't he, this geezer – or your granddad?'

---

[1]   This handful of fans, not all girls, came from a faction known as the Bromley contingent who were part of the original punk scene. One of them wore a swastika arm band.

Looking at a very young Siouxsie Sue, Grundy asked, 'Are you worried or are you just enjoying yourself?' Coyly stroking her hair, Siouxsie answered, 'Enjoying myself ... I've always wanted to meet you.' Grundy seized his moment: 'Have you really? We'll meet afterwards, shall we?' In what became the key part of the interview, the presenter's flirty come-on gave Jones a chance to feign moral indignation and challenge their interviewer's salacious intent:

> Jones: You dirty sod! You dirty old man!
> Grundy: Well keep going, chief, keep going. Go on – you've got another five
>   seconds – say something outrageous.
> Jones: You dirty bastard.
> Grundy: Go on, again.
> Jones: You dirty fucker!
> Grundy: What a clever boy.
> Jones: What a fucking rotter!

Until the exchange between Grundy and Siouxsie, Jones had been quietly smoking, drinking, and looking away from his interrogator: 'When he asked Siouxsie if she'd meet him afterwards, Steve went into Warp Factor Five and weighed right into him.'[2] The flummoxed presenter slumped in his chair and finished with, 'Well, that's it for tonight. The other rocker, Eamonn – I'm not saying anything else about him – will be back tomorrow. I'll be seeing you [audience] soon. I hope I'm not seeing you [Pistols].'[3] As the camera panned in on Grundy and the credits rolled, Jones stood up and started grand-standing, turning the studio into a party.[4] The Pistols seemed triumphant, and the presenter agitated.

The interview has become an event in history. In 2007, *The Guardian* published a full CD recording and transcript booklet of it, as part of their 'Great Interviews of the Twentieth Century' series. While it may not readily bear comparison with other momentous episodes in the series (which included interviews with Fidel Castro, Richard Nixon and Adolf Hitler) in a sense the world was changed by it. My aim here is to consider exactly what it means, more than three decades later. On their 1978 EP, the Television Personalities asked, 'Where's Bill Grundy Now?' What follows will attempt to answer that question, starting (improbably) with a celebrated dictum from Karl Marx:

---

[2]   Glen Matlock, *I Was A Teenage Sex Pistol* (London, 1996), p. 127.

[3]   The 'other rocker' was in fact *Today*'s other anchor, Eamonn Andrews. Famous in his own right as host of the show *This Is Your Life*, the Dublin-born Andrews had a completely different style to Grundy. It is interesting to ponder how different history might have been if he had interviewed the band.

[4]   Some accounts suggest that Grundy can be seen mouthing 'Oh, shit' as the credits rolled. Whether these were his words or not, they convey a popular interpretation of the event.

> Marx begins his *Eighteenth Brumaire Of Louis Bonaparte* with a famous
> paragraph: 'Hegel remarks somewhere that all facts and personages of great
> importance in world history occur, as it were, twice.' He forgot to add: the first
> time as tragedy, the second time as farce.[5]

This statement about the return of historic phenomena is particularly appropriate,
and not just because the *Today* interview was a fiasco that dogged its participants:
the interview can be productively examined by focusing on the relationship
between its implication in historic narratives, its actual content, and our own 'out
of context' experience as contemporary viewers. Not only do these three elements
sustain interest in the footage by mutually supporting each other, but in subtle and
important ways they also change the meaning of what we see. It is not just that
we do not have access to the totality of the past; it is also that what contemporary
viewers are sold is not quite what they actually get. Consequently, the real question
is why the encounter between Grundy and the Sex Pistols remains so valuable.

Music fans and researchers have never been allowed to forget the *Today*
interview. It has been depicted as an accident, and yet as an inevitable turning
point in the cultural explosion of punk. As a historic moment, it is celebrated as
something that was impromptu, rather than calculatedly arranged and, as with all
emotional expressions, commentators authenticate its sincerity by emphasising that
it was unplanned. The conventional account of events relates that the programme's
original guests, Queen, had to cancel their appearance; consequently, one of EMI's
most extrovert and self-aggrandising hustlers (Eric Hall) persuaded *Today* to
feature a new act that evening; neither the Sex Pistols nor Grundy were enthusiastic
about the interview; both parties had been drinking in the green room beforehand;
and the interview was broadcast live, with no opportunity for editing.[6] This oft-
repeated reading of the interview suggests that it almost never happened, a point
designed to qualify it as a genuine iconic moment whose repercussions have given
it value for music historians: it mediated punk as an offensive attitude, shocked the
nation, and set in train a gradual implosion of the Pistols. Virtually every book on
the history of punk makes reference to it, some providing a partial or full transcript
of the occasion. For most biographers, it indicates a rupture, a moment when the
punk crusade found a voice on a national level. Phil Strongman's introduction to
his 2007 history of punk is typical:

> This book is roughly divided into two sections – underground and overground.
> Or, to put it in crude terms, before and after Grundy. For it was the live TV 'swear-
> in' on Bill Grundy's *Today* programme in December 1976 that first sent punk

---

[5]   Bruce Mazlish, 'The Tragic Farce Of Marx, Hegel And Engels: A Note', *History &
Theory* 11/3 (1972), p. 335.

[6]   For an extended description of the context of the interview, see Jon Savage,
England's Dreaming (London, 1991), pp. 255–69; Brian Southall, *The Sex Pistols: 90 Days
At EMI* (London, 2007).

shockwaves, and headlines, around the UK and then, albeit more faintly, around the entire world. For many, perhaps most, of those then involved, it irrevocably damaged the small, original 'scenes' in both London and Manchester, but it also made sure that those scenes would become legendary – that their influence would also be felt across continents, cultures and then-unimagined genres. Because one of the most important things about punk – hiding beneath its tendency to divide – was its ability to bring people together.[7]

In this reading, the interview is understood as a turning point in the history of punk because it disturbed authentic, urban music scenes. While it would be romanticising events to say that it disrupted the organic wholeness of punk as a subcultural scene, it clearly located its actors in public consciousness.[8] Even though the Sex Pistols had been interviewed on television before, *Today* mattered because it made the band and its following infamous, fixing their media image in a shockingly defiant moment of profanity. In other words, it set the frame for public interpretations of this new youth movement on a national level.

Swearing was common in everyday life well before *Today* – as a way of denoting anger, of being vulgar, of signifying disaffection or, arguably, of expressing class affiliation. It was heard frequently in the context of X-rated cinema, and occasionally in recorded popular music, but rarely on television, and never at tea-time. As a result, the shock waves from the interview were instantaneous. One disgusted viewer, an Essex lorry driver named James Holmes, reportedly kicked in his television set. Just after the group left Thames Television studios, a police van arrived there. Although the programme had only been broadcast in the London region, re-runs of the footage elsewhere on evening news shows ensured that it became a prominent story. A spate of front-page reports in the tabloid press – one notably headlined 'The Filth And The Fury'[9] – helped spark a national outcry in the days that followed. The Sex Pistols were transformed into folk devils. Almost all dates on the band's planned tour with Johnny Thunders and the Heartbreakers were cancelled, when local civic leaders banned punks from their venues. The Sex Pistols and their unruly followers became a national symbol for youth-as-trouble.

Thus, the interview is recounted as the dividing line that introduced punk to the general public, and exposed the music as a cultural response to the decaying state of Britain. Here, punk rock is read romantically and, to some extent rightly, as a rebellious outburst, a dose of anarchy to counter the boredom felt by young people who, in an age of high unemployment, had not been offered a future. *Jubilee* (Derek Jarman, 1978) supplied a cinematic illustration: starring (Sex Pistols' manager) Malcolm McLaren's protégé Jordan as Amyl Nitrate, it portrayed a bleak vision of

---

[7]   Phil Strongman, *Pretty Vacant: A History Of Punk* (London, 2007), p. 13.

[8]   The Damned were beginning to escape the London pub rock circuit with their 'New Rose' single in October 1976, and the Sex Pistols had already appeared on television, on BBC's *Young Nationwide*.

[9]   *Daily Mirror*, 2 December 1976, p. 1.

Britain as a broken, anarchic society. The young scavengers who dressed as punks revelled in meaningless violence and shocking perversion; they signalled the rapid decline of Britain's collective community, but also had fun hastening its end. As flamboyant recording impresario character Borgia Ginz explains in the movie, 'As long as the music's loud enough, we won't hear the world falling apart!' The film did not show how the wild children of punk had emerged, but by 1978, the nation already knew: *Today* had long since marked their appearance on the public stage.

As history, *Today* was seen as the moment that unleashed punk on an unsuspecting nation. It caused an outcry that could be read as 'the end of the beginning' of the genre because, after it, punk was understood primarily as an attitude born of its extensive media coverage. The band's members were reviled as the offenders of middle England, caricatured as offensive celebrities, frozen as victims of their own actions, and sent on the almost inevitable road to disaster. The programme's significance was not lost on Matlock: 'If there's one thing that everyone – even if they've never listened to a rock'n'roll record in their life – knows about the Sex Pistols, it's that we appeared on the Bill Grundy show, we swore.'[10]

A first step to understand how cultural norms frame our interpretation of the *Today* interview is to examine its relationship to music. Martin Cloonan has noted that it was important precisely because the Sex Pistols' archetypal moment was *not* a musical one.[11] But although the band performed no live music, its appearance was nonetheless a performance; indeed, the interview was the most significant performance that the Sex Pistols ever gave. *Today* is, therefore, not a source of supplementary information about the Sex Pistols. Instead, it remains their ur-text: an encapsulation of the attitude that frames the music. To put this another way, if *Today* had never happened, the band's songs might have been heard differently. In that sense, the Sex Pistols effectively entered the public realm of popular music as both *unmusical* and *unpopular*. *Rolling Stone* reflected: 'So this is how legends are born. Not with a song, or even a death, but with an expletive.'[12] In his own celluloid dissertation on punk, *The Great Rock'n'Roll Swindle* (Julien Temple, 1980), McLaren asked 'Haven't you understood anything yet? Didn't you realize that these kids didn't buy these records for the music? If that was the case this thing would have died the death years ago.' The idea of buying records but not for music seems contradictory, and the combination of legendary infamy and the strange gap where the music should have been has created a very distinct interpretation of *Today*. Documentaries and other commentaries rarely, if ever, talk about Jones's guitar playing and musicianship; they seem irrelevant, perhaps even contradictory, to the myth of Jones as the disaffected everyman. He was making

[10] Matlock, *Teenage*, p. 123.

[11] Martin Cloonan, *Banned: Censorship Of Popular Music In Britain 1967–1992* (Aldershot, 1996), p. 147.

[12] Mick Brown, 'UK Report: Sex Pistols And Beyond', *Rolling Stone*, 27 January 1977.

a stand, not playing along. Even so, as a famous performance, the interview has sometimes attracted a musical interpretation: 'Once it got beyond its tepid start, the resulting broadcast was roughly equivalent to the "Anarchy" single.'[13] Such comments do not seek to infer that the interview itself was musical. Instead, they suggest that because the Sex Pistols' songs, and this interview, are performances, it is difficult not to liken the moment to a musical triumph – to compare it with the way in which rock bands usually find fame. Such modes of narration subtly frame our own interpretations.

Given the weight of such narratives, what happens when we watch the footage again? Those who saw the original broadcast can act as its privileged interpreters:

> Newly arrived in London, and living in a squat in Willesden, I remember how the Pistols' TV appearance divided my household in a microcosm of the national debate that raged the next day. I knew which side I was on. For the first time, I had found a pop group who had not come to me second-hand via older lads' record collections and reminiscences.[14]

Such experiential accounts of viewing-in-context guide interpretations of what we see as contemporary viewers. To watch the footage now is to be invited back to 1976, as if to see it for the first time.[15] In that sense we are encouraged to construct a memory of a moment that many of us never actually experienced. Elsewhere (borrowing from Beatles' biographer Ray Coleman) I have labelled these confabulations 'imagined memories'.[16] Within film studies, Alison Landsberg calls them 'prosthetic memories', in a way that highlights the illusory nature of remembering something on the basis of its media footage:

> Because the mass media alter our notion of what counts as experience, they might be a privileged arena for the production and circulation of prosthetic memories. The cinema, in particular, as an institution which makes available images for mass consumption, has long been aware of its ability to generate experiences

---

[13]   Theodor Gracyk, *I Wanna Be Me: Rock Music And The Politics Of Identity* (Philadelphia, 2001), p. 2. More evidence for this subtle process of 'musicisation' comes from Virgin Records who released the *Today* interview, under the title of 'Fucking Rotter' on the Sex Pistols' album *Some Product*. In 2008, the broadcast was also included on Delta Records' *The Sex Pistols Raw & Live*.

[14]   Sean O'Hagan, 'Guerillas In Our Midst', *The Observer*, 20 February 2000.

[15]   Consider the statement, 'I'd never felt the call to arms, even when glancing up from my tea to watch the now-legendary Bill Grundy interview with the Sex Pistols', in Roger Sabin (ed.), *Punk Rock: So What?* (London, 1999), p. 174. While the response may be different to O'Hagan's, the idea of the interview drawing a line is re-affirmed.

[16]   Mark Duffett, 'Imagined Memories: Webcasting As A "Live" Technology And The Case Of Little Big Gig', *Information, Communication & Society* 6/3 (2003), pp. 307–25.

and install memories of them – memories which become experiences that film consumers possess and feel possessed by.[17]

In addition, she suggests that fictional feature films that explicitly play with the theme of prosthetic memories might also be read as allegories for the power of the corporate media. False, media-created memories emerge as a central theme in a series of movies from *Blade Runner* (Ridley Scott, 1982) through *Total Recall* (Paul Verhoeven, 1990) and *New Nightmare* (Wes Craven, 1994) to *Strange Days* (Kathryn Bigelow, 1995). Although Landsberg does not dwell on this point, the release dates of these films are significant, in that they parallel the mass adoption of video, satellite television, and internet technologies. In the contemporary era, the extension of prosthetic memory and of digital archiving have gone hand in hand. And just when these technologies allowed their users to store away recorded moments, ideas that erode the ontological basis and unity of historical narratives have gained ground.[18] For Landsberg, the power of film is its ability to provide viewers with sensory stimulation, helping their media-based imagined memories to appear real.[19] The limiting horizon of her theory is that the media do not 'create and implant' memories (a 'media effects' argument); instead, it is viewers who make use of the sensory data offered by electronic media to confabulate memories that are also made important by narratives. In a kind of symbiotic process, the stories that contemporary viewers read, see and hear about the historic place of the *Today* interview make it significant and, in turn, the availability of the footage helps to affirm and support those same stories.

If not all punk fans actually shared the experience of watching the interview live on its original broadcast, O'Hagan's recollection of the divisive nature of the controversy does not quite imply the creation of prosthetic memory. Narratives around the programme do not invite contemporary viewers to see themselves as participating in the interview (even though they may also image such a scenario). Instead, the narrative invites us to imagine watching the show as it was first transmitted (in 1976, in London) so that we can share in the radicalising experience that infected its original viewers. To watch *Today* now is therefore to be invited back into a specific historic experience of television viewing. Contemporary viewers are subtly encouraged to image themselves in its original

---

[17] Alison Landsberg, 'Prosthetic Memory: *Total Recall* and *Blade Runner*', in Mike Featherstone and Roger Burrows (eds), *Cyberspace Cyberbodies Cyberpunk* (London, 1996), pp. 175–90.

[18] See Fredric Jameson, 'Postmodernism And Consumer Society', in Hal Foster (ed.), *The Anti-Aesthetic: Essays On Postmodern Culture* (New York, 1999), pp. 111–25; this was presented in part as a Whitney Museum Lecture in 1982, before the works of Lyotard and other European postmodernist writers were translated into English.

[19] Also see Alison Landsberg, 'Prosthetic Memory: The Ethics And Politics Of Memory In An Age Of Mass Culture', in Paul Grainge (ed.), *Memory And Popular Film* (Manchester, 2003), pp. 144–61; Alison Landsberg, *Prosthetic Memory* (New York, 2004).

television audience watching the live broadcast. The self-evidential nature of the footage as offensive tea-time viewing may help to authenticate our shared experience of also being viewers (along with O'Hagan) yet we can never quite be there. Indeed, it problematises Landsberg's distinction between 'authentic' and 'inauthentic' memory: those of us who were not watching Thames Television that night *have* seen the footage, as the memory suggests, even if we did not see it in its original time and place. We (literally) see *what* the first viewers saw, but we cannot meaningfully see it *in the same way* as they did. The associated narratives, frequent syndication and recycling of the clip invite all viewers – original and contemporary – to confabulate, by following narrative cues that the audience in 1976 never had. Although original viewers can still recount their first experiences of seeing the interview screened live, their interpretations are, nonetheless, shaped by the later meanings that have over-determined the footage. As a ritually repeated piece of television punctum, the *Today* interview therefore comes to us as already having been viewed before.

In an age of preservative digital media, how should the predicament of recorded culture be interpreted? The Sex Pistols/Bill Grundy clip is now an intellectual property, and has been licensed to a variety of media outlets; in July 2008, *New Musical Express* reported that the owners of the footage, Fremantle Media, had revealed that the clip was the most-requested by TV companies, making it a popular culture equivalent of the Zapruder footage.[20] As electronic archives make recorded fragments of the past more accessible than ever, one might argue that recorded moments lose their vitality; they become perpetually repeated and recycled, like so many 'broken records'. Since we now live in the archive, our linear experience of historic time seems to have lost much of its meaning and momentum: it is 'as though we were unable today to focus our own present, as though we have become incapable of achieving representations of our current experience'.[21] Fredric Jameson adds that contemporary society has made the importance of 'now time' and the status of history as a unanimously-agreed narrative disappear, leaving us to experience life in a pretty vacant perpetual present. Perhaps this timeless, mediated world is the 'no future' of which the Sex Pistols sang. An evasion of the present sits alongside society's inability to deal with time and history in a traditional way and, in the absence of historical continuity, nostalgia becomes a popular mode of personal experience, not least because the repeated screening of iconic moments reminds us of a longing for times past.[22] In this schema, the media usurp organic memory, and repeated viewings reduce the resonance of key moments; they fade, just as they do when 'children repeat a phrase over again until its sense is lost and it becomes an incomprehensible incantation'.[23] The

---

[20]   Abraham Zapruder's 18-second film of President Kennedy's assassination in Dallas, on 22 November 1963.

[21]   Jameson, 'Postmodernism', p. 117

[22]   Ibid., pp. 116–17.

[23]   Ibid., p. 120.

endless extension of inconsequential coverage then orientates our interpretation of everything, encouraging us to look back with hindsight more rapidly, upon even recent events:

> Our entire contemporary social system has little by little begun to lose its capacity to retain its own past, has begun to live in a perpetual present and in a perpetual change that obliterates traditions of the kind which all earlier social formations have had in one way or another to preserve. Think of how the media exhaust news: of how Nixon and, even more so, Kennedy are figures from a now distant past. One is tempted to say that the very function of the news media is to relegate such historical experiences as rapidly as possible into the past. The informational function of the media would thus be to help us forget, to serve as the very agents and mechanisms for our historical amnesia.[24]

However, Nixon and Kennedy, or indeed the Sex Pistols of 1976, are *not* forgotten. Instead they squarely take up their place as icons in popular memory. Good or bad, famous or infamous, they have become part of our cultural furniture. In that sense, the *Today* interview is still with us. Nostalgia thus seems inappropriate as a term for describing the urge to so frequently revisit these media moments, since their footage has never really gone away.[25] The interview is better understood as a recurring and commodified fragment of the cultural past. Alongside its historical significance, its endless circulation now plays an equal role in making it part of collective memory.

The 'broken record' analogy is only one way to see our recycled past. Landsberg has argued that all memories (including those imagined) function as much more than recollections, since they also act in the present as 'building blocks' of personal and collective identity.[26] In that sense, she suggests, the broken, pessimistic version of historic experience put forward by Jameson misunderstands that in contemporary experience memories primarily function to give us a purpose. These two disparate versions of archival experience (the 'broken record' and 'building block' interpretations) are correct in different ways. We *are* overly familiar with the *Today* footage, and yet still strangely inspired by it. By first applying the 'broken record' perspective to the interview and the way it has ricocheted through popular history, I will suggest that when contemporary viewers watch it, they watch an adolescent ordeal that was quickly recycled to entrap its participants. In other words, it happened first as tragedy, and secondly as farce.

In order to explain the drama of gender that unfolds in the interview, it is necessary to resume a close reading of the footage itself. One of the more interesting

---

[24]   Ibid., p. 125.

[25]   As Svetlana Boym's definitive discussion makes clear, nostalgia is about personal loss and longing for something absent; see *The Future Of Nostalgia* (New York, 2008). It therefore seems inappropriate to apply it to media-based generational remembrances.

[26]   Landsberg, '*Total Recall*'.

aspects is the way in which masculinity is played out. All the participants displayed slightly different gender identities, and it is the interaction between those identities that makes the interview meaningful. Drummer Paul Cook, who was nearest to Grundy, looked diligent and remained silent, briefly smirking and covering his face when Jones began swearing. Next to Cook, Matlock seemed cheerful, boyish and slightly bemused; he was making sense of the process from within it. Rotten, furthest away from Grundy, restlessly rocked in his chair, the epitome of the misunderstood adolescent. Finally, Jones (who was wearing Vivienne Westwood's Seditionaries 'tits' t-shirt and leather trousers) appeared to be the boldest rebel, nonchalantly drinking and smoking. Of the four, Jones had the most 'normal' haircut, and it is notable that he took the lead, when one might have expected Rotten (or later, Sid Vicious) to assume that role.[27]

In contrast to the band's display of various adolescent masculinities, Grundy seemed tired but relaxed, crossing his legs and slumping in his chair. From the first sentence of his interrogation, the swaggering, middle-aged presenter positioned his quarry as another in the parade of youth phenomena coming after teds, mods and hippies; he had seen the cycle of youth culture before, and indicated his weariness towards it. Although history read punk as a new phenomenon, the Rolling Stones had, long before 1976, already proven that rock stars could behave 'badly'; indeed, in the wake of the programme, many critics compared the Sex Pistols to the Rolling Stones. The presenter implied that the Sex Pistols made those bad boys of the last generation seem comparatively well behaved, and his introductory vignette therefore attempted to map a place for the band in relation to both youth culture and to himself:

> They are punk rockers – a new craze they tell me. Their heroes – not the nice clean Rolling Stones. You see, they are as drunk as I am. They are clean by comparison. They're a group called the Sex Pistols and I'm surrounded now by all of them. Just let us see the Sex Pistols in action.

When he wrote himself into the narrative by saying, 'they are as drunk as I am', Grundy both separated himself from the public and distanced himself from the band, competing with them to determine who was the biggest rebel. He soon put his first question: 'I am told that that group has received £40,000 from a record company. Doesn't that seem to be slightly opposed to their anti-materialistic view of life?' To address them in the third person, while talking directly to them as 'that group [with] their anti-materialistic view', emphasised the separation between them. He also assumed that the Sex Pistols were against materialism (like the hippies before them) and hypocritical for that. His comment framed the movement as yet another dreary, youth cultural phenomenon that had nothing new or worth taking seriously. When he then asked what they had done with the money, the expletive in Jones's

---

[27] Writing in *Rolling Stone* a month after the interview, Mick Brown mistakenly said that it was Rotten who had called Grundy a rotter. See Brown, 'UK Report'.

reply – 'We've fucking spent it, haven't we?' – was ignored. Commenting later on this apparent failure to notice the swearing, Jones suggested that Grundy was drunk and unprofessional, and had already stopped listening. After they explained that their money had all disappeared 'down the boozer', Grundy's tactic was to feign shock: 'Really?! Good Lord!' His mocking, obviously false indignation was important in adroitly positioning him not only as disrespectful to the Sex Pistols, but also somewhere outside his potential role as a conventional, morally disgusted member of the establishment. Grundy saw himself as a tricky rogue, comically dancing around the band members, challenging them, but carefully avoiding the shackles of duty that might come with his role as a representative of the general public. Ultimately, when Jones turned the tables, that separation from the public was what entrapped him.

Although historians have portrayed the incident as a shock to the national system, popular culture quickly absorbed the incident as farce through repetition. Once it was transferred out of its sensitive tea-time slot, the segment could be repeated (sometimes with the expletives deleted) on news bulletins and re-runs where adults could find it, on late night music documentaries and film compilations, as part of punk merchandise, and eventually as uploaded content on websites like YouTube. This relocation shifted the footage from its birthplace on live television into a category similar to the Certificate 18 feature film – a media form in which swearing has engendered much less of a shock response from the audience. As the event was recycled, it was soon presented in various parodies. Comedy trio the Goodies quickly spoofed the moment with their own footage of Ronald McLeod dressed as 'Bill Grumpy'. Wearing a nose chain and punked-up suit with 'SCUM' written on it, McLeod swore frequently as he interviewed rebelliously 'nice' Tim Brooke-Taylor; the intended message was that Britain had perhaps over-reacted to an episode of mere bad language and that Grundy was the godfather of punk.

Three years later, after the Sex Pistols had split, McLaren returned to the incident in *The Great Rock'n'Roll Swindle*, where he declared:

> It was all going smoothly … our record company was footing the bill for a nationwide tour – the only problem being the Sex Pistols, a band that couldn't play. I must admit, I was a bit stumped at this point, but fortune played into our hands. The record company came up with the Bill Grundy show. It was my task to make absolutely sure that none of us would ever return to normality.

Next, a middle aged man in jeans, a t-shirt and a waist coat (presumably meant to be the disgusted lorry driver) is seen in his living-room, feeding scraps of his cooked breakfast to his dog. Grundy's words blare out from a television, spoken in a rather camp, distinctly upper-class voice. The set reads 'Censored by Thames TV' as Jones intones: 'You dirty sod! You dirty old man! You dirty fucker! What a fucking rotter!' Outraged by such vulgarity, the viewer leaps to his feet and smashes the television in anger. A montage of news headlines then appears.

Through the 1980s and 1990s, interest in *Today* continued unabated: the Television Personalities' track was re-released in 1980, and again in 1992. In 1993, a re-creation of the interview was included in *The Buddha Of Suburbia* (a BBC mini-series adapted from Hanif Kureshi's novel) in which television anchorman Bob Welling (of BBC's nightly *Nationwide* magazine show) took the interviewer's chair. In 2000, surrealist comic Harry Hill performed his own version of the interview on Channel 4's *Harry Hill Christmas Special*, defending the Queen as he lambasted a clutch of punk comics. With the passing of time, the interview now seems a little shorn of its shock value.

However, as the controversy over the obscene telephone calls broadcast on Radio 2 by Jonathan Ross and Russell Brand demonstrated in 2008, British media audiences can still be concerned about swearing and vulgarity in the media, at least in certain contexts. In 2006, a poll of 2,000 UKTV Gold viewers placed the *Today* interview sixth in a list of the 'Most Shocking TV Chat Show Moments', behind the Bee Gees walking out from BBC's *The Clive Anderson Show* in 1996, and – more famously – Grace Jones's assault on her host during ITV's *The Russell Harty Show* in 1981. Now that swearing has become commonplace on television (at least, after the 9.00 p.m. 'watershed') the play fight between Harty and Jones may appear more shocking to viewers than the symbolic violence between Grundy and the Sex Pistols. The *Today* clip remains in circulation as a funny, silly moment that outraged tabloids and ordinary, 'decent' British people at a particular moment, but somehow can no longer deliver the kind of voltage it once did: 'Anybody who could see that footage now, and see how tame it was, would be stunned as to why it became an enormous rip in the cultural fabric of Britain in the late 1970s.'[28] Even so, it continues to possess an enduring status as an iconic moment of British television: it has appeared in a graphic novel telling the story of the Sex Pistols;[29] Jones has mooted the idea of licensing his re-recorded swearing as a ring tone; there is even a Sex Pistols tribute act now called The Bill Grundy Show. In that sense, the *Today* interview has certainly returned as farce.

While the lighter side of the encounter still echoes in the public imagination, what lends most credence to the 'broken record' approach is that continued interest has, perhaps inevitably, trapped the programme's participants inside the claustrophobic confines of cultural memory.[30] Almost instantaneously, the young punks went from 'flies in the ointment' to 'flies trapped in amber', their bodies aging, but their accepted meaning frozen by an image of their past. In that sense the footage also functions to anchor the most compelling narratives about its

---

[28]   Music journalist Gary Mullholland, speaking in *The Sex Pistols: Punk Icons* DVD (Classic Rock Legends, 2006).

[29]   Jim McCarthy and Steve Parkhouse, *The Sex Pistols: A Graphic Novel* (London, 2008).

[30]   Bill Grundy himself died of a heart attack in 1993, although some stories suggest that he died in a car accident; the implication – in line with the Sex Pistols fiasco – is that his demise came through his own carelessness.

participants and, if new facets of their personalities come to light, they have to conform with the events of *Today* if they are to make sense. This can be illustrated by considering the images of two survivors from the interview: Steve Jones and Johnny Rotten.

The interview gave Jones a reputation as a delinquent 'boy' willing to break taboos and utter profanities; and he was, therefore, framed as a crafty opportunist in a wider sense. A focus on his immature opportunism has continued in portrayals of his criminal delinquency, his lack of spoken manners, and his hedonistic sexuality. References to this persona also appear in the frequent characterisations of Jones as a kleptomaniac, particularly in *The Great Rock'n'Roll Swindle*, where he is portrayed as an errant delinquent, jokingly playing the part of a hardboiled private eye; McLaren contextualises the band by saying, 'Assemble four kids. Make sure they hate each other', as their roles are revealed: McLaren is 'the Embezzler', Rotten 'the Gimmick', and Jones 'the Crook'. He evokes a history going back to the Gordon Riots of 1780, in which 'the London mob created anarchy in the UK'. As the baying crowd carries effigies of Jones and the other outlaws on the way to their public hanging, McLaren whispers, 'In our case there was Steve Jones, 18 years of age, a brilliant cat burglar. In one instance nearby, at Rolling Stones' Keith Richards's house, he managed to steal a colour TV, a load of nice fur coats and a bunch of guitars'. Jones's appearance in the movie has him lighting a cigarette at night in Soho, saying, 'The first time I laid eyes on McLaren, he was chasing me down the Kings Road on account of the clothes I'd nicked from his shop'. He explains that he has entered into arrangements with Malcolm, and threatens, 'But if he rips me off, I'd break his fucking legs'. He smashes down the door of the Glitterbeast office and steals from a safe, while his voiceover states, 'The clues were in front of me in black-and-white, but I never learned to read or write'. By the time of the film's release, *Today* had already made Jones infamous and, in some quarters, celebrated for his use of profanity.[31]

In addition to his edgy criminal side, Jones is also portrayed (like his adversary Grundy) as a shady sexual opportunist, a dirty old man, and a rotter with women. On the commentary track to *The Great Rock'n'Roll Swindle*, director Julien Temple explains: 'There is something about Steve that goes deep into that kind of pre-war Cockney humour. He's a bit like a Sid James figure in a way. I don't know, there's something like a *Carry On* figure, and we certainly played with that.' The interpretation of the Sex Pistols' actions as comedic – as *Carry On* or as music hall – offers a way for them to escape responsibility for what happened on *Today* and in its aftermath. Nevertheless, the salaciousness of the *Carry On* series is clearly part of Jones's character in *The Great Rock'n'Roll Swindle*, and has continued to be one aspect of his image. While Sid Vicious became the poster boy for a kind of all-round nihilistic irresponsibility, portrayals of Jones's irresponsibility channel it through his criminal and sexual appetites. In the film, his bad language, inability

---

[31] Jones continued to play up to his image. Even excluding the Grundy re-enactment, he says 'fuck' at least eight times, and 'cunt' at least three times, in the film.

to settle with one mate, and the reckless way he uses women all mark him out as a delinquent male.

Today helped to create this public image, casting a myth of him as a young man ready to seize any chance coming his way, and break polite codes of conduct at a moment's notice. The myth is also tied to the absence of a father figure. In *The Filth And The Fury* (Julien Temple, 2000), the guitarist explains that he never knew his own father (a boxer named Don Jarvis); he grew up feeling unwanted, and drifted into a life of crime that included theft in and around London's Shepherds Bush.[32] Since the heyday of the Sex Pistols, and outside his musical and associated commitments, Jones has continued to capitalise on this image, in various ways: he played the guitarist of the Looters in *Ladies And Gentlemen, The Fabulous Stains* (Lou Adler, 1982) and introduced the DVD documentary *Hooligans And Thugs: Soccer's Most Violent Fan Fights* (BBF Media, 2003). Jones's image thus represents a cautionary tale about how boys might fend in the absence of responsible guidance. His reputation makes him seem overly casual, and unable to take from the world without ignoring where its limits might lie.

Meanwhile, Johnny Rotten has remained trapped in what is perhaps an even more juvenile role. Interviewed by Australian film-maker Peter Clifton in 1983, Rotten implied that he was only just beginning to come to terms with his spell in the Sex Pistols. When asked about revivalist trends on the rock scene, he snarled:

> I think that's regression, in a way and I'm not for that. It's like, yeah, that rockabilly trend thing. That's escapism and that's not on. You've got to progress and you've got to be able to live in your modern, urban-day society. That is very important. Keeping on harping back to the past makes you somehow irrelevant instantly. It just shows you up for the fool you are – your lack of ideas. It's also a fear and a paranoia, and I'm not interested in people that behave that way. You can have respect for the past, but you needn't live in it. For quite a period, right, I did go out of my way to pretend that it never happened, and that was very stupid and silly of me. I've changed my mind, and now I can perform old Pistols numbers and not see it as a threat, it fits in very well [but] I can't see myself doing, for instance, 'Jumping Jack Flash', for the next 15 years.[33]

At the time, Rotten was fighting the tide, drowning in audience expectations based on memories of the events of the previous decade. His image shifted from that of being an awkward rebel, to staying stuck in a kind of perpetual adolescence, touting his romantic creed that each individual should remain true to themselves in their life and art. Although Rotten gained respect under his own name during the 1980s as the creative musician in Public Image Ltd, he never escaped the long

---

[32]   Jones's wiki page claims that he had 14 convictions, a council care order, and spent a year in a remand centre.

[33]   This interview can be seen as an extra on the DVD release of *The Punk Rock Movie* (Don Letts, 2008).

shadow of the Sex Pistols, nor could he. By the mid-1990s his interpretation of the *Today* interview was that 'Really, all I'd seen was a bunch of spotty kids being naughty',[34] comments which led John Strausbaugh to describe him as 'a rather tame provocateur, a kind of middle-aged brat, more annoying than anarchic'[35] and a fallen symbol of youth rebellion.

However, it may be more relevant to consider the extent to which Rotten has been inevitably trapped by his own reputation. In one early interview he stated, 'You start off in school and they take your soul away ... so when you leave school, your only future is getting married, and by the time you're about 29 you've got two kids – you just want to commit suicide'.[36] Yet in 1982, the singer married German media heiress Nora Forster, a woman 14 years his senior. Forster had previously dated Chris Spedding, and was the mother of Ari Up of the Slits. Despite being just six years older than her, Rotten became Ari's stepfather, and saw her children as his grandchildren. He has largely kept this unconventional family unit out of the media, perhaps out of a desire for privacy, perhaps because the idea of family life does not fit his rebellious image. In 2000, his circumstances were seen in these terms:

> And John Lydon is holed up in Los Angeles, where he hosts a cable show called *Rotten TV*, and plays the cartoon punk whenever and however it suits him. Really, though, there was nowhere else for any of them to go after punk.
>
> 'No future' howled Johnny Rotten back then, little knowing that he was singing ultimately of himself.[37]

Such descriptions of Rotten as a 'cartoon punk' or 'middle-aged brat' aptly identify the unchanging nature of his image. His return to British television in 2004 – as a reality show contestant on ITV's *I'm A Celebrity, Get Me Out Of Here*, and as an eccentric bug hunter in Discovery TV's *John Lydon's Megabugs* – prompted the hosts of Channel 4's *Richard And Judy* (Richard Madeley and Judy Finnigan) to comment in 2005 that his career had stretched 'from anarchy to arachnology'.

While the 'broken record' theory might suggest that *Today* fixed its actors in their roles, what made the programme a 'building block' (an ongoing cultural inspiration) is that it was about four young people finding their way in the absence of mature guidance. The interview itself seems to have a dreamlike quality about it, not merely because contemporary viewers are literally seeing it out-of-time (and because they have also seen it out-of-time many times before), but also because it suggests a symbolic subtext as a masculine rite of passage.

---

[34] Rotten's comments here are taken from the Australian TV documentary *The Story Of Rock'n'Roll* (Channel 9, 1995).

[35] John Strausbaugh, *Rock Till You Drop* (London, 2002), p. 205.

[36] Rotten can be heard saying this in *The Great Rock'n'Roll Swindle*.

[37] O'Hagan, 'Guerillas'

The band's symbolic father, Malcolm McLaren, was in close attendance, and yet he was in some ways a rather gutless father figure. It was he who had forced them to appear on the show by threatening to dock them a week's wages. Like Grundy, McLaren also called them 'boys', and his response to the controversy was to re-assert the childish status of his 'sexy young assassins' by saying 'boys will be boys', and refusing to accept any responsibility for the incident at the time:

> All the time I could see Malcolm behind the cameras. He had his head in his hands. I couldn't hear him but he looked like he was laughing. Not because he thought it was funny but out of nerves. He was shitting himself. His attitude was, oh no, you've gone and done it now, what the hell are we going to do? A long way from the idea that a lot of people had that it was all his scheme. There was no little Malcolm the Machiavellian telling us to go and swear our heads off on TV so we could scoop all the publicity … Straight after the show, we walked out through the studio still having a bit of a laugh about it all. I wanted to get back in the green room for another drink. But Malcolm was having none of it. He literally dragged me out of the building and shoved me into the motor with the rest of them.[38]

Jon Savage offered a similar observation: 'McLaren was unable and unwilling to give them the emotional support – even nursemaiding – they now more than ever required.'[39] Equally, Grundy himself was never the stable patriarch; by goading the young rebels into a response that would test their limits, it was as if he were a naughty teen leading even more childish boys astray.[40] Although it has been suggested that the Sex Pistols were knowingly cast as 'the ugly face of disaffected youth' and Grundy as 'the establishment's policeman',[41] his role is unconvincing. Indeed, if he was 'the establishment's policeman', he was more akin to Clint Eastwood's Dirty Harry, in his tendency to ignore the protocols of his own institution and injudiciously pursue his quarry.

In 1977, Grundy appeared in BBC's *The Punch Review*, where he created a parody of himself as the epitome of irresponsibility, the world's worst drunk; television presenter and music entrepreneur Tony Wilson claimed that while at Granada TV, Grundy would regularly come in to work drunk, and shout abuse at the canteen staff: 'he really didn't give a shit'.[42] Thus, while Grundy parodied himself as unprofessional, he also lived out (to an extent) the parody. His 'as drunk as I am' quip was actually designed to put the Sex Pistols in his *low* category. The

---

[38] Matlock, *Teenage*, p. 127.

[39] Quoted in O'Hagan, *Guerillas*.

[40] 'The moment John Lydon actually swears, and Bill Grundy picks him up on it, he goes, "Oh, nothing," and he looks like a little kid who's been told off.' Music journalist John Robb, speaking in *The Sex Pistols: Punk Icons* DVD (Classic Rock Legends, 2006).

[41] Gracyk, *I Wanna Be Me*, p. 3.

[42] Strongman, *Pretty Vacant*, p. 151.

line that followed ('they are clean by comparison') left its object ambiguous: were the Sex Pistols clean compared to the Rolling Stones, or were they clean compared to Bill Grundy? In the wake of his two-week suspension from Thames TV, it was unsurprising that the Goodies represented *him* as the rebel. In his accidental role as the unwitting godfather of punk, Grundy succeeded in portraying the Sex Pistols as foul-mouthed yobs, only to be disciplined and given an image that was as irresponsible and controversial as the musicians he had harangued. When the Television Personalities' 'Where's Bill Grundy Now?' was first released, its sleeve featured a phallic picture of Grundy, castrated by the Sex Pistols incident, standing erect, but with his head missing. The figure of Bill Grundy endures not so much as a gentle or staunch father, but as a blustering, errant one.

In his survey of punk's gender politics, Nathan Wiseman-Trowse has pointed out that groups like the Sex Pistols were notable for their absence of female figures:

> This struggle against the feminine as a shackle is further articulated throughout punk, whether in the body-horror of the Sex Pistols' 'Bodies' or The Clash's pseudo-military posing. The gang/band is consistently articulated as a masculine unit, untamed by the family or by femininity in any fashion. The phallic preoccupations of punk are evident in the band names alone: the Sex Pistols, the Buzzcocks, the Members, Stiff Little Fingers, Penetration.[43]

Following on, I want to suggest that the *Today* interview is structured around the absence of a masculine father figure. By father figure I do not mean a biological father, but a paternal symbolic figure: an authoritative elder who can take responsibility, care for others, and provide an example to those around him. During the opening sections, Grundy's cadence is strange because some of the band are reading from the auto-cue, and unsettling him. Just before Grundy says 'in action', Jones pre-empts him and pumps a fist in the air. The mischief – one might even say, the anarchy – has already begun. The juvenile, perhaps even infantile, masculinities of the Sex Pistols are never quite held in check, as neither their manager nor their interviewer is able to guide or restrain them.

What ensues is the creation of a generation gap from both sides. In that sense, the presenter came to represent something more than himself, as Matlock's comment sutured him into a patriarchal position. 'He's like your dad, this geezer' was unusual because it acted as a meta-commentary, creating a semantic perspective from outside the interview, directly labelling the programme's host right in front of him. It was a way to laugh at Grundy, to frame his efforts to mock the band. A combination of Matlock's meta-commentary and the presenter's fake indignation helped to mark out generational boundaries and cement Grundy in his role as a corrupt and inadequate patriarch. He was, in fact, a father of six

---

[43]   Nathan Wiseman-Trowse, *Performing Class In British Popular Music* (London, 2008), p. 129.

(a point occasionally mentioned in histories of the incident) but on this evening, his arrogant, self-interested and disrespectful stance signified everything that was wrong with the older generation and the society that they had created. It was hardly surprising that the 'rotter' appellation was later employed in an attack on irresponsible record industry executives. During a scene in *The Great Rock'n'Roll Swindle*, Jones enters a sleazy hotel in Kings Cross, where Client Number One – MAMIE Records boss Ed Bird – is awaiting trial on a child molestation charge.[44] Bird declares that McLaren will never work again, adding, 'We don't take risks in this business anymore – we don't need to!' Spitting at him and ruffling his hair, Jones counters, 'You dirty old man! What a fucking rotter!' By this time, the ransom note styling and title of their first album (*Never Mind The Bollocks Here's The Sex Pistols*) had already helped brand the Sex Pistols as outlaws willing to hold their record company hostage. As Toyah Wilcox, in her role as the aptly-named punk girl Mad, explained in *Jubilee*: 'the world is no longer interested in heroes'.

From this 'building block' perspective, their appearance on *Today* was a rite of passage for the 'boys' in the Sex Pistols in which the narcissistic side of their individuality was tempered with a kind of fortitude. Their use of street language at a time when it was unheard of on British tea-time television took courage. The widespread indignation that would rain down on them and Grundy would show that they had evoked a threat of retributive violence, whether symbolic or real; one fan advised Rotten to 'take care and stay away from the crowbars, chains, knives or whatever else may be coming your way'.[45] For every punk in the wake of *Today*, simply to be honest to yourself was to be tested, and to be tested was to find your independence. Two weeks after the broadcast, the UK music weekly *Sounds* concluded that 'to turn up to a Sex Pistols' show nowadays is to make a statement to the world that you care about rock'n'roll, and don't give a Bill Grundy what the yellow press thinks'.[46] The band's (non-musical) performance in the face of opposition inspired fans across the world.[47] Two years after the incident, two female fans who wrote to the band used their own swearing as a badge of authenticity:

---

[44]   MAMIE is a fictional but obvious amalgamation of EMI and A&M Records, the major labels that had briefly courted the Sex Pistols.

[45]   This, and subsequent, quotations from Sex Pistols fan mail come from the 'England's Dreaming' punk archive donated to Liverpool John Moores University by Jon Savage. My thanks to the Special Collections curator, Emily Burningham.

[46]   Pete Silverton, 'Pistols, Clash, etc.: What Did You Do On The Punk Tour, Daddy?', *Sounds*, 18 December 1976.

[47]   'I can remember watching it and thinking "My God, these people are speaking just like I speak to my friends. These are real people. They are not this anodyne thing that the camera normally makes people. They are real. They speak just like I do" and it was such a liberating experience just to see real people on television'. Ian Fortnam, speaking in *The Sex Pistols: Punk Icons* DVD (Classic Rock Legends, 2006).

You four were the best thing that ever hit the music scene. You were really different, individualists … John, don't get the impression that we only like you for your fame (and fortune!); it's not like that … You are you, you don't give a fuck about what people expect you to do, you just want to be yourself … We are two 16-year-old Dublin girls who are individualists. We don't give a fuck about anyone's views. We have our own views on life and that's all that matters.

After the group split, another fan wrote, 'I thought you had the guts to stick it all out'; a female fan from Japan asked, 'Are you a man or a mouse? If you are a man, you have to play the man'. These fans understood that in a society offended by bad language, to swear and not care takes guts, and that to define oneself as a rebel is a form of masculine bravado. *Today* represented a moment of masculine testing, a showdown in which Grundy inadvertently helped the Sex Pistols to sacrifice his career, as the lyrics of 'Where's Bill Grundy Now?' astutely observe: 'he set them up and they knocked him down'. Speaking in *The Filth And The Fury*, Jones recalls how Grundy 'started provoking us and we coated him off'. Doing that and withstanding the furious national response allowed the 'boys' in the Sex Pistols to discover their strength.[48] At the conclusion of the interview re-created in *The Great Rock'n'Roll Swindle*, the 'Bill Grundy' voice insists, 'Carry on lads, swearing all the more'.

So, to focus on the question that has been addressed throughout this chapter: Where is Bill Grundy now? My aim has been to examine the interview as a founding myth of the punk attitude. If the past is the unknowable totality of what happened in the encounter, history represents the stories that continue to make it meaningful. Narratives about *Today* still circulate; they act to promote the footage more than three decades after its broadcast, and encourage us to visit and revisit it as intrigued viewers. But what do we actually see? How might this relatively unstudied ur-text of punk be understood? To discover where Bill Grundy is now requires us to do more than to appreciate that swearing today is more frequent and less contentious than it was. If historical narratives and practices of viewing support each other there are, nevertheless, places where their meanings conflict, and what viewers are sold is not what they get. Although the *Today* interview was improvised, it was the product of a media collaboration, as Thames TV and EMI were part of the same over-arching corporate structure. Watching the footage today, viewers are sold an organic memory, and they get an arranged one; they are sold an impromptu moment, and they get a re-run; they are offered shock in context, and they get a farce out of context, a contemporary experience of viewing masquerading as a memory of watching the world change. If the interview made swearing and not caring the *sine qua non* of punk, it is the Dorian Gray quality of its footage that has since become important. The anarchic 'now time' ethics that made punk so exciting have since been contradicted by the consequences of

---

[48]   Compare this with the myth recounted in Sigmund Freud, *Totem And Taboo* (London, 2001) where the young bucks kill their father.

time both moving on and standing still, relegating the first national gasp of the movement to history, but repeating our experience of media viewing to create an imagined memory. The significance of the interview has fixed its participants in their most famous moment, but also acts as a constant reminder of the punk attitude. Does this frozen portrait of generational conflict and the stilted media careers of its aging participants mean that the *Today* interview has lost all its inspirational charge? I think not, for it is in our current reading and viewing that England's still dreaming, Johnny Rotten and Steve Jones are still youngsters, the Sex Pistols are still together, and they are making a stand.

Chapter 7

Indie On The Box: The Contribution Of Television To UK Independent Music From *C86* To Britpop

Rupa Huq

Much current scholarship on pop examines how its form is ever-changing as a result of technological advance. This chapter considers a time when the upper-case maxim of Julie Burchill and Tony Parsons – 'IT'S ONLY ROCK AND ROLL, AND IT'S PLASTIC, PLASTIC, YES IT IS!!!!!!'[1] – held true, by concentrating on the portrayal of British indie music on mainstream television in the 1980s. It then moves on to consider the representation of Britpop in the mid-1990s which, it is argued, spelled the death knell for the traditional indie scene. Finally, it traces developments to today's unprecedented fragmentation of musical markets in a multi-channel era. Among the examples discussed, the Smiths are presented as a noteworthy case study for their deliberate rejection of the conventional vehicle of pop television communication in the 1980s – the pop video – in favour of live, studio-based performance (either miming or playing). The concluding discussion considers how television's treatment of indie music in the past might inform future approaches to popular music.

Pop Flashback: Reviving *Top Of The Pops* In 2008

London, Christmas Eve 2008: in the midst of the festive period's BBC-TV schedules is a late-night showing of the nostalgia-inducing, vintage pop-clip show *Top Of The Pops 2*. The programme, which ended its regular run in 2007, is experiencing something of a seasonal rejuvenation. Unlike its bigger brother, *Top Of The Pops* (from which it derives its material) *TOTP2*, as it is commonly abbreviated, was always about retrospectivity, rather the here-and-now. Tonight's episode contains some dependable curios, such as black-and-white footage of Arthur Brown's 'Fire' (complete with studio pyrotechnics) and a mid-period, long-haired Cliff Richard singing 'We Don't Talk Anymore'. However, the most arresting sight of the broadcast is Manchester's four-piece band the Smiths

---

[1]   Julie Burchill and Tony Parsons, *The Boy Looked At Johnny: The Obituary Of Rock And Roll* (London, 1978), p. 96.

performing 'What Difference Does It Make?' The gangling young vocalist, Stephen Patrick Morrissey, appears bespectacled, attired in textured white shirt, arms manically waving, as he spins around the stage, while the camera zooms in on the small bunch of daffodils in the back pocket of his jeans. Meanwhile, guitarist Johnny Marr, sporting a Brian Jones haircut, grins in the background and chimes out powerchords. Bassist Andy Rourke and drummer Mike Joyce perform their respective roles in dependable fashion. It is 1984, and colourful balloons festoon the setting. The prevailing socio-economic climate, like the minor key of the mournful yet insistently pounding tune, is bleaker than the set (which is backlit in pink) and the cheery studio audience suggest. Unemployment is heading northwards, soon to hit three million, and industrial relations are crippled by a protracted miners' strike. Yet the forced jollity around a band which frequently has the terms 'depressing' and 'social realism' applied to it, illustrates at once the contradictions of indie music on British pop TV, at a time when the fortunes of the two were inextricably entwined.

Blur's Alex James has written: 'The two most important things in the world when I was growing up were *Top Of The Pops* and *Smash Hits*.'[2] From the standpoint of 2008, many of what were long taken to be axiomatic staples of pop in the UK have been refined and re-defined in the twenty-first century, while others have simply faded away. In the first category, pop has outgrown simply being consigned to columns of new releases reviewed to reach the front pages of the red-top newspapers where artists' actions are detailed daily. At the other end of the spectrum, pop now commands its own broadsheet newspaper supplements: the publication by *The Observer* of a monthly music magazine neatly demonstrates a greater youth-orientation within its readership. In the second category, of those pop cultural co-ordinates that are no longer there, many of the traditional popular music weeklies have gradually been squeezed out by the widespread availability of pop news, features and interviews from elsewhere. There was a time when 'the music press' was always factored into the conclusions of UK chroniclers of pop but, as an entity, this has shrunk dramatically. *Sounds* (1970–91) and *Melody Maker* (1926–2000) have disappeared, as has the comparatively tabloid *Smash Hits* (1978–2006). *New Musical Express* (1952–) continues, backed by a web-presence. *Top Of The Pops* is a similar example of a pop mainstay rationalised out of existence. From 1964, the programme was a constant of Thursday night programming and a weekly highlight for teenage audiences; from 1994, it also spawned the spin-off *Top Of The Pops 2*, which combined archive footage with occasional clips of current acts, often recorded during sessions for the parent show. *Top Of The Pops* itself was finally axed in mid-2006, in the face of declining audiences.

In late 2008, the news that *Top Of The Pops* was to be revived for a one-off Christmas special caused an outpouring of nostalgia in the popular press. Mark Simpson had earlier written of its longstanding hypnotic power over the

---

2   Alex James, *Bit Of A Blur* (London, 2007), p. 113.

nation's youth, invoking a phrase of 1960s/1970s British Labour Prime Minister Harold Wilson in his prose: 'Then suddenly, in the early seventies, thanks to the "white heat of technology" and hire purchase, *Top Of The Pop*s was a Technicolor dream. A land of Oz to which the twister of pop could snatch away any young person trapped in one of those grey, ugly, new houses in the suburbs.'[3] The idea of escapism has been a constant of pop, and *Top Of The Pops* had offered the perfect vehicle to effect this for successive generations. It had also been a fixture of Christmas Day afternoon viewing, when its annual countdown of the year's best-selling singles routinely preceded the Queen's Christmas message to Britain and the Commonwealth. The re-instatement of *Top Of The Pops* brought with it a one-off *TOTP2* and the 24-year-old clip of the Smiths. As the track ended, the voice-over from former BBC Radio 1 afternoon-show host Steve Wright insisted that 'the DJ they wanted to hang wasn't me', alluding to the 'hang the DJ' chorus of the band's 1986 hit 'Panic'.

In its presentation of a previously self-styled collection of social misfits as part of our pop heritage, BBC-TV was playing a part in bringing about the transformation of the Smiths' reputation, from edgy indie oufit to national treasures. Yet, just as *Top Of The Pops* had at times been shunned by 'alternative' acts – The Clash notably refused to play the show throughout their career due to its miming policy – indie had not always enjoyed the programme's approval. In the 1980s, when the term was first popularised, it had connotations of being 'alternative' and 'anti-establishment'. It is this aspect of the genre which I will turn to next.

Defining Indie

In his study of 1980s indie music, Mathew Bannister rightly notes that 'genres are not just made out of "what is already here" but are also shaped by "what is not"'.[4] Accordingly indie defined itself, insofar as this was possible, against the dominant chart-topping 'New Pop' of the day: 'the glamour, androgyny and self-conscious artifice of 1980s New Pop (Culture Club, Duran Duran, Human League), which in many ways, indie rock was reacting against'.[5] Musically, the acts associated with indie were primarily male, guitar-based outfits containing echoes of 1960s beat groups and a good dose of 1970s punk, sonically and attitudinally. Sartorially, indie bands sported a 'dressed-down' aesthetic or thrift store look – denims, checked shirts, or black clothing being most dominant. The message they promoted was, in the main, a set of anti-establishment sentiments. The prevailing politics of the time in the UK were the monetarist leanings of the Thatcher government, against a backdrop of economic recession, and upwardly spiralling unemployment

---

[3]   Mark Simpson, *Saint Morrissey* (London, 2004), p. 65.

[4]   Matthew Bannister, *White Boys, White Noise: Masculinities And 1980s Indie Guitar Rock* (Aldershot, 2006), p. 58.

[5]   Ibid., xxii.

which reached three million during the decade. The causes to champion included opposition to the war against Argentina over possession of the Falkland Islands in 1982, and support for those on strike in the bitter and prolonged miners' dispute during 1984–85. However, when taken literally, 'indie' is an economic term to describe labels owned and run independently of the mainstream recording industry. Strachan even defines 'micro-independent' labels as 'small-scale operations usually run from private addresses by one or two individuals who undertake all the tasks necessary for the commercial release of a recording themselves'.[6] In theory this should not implicate any musical or fashion styles.

The boundaries between what is understood as indie and what is taken to be mainstream are exceptionally elastic. Among the indie bands named by Bannister are Joy Division, My Bloody Valentine, the Smiths, The Jesus and Mary Chain (UK), Dinosaur Junior, REM (USA) and the Chills (from his native New Zealand). Only the first three of these however were signed to genuinely independent labels for their entire careers. Other bands associated with indie, but contracted to major labels, included Echo and the Bunnymen (RCA), Lloyd Cole and the Commotions (Polygram), Prefab Sprout (Kitchenware/Epic) and the Mighty Lemon Drops (WEA). The acquisition of an indie label by a major label would usually signal an effective takeover of its primary recording and marketing functions. When Glasgow's Postcard Records was bought by Polydor (alongside the signing of the band Orange Juice) *The Face* reported that within the new set-up, Postcard would be 'little more than a trademark'. However, it did also state that 'what Orange Juice have secured sees as close to complete control as any young band is likely to get … including the continued use of the Postcard name for what Postcard chief Alan Horne terms "conceptual unity"'.[7] Later indie acts were subsequently signed to majors, such as the self-styled 'second favourite of every Smiths fan', the Wedding Present, who made the transition from Reception to RCA. A less common situation saw successful chart acts signed to independent labels, such as the stable of acts on the PWL label (owned by the Stock-Aitken-Waterman triumvirate, whose best-known performer was Kylie Minogue, and which produced the best-selling single of 1988, Rick Astley's 'Never Gonna Give You Up'). While it might be possible to fill an essay with the portrayal of 1980s indie-stars on television by discussing episodes of *Neighbours*, I wish to discuss conventionally understood indie acts and their relationship with television for the remainder of this section, with a particular concentration on the Smiths, who, in many ways, were the archetypal indie band.

The characteristics of New Pop helped to shape the pop programmes of the 1980s. Most were studio-based, with colourful neon lighting. Ian Gittins's description of *Top Of The Pops* echoes the image recalled above by Simpson: 'For its part, *TOTP* happily became a weekly Club Tropicana. Zoot suits, vertiginous hair

---

[6]   Robert Strachan, 'Micro-independent Record Labels In The UK: Discourse, DIY Cultural Production And The Music Industry', *European Journal Of Cultural Studies* 10/2 (2007), p. 247.

[7]   'Postcard Defunct As Orange Juice Go Major', *The Face*, November 1981.

and cheerleaders planted in the audience were, as a presentational style, as zingy and upbeat as the music it introduced.'[8] Meanwhile, Billy Bragg has explained how his particular message was erased from the show, so as not to threaten the prevailing climate:

> Steve Wright was hosting the show, and he came over at rehearsal, and asked me to explain the politics of the song to help him with the intro ... I talked him through it and he listened thoughtfully and nodded a lot. Then, when he came to it, he just said, 'Ladies and gentlemen, it's Billy Bragg!' The show was full of bands like Wham! shoving shuttlecocks down their shorts. I felt like a fish out of water.[9]

The pop programming policy of the 1980s was also evident in the redesigned set and title of BBC2's *Whistle Test*, the influential music series that had started life as the *The Old Grey Whistle Test* in 1971. Sightings of pop acts could be also seen on mainstream entertainment programmes, such as the daily lunchtime magazine show *Pebble Mill At One* (BBC, 1973–86) and the thrice-weekly evening chat-show *Wogan* (BBC, 1985–92), usually miming to their discs to promote them. In addition, there were children's programmes such as *Saturday Superstore* (BBC, 1982–87) in which pop groups would not merely mime to their records, but also take part in quizzes and general tomfoolery, and its successor, *Going Live* (BBC, 1987–92); ITV responded with *Number 73* (1982–88) and *Get Fresh* (1986–88).

The jewel in the crown, however, was still *Top Of The Pops*. Many performers have related how an appearance on the programme confirmed their induction into the pop pantheon. Simpson suggests that Morrissey knew that the Smiths had 'made it' when they were asked to appear on the show to perform their second single 'This Charming Man': '*Top Of The Pops*, the loved-and-hated tacky TV chart show institution where he had seen so many of his heroes, Sandie, Bowie, Bolan, Sparks. The hopeless fan(atic) had finally become a *star*.'[10] For a band that refused to make promotional videos in the early part of its career, appearances on the show were critically important in showcasing its music. Simon Reynolds has asserted that 'Morrissey is a character in a pop era of nonentities'.[11] Although I cannot dispute the first part of the claim, there were several larger-than-life pop personalities of the 1980s with whom Morrissey competed. But on *Top Of The Pops*, all were equal: indie and New Pop had adjacent dressing rooms. In an early article introducing band members to readers, the first factual credentials stated about them are their broadcast appearances, before moving on to music press acclaim: 'They've been on *Top Of The Pops*, *Round Table*, *The Old Grey*

---

[8]   Ian Gittins, *Top Of The Pops: Mishaps, Miming And Music* (London, 2007), p. 93.

[9]   Ibid., p. 91.

[10]   Simpson, *Saint*, p. 99.

[11]   Simon Reynolds, *Blissed Out* (London, 1990) p. 22.

Whistle Test. They've been in *Sounds*, *NME*, even *Rolling Stone*';[12] the band's self-portrayal is very much about lead-singer Morrissey as the central performer, while the musicians appear to be cast in a supporting role.

When the posthumous video compilation *The Smiths: The Complete Picture* was released by WEA in 1992 following the collapse of Rough Trade (with whom the band remained throughout its existence), the lack of formal video segments meant that six of the 12 tracks were culled from television pop programmes. 'This Charming Man', in which the band perform in a sunlit building, carpeted with flowers, is a promo-style video clip filmed for Channel 4's *The Tube* (1982–87) and five are *Top Of The Pops* studio appearances; only in the first of these does Morrissey have a microphone. Reynolds has drawn the contrast between New Pop's 'soundtrack to the new yuppie culture' and 'the Smiths [who] glamorized debility and illness, advocated absenteeism, withdrawal and failure to meet quotas of enjoyment' (as evidenced, perhaps, in the single 'Heaven Knows I'm Miserable Now'). He goes on to group this 'misfit' status with other indie fellow-travellers: 'The profound embarrassment of Morrissey's dancing turned the lack of oneness with your body into glamour. All the self-squandering and deficiency of lifeskills that animated The Birthday Party and The Fall, the Smiths turned into glamorous, consumable pop, two minute blasts of otherness in the charts'.[13] Of the three, it is the Smiths who appeared in the nation's living rooms most frequently, because of their penetration of the UK singles chart. The implication is that they were something of a cross-over act, or even a Trojan horse, transgressing the boundary between indie and pop. By entering the Fab 40 (as Radio 1 would term the charts) the band was granted a passport to prime-time television slots, rather than being relegated to late-night radio shows – the best known proponent of all three bands throughout the 1980s was radio DJ and occasional *Top Of The Pops* presenter, John Peel.

Top Of The Pops was a show in which the acts mimed; no pretence was ever made of it being anything other than that. While other acts would seek to conceal it within the conventions of video, Reynolds has noted how Morrissey's stage persona uniquely placed him to carry this off. His performances in *The Complete Picture* progressively show how the early trademark adornments (NHS spectacles, foliage in back pocket, bunches of flowers brandished like whips, hearing aid) appear less and less. In this sense, Morrissey joins other rock performers who use their bodies to sell their music: 'the physicality of the body … Jagger's hips, Hendrix's cock, Bolan's grin, Prince's tongue, Morrissey's nipples (one of the few options of indecency left to revel, to splay oneself as play *thing*)'.[14]

This observation has a specific context. In the television performance of 'Heaven Knows I'm Miserable Now' (at the lines 'Would you like to marry me? And if you like, you can buy the ring') Morrissey theatrically opens up the oversized blouse

---

[12]   Katy Neville, 'The Post Cool School', *The Face*, February 1984.

[13]   Reynolds, *Blissed Out*, p. 24.

[14]   Reynolds, *Blissed Out*, p. 45.

he is wearing (possibly with Velcro fastenings) to reveal the words 'MARRY ME' scrawled in ballpoint pen across his chest:

> The Smiths invariably went the extra mile to ensure that their string of eagerly-received mid-1980s appearances were out of the ordinary. Suavely introverted in NHS specs and hearing aid and waving gladioli at the throng, Morrissey seemed like an emissary from an edgier, more curious world.[15]

Johnny Marr agrees that '*TOTP* was a fantastic forum for Morrissey, and a great platform for his ideas … They quite rightly became talking points in our band's history'.[16] The band appearing barefoot, while Sandie Shaw provided the vocals for 'Hand In Glove' was another memorable example (although Morrissey himself did not appear on that occasion).

When not performing, Morrissey was the band's spokesperson. When, in 1985, the Smiths were featured on *Granada Reports*, it is Morrissey's status (and the opening line of their *Meat Is Murder* album – 'Belligerent ghouls run Manchester schools') that prompt much of the questioning from TV journalist and Factory Records chief Tony Wilson. In a rehearsal studio in Chorlton-cum-Hardy, the rest of the band casually shrug off claims of their second-fiddle status, Rourke claiming that Morrissey 'deserves all the attention he gets' (although he and Joyce would later sue Morrissey and Marr over unpaid royalties). In a *Whistle Test* appearance from the same period, Morrissey and Marr are filmed talking together to camera, explaining their new album, and putting down tracks in the recording studio. When the show's presenter (and *Smash Hits* editor) Mark Ellen comments that most see Morrissey as an 'an ailing early Victorian romantic with a health problem', he answers that the accusation 'isn't really, as far as I'm concerned, a slur'. At times, children would appear with the Smiths, such as the schoolboy who joined them on *The Tube* when they performed 'Panic' in 1986. Other television outings were on children's programmes, such as *Data-Run* (TV-AM, 1983–84) in which Morrissey is introduced by puppets before reminiscing at his former primary school and singing 'This Charming Man' with some of the pupils, and *Charlie's Bus* (TV-AM, 1984) in which Marr and Morrissey visit Kew Gardens with a group of children for an impromptu performance with Sandie Shaw. Such combinations of pop with other formats have long endured in British broadcasting (see the chapter on the early TV appearances of the Beatles). However, in an era of multi-channel programming, where sections of the population are segmented off into what are presumed to be separate audiences, it seems unlikely that such shows could work now.

---

[15] Gittins, *Top Of The Pops*, p. 145.

[16] Ibid.

1980s Alternatives: The Beginnings Of Deregulation

The 1980s were a decade in which the UK underwent major changes socio-politically and in terms of cultural infrastructure. Today, Channel 4 is a broadcasting staple, with a familiar roster of celebrity-themed 'reality' programmes, but when it first appeared in 1982 (as the UK's second commercial station, backed by considerable subsidy and regulated by Parliament) it threatened to disrupt television's conventional ethic through its 'shock' tactics, broadly oppositional stance (against the Thatcher government and/or the rival BBC), and its 'in yer face' disregard for tradition. In a retrospective interview, the channel's former Head of Education, Naomi Sargant has recalled that 'at one point, virtually every factual series, whether it was education, youth, religion or current affairs included the women camped on Greenham Common, even my over-60s show'.[17] The programme that introduced Channel 4's youth and pop output was the Friday night series *The Tube*; it broke with the *Top Of The Pops* concentration on chart stars by giving a platform to many unsigned acts and by including a significant number of bands signed to independent, rather than major, labels.

For Bannister, 'the positioning of indie as local (as opposed to global) was also continuously with the sense that indie music was now carrying the flag for innovative pop/rock'.[18] Regionalism had always been a key part of indie. This was reflected in the way that micro-scenes came from different parts of the country, often with their own associated labels, such as Glasgow's Postcard Records (later subsumed with Polydor) and Coventry's Two Tone (subsequently licensed to Chrysalis); Leeds became strongly associated with the goth scene, and its bands such as the Mission, Sisters of Mercy and The Cult. This regional diversity was also reflected in indie on television: a decade earlier, Joy Division of Manchester's Factory Records received their first television exposure performing 'Shadowplay' on Granada's *So It Goes* (1976–77), and in the early 1980s *The Oxford Road Show* (1981–82), which was broadcast nationally from the BBC studios in Manchester, included a slew of local talent such as Liverpool's The Mighty Wah! (whose label, Zoo Records, was acquired by RCA). And one of the most distinctive features of *The Tube* was that it was broadcast weekly from Newcastle upon Tyne, thus obliging big name acts from overseas to make the extra journey north-eastwards, after flying in to London.

Former station controller Liz Forgan has since named *The Tube* as one of several landmark features of the new channel when it was launched in 1982: 'The injection of argument rather than just opinions, the admission to the screen of large numbers of black and Asians, *The Tube* making *Top Of The Pops* look like a vicarage tea party, and the new deal with the film business through Film On Four, some marvellous drama – in all those ways, Channel 4 did completely shake up

---

[17]   Peter Catterall (ed.), *The Making Of Channel 4* (London, 1999), p. 151.

[18]   Bannister, *White Boys*, p. 58.

British television'.[19] Not only did the programme's freedom from a 'countdown' chart formula and its Newcastle home distance it from its BBC rival, but it also found space for quirky, non-musical items, such as the first airings of comedy duo French and Saunders, long before the pair became household names of reliable major channel entertainment. The show's reputation for shock-value was enhanced by its willingness to broadcast material such as Frankie Goes To Hollywood's explicit video for 'Relax', a song whose gay sex references had led to a ban on BBC radio and television, and helped catapult it to the Number One position in the UK singles chart.

However there were some other curiosities that are not remembered in such reverential terms, if indeed they are remembered at all. As a ten-year-old when Channel 4 launched, my early memories include that of *Minipops* (1983) in which current hits were performed by young children dressed as the original acts – a concept which combined the idea of a junior talent show with the cover version albums of Woolworth's Winfield record label. Sargant has since acknowledged that the programme was somewhat incongruous with the rest of Channel 4's output, and attributed responsibility to the constraints of the entertainment budget and the then Commissioning Editor, Cecil Korer: 'That was, of course, pretty ludicrous for Channel 4.'[20] The slightly 'rough around the edges', almost DIY ethos of Channel 4 was well suited to indie and very fitting, given that the station's remit was quite different to any other channel. No programmes were made 'in-house', but were commissioned from outside programme-makers, the majority of whom were independent production companies. One such pop-magazine programme was *Earsay* (1984) presented by Gary Crowley and Nicky Horne; an early edition featured a lengthy interview in which Morrissey talked about his teenage depression.

A significant event in the 1980s that has attracted much academic attention was the advent of MTV, the first satellite channel of wall-to-wall music video, which immediately privileged the form of the video clip over the live performance.[21] Many of those who analysed this development hailed it as a prime example of postmodernity in pop. Simon Frith has observed that the act of constructing pop video allows a degree of control to performers and their entourages not afforded to them when they appear on traditional pop performance shows on the terms of the programme-makers. Of course, they operated within the boundaries of taste and decency, and the requirements of the 'watershed', but did not take long to become

[19]   Catterall, Channel 4, p. 128.

[20]   Ibid., p. 158.

[21]   See, for example, R. Serge Denisoff and William D. Romanowski, 'MTV Becomes Pastiche: Some People Just Don't Get It!', *Popular Music And Society* 14/1 (1990), pp. 47–61; Simon Frith, Andrew Goodwin and Lawrence Grossberg (eds), *Sound And Vision: The Music Video Reader* (New York, 1993); E. Ann Kaplan, 'Feminism(s)/Postmodernism(s): MTV And Alternate Women's Videos And Performance Art', *Women And Performance: A Journal Of Feminist Theory* 6/1 (1993), pp. 55–76.

an indispensable part of the process of televising pop: 'The pop video is important not because it compels musicians to perform in quite new ways (though it may sometimes do this), but in the way that it necessarily draws on (and therefore brings to our attention) established performing conventions and adapts them to new technological and selling conditions.'[22] The making of a promotional video to be aired on MTV (and even *Top Of The Pops*, which increasingly featured them) became a part of the budget of the release of every single, certainly on all the major labels. They reflected their times: Duran Duran and Spandau Ballet were frequently presented in exotic settings and locations that displayed the fruits of their new-found wealth. Their 'travelogue' style of clip was mocked by The Mighty Wah! in the lyrics of their single 'Weekends', in which they disdainfully listed among their leisure options, 'or swan on a beach in Sri Lanka, just like Duran Duran'. The contrast with a rather more muted aesthetic was stark: indeed, many of the memorable pop tracks of the 1980s remain memorable precisely because of their accompanying videos. Robert Palmer's 'Addicted To Love' and Peter Gabriel's 'Sledgehammer' dramatically re-launched the careers of both acts, the arresting imagery of their respective videos propelling them to the playlists of music television in a way that the songs alone could not have done. Even if performers were deceased or unavailable, a 'posthumous' video release could be arranged, as in the case of Nina Simone's 'My Baby Just Cares For Me' and Jackie Wilson's 'Reet Petite' (with its plasticine figures). Television advertisements for Levi's jeans helped to revive the record sales careers of Sam Cooke and Marvin Gaye in the same decade. Indie artists too could not afford to ignore the medium of video, and it would be facile to draw too much of a distinction between indie and mainstream productions. Often, there were significant points of overlap, such as the Housemartins' 'Happy Hour' video, which featured animated plasticine figures of the band members.

In 1986, *New Musical Express* compiled an audio-cassette of tracks from its favourite bands entitled *C86* that itself became shorthand for the jangling guitar music affectionately referred to in the music press as 'shambling' bands.[23] By this point, Channel 4 had begun to broadcast *The Chart Show* in the *The Tube*'s Friday night slot, during its inter-series break. This programme had no presenters; instead, the hour-long show consisted entirely of video clips grouped into different charts. The UK singles chart was a constant, but 'specialist' charts (heavy metal, dance) were rotated for full airings of tracks. At other times, viewers could look further at the album chart (which, for much of the decade, seemed to be topped by Dire Straits' *Brothers In Arms*). Once a month, it was the turn of indie. On these occasions, a chart rundown was presented, in the style of a video-play; exaggerated graphics on the screen fast-forwarded tracks, pausing to play some of them.

---

[22] Simon Frith, *Performing Rites: On The Value Of Popular Music* (Oxford, 1996), p. 224.

[23] Acts featured on the cassette compilation included Primal Scream, the Mighty Lemon Drops, the Soup Dragons, Half Man Half Biscuit, and The Wedding Present.

During instrumental breaks, when the viewer had no lyrics to study, information flashed on-screen in dot-matrix style pixelated type. Over Half Man Half Biscuit's 'Dickie Davies Eyes' (a playful take on Kim Carnes's 'Bette Davis Eyes') an announcement about the band's postponement of tour dates appeared, including the message, 'Get well soon, and stop smoking, Nigel'. This technique has since been used extensively on all music channels, and even in news programming.

It was in the indie chart slot that I was exposed to the sight of New Order's 'True Faith' video, directed and choreographed by French mime artist Philippe Decouflé (featuring colourfully-attired dancers in inflatable suits turning somersaults and slapping one another) and the ramshackle amateur-looking video of 'Rules And Regulations' by Birmingham lo-fi guitar girl band We've Got A Fuzzbox And We're Going To Use It: within three years, they were appearing on *Top Of The Pops* as a polished girl group, signed to WEA. The Soup Dragons effected a similar change in career direction between their early appearances on *The Chart Show* (performing 'Soft As Your Face') and their later chart success with 'I'm Free', issued on the back of the Madchester indie boom in 1990. The indie segment of *The Chart Show* (and Channel 4 itself) were sometimes subject to moments where still-photos covered up for a lack of moving content: in its infancy, there were sometimes insufficient advertisers to fill a commercial break, necessitating the on-screen display of the programme's logo to the sounds of musak. Similarly, indie chart acts without a video (such as House Of Love's 'Destroy The Heart') had to be content with a simple photograph of the band to accompany their songs.

New televisual opportunities for pop continued to emerge throughout the 1980s. Channel 4's *Network 7* (1987) was the first programme in a pioneering genre known patronisingly as 'Yoof-TV', created and fronted by young production teams for young audiences. Characteristic of the format was fast editing, gravity-defying camera angles, and ticker-tape captions, although on such shows pop was given less importance than some of the social issues in the run-up to the 1987 General Election. *Network 7*'s founding producer Janet Street-Porter later took a refined version of the show to BBC2 under the title *Def II* (1988–94), which extended the links between music and news/documentary topics by investigating subjects like racism or homophobia in rap. Other new initiatives included BBC2's culture and entertainment-focused *The Late Show* (1989–95) which included pop music in its brief. However, serious arts programming still tended to give indie music a wide berth. One exception was an edition of ITV's *The South Bank Show* in 1987 devoted to the Smiths; another was the performance by the Stone Roses of 'Waterfall' on *The Late Show* in 1989, during which the failure of the power supply led vocalist Ian Brown to shout angrily at the camera crew and the show's visibly shaken presenter, Tracy Macleod.

The Advent Of Britpop

A large part of Bannister's definition of indie – 'small groups of white men playing guitars, influenced by punks and 1960s white pop/rock, with a broader discourse and practice of (degrees of) independence from mainstream musical values'[24] – also applies to Britpop. The term came into use in 1995, to describe a set of musical acts emerging in the wake of US grunge. Musically, the sound harked back to the 1960s beat era (the Beatles, the Rolling Stones, the Animals, The Who) with a nod to 1970s punk attitude. Bands associated with Britpop included Pulp (from Sheffield) and, most notably, Oasis (from Manchester) who became locked in an ongoing rivalry with Essex band Blur; a second wave of signings (and lesser achievers) included Marion, Lodger, Rialto, Gene and Menswear. Without exception, they were all-male, guitar-driven groups. Other bands, such as Elastica, Sleeper and Echobelly, were led by women singer-instrumentalists. A further category of Britpop acts included pre-existing bands, to whom a new lease of life was offered in becoming retreads: Ocean Colour Scene had been part of the early 1990s 'baggy' scene before their re-invention as Britpop, in much the same way as prog-rockers the Guildford Stranglers had emerged anew, clutching at the coat-tails of punk. The (female-led) Lush, who had been prime movers in the contemplative, reverb-heavy guitar scene known as 'shoe-gazing', made a comeback with a Britpop-style album of more straightforward, hook-laden guitar pop. And groups from earlier eras were hailed as godfathers of the movement, notably the Kinks and The Jam (who were themselves related through The Jam's cover version of the Kinks' 'David Watts').

However, there were also significant distinctions between Britpop and indie. In the 1980s, indie had been found on a variety of regional labels (Factory, Two Tone, Postcard, Zoo). By contrast, Britpop appeared to be a metropolitan movement that was not just London-centric, but concentrated around specific locations in the fashionable North London district of Camden. The Good Mixer pub assumed a landmark status as the natural habitat of Britpop acts, and became a magnet for those associated with the scene, as Alex James has recalled: 'Graham [Coxon] had moved to Camden, and sometimes I went to see him there in The Good Mixer public house … He had become the king of a strange people who all looked like him, and he held his court at The Mixer.'[25] Even Britpop kings Oasis came from Manchester's suburban Burnage, rather than the inner-city hell they implied as their original habitat. In fact, the band very quickly relocated to the more salubrious, 'stockbroker' belt of London, where Noel Gallagher achieved notoriety for the 'all back to mine' parties he threw at his 'Supernova Heights' home in Belsize Park. This ostentatious rock-star excess was the opposite of the dressed-down and austere aesthetic of indie. Significantly, Britpop of the 1990s dined at the high table of contemporaneous electoral politics (such as Noel Gallagher's role as court jester at Tony Blair's early celebrity gatherings at 10 Downing Street),

---

24   Bannister, *White Boys*, p. 8.
25   James, *Blur*, p. 113.

whereas indie of the 1980s sought to be a thorn in its side – although this is, in part, explained by the election of a Labour government on a tide of popular optimism, after the easy hate-figure of Margaret Thatcher.

Britpop On The Box

Television references to Britpop were often indirect: Blair's 1996 Labour Party Conference speech, in which he declared that 'Labour's coming home', was a direct paraphrase of the Lightning Seeds' song for that year's European Soccer Championships, 'Football's Coming Home'. Nevertheless, TV played a crucial role in the development of Britpop (which has become rather nostalgically mythologised since BBC4's 'Britpop Night' in 2006). In 1995, BBC2's *Britpop Now* presented twelve acts, performing live in the studio, introduced by Blur's Damon Albarn. The non-inclusion of Oasis was officially explained by the fact that the band were touring in Europe at the time of the recording, although there has been speculation that their absence was because of the band's resentment of Albarn. *Top Of The Pops*, which continued throughout the Britpop era, was the more natural showcase for these groups. James has described the show as a 'fundamental force' and noted its rite of passage significance:

> There weren't many things that were exactly as I thought they'd be, but appearing on that show was like walking in the television. It was almost magical. Practically everyone there seemed hardly able to believe they were inside it. There was always a wide-eyed, open-mouthed glee about the studio audience. The acts on *TOTP* were just part of the spectacle. Everybody mimed, which made it even more unreal and dream-like ... All the other bands came to watch us mime 'Girls & Boys', and the audience went berserk at four grown men, pretending to play their instruments. It was brilliant.[26]

In the 1990s *Top Of The Pops* was joined by a new stable of programmes, where live performance was the driving force. Channel 4's Friday night *The Tube* slot was occupied by *The Word* (1990–95) initially presented by the streetwise Mancunian Terry Christian, before the 'cockney' Mark Lamarr (actually from Swindon) replaced him. The clinical, white studio, populated by an adoring audience recalled in some ways the sets of ITV's *Ready Steady Go!* (1963–66). The programme included freakshow antics of the public and a sometimes raucous studio crowd. It featured both grunge and Britpop: Nirvana appeared, as did the female US grunge band L7, and Blur's 'Girls & Boys' was performed here, before it charted. The series ended before Britpop came fully into its own but its successor, *TFI Friday* (1996–2000) presented by Chris Evans, had many similar features. The white studio disappeared and Evans interviewed guests from his desk (as opposed

---

[26]   James, *Blur*, p. 114.

to *The Word*'s sofa) but the boisterous audience in festive mood remained; the programme even had a bona-fide Britpop theme-tune in 'The Riverboat Song' by Ocean Colour Scene. Channel 4's *White Room* (1995–96) which foregrounded music as central rather than incidental, was presented by veteran indie DJ Mark Radcliffe. This was an interesting choice: Radcliffe had begun his BBC Radio 1 career anonymised, concealing his physical appearance beneath the hood of his duffel coat. *White Room* featured live acts, many of whom were drawn from the Britpop/indie stable, and departed from the strictures of *Top Of The Pops* by encouraging collaborations, such as that between Damon Albarn and the Kinks' Ray Davies. *Later ... With Jools Holland* (BBC, 1992–) has consistently placed the emphasis on live performance and musicianship, and has featured all the major Britpop bands during its long run. (Among the associated spin-off projects was the 34-track DVD *Later ... With Jools Holland: Cool Britannia Volume 1* in 2004, followed by *Volume 2* in 2005).

One of the novelty aspects of *Later ... With Jools Holland* comes at the start of the show where, on a weekly basis, all the performers collectively jam in the circular studio as the camera pans round them, one by one: Britpop, world music, roots, reggae, country and other genres do not just have adjacent dressing rooms, but here they trade licks with each other. Morrissey has always looked resolutely uncomfortable in such settings. Indeed, a further sign of his growing respectability was his appearance on Radio 4's *Desert Island Discs* in 2009.[27] The programme was memorable for Morrissey taking the driving seat from the show's fawning presenter Kirsty Young: when questioned about his personal life, he moved the conversation on by announcing, 'and the next record is ...'

Conclusion

The changes in British music from indie in the 1980s to Britpop in the 1990s have, in some ways, come full circle. Much of the 'humble' demeanour of indie was replaced by the self-aggrandizement of Britpop. Creation Records chief Alan McGee bought Noel Gallagher a Rolls Royce saloon (despite the fact that he was unable to drive it) and the cover of the third Oasis album (*Be Here Now*) pictured a Rolls Royce crashing into a swimming pool. However, as Simpson has soberly pointed out:

> The bragging materialistic self-importance of all this was somewhat punctured, however, by the fact that by the late nineties, the Spice Girls, the manufactured 'girl power' band whose professed inspiration was Margaret Thatcher, and who seemed to be a feisty bollocked version of eunuch boy band Take That (who

---

[27] First broadcast in 1942, *Desert Island Discs* is the BBC's (and the world's) third longest-running radio programme. Only *The Daily Service* (1928–) and *A Week In Westminster* (1929–) have longer histories.

in turn seemed to be modelled on the Village People), outsold Oasis, Blur and Suede put together.[28]

Again, the televisual imagery of the Spice Girls was just as potent as the music. Particularly memorable was the sight of lead singer Geri Halliwell/'Ginger Spice' clad in her Union Jack dress, which had only been made possible by the popularisation of the emblem through New Labour's Cool Britannia initiative. The group quickly outgrew television with their film *Spice World* (Bob Spiers, 1997).

One of the features of Britpop its defenders saw as most important was its manifesto of being authentic (real instruments) and homegrown (UK-originating) music after a period where synthetic electro dance sounds and pop from the other side of the Atlantic had enjoyed ascendancy in the techno and grunge scenes. Yet, since its high watermark in 1997, its parent style indie has become increasingly fragmented, as have the media that communicate pop to the wider public. With the currency of the singles chart devalued, we inhabit an age where music is intangible – stored in files to be electronically transferred, rather than on pieces of plastic housed in cardboard. Web 2.0's climate of democracy in musical participation (consumption, performance, production and criticism) is now a given. To the extent that Britpop was the final nail in the coffin of indie, we have now moved to a situation where a hyper-indie scene occupies the space that the old independent scene used to inhabit. Groups such as the Arctic Monkeys have made their breakthrough not through the traditional 'payment of dues' of gigging and releasing records, but via the web. The DIY ethos of indie has in some ways 'won' but, in other respects, the popularity of TV shows such as *The X Factor* (ITV, 2004–) which create overnight stars through televised talent contests of nostalgia pop cover-versions suggests that the mainstream too has become a hyper-real version of mainstream. Whereas once whole families would gather around 'the telly' for *Top Of The Pops*, YouTube and catch-up services such as BBC's i-player (whose slogan is 'making the unmissable unmissable') mean that 'the small screen' is no longer restricted to television, but may equally be a laptop monitor or mobile phone. Where the technology takes us next is anybody's guess. What does remain certain however is that there is still a strong and continuing relationship between indie and the box.

---

[28] Simpson, *Saint*, p. 173.

PART III
Comedy And Drama

Chapter 8

Dad's Army: Musical Images Of A Nation At War*

Sheila Whiteley

On 14 May 1940, Anthony Eden made his first speech as Secretary of State for War. The fall of European allies in the spring of 1940, when Britain was militarily separated in Western Europe, had highlighted the possibility of a Nazi invasion and Eden emphasised the need for Local Defence Volunteers to 'come forward and offer their services ... this name describes its duties in three words. You will not be paid, but you will receive uniforms and will be armed'. Within 24 hours of the broadcast, 250,000 men, aged between 17 and 65, had put down their names; by the end of the month, the number was between 300,000 and 400,000; by the end of June, it had risen to 1.5 million. The Home Guard, as it was re-christened, was finally disbanded on 31 December, 1945.[1] Two decades later, on 31 July 1968, Dad's Army was launched on BBC1 as a six-part series[2] that would eventually run for nine years and 80 episodes.

Set in the fictional, South coast town of Walmington-on-Sea, and hence in the frontline of a possible invasion from across the English Channel, the series centres around the exploits of a group of men who have enrolled as Local Defence Volunteers (the Home Guard) – a strand of the Armed Services known affectionately as 'Dad's Army'. The effectiveness of the comedy lies in the relationship between the characters, in the platoon's constant bungling of seemingly straightforward instructions, and – because of their age and other disabilities – their inability to take an active role in the war. With humour ranging from the class-based tension between platoon commander Captain Mainwaring (Arthur Lowe) the grammar-school educated bank manager, and Sgt Arthur Wilson (John Le Mesurier) his

---

* This chapter is dedicated to my grandson, James Kearney.

[1]   The name was changed from Local Defence Volunteers to Home Guard in July 1940 on the instructions of Winston Churchill, who considered the original to be uninspiring.

[2]   *Dad's Army* was written by David Croft and Jimmy Perry, and its success as a television series led to radio adaptations, a film in 1971, and a stage version, originally in the West End and then on tour in 1975 and 1976. There have also been many television repeats (it is still shown today on BBC2) as well as video, DVD and audio cassettes of the series, In 2000, it was ranked 13th in the BFI's list of the 100 Greatest British Television Programmes, and in 2004 it was voted into fourth place in a BBC Poll to find Britain's Best Sitcom.

genteel bank clerk and second-in-command, and slapstick comedy and jingoistic barbs from Lance-Corporal Jones (Clive Dunn), the range of characters – the effete vicar, the belligerent greengrocer/air-warden, the cosseted mother's boy, the spiv – create a humorous and nostalgic picture of wartime England and the efforts of the Home Guard to protect the home counties from invasion. Its success was arguably due to the ways in which it foregrounds a sense of national identity that was perceived by viewers as both amusing and authentic.[3] While this could be attributed to co-writer and creator Jimmy Perry's real life experience in the Local Defence Volunteers,[4] it cannot account for the unprecedented popularity of a series about a largely forgotten aspect of Britain's defence during the Second World War. Four years after the series began, Arthur Lowe commented: 'We expected the show to have limited appeal, to the age group that lived through the war, and the Home Guard. We didn't expect what has happened – that children from the age of five upwards would enjoy it too.'[5]

Questions thus arise about the ways in which the characters and situations in *Dad's Army* relate to popular memory, so creating a dialogue between past and present; about the manner in which the series relates to the war as a 'myth of origin', reminding viewers of 'who they are'; and why both are essential ingredients in the construction of national identity. After exploring these issues, I then move to a specific discussion of the ideological significance of music during the Second World War and thence in *Dad's Army*; this will include a consideration of the opening theme and instrumental outro, of the ways in which songs of the 1930s and 1940s are used to link scenes within the episodes and, not least, how they create a sense of ironic humour while defining and recapturing the mood of the period.

Mythscapes, Popular Memory And National Identity[6]

While it is possible to interpret both myth and popular memory as cultural constructs, they nevertheless provide distinctive ways of shaping national identity, especially in times of conflict and war. Historical memory is not a copy of the 'real' past, but rather can be made and remade according to changing needs. The destruction of war can be set in opposition to often homely images, the freedom to walk where one pleases, freedom of speech, and even those everyday characteristics

---

[3]   The series regularly attracted 18 million viewers.

[4]   Perry was 15 when he joined the local 10th Hertfordshire Battalion, and admits a passing resemblance to the character of Private Pike. An elderly lance-corporal in the same battalion became a model for Lance-Corporal Jones.

[5]   Deirdre MacDonald, 'Arthur Lowe Talks To Deirdre MacDonald', *Radio Times*, 18 March 1972.

[6]   The concept of mythscape was coined by Duncan Bell, 'Mythscapes: Memory, Mythology And National Identity', *British Journal Of Sociology* 54/1 (2003), pp. 63–81.

held in common such as a cup of tea, a red pillar box, the pub, the sound of Big Ben.[7] In contrast, national myths draw, as Neil Kelly has noted, 'on commonly shared heroic or subjugated backgrounds and serve as focal points around which people can rally to a good cause, not least at times of war when killing and self-sacrifice become the means to a greater end'.[8] Imagined heroes, such as King Arthur and Robin of Locksley, sit alongside Nelson and Drake and can be evoked as guarding the spirit of England, encouraging its people to have faith; while the image of Britain ringed by an 'uncrossable sea, has been, perhaps, the most potent of England's ethnoscapes, both as a military bastion and as a peaceful idyll, as invoked in John of Gaunt's eulogy (*Richard II*, Act II, Scene I):[9]

> This fortress built by Nature for herself
> Against infection and the hand of war;
> This happy breed of men, this little world,
> This precious stone set in the silver sea,
> Which serves it in the office of a wall,
> Or as a moat defensive to a house,
> Against the envy of less happier lands;
> This blessed plot, this earth, this realm, this England.

While such signifiers of national identity are powerful in evoking a sense of pride in country, memories of the First World War, in which almost a million British had died and a further two million had been wounded, had resulted in a reluctance to enlist in the armed services.[10] When war broke out in September 1939, Britain could only raise 875,000 men, and in October, the Government announced that all men aged between 18 and 41 who were not working in 'reserved occupations'

---

[7]   John Baxendale, 'You And I – All Of Us Ordinary People: Renegotiating "Britishness" In Wartime', in Nick Hayes and Jeff Hill (eds), *Millions Like Us? British Culture In The Second World War* (Liverpool, 1999), pp. 298–300.

[8]   http://knol.google.com/k/neil-kelly/the-use-of-mythology-in-the-creation-of/nu0k105zuhiv/2#.

[9]   Anthony Smith, 'Set In The Silver Sea: English National Identity And European Integration'. *Workshop: National Identity And Euroscepticism. A Comparison Between France And The United Kingdom*, (Oxford, 2005) p. 4. It is interesting, in this context, to note the foregrounding of England. While this relates historically to the separation (at the time) and, hence, independence of Scotland and Ireland, it is also apparent that the geographical location of *Dad's Army* and its cast of characters are English – with the exception of Private James Frazer (John Laurie) the local undertaker, a Scot and the only member of the platoon to be portrayed as a villain, in episodes such as 'The Soldier's Farewell', 'Two And A Half Feathers' and 'If The Cap Fits'.

[10]   Sonja O. Rose, *Which People's War: National Identity And Citizenship In Wartime Britain 1939–1945* (Oxford, 2004), p. 9.

were liable for call-up.[11] Posters featured Britannia leading the call to arms against a background of sea and warships, with prominent images of the armed services, police, nurses, fire service and Home Guard, as well as a mother and child and the words 'England Expects' in large capitals (centre top) and 'National Service' (centre bottom).[12] While there is little apparent ambiguity in the poster's message, it is nevertheless interesting to recall the concept and function of myth which, as Barthes observes, 'has the task of giving a historical intention a natural justification and making contingency appear eternal',[13] while 'the text loads the image, burdening it with a culture, a moral, an imagination'.[14]

Britannia, the name given by the Romans to the province of England and Wales, had been anthropomorphised into a woman, wearing a helmet and bearing a trident and shield, in the late seventeenth century. The poem 'Rule Britannia' (James Thompson, 1700–1748) had been set to music by Thomas Arne (c.1740) and its associations with freedom and nationalism have made it an 'alternative national anthem', assisted by its rousing chorus:

> When Britain first at Heav'n's command
> Arose from out the azure main;
> This was the charter of the land,
> And guardian angels sang this strain:
>
> Rule, Britannia! Britannia, rule the waves:
> Britons never will be slaves.

The association of freedom with duty (as connoted by the extract from Nelson's signal from his flagship HMS Victory on 21 October 1805 at the onset of the Battle of Trafalgar), the significance of Britain as an island state surrounded by sea and, hence, the importance of 'rul(ing) the waves',[15] the Union Jack emblazoned on Britannia's shield, and the inference that England Expects (every one to do

---

[11]   Conscription was by age, and in October 1939 men aged between 20 and 23 were required to register in one of the armed services. As the war continued, men from other age groups were also conscripted and, in 1941 single women aged between 20 and 30 were also required to sign up for reserved occupations, mainly in factories or farming.

[12]   See Government Campaigns Military Political Recruitment Poster Britannia (http:// images.google.co.uk/-imgres?imgurl=http://www.advertisingarchives.captureweb.co.uk/ images/trueimages/30/55/40/74/30554074-1).

[13]   Roland Barthes, *Image-Music-Text* (London, 1977), p. 117.

[14]   Ibid., p. 26.

[15]   Trafalgar was the decisive naval battle of the Napoleonic Wars and gave Britain control of the seas, so removing the possibility of a French invasion and conquest of Britain. Shipping lanes were also of vital importance during the Second World War, with the Atlantic as the major theatre of operations. Before the Allies could build an army to take to Europe or Africa, they had to secure the shipping lanes to England.

their) National Service provide a powerful definition of nationhood at war, of duty, and an 'equality of service' whereby 'individuals are invited to see themselves as national beings regardless of their other loyalties and preoccupations' and, as such, to serve their country.[16]

The significance of being an island at war, and hence subject to invasion, was also important to the role of the Home Guard who were identified as the country's first line of defence. The mission for 'Dad's Army' was to defend: to promote freedom rather than militarism and to guard the homeland.[17] Freedom and home are thus brought into association, and England is projected as a nation of community 'where we experience the emotional security of being perpetually "at home" ... a historically shaped cultural construction meant to apply broadly, and a cultural concept that answers the question for individuals "who am I", so producing a collective and individual identity'.[18] Exemplified by the flag, as symbolic of national identity and, hence, a self-identification of inclusion/exclusion, the opening titles for *Dad's Army* feature an animated sequence of swastika-headed arrows approaching Britain. Germany and Britain are thus set in opposition: aggression versus peace, tyranny versus freedom and, within the context of the series, belligerence versus the volunteer spirit.[19]

While this sense of national belonging and community spirit is given a specific focus in images of the Blitz (air-raid sirens, plummeting bombs, people picking their way through the debris of their homes) the choice of a rural location for *Dad's Army* resonates with the myth of an unchanging England, characterised by its countryside and village life. A Mass Observation survey, compiled in September 1941, had asked participants to 'write freely on "What Britain Means To You" ... At the top of the list came the countryside, [England's] fields, her woods, her homes, her Wordsworth'.[20] In other words, nation is imagined as a place we have always inhabited, small-scale, homely, rural, so constructing a potent ideological discourse of 'the people' which emphasises continuity, permanence, stability and

---

[16] Rhetorics of nationhood are strategies deployed to manage or organise the differences among people, so that the national 'we' becomes a politically and emotionally powerful vision. See Rose, *Which People's War*, p. 9.

[17] Prime Minister Winston Churchill revived the concept of nation as a historic linguistic community, and then as a heroic narrative based on freedom rather than patriotism or militarism. Britain's historic mission was identified as the defence and promotion of freedom – not just her own, but for all the world. See Baxendale, 'You And I', p. 308.

[18] Rose, *Which People's War*, p. 11.

[19] Baxendale, 'You And I', p. 314.

[20] Baxendale points out that Mass Observers were not a typical sample of the population, and their responses were filtered through [co-founder] Tom Harrison's judgement on what to include in the file report and his subsequent article in *World Review*. Even so, it is interesting to note that many rejected the older idea of nationhood which was perceived as 'gunboats, missionaries and prestige' and few cited the royal family or patriotic songs. See 'You And I', p. 303.

ordinariness, and where the threat of invasion necessitates caution, epitomised by the slogan 'Careless Talk Costs Lives'.

Contemporary British propaganda, including such films as Ealing Studios' *Went The Day Well* (Alberto Cavalcanti, 1942) reflected on the nightmare of occupation and the need for nationwide vigilance. Set in the fictitious village of Bramley End and told in documentary-style flashback, the film relates the arrival of a battalion of Royal Engineers demanding accommodation. Initially welcomed by the villagers, doubts begin to arise about their true identity, and it is discovered that they are intended to form the vanguard of a German invasion. The occupants of the village are rounded up and held prisoner in the local church. They attempt to escape and warn the Home Guard, but are betrayed by the village squire who is revealed to be a German spy. The Germans ambush and kill the Home Guard but are eventually defeated. The message of the film is encapsulated in the opening quotation, taken from the poetry of John Maxwell Edmonds (1875–1958):

> Went the day well?
> We died and never knew
> But, well or ill,
> Freedom, we died for you.

Such anxieties about the threat of invasion and the need for caution, which were persistently emphasised by the Ministry of Information (2.5 million posters were distributed in the early months of 1940: 'Lives are lost through conversation, Here's a tip for the duration, When you've private information, Keep It Dark!') are given a humorous twist in 'The Deadly Attachment', possibly the most famous episode of *Dad's Army*.[21]

> German U-boat Captain: I am making notes, Captain, and your name will go on
>   the list; and when we win the war you will be brought to account.
> Captain Mainwaring: You can write what you like. You're not going to win the
>   war!
> U-boat Captain: Oh yes, we are.
> Mainwaring: Oh no, you're not.
> U-boat Captain: Oh yes, we are!
> Private Pike: [*Singing*] Whistle while you work, Hitler is a twerp,
>   He's half-barmy, so's his army, whistle while you work!
> U-boat Captain: Your name will also go on the list! What is it?
> Mainwaring: Don't tell him Pike!

---

[21]   'The Deadly Attachment' was transmitted on 31 October 1973. Mainwaring's platoon is instructed to guard a captured U-boat crew until a military escort arrives. The escort is delayed and the Germans have to be guarded overnight.

The play on pantomime banter, Pike's (Ian Lavender) singing of a popular wartime adaptation of the song from Disney's *Snow White And The Seven Dwarfs* (David Hand, 1937),[22] and Mainwaring's bungling attempt to prevent Pike's name from going on 'the list', reference the conventions of 'amateurism and incompetence, which, in English popular culture, is concerned with all those notions of "muddling through", determination and pluck which are summed up in the idea of the "Dunkirk" spirit … and is offered in its original 1960s context, as a conservative political counterpoint to Harold Wilson's modernizing "white heat of technology", a concept always rather alien to the British national psyche'.[23]

The identification of courage, cheerfulness, resolution and 'muddling through' were qualities that, with hindsight, were most commonly drawn into association by contemporary films, broadcasts, the press, and by such writers as J.B. Priestley, who had worked with the Local Defence Volunteers on the Isle of Wight, and had stressed 'ordinariness', along with patience and good humour, as typically English characteristics. As a construction of national identity, the myth of 'ordinariness', through which class divisions were forgotten as the nation pulled together to defeat the common enemy,[24] was powerful, although it should be noted that such propaganda posters as '*Your* Courage, *Your* Cheerfulness, *Your* Resolution Will Bring Us Victory'[25] were greeted with a certain scepticism by those hardest hit by the Depression, and for whom the obligations of war meant even greater deprivation.[26] Nevertheless, the People's War, as it was (and still is) popularly called, is remembered as a time 'when the British pulled together to defeat the Nazi enemy in a war that until the middle of 1944 had produced more deaths among civilians in Britain than among those who were in the fighting services … World War II is remembered as Britain's finest hour when people – both the ordinary people and the privileged – put aside their everyday involvements and individual concerns, joined hands, and came to the nation's defence'.[27]

---

[22]   'Whistle While You Work' was originally performed in the UK by Billy Cotton and his Band.

[23]   Hayes and Hill, *Millions Like Us*, p. 325.

[24]   Although the village squire's Nazi status (in *Went The Day Well*) was a possible reminder that rank and hierarchy do not necessarily align with national security or patriotism.

[25]   1939 Ministry of Information poster, designed by A.P. Waterfield.

[26]   'It is true that millions of ordinary people made terrible sacrifices in the war, but sacrifice was far from evenly shared. While workers put up with rationing it was business as usual at the Savoy. Restaurants, which were mainly used by the rich, were not subject to rationing. The wealthy escaped the blitz by spending their nights in country houses. East Enders had to sleep in the Essex fields because no proper bomb shelters had been built. It was only action by left wing militants that forced the authorities to open up the tube stations at night for shelter.' See Chris Lyneham, 'The People's War', *Socialist Review* 176, June 1994, p. 1.

[27]   Rose, *Which People's War*, p. 2.

More than half a century on, similar characteristics emerged when the BBC invited the public to contribute its memories of the Second World War to a website between June 2003 and January 2006. 'The People's War' web archive contains 47,000 personal recollections, 'a legacy of people who lived and fought in World War II ... with many of its stories showing considerable pride in Britain's record of standing alone during 1940–41, and nostalgia for the cheerfulness and cohesion of society during the war-time years'. However, as Purdue had commented, 'the accuracy of this image of Britain at war can, of course, be challenged. It comes to us filtered by films, journalism, books and TV series; even for those who lived through the war what have become standard accounts and images may overlay memories'.[28] Nevertheless, as a myth of origin, the war remains a potent signifier of 'who we are' and, in terms of popular history, it continues to occupy a key place in creating and organising memories and experiences.

Who Do You Think You Are Kidding, Mr Hitler?

While myths and historical memory are integral to the construction of national identity, it is also significant that popular culture acquires much of its meaning at moments of national uncertainty. Music, in particular, came to stand for the specificity of war-time experiences. Choir and brass band concerts were broadcast regularly by BBC radio; for workers in factories and munitions there was *Music While You Work*, and the popularity of big bands led to regular broadcasts by Henry Hall, Billy Cotton, Mantovani, Victor Silvester, Ambrose, and Ivy Benson with her 'all-girl' orchestra. Not least, popular songs became associated with the everyday situations of wartime Britain, the blackout, rationing, the comedies of service life and, especially, love and partings. For every situation, there was at least one special song that would conjure up and heighten emotions: 'We'll Meet Again', 'We'll Gather Lilacs', 'Roll Out The Barrel', 'I'm Going To Get Lit Up'.[29]

> At the level of popular assumption, the belief that music produces sense, or conveys meaning, is unquestioned. Yet such unquestioned assumptions mask a number of questions. First, what *kind* of meaning is music supposed to convey – affective, cognitive, referential? Then, how is the process supposed to work?[30]

But, while it is tempting to simply interpret songs/music as somehow reflecting the experiences of a nation at war, it is rather how they produce, create and construct the quality of those experiences that is significant. With emotions heightened by several years of dockside and station farewells, and the hope of leave-time

---

[28]   Bill Purdue and James Chapman are co-authors of the Open University study pack, *The People's War?* (http://www.open2.net/history/whosewar.html).

[29]   See Michael Leitch, *Great Songs Of World War II* (London, 1985), p. 5.

[30]   Richard Middleton, *Studying Popular Music* (Milton Keynes, 1990) p. 172.

reunions, a song's promise that 'we'll meet again' is not simply about boosting morale. It also defines the ways in which individuals and groups understood and negotiated everyday life across and beyond the duration of war, describing 'the social in the individual and the individual in the social ... and so providing an experience of the *self-in-process*'.[31] The musicalisation of such war-time signifiers as partings ('Wish Me Luck As You Wave Me Goodbye'), optimism ('Blue Skies Are Round The Corner'), home-centredness ('I Haven't Said Thanks For That Lovely Weekend') and safe return from missions ('Coming In On A Wing And A Prayer') relies on the pertinence of the text, its social context, and the ways in which listeners' needs are built into the words/music. For the most part, the language is everyday, familiar, rooted in the here-and-now of the war and, as such, there is a sense of identification through which the listener is located in the text, and thus in the experience communicated by the song. The music/lyric relationship in ballads where 'words and music merge into unified emotive phrases' and where the music 'becomes a vehicle for the singer's intimate, conversational address to the individual' provides one such example, suggesting a structural relationship between the social experience and the musical form.[32] It is also apparent that the wider musical context of dance-bands and their performing situations (nightclub, dance hall, movie, radio) were significant in producing meaning: the jitterbug began early in the war, accelerating with the arrival of GIs, and was characterised by rhythmic excitement; while novelty dances, such as the 'Blackout Stroll', resonated with dance-hall flirtations as the lights went out and everyone changed partners ('Everybody do the Blackout Stroll, laugh and drive your cares right up the pole'). 'The aesthetic thus describes the quality of the experience'[33] and the music 'in so far as it is a cultural activity ... is also communicational activity'.[34]

This sense of communication is important. Above all, the songs of the Second World War were about optimism, and songs having a remotely defeatist content were censored. 'As far back as 1936, the Lord Chamberlain had banned jokes and songs about Hitler when a song, "Even Hitler Had A Mother" was blue-pencilled. Once war was declared, the ban was lifted but relatively few songs "knocking the enemy" became popular'.[35] Patriotism in music, however, was celebrated:

> With a certain patriotic logic, the BBC blacklisted composers whose copyright was held in enemy countries, while exempting certain popular works such as Leoncavallo's *I Pagliacci*, a performance of which, in September 1944 attracted an audience of over twenty-five per cent ... The Proms also enjoyed unprecedented success, and such well-staged coups as the premiere of Shostakovich's *Leningrad*

---

[31]   Simon Frith, 'Music And Identity' in *Taking Popular Music Seriously: Selected Essays* (Aldershot, 2007), p. 294.

[32]   Middleton, *Studying Popular Music*, p. 229.

[33]   Frith, 'Music And Identity', p. 294.

[34]   Gino Stefani, 'Sémiotique En Musicologie', *Versus* 5 (1973), p. 21.

[35]   Leitch, *Great Songs Of World War II*, p. 5.

Symphony in June 1942 (smuggled out of Russia by diplomatic bag) maintained the Music Department's high profile.[36]

It was, however, the song 'There'll Always Be An England' (composed by Ross Parker and Hughie Charles) that best summed up the country's mood at the onset of hostilities. 'Sung by a boy soprano, dressed in a midshipman's uniform, it went straight to the top of the bestseller's list and became the first great hit of the war.'[37] Its success was followed by 'Hang Out Your Washing On The Siegfried Line' (composed by Jimmy Kennedy and Michael Carr),[38] sung by music-hall performer Bud Flanagan, in which 'comic domesticity is set against Nazi militaristic pretensions'.[39] 'It was to prove one of the most misguidedly optimistic songs of the war, written some months before the Allies' defeat in Europe ... although its cocky assertions about the future of Hitler's most strongly fortified defence line infuriated the Nazis who claimed it was written by the "Jewish scribes" of the BBC.'[40]

This relationship of music to what has been termed a 'structure of feeling'[41] provides a particular insight into the significance of myth in constructing a common stock of understandings which can then be attached to the music. The *tempo di marcia* of 'Hang Out Your Washing On The Siegfried Line', with its satirical hint of a German 'oompah' band,[42] connects Nazi Germany with Wagnerian mythology and anti-semitism against a backdrop of music-hall humour and optimistic bravado ('if the Siegfried Line's still there ...'). Conversely, the Germans interpreted the song as 'Jewish': 'This is not a soldiers' song, because soldiers do not brag', railed the German radio.[43] In contrast, the marching rhythms, simple harmonies and timeless construction of Englishness in 'There'll Always Be An England' resonates with the myth of an unchanging homeland – a cottage small, an English lane: 'England = us, and like us, there'll always be an England'.[44] As Lévi-Strauss has noted:

> Music and mythology are like two offshoots of language, each branching off in its own direction. They are both languages lacking in something. Music is

[36]   Hayes and Hill, *Millions Like Us*, p. 76.

[37]   The song was featured in the Carroll Levis film *Discoveries* (Redd Davis, 1939), an offshoot from his radio talent show. See Baxendale, 'You And I', p. 296.

[38]   The Siegfried Line was a chain of fortifications along Germany's Western border. The song was written by Jimmy Kennedy for the British Expeditionary Force when he was in the British Army's Royal Artillery during the early years of the war.

[39]   Baxendale, 'You And I', p. 296.

[40]   Leitch, *Great Songs Of World War II*, p. 30.

[41]   Sheila Whiteley, Andy Bennett and Stan Hawkins (eds), *Music, Space And Place: Popular Music And Cultural Identity* (Aldershot, 2004), p. 3.

[42]   Baxendale, 'You And I', p. 296.

[43]   Leitch, *Great Songs Of World War II*, p. 30.

[44]   Baxendale, 'You And I', p. 296.

language without meaning (*la musique c'est le langage moins le sense*) and therefore it is easy to explain why a listener to music feels an irresistible need to fill this gap with meanings provided by himself. In an analagous way, myths, i.e. systems of meaning, can detach themselves from their verbal foundation to which they are not as strictly bound as ordinary language. Consequently, it is valid to consider myth and music as closely related when observing their specific sign structure ... [and while] the tonal structures may be imbued with many different semantic contents ... this does not prevent the firm interweaving of myth and music in a given cultural context.[45]

Despite, then, the apparent cohesion of the march with militarism (on-the-beat, heavily accented, 4/4 rhythms originally intended to facilitate marching[46]), its meaning is not fixed; rather its connotations relate to particular histories and associations: 'Red, white and blue? What does it mean to you?'.[47] 'Colonel Bogey' provides a succinct illustration: written in 1914 by Lieutenant F.J. Ricketts (1881–1945), a British Military bandmaster and Director of Music for the Royal Marines, it became the authorised march for the Kings Own Calgary Regiment (Canada). The tune subsequently, and forever, became associated with *The Bridge Over The River Kwai* (David Lean, 1957) when it was whistled by British prisoners of war in a Japanese prison camp.[48] Its subtext ('Hitler has only got one ball') had originated at the onset of the Second World War and although the words are not sung in the film, they were sufficiently well-known for the humour to be understood: 'Meaning is thus the consequence of an intense dialectical interaction between text, other adjacent texts (lyrics, images, movement) and social, cultural and biographical centres.'[49] As such, while the march rhythm and tempo imply a militaristic association, the ways in which such formal structures were used in popular songs of the period could range from the romantic 'Lili Marlene'[50] to action songs such as 'Praise The Lord And Pass The Ammunition' (Frank Loesser) and the humorous 'Kiss Me Goodnight Sergeant Major' (Art Noel and Don Pelosi). 'Der Fuehrer's Face' (Oliver Wallace) provides a particular insight into the ways in which many wartime experiences were assimilated by a cheerful vulgarity that

---

[45]   Claude Lévi-Strauss, quoted in Eero Tarasti, 'On Music And Myth', in Derek B. Scott (ed.), *Music, Culture And Society: A Reader* (Oxford, 2000), pp. 46–7.

[46]   According to the speed of the march, this could also be in 2/4.

[47]   'There'll Always Be An England'.

[48]   The movie was filmed in Sri Lanka between November 1956 and May 1957, and was released in October 1957.

[49]   John Shepherd, *Music As Social Text* (Cambridge, 1991), p. 175.

[50]   The words were written in 1915 by Hans Leip, a German schoolteacher who had been conscripted into the Imperial German Army and was published as a poem in 1937 ('Das Lied Eines Jungen Soldaten Auf Der Wacht'). It was set to music by Norbert Schultz in 1938 and, because of its popularity with both German and English troops, a version was recorded by Anne Shelton with words by Tommie Connor.

harks back to music-hall slapstick; the words "Ve iss der Master Race' were given the rejoinder 'Ve Heil! Heil! Right in Der Fuehrer's face' and punctuated by a 'raspberry'. Lewis has observed that 'people look to specific musics as symbolic anchors ... as signs of community, belonging and a shared past'[51] and it is in this context that the theme tune to *Dad's Army* has a particular resonance.

Regarded by many as an actual wartime song, the upbeat music and bantering, yet fiercely patriotic, tone of the lyrics is reminiscent of music-hall and was intended as a pastiche of war-time songs.[52] The two-bar introduction, with its orchestra pit connotations, evokes memories of Leeds City Varieties and the Players' Theatre in London, and heralds the iconic sound of Bud Flanagan. Already associated with such songs as 'Hang Out Your Washing On The Siegfried Line' and 'Underneath The Arches' (which he sang with his partner Chesney Allen) and comic routines in the Crazy Gang, his voice chimes with popular perceptions of London's East End – it is Cockney, ordinary, whimsical, and defiant:

> We are the boys who will stop your little game.
> We are the boys who will make you think again.

Perry's choice of Flanagan as vocalist was astute and, while it related to memories of his childhood idol, the link with music-hall within a framework of wartime entertainment gives the song both an affective and contextual frame of reference.

Music-hall, as part of Britain's cultural heritage, has been recognised as 'a truer reflection of the life and culture of the urban classes than was to be found in any other artistic form. It dealt with a whole range of familiar experiences, framed by common references and attitudes'[53] and its legacy – the concept of 'wartime entertainment' and its associations with optimism, attitude, and 'serving the country' – was important in mediating not only 'what happens', but also 'how it happens'. In particular, 'certain patterns of life and feelings are strengthened, affirmed and expressed'[54] through contemporary songs and the special relationship established between performer and audience, as discussed previously. Concerts, plays and variety shows, featuring such well-known entertainers as George Formby and Arthur Askey[55] were staged by ENSA (Entertainments National Service Association) and while these were of their time and place, their resonance within 1960s popular culture continued in the BBC-TV variety series *The Good Old Days* (1963–83) and *It Ain't Half Hot, Mum* (1968–77), Croft and Perry's

---

[51]   G.H. Lewis, 'Who Do You Love? The Dimensions Of Musical Taste' in James Lull (ed.), *Popular Music And Communication* (London, 1992), p. 144.

[52]   The lyrics were composed by Dick Perry, the music in collaboration with Derek Taverner. Bud Flanagan was paid a fee of one hundred guineas.

[53]   Stuart Hall and Paddy Whannel, *The Popular Arts* (London, 1964), p. 56.

[54]   Ibid., p. 46.

[55]   Arthur Askey was the vocalist on 'It's A Hap, Hap, Happy Day' which is given a brief excerpt in *Dad's Army*.

'sequel' to *Dad's Army*. As a high profile wartime entertainer, Flanagan thus comes across as both a contemporary of, and spokesman for, the nation in his 'cock a snook' attitude towards 'Mr Hitler':

> Who do you think you are kidding, Mr Hitler,
> If you think we're on the run?

The credibility of the song and the sense of 'being of its time' are given additional weight by the inclusion of snippets of wartime songs to link the various scenes in *Dad's Army*.[56] Rationing, for example, 'had produced its own crop of food songs',[57] including 'Run Rabbit Run' (Noel Gay and Ralph Butler). Originally composed for Gay's West End show, *The Little Dog Laughed* (which opened on 11 October 1939, at a time when most of the major London theatres were closed) it was sung by Flanagan and Allen, who subsequently changed the lyrics to 'Run Adolf, Run Adolf, Run, Run, Run' in a jibe at the Luftwaffe.[58] Although the series featured only a brief quote from the song, its double associations with Corporal Jones's butcher's shop (and his favouring of special customers with an extra sausage) and his boyish enthusiasm for combat added its own humorous connotations. It is thus appropriate that the closing credits of *Dad's Army* should feature an instrumental march version of 'Who Do You Think You Are Kidding, Mr Hitler?' Played by the Band of the Coldstream Guards, conducted by Captain (later Major) Trevor L. Sharpe, and ending with the air-raid warning siren sounding all-clear, it adds a final touch of nostalgia. The caption 'You have been watching' is followed by vignettes of the main cast: 'Dad's Army' have done their best, 'so watch out Mr Hitler, if you think old England's done!'

To return finally to the question of how the music for *Dad's Army* continues to produce meaning for its viewers, it is suggested that the ways in which individuals remember the past occupy certain narrative spaces that relate to popular memory. This, in turn, creates a dialogue between past and present, reminding viewers of 'who they are' (cheerful, optimistic, pulling together in times of trouble).[59] In

---

[56] These included recordings by such well-known big bands as Jack Payne's Orchestra ('There'll Always Be An England'), Jack Hilton and his Orchestra ('Blue Skies Are Round The Corner') and music hall artist Gracie Fields ('Wish Me Luck As You Wave Me Goodbye').

[57] Leitch, *Great Songs Of World War II*, p. 5.

[58] On 13 November 1939, soon after the outbreak of the Second World War and also soon after the song was premiered, Germany launched its first air raid on Britain, on flying boats sheltering in Sullom Voe, Shetland. Two rabbits were supposedly killed by a bomb drop, although it is suggested that they were in fact procured from a butchers' shop and used for publicity purposes. Walter H. Thompson's television biography, *Churchill's Bodyguard* (UKTV History, 2005) rates the song as the Prime Minister's favourite.

[59] As characteristics of the nation, these 'mythical' associations can be drawn on for situations as diverse as The People's War (reminding us of the stand taken by parents,

effect, *Dad's Army* and its associated music not only recall (albeit in a humorous form) the role the Home Guard played in the Second World War, but also construct those experiences for the viewer, using identifiable characters whose exploits are not that far removed from those recalled in *The Real Dad's Army* (a documentary series broadcast on Channel 4 in 2006). The use of both pastiche and original wartime songs is an important part of this process of identification, evoking and organising shared memories, signalling attitude, humour, nostalgia, and – above all – recreating what it meant to be part of 'old England' during the people's war. It was a technique subsequently used in the BBC1 series *Goodnight Sweetheart* (1993–97) reminding us once again that our memories of Britain at war come to us filtered by such series as *Dad's Army* and that, as a national myth, the combination of optimism and amateurism was a force to be reckoned with.

---

grandparents and so forth), at international football matches, or – at its extreme – by the National Front or British National Party. As a cultural process, the 'idea' of Englishness/ Britishness can become a statement of identity, a cultural frame of reference, and an expression of nationalism.

Chapter 9

Little Ladies: *Rock Follies* And British Television's Dramatisation Of Rock Music

Peter Hutchings

Rock Follies (ITV, 1976) and its sequel *Rock Follies Of '77* (ITV, 1977) are rare items indeed: British television drama series that are set in, and take explicitly as their main subject matter, the world of rock music. Of course, numerous music-based shows have shown up on British television over the years, but surprisingly few dramas have engaged with rock or popular music: *Tutti Frutti* (BBC, 1987) which dealt with the exploits of a touring rock band, and the more fantastical likes of *Miami 7* (BBC, 1999) spring to mind, but little more. Given the pervasiveness of rock and pop music in British culture since the 1950s, the paucity of rock-themed television dramas throughout that period – and the few exceptions to the rule – surely merits some consideration.

In an important account of what he sees as the complicated historical relationship between rock music and television, Simon Frith offers some possible reasons why television might have generally struggled to bring music, and especially rock and pop music, to the centre of attention in any televisual format.[1] First and foremost is the poor sound quality of most television sets; indeed, 'television sound has become relatively worse over the years as the quality of recorded and radio sound has improved, with the development of hi-fi recording techniques and FM/VHF transmission'.[2] Associated with this is the fact that, for Frith at least, television is primarily a visual medium that lacks the enveloping experience offered by listening to music, so that music on television therefore functions more as a prop for visuals than as a key element in its own right. So far as rock and pop music in particular are concerned, he notes that while young people have been the primary audience for this kind of music, they were also – at least until the advent of MTV in the 1980s – the section of society that watched television the least. Hence the rather awkward address adopted by pop music shows from the 1950s through to the 1970s as they sought to appeal both to young people and to their parents.[3]

---

[1]   Simon Frith, 'Look! Hear! The Uneasy Relationship Of Music And Television', *Popular Music* 21/3 (2002), pp. 277–90.

[2]   Ibid., p. 279.

[3]   For a detailed discussion of such programmes on British television, see John Hill, 'Television And Pop: The Case Of The 1950s', in John Corner (ed.), *Popular Television In Britain: Studies In Critical History* (London, 1991), pp. 90–107.

Clearly, these issues will also apply in various ways to television drama. However, the staging of popular music within dramatic contexts also poses another set of problems for programme-makers – not least, coming to terms with the tensions between what they might attempt to do on the small screen and what filmmakers with much greater resources had done, and were continuing to do, on the big screen. Musical drama – and both *Rock Follies* series are as much musical dramas as they are dramas about music – had initially been the province of the stage but, from the 1930s onwards, cinema, and Hollywood in particular, had developed a formidable expertise in the production of musicals, to the extent that the musical had quickly become the epitome of all that was glamorous and escapist about the cinematic medium itself. Admittedly, that tradition appeared to be stuttering at the time that *Rock Follies* came along, with decidedly 'old-fashioned' and relatively unsuccessful musicals such as the Barbra Streisand vehicle *On A Clear Day You Can See Forever* (Vincente Minnelli, 1970) and Lucille Ball's *Mame* (Gene Saks, 1974) mingling with more modish attempts to incorporate rock music into the musical, notably through the 'rock opera' format of *Jesus Christ Superstar* (Norman Jewison, 1973), *Godspell* (David Greene, 1973) and *Tommy* (Ken Russell, 1975). Later in the decade, the youth-oriented and extraordinarily successful *Grease* (Randal Kleiser, 1978) not only made full use of the new Dolby sound system (prompting one critic to later comment that 'the film is as much a rock concert as a movie') but also re-fashioned the musical into modern blockbuster form.[4] In the meantime, and despite the box-office failure of some of the contemporary musicals, the release of the nostalgia-laden *That's Entertainment* (Jack Haley Jr, 1974) and *That's Entertainment Part II* (Gene Kelly, 1976), both of which comprised clips from classic MGM musicals of yester-year, helped to remind 1970s audiences not just in the US, but internationally, that when it came to screen musicals, Hollywood knew best.

This then was the apparently unpromising context out of which *Rock Follies* and its sequel emerged: products of a televisual medium characterised, at the time, by relatively poor sound quality in comparison with the standard of sound reproduction in other media, and also, in a pre-high definition television era, by a lower standard of image quality and production values than was evident in cinema, and more particularly in the Hollywood-centred approach that had overwhelmingly defined what a popular musical drama should look and sound like. To do what *Rock Follies* attempted to do, not just to tell stories about the world of rock music but to integrate specially composed musical numbers into the narrative, might, in that context seem inadvisable, unduly ambitious, hubristic or possibly just crazy.

And yet *Rock Follies* and *Rock Follies Of '77* can both be seen as successful, in most senses of that term. At the time of their original transmission, audience ratings were good, and the critical response to the shows was, if not uniformly positive, usually at least respectful, and often enthusiastic. In addition, the soundtrack album

---

⁴   Charles J. Maland, '1978: Movies And Changing Times', in Lester D. Friedman (ed.), *American Cinema Of The 1970s* (Oxford, 2007), p. 226.

from the first series reached Number One in the UK album chart, with, perhaps inevitably, the second series also generating a commercially released soundtrack. While *Rock Follies* has never attained the canonical status of other television dramas from the 1970s (not least those dramas written by Dennis Potter which also incorporated musical numbers, but in a different way from *Rock Follies*) and has not been repeated on British television since its original transmission, it has continued to be remembered (as a glance at Internet sources quickly demonstrates) with the re-release of the two *Rock Follies* albums in 2000, and the release of both *Rock Follies* and *Rock Follies Of '77* on DVD in 2002 further helping to keep the show in the public eye.

However, the nostalgia that this has involved, and indeed the passage of years since the show's first transmission, has helped to obscure what was bold and experimental about *Rock Follies*, for this was a show that aspired to be new and innovative, in part through pushing back boundaries so far as its subject matter was concerned, but also in formal terms. In particular, its commitment to exploring the aesthetic possibilities of video both dates it (as will be discussed below, pre-high definition forms of video have since the 1970s become a deeply unfashionable recording system for high-end television drama) and identifies it as a potential case study through which one can consider televisual aesthetics during the 1970s and perhaps more generally. Thinking about *Rock Follies* in this way requires us to return to some of the apparent intrinsic 'weaknesses' of television – notably the impoverished image and sound quality – and to begin to think about these not so much as limitations to be overcome (or not overcome, as the case might be) but rather as enabling or facilitating particular kinds of drama, that might relate to drama as it exists in other media, but which have their own distinctive aesthetic characteristics. In the case of *Rock Follies*, both series display a clear awareness of cinematic sources for musical drama, and on this basis they proceed to appropriate, reject or critique the development of their own determinedly video-based televisual identity.

Video And 'Heightened Reality': The Drama Of *Rock Follies*

The first six-episode season of *Rock Follies* was broadcast on ITV between 24 February and 30 March, 1976. The sequel, *Rock Follies Of '77*, had its first three episodes transmitted between 4 May and 18 May, 1977, at which point industrial action at Thames Television (the show's production company) brought transmission to an abrupt halt. The final three episodes were eventually broadcast between 22 November and 6 December, 1977. All episodes were scripted by US writer Howard Schuman, who also provided the song lyrics; the music was composed by Andy Mackay, a founder member of Roxy Music. The two series recounted the exploits of the all-female rock group the Little Ladies, from its formation, through a range of trials and tribulations, to – at the end of *Rock Follies Of '77* – a bittersweet conclusion in which a reformed Little Ladies, minus two of the original members, stands on the verge of international stardom.

The narrative trajectory is, on the surface at least, a conventional one. The idea that fame has a price, and that the road to stardom will involve considerable sacrifice, is hardly original, and indeed, British cinema had offered two rock-themed versions of this kind of story immediately prior to the production of the first *Rock Follies* series, in *Stardust* (Michael Apted, 1974) and *Flame* (Richard Loncraine, 1975). In both films, rock performers (David Essex in *Stardust*, Slade in *Flame*) are originally based in musical and performance contexts characterised positively in terms of spontaneity, authenticity and being true to one's roots. By contrast, their commercial success involves their being transformed by a corporate music business into a branded and manufactured product, that diminishes their freedom and creative integrity in a process unambiguously presented as alienating and destructive. Accordingly, *Stardust* concludes with the death by drugs overdose of its rock star, while, more bathetically, the rock group in *Flame* simply splits up and goes home. In effect, what we are presented with is the pathos of success, of commercial success in particular, defined as a selling-out to those corporate interests that form the music scene, but which at the same time exploit and ultimately waste what is valuable about rock, namely its energy and its general unpredictability and liveliness.

Ostensibly at least, *Rock Follies* and *Rock Follies Of '77* offer comparable scenarios. The early episodes of the first series traces the formation of the Little Ladies, from their initial meeting while working on a revival of an old stage musical, *Broadway Annie*, to the fateful moment where they first sing a rock song together, not for commercial or career purposes, but purely for fun while relaxing in a pub (the song is 'Blueberry Hill', a rock'n'roll classic as performed by Fats Domino in the mid-1950s, even though it was first published in 1940; it is the only song of note in either series not to be written by Schuman and Mackay). This initial performance can in fact be seen as their original moment of authenticity, signifying an appealing talent in them that is innate, spontaneous and unmediated, especially in contrast to some of the old-fashioned numbers they had earlier sung for the stage musical, and which their later development within the music industry will slowly, but inevitably, attenuate and destroy.

The mid-section of *Rock Follies* depicts the group's adventures on the road during an impromptu tour where, despite setbacks, this positive energy is maintained, before – in the last two episodes – they finally achieve a degree of commercial success when they are taken up by a wealthy businessman who restyles both their appearance and their music (twice-over) according to what he sees as the latest commercial fads – first turning them into a mock 1930s-style chanteuse combo, and then remaking them as the retro-World War Two band, the Victory Girls. The negatively presented commercialisation of the Little Ladies is even more evident in *Rock Follies Of '77*, in which, under new management, they are introduced yet more forcibly into a music industry defined as a promoter of all that is superficial and inauthentic, and in which they are repackaged and restyled yet again – this time including a change of line-up – to reflect what the market is seen to require. Unsurprisingly in this context, the question of the group's identity becomes increasingly an issue as the drama progresses and the Little Ladies move ever further away from that prelapsarian 'Blueberry Hill' moment.

Having noted this, neither of the *Rock Follies* series is quite the same as *Stardust* or *Flame*. While the movies opt for a dour, downbeat realism, *Rock Follies* offers instead something that is both more stylised and more in keeping with its televisual nature. *Rock Follies* was shot entirely on video in the studio; this was not an uncommon practice in 1970s British television drama, although combining interior video sequences with filmed exterior scenes was probably the more common approach, especially for adult-centred popular drama of the *Rock Follies* kind. One of the strategies deployed by both *Stardust* and *Flame* to enhance their realist credentials (shooting on location) was therefore not available to the *Rock Follies* programme-makers. But another was: the introduction of content not seen or heard before in the medium. The first series of *Rock Follies* duly obliges with some risqué subject matter, notably an episode about the porn industry and an early television use of the word 'wanking'. Indeed, *Rock Follies'* studio-bound nature might be seen as further inhibiting any claims to realism, especially in the context of British television of the 1960s and 1970s where a new and often critically privileged kind of social realism involved both shooting on film and taking the cameras out of the studio and into the 'real' world – and, in so doing, blurring the distinction between television and cinema.[5]

From this perspective, *Rock Follies* might appear defiantly old-fashioned in its attachment to studio drama of the kind which, by the 1970s, was seen not just by critics but by many key practitioners within television drama itself as unduly theatrical and limiting. An exchange between writer-producer Russell T. Davies and Howard Schuman on the occasion of the 2002 DVD release of *Rock Follies* is interesting in this respect. Davies, writer of *Queer As Folk* (Channel 4, 1999–2000) and BBC's long-running *Doctor Who* from 2005 to 2010, and a key figure in contemporary British television drama, expresses a modern scepticism about the value of pre-high definition, video-based drama when he comments to Schuman: 'The whole thing was shot on video. Didn't you find the lack of film and exteriors stifling?' Schuman defends video thus: 'We'd decided it would be highly stylised, all in studio and all on video. If we'd shot on celluloid in real rock venues, we would have been in the realm of verisimilitude or documentary. For heightened reality, video had tremendous possibilities and it freed me.'[6] Confirming that this is not just a retrospective justification of the programme, Schuman also commented at the time of *Rock Follies Of '77* that he was aiming for 'reality through stylised means'.[7]

---

[5] See Lez Cooke, *British Television Drama: A History* (London, 2003), pp. 56–127.

[6] Russell T. Davies, 'First Ladies Of Rock', *The Observer Review*, 16 June 2002, p. 9.

[7] Tony Gould, 'Rock Political', *New Society*, 9 June 1977, p. 514.

It is worth considering here precisely where this 'stylisation' lies in the programme, and what its relation is to the representation not just of rock music but of the music industry generally. Not unexpectedly, given that Schuman is a writer, it manifests most obviously in the writing, and particularly in characterisation. A number of *Rock Follies* characters are clearly meant to be seen as caricatures, mouthing meaningless catchphrases and generally serving to illustrate, usually for satirical and comic effect, the idiocy of particular attitudes, beliefs and habits. One thinks here in particular of the left-wing activists running the communal house in which one of the Little Ladies lives during the first series, who are variously presented as egotistical, selfish, deluded and hypocritical, or of the inane and self-important impresarios and music journalists who populate *Rock Follies Of '77*.

However, this sense of a 'heightened reality' can also be applied to some of the programme's more prominent characters, who often seem to exist on the cusp between a stereotypical function and layers of psychological complexity. Take the three founding members of the Little Ladies, for example – a schematically designed group if ever there was one. Devonia Rhodes, known as Dee (Julie Covington) is the chirpy, working-class member who habitually refers to everyone she meets (in the opening episodes at least) as 'cock'. Anna Ward (Charlotte Cornwell) is the middle-class one, an actor tired of playing Ophelia and wanting to experience the delights of the counterculture that she missed the first time round. And Nancy Cunard de Longchamps, known mercifully as Q (Rula Lenska), is the improbable one: coming from an upper-class milieu with an arriviste shop assistant mother who married into wealth, she yearns to be a cabaret singer, but spends much of her time appearing in soft core porn movies.

Their subsequent development as characters is, in certain respects at least, informed by stereotypical assumptions about how people from particular social strata behave. Thus, the working-class Dee is the most down-to-earth and direct, the one who is most concerned about the prospect of selling out to the establishment and associated issues of authenticity. Anna, by contrast, is the most introspective and intellectual of the group and, especially in the second series, the most psychologically troubled, the most attracted to the idea of the group, but ultimately the most destructive of it. And Q, largely detached from traditional class structures, remains the most passive and accepting of the three. At the same time, their relationships with each other and the people with whom they live and work are explored in some detail. In particular, the Little Ladies' shifting relationships with their respective boyfriends, and their taking on new lovers as the series progresses, becomes a way of articulating their changing sense of themselves and their own identities.

What emerges then is a drama in which all the characterisations are stylised to some degree, but where some are also nuanced and coloured (not least by some charismatic and lively performances from the actors playing the Little Ladies) without ever completely leaving behind that formative stylisation. This takes place in a televisual world for which, as noted above by Schuman, photographic verisimilitude is neither an option nor desirable. One can argue in fact that it is precisely the lack of visual detail associated with video-based recording techniques that facilitates a kind of impressionistic treatment of setting, where often those settings are not meant to be seen as realistic in any significant way, but rather denote some broader attitude or practice that the series wishes to satirise.[8] An interesting example of how such an approach can be modulated to achieve particular dramatic effects is the extended media junket sequence on a train in the 'The Hype' episode from *Rock Follies Of '77*. This comes in two sections, the first of which is a hyper-stylised musical number set on board a train, the second a more realistically presented, albeit still studio-bound and stereotype-bound, scene on a train, with the musical number bracketing the dramatic scene. The fact that the train in the musical part of the scene is clearly not really a train, and is not really going anywhere, underlines not just the anxiety expressed by the Little Ladies (in the other part of the sequence) about their lack of control over the media hype with which they have become involved, but also the illusory nature of the media marketing process, while the representation of the press junket itself gives some context, detail and specificity to that anxiety. Given that both elements of the sequence are stylised, it is not a question of a fantasy scene revealing some new aspect of a realistic scene, but rather of a sequence operating in two distinct, mutually interactive registers.

A related sense of a world that is shaped by fashion, fad and image manifests elsewhere in both series – in the Biba Nova and World War II-retro Blitz clubs in *Rock Follies*, and in the more downmarket Aggro club in *Rock Follies Of '77*. The owner of the latter confides to Dee that when country-and-western music had been in fashion, the club had been called The Rio Grande, then restyled as The Top Hat when elegance was 'in', and since the appearance of punk has become The Aggro (with punk itself clearly marked as just another passing musical fad; indeed by the end of the series the previously pro-punk journalist is proclaiming that punk is dead).[9]

This presentation of a world lacking in permanence or integral values might help to explain the series' attitude towards politics and political movements. At first glance, the *Rock Follies* series both appear to offer some left-wing and radical qualities – the portrayal of women making their own way in a man's world, an accompanying critique of oppressive male behaviour (in particular, Dee's boyfriend Spike is anatomised, critiqued and reconstructed in the course of the two series), a sympathetic account of left-wing publishing in *Rock Follies Of '77* and, also in the latter series, a non-judgemental portrayal of a gay relationship. However, this

---

[8]   Clearly such an approach, which involves less detailed set design, is well suited to the lower budgets of television production in comparison with film, although *Rock Follies* arguably foregrounds this to an extent that was unusual in popular television drama of the 1970s.

[9]   These comments from the Aggro owner offer a sly comment on the first *Rock Follies* series, in which the Little Ladies first played in a country-and-western pub before moving onto to the elegance-themed Biba Nova club.

never translates into support for any explicitly political position or programme. The negative portrayal of the communal house in the first series has already been mentioned in this regard. More striking yet, especially given that the series deals with an independently-minded female rock band, is the marginality of feminism in the drama. One might argue that some of the Little Ladies' attitudes, and a number of their songs, deploy the language and attitudes of 1970s feminism, but the only significant explicit reference to feminism occurs in the opening episode of *Rock Follies Of '77*, during the production of a TV advertisement for convenience food that features the Little Ladies and which unambiguously co-opts feminism for commercial purposes: as the jingle puts it, 'You're a liberated lady with Wonder Woman frozen food'. When informed that the ad-makers want to raise female consciousness, Dee responds, 'That's like having a seminar on feminism in a harem'. And that's about it so far as feminism is concerned.

Bearing all this in mind, it does seem that what both series are exploring through the figures of the Little Ladies, and doing so with increasing desperation, is the question of how one is to live in a world wholly defined in terms of mediated commercial imagery. When organised resistance has already been absorbed and turned into the latest fashion or marketing device, how is value and integrity to be found; how, in other words, does one escape 'the hype'? The answer is hard to articulate, but it is consistently shown to have something to do with music and performance.

With Feeling: The Songs In *Rock Follies*

In his history of British television drama, Lez Cooke notes an interesting connection between *Rock Follies* and Dennis Potter's *Pennies From Heaven* (BBC, 1978). For Cooke, the songs in both series represent a happiness that is otherwise unattainable for the main characters, so that 'it is only through their music that the Little Ladies in *Rock Follies* can keep their dream of stardom and success alive amid the dour reality of life on the road in a 1970s Britain also spiralling into recession'.[10] Like a number of other critics, he also argues that the interruption of broadly realistic narratives by fantasy-based musical numbers creates a Brechtian-like distancing effect that enables an audience to view the drama from a different perspective, which lies outside the comforting predictability of conventional realism. However, such a reading of *Rock Follies* is reliant on the main body of the drama consistently exhibiting a naturalistic realism which, as has already been observed in regard to Schuman's notion of heightened reality, does not appear to be the case. Some of the songs in *Rock Follies* might move us yet further away from realism, but that is in the context of an overall narrative that constantly presents us with provocative stereotypes and stylised settings and situations. It is also the case that these songs sometimes seem to be serving very different functions within the narrative, with

---

[10]   Cooke, p. 122.

this permitted by the fact that, unlike the pre-existing 'found' songs deployed in *Pennies From Heaven*, they were written especially for the show in the manner of more traditional forms of musical drama.

As already noted, the opening episodes of *Rock Follies* juxtapose an energetic rendition of 'Blueberry Hill' with the enervated, old-time stage musical *Broadway Annie*. The commercial failure of the musical in the second episode does not just provide the impetus for the formation of the Little Ladies group, but also seems to mark the moment when *Rock Follies* invokes the traditional musical drama format, if only to distance itself from it. At the same time, the aspirational showbiz 'names up-in-lights' theme of *Broadway Annie* clearly resonates with the Little Ladies' ambition to be successful in the business and, indeed, certain aspects of the stage and cinematic musical are retained in the series, if only periodically or residually.

For example, *Rock Follies*' depiction of ups and downs in the music business aligns it with the backstage musical format that was particularly popular during the 1930s (and of which *Broadway Annie* is clearly an expression). In both, the presence of songs is explained by their being part of a performance for an audience located within the world of the drama, or as rehearsals for that performance. In the case of *Rock Follies* and *Rock Follies Of '77*, a number of the songs, far from being non-naturalistic interventions, are performed on stage, in rehearsal halls, and in recording studios, as a normal feature of the lives of professional musicians. Their function in this respect is, in part, to demonstrate the credibility of the Little Ladies as a viable and worthwhile band. However, the aggression displayed by these songs in both their pounding rhythm and in Schuman's lyrics also helps to give a sense of the band's attitude and in particular its resistance to, and anxiety about, being told what to do by others. An anti-authority stance drives 'OK' ('You want a victim, there are plenty to spare there, OK? But you ain't picked one, so get out of my hair, beware, OK?'). 'Loose Change' invokes a female rejection of parental authority ('And she isn't going to wind up like her parents'). 'Good Behaviour' tells of a wife's escape from an unhappy marriage, albeit into what, in retrospect, looks like a ladette-like hedonism ('Booze and music for me again, and a crop of fancy men, with black cigars, panama hats, driving Jaguars, hey hey hey, I'm free again'). And the faux-punk 'Jubilee' expresses a working-class aggression directed against a consumerist world ('Stay away from my street, ten per cent are out of work, and some disloyal little burke might shout a foul obscenity about the Silver Jubilee').

The extent to which the assertiveness evident in these songs is more than just a stance is, as noted above, an important issue being worked through in the drama, and the songs themselves could reasonably be seen to function as repeated assertions of an attitude that is hard for the Little Ladies to maintain outside their performances. Interestingly in this respect, 'The Band Who Wouldn't Die', a song featured early in the second series (which is the series that focuses most explicitly on the media management of the group), retains the assertive beat of these other songs, but modulates their meaning through the introduction of vulnerability and self-doubt into the lyrics. These lyrics initially refer to the conclusion of the first series, during which the club in which the Little Ladies were working was blown up as part of an insurance scam ('The club exploded, we were shaking'), then describes a conversation between the band-members and a journalist who wants to depict them as heroines because it makes for a better story ('We're pretty frightened. No, you're not … you're full of British pluck, your spirit's red hot, that's the story for my reader') with eventually the band accepting this fictional persona ('Even we believed the lie, we're the band who wouldn't die'). A related scepticism about commercial success is also evident in the first series' 'Sugar Mountain' ('Sugar Mountain, where the rock stars go, when they hit the charts and let their egos grow, Sugar Mountain, it's so lush and cool, you float on Valium in your swimming pool') and also in 'Rollercoaster' ('Our future's in the hands of some technician who is out of sight, an unknown guy at the controls, controls our rocks, controls our rolls, our head is full of panic, and we're sure we're gonna die tonight').

An alternative method employed by screen and stage musicals to introduce songs into the drama is to have characters spontaneously burst into song, but this occurs only rarely in either of the *Rock Follies* series.[11] Instead, they create a series of numbers explicitly marked as being outside the 'real' world of the drama; this is achieved through the often minimalist design exhibited in such sequences, through camerawork and editing built around the theme and rhythm of the songs, and sometimes through the use of video techniques that electronically distort the image in some way or other. Sequences of this kind clearly look forward to the rock video in their formal organisation, but they also stand in a particular relation to the narrative in which they are embedded, to the extent that it is hard to think of them as 'fantasy' numbers, at least in the escapist sense of that term.

Some of these songs take the form of interior monologues, as characters muse on the problems that beset them: each of the Little Ladies has at least one of these numbers, while the more unusual 'In My Cans' (in *Rock Follies Of '77)* allows all of them to express inner doubts in the form of a voice-over (or, more accurately, a sing-over) during the recording of their first single, 'OK'. Others, and particularly those that appear towards the end of episodes, act both as a summation of the preceding drama and a reflection on or emotional response to it. Indeed, many of these songs can be seen to provide musical expressions of emotional states that offer an immediacy and directness not available elsewhere in the drama while, in some cases, also possessing a complexity of their own.

Two notable examples of this from the first series are 'Stairway' and 'The Road', each of which balances elements of doubt and anxiety, largely articulated through the lyrics, against a simple melodic refrain conveying a hope and longing that seems largely beyond words. So, in 'Stairway' – sung as the Little Ladies are about to embark on their career as a rock band – the questions ('Is it glittering,

---

[11]   The only significant exception is the 'Wolf At The Door' number in *Rock Follies Of '77*, and even this is sung in a club after a gig, and so could pass as an impromptu jam session if it were not so polished in its delivery.

peeling, gleaming, decayed? Will your dreams be fulfilled, surpassed or betrayed?') are followed by an affirmative response ('Go up the stairway, it's time to climb') accompanied by images of the band-members, their arms held upwards, ascending a stylised staircase. Significantly, this song is repeated at the end of the series; now, the staircase is fire-damaged, the Little Ladies' clothes are torn and their dreams in tatters, but the affirmation of 'climb the stairway' bestows a note of hope as the series ends. Similarly, 'The Road', which concludes the episode in which the band has been touring, juxtaposes the dispiriting ('They grip your hands and they grope your thighs, and they swallow you up with their hungry eyes') with the epiphanic ('But you keep on having these incredible highs, on the road, on the road') with the first 'road' extended to convey a sense of freedom that is possibly only available via musical recollection, and which does not manifest in any obvious way in the dramatic scenes depicting their life on the road.

It seems from this that what many of these musical numbers do, both in the 'back-stage' and 'extra-narrative' versions, is develop *Rock Follies'* emotional register in a way that its non-musical dramatic scenes cannot really do by themselves. Moreover, they do this in a manner that permits complexity and contradiction. While some of the more satirical songs might deliberately push the viewer away from particular dramatic situations in order that he or she might see them differently, others invite an affective involvement with the Little Ladies and all their issues and problems. Even at their most stylised, they work to draw viewers into, and to deepen their sense and understanding of, this distinctive world. In a different context, John Mundy, writing about the musical drama *Blackpool* (BBC, 2004), considers the ability of popular songs to enrich television drama: 'Taken together, the songs and their performance provide an exuberance that would simply be missing in a conventional drama, a dimension in which affective states are more directly addressed than would otherwise be the case. Given the central importance of music and song in this construction, it is hard to know why television drama has consistently ignored this particular aspect of its vocabulary.'[12] If nothing else, *Rock Follies* underlines the validity of Mundy's point in both its innovative accomplishments and in the fact that there are very few British television dramas quite like it.

The Real Life

At the time of their original transmission, the two *Rock Follies* series generated a range of critical responses, none more intriguing than the wholly negative review of the first series provided by *New Musical Express* or the much more positive review of both series in *New Society*. The opening lines of the *NME* article announces:

---

[12] John Mundy, 'Singing Detected: *Blackpool* And The Strange Case Of The Missing Television Musical Dramas', in *Journal Of British Cinema And Television* 3/1 (2006): p. 67.

'To hell with objectivity. I hate *Rock Follies*. I found the plot cumbersome and the script foolish. I disliked the fundamental inaccuracy of the "real bits", remained un-entranced by the "surreal bits"'.[13] The rest of the article, which encompasses an edgy interview with Schuman and Mackay, strongly conveys the impression that this is not actually a show about the rock business and that indeed 'rock and TV drama basically don't mix'. Interestingly, Tony Gould's account in *New Society* also concludes by suggesting that while *Rock Follies* may not be primarily about the world of rock music, it is nonetheless using it to make points about other things: 'In the end *Rock Follies* is about success and failure, and not only in rock. The music business is the microcosm, and rock provides a suitable metaphor because rock is all about power.'[14]

If we accept either assertion, then we probably have to agree that *Rock Follies* does not tell us much about the music business. Instead, its distinction lies in the way that it uses rock music inventively and expressively to tell an emotionally involving story, and simultaneously uses the music business setting to illustrate what it sees as broader social trends, not least a diminution of any sense of the real in a new, image-based society organised around short-term sensations and fads. That the only kind of resistance and authenticity it can muster in the face of these changes comes in the form of rock music, and that this resistance is so fragile and vulnerable, arguably taps into a wider set of beliefs and anxieties about the attraction, necessity and danger of commercial success that have become embedded in rock history.

In the final moments of the final episode of *Rock Follies Of '77*, Dee and new band member Roxy (Sue Jones-Davies) are joined by ex-band members Anna and Q. It is an illusory reunion with the four singers not actually sharing the same space, but superimposed there electronically. Nevertheless, they sing together for the last time:

> Yes clasp my hand
> And hold it tight
> And help me get through the real life.

As is so often the case in *Rock Follies*, this is a moment where success and failure are inextricably bound together, and where desire and fantasy are thwarted, but also – again characteristically for the series – where there is hope, energy, resistance, not necessarily in the words of the song, but in the melody and in the sound of human voices. For all the schematic designs and broad strokes of the programme as a whole, it is an affecting moment, and at its end there is a sense of loss. The credits roll, and we see, as in preceding episodes, the *Rock Follies* title as a neon sign, with some of the letters turning on and off. And then comes the series' final dark joke – the title is briefly but unmistakeably rendered as 'Lies'.

---

[13]   'Schlock Jollies', *New Musical Express*, 10 April 1976.

[14]   Gould, p. 514.

Chapter 10

Pop Half-Cocked: A History Of *Revolver*

Richard Mills

The eight episodes of ATV's *Revolver* (1978) provide a window through which to scrutinise key elements of late 1970s popular culture. They bridge the gap between the progressive concerns of *The Old Grey Whistle Test* (BBC2, 1971–87) and the post-punk aesthetic of *The Tube* (Channel 4, 1982–87) in the early 1980s, reflect the musical chaos of that intervening period, and do so in a bold and confrontational manner. Fictionally located in an excessively seedy nightclub, and introduced by a cynical and antagonistic manager (played by Peter Cook) with little interest in music, *Revolver* fused elements of popular music, television comedy and political satire.

The fact that not all of the featured acts achieved major commercial success does not detract from their importance as cultural indicators of trends in popular music in the late 1970s. Indeed, the programme was knowingly designed as a vehicle to highlight the post-punk and New Wave musics that followed the original punk explosion led by the Sex Pistols and The Clash in 1976–77. The significant components of *Revolver*'s brief existence may be summarised in four statements: first, it was an innovative postmodernist text that failed because of its self-consciousness; secondly, it was a programme that exemplified 'the way fans intervene in industrial-produced television products';[1] thirdly, its structure, contents and location give it a unique place in British broadcasting history; fourthly, the show revealed many of the popular conventions and fashions of a particular time and place.

Design, or intentionality, is central to *Revolver*. For the first time on British television, the presentation of popular music is truly postmodern, in the sense that the programme is historically placed to benefit from hindsight, not least through its deliberate mimicry of ITV's *Ready Steady Go!* (1963–66). In pre-planning meetings, music producer and entrepreneur Mickie Most explicitly stated that he wanted it to be 'a new *Ready Steady Go!*'[2] With *Revolver*'s audience and cameras constantly on screen, and the mechanics of the show's production on display to the viewer, 'you knew you were watching a TV programme'.[3] Contemporary understandings of fandom are also key to the programme's objectives, and are

---

[1] Lisa A. Lewis (ed.), *The Adoring Audience: Fan Culture And Popular Media* (London, 1992), p. 5.

[2] Chris Hill (co-presenter of *Revolver*), personal interview, 18 September 2009.

[3] Ibid.

included in its central conceit, which sees the disgruntled club manager forced to book bands against his will. Unlike much popular music on television, there is no clear demarcation between the (active) producer and (passive) consumer of music; the camera devotes as much time to the studio audience as to the bands, illustrating Jenkins's observation that 'fandom here becomes a participatory culture which transforms the experience of media consumption into the production of new texts'.[4] Yet there are limits to this 'poaching': although the line between producer and consumer becomes blurred, 'it occurs quite precisely within the economic and cultural parameters of niche marketing whereby fan-consumers and producers are more closely aligned'.[5] Thus, throughout *Revolver*'s short life, the audience and the producers are in an uneasy alliance: the audience are being manipulated and they know it.

The show was produced and broadcast by ATV in 1978. Following a 45-minute pilot in May, seven 30-minute editions were subsequently screened from July to September. By bringing post-punk music into the mainstream, it was intended to be an edgy riposte to the perennial success of BBC's *Top Of The Pops* (1964–2006). The line-up in the pilot show (Episode 1) achieved this aim, and also created a certain notoriety by featuring the Tom Robinson Band's 'Glad To Be Gay', which *Top Of The Pops* had refused. Other performers were Steel Pulse, XTC, Rich Kids (whose members included a pre-Ultravox Midge Ure on vocals and ex-Sex Pistol Glenn Matlock on bass), John Dowie, and Ricky Cool and the Icebergs; the only commercially successful performer was Kate Bush.

Added to this unpredictable mix was the presenter Peter Cook. He was isolated from the bands in a separate studio, and appeared on a large screen to taunt the live audience. His remit was to be deliberately provocative in the role of an ill-tempered club manager who has been forced to let his premises to the television company. He was given free rein to abuse the bands, and his acerbic introductions established a tone that satirises the reverential and serious approach of *The Old Grey Whistle Test* and Granada's punk-dominated *So It Goes* (1976–77), and anticipates the irreverence of *The Tube*. However, the studio audience reacted to Cook's 'misanthropic elitism' with violent gestures and heckling, giving his performance (especially its racist and sexist elements) a different meaning than that intended by the producers. The sexist and racist codes would not go unchallenged either by a television or studio audience.

In 1978, Cook was one of Britain's best-known and most active entertainers. His mordant style was already well known to television viewers, through *Not Only ... But Also* (BBC, 1965–66 and 1970–73), and seemed particularly well suited to illustrate the shifts in British comedy and British popular music at this time. Following the enormous success of the revue *Beyond The Fringe* at the 1960 Edinburgh Festival, in which he appeared with Dudley Moore, Jonathan Miller and Alan Bennett,

---

[4]   Henry Jenkins, *Textual Poachers: Television Fans And Participatory Culture* (London, 1992), p. 46.

[5]   Matt Hills, *Fan Cultures* (London, 2002), p. 40.

Cook's anti-establishment brand of humour had made a huge contribution to British cultural life, and was largely responsible for the satire boom which swept Britain in the 1960s. In addition to *Not Only ... But Also*, he had written and/or appeared in a string of television comedy and drama productions, including Miller's *Alice In Wonderland* (BBC, 1966), *An Apple A Day* (BBC, 1971) and *Eric Sykes Shows A Few Of Our Favourite Things* (ITV, 1977). His movie appearances included *The Wrong Box* (Bryan Forbes, 1966), *Bedazzled* (Stanley Donen, 1967), *Monte Carlo Or Bust* (Ken Annakin, 1969), *The Bed Sitting Room* (Richard Lester, 1969), *The Rise And Rise Of Michael Rimmer* (Kevin Billington, 1970) and *The Adventures Of Barry McKenzie* (Bruce Beresford, 1972). In 1962, along with Nick Luard, he had bought a controlling 75 per cent share in the fortnightly satirical publication *Private Eye*. The magazine had a huge influence on, and occupied a unique place in, British public life: among other things, it uncovered the Profumo scandal in 1963 and, in so doing, contributed to the downfall of the 13-year Conservative government in the 1964 General Election. And in the mid-1970s, Cook had presented two all-star comedy shows to raise funds for Amnesty International – *Pleasure At Her Majesty's* (1976) and *The Mermaid Frolics* (1977) – that became the template for *The Secret Policeman's Ball* charity events from 1979.

When *Revolver* was filmed, Cook was at his most sarcastic and scabrous. The notorious *Derek And Clive* albums (with regular partner Dudley Moore) had attracted new levels of condemnation for their alleged obscenity. *Derek And Clive Live* (1976), *Derek And Clive Come Again* (1977) and *Derek And Clive Ad Nauseam* (1978) made explicit the undercurrents of vulgarity and 'bad taste' that had always been implicit in the British comedy tradition, and matched perfectly the cynical punk aesthetic of *Revolver*:

> Sarcasm, it's said is the lowest form of wit and Cook sinks to the challenge admirably. But it's not just the jokes that make Cook so essential to *Revolver*; it's the whole psychological baggage that he brings to the role of unwilling host. Look at him, in his office full of ashtrays, bottles, and bad memories, not caring less, slumped in his chair, cigarette in hand, jaded eyes mentally daring the audience to rise up and attack him. Come on, burn me at a stake, he seems to be thinking; do something, if you've got any guts.[6]

Cook's co-host on the show was Chris Hill. A former disc jockey (with a liking for the music of Georgie Fame, Geno Washington and Chris Farlowe), he went on to found Ensign Records and sign punk bands such as the Boomtown Rats. His irreverence matched Cook's: he was dismissive of many of the post-punk bands, and preferred the soul and funk performers who appeared on the programme.

---

[6]   Paul Hamilton, 'Revolter', in Peter Gordon, Dan Kieran and Paul Hamilton (eds), *How Very Interesting: Peter Cook, His Universe, And All That Surrounds It* (London, 2006), p. 216.

Although generally pleased with the pilot (which was transmitted at 6.45 p.m. on a Saturday evening) ATV's wary executives moved the subsequent shows to a late-night Saturday slot. The first of the series proper (Episode 2) contained a selection of relatively unknown performers (the Autographs, Hi-Tension, the Boyfriends, the Lurkers, Kandidate), commercially successful punk acts (the Boomtown Rats, the Stranglers), and an additional segment that was to become a permanent feature of the series: classic footage from the ATV archives (Julie Driscoll). Viewed today, this episode revels in a studied unprofessionalism that makes it a landmark in British popular music television history. *The Old Grey Whistle Test* is never this indecorous; *The Tube* lacks its tension. The bands on display are representatives of a post-punk subculture who, although they were promoted by major record companies, were broadly unsuccessful and remained outside the commercial mainstream. The programme was their only chance of fame – and they mostly failed. Its dingy, anarchic aesthetic (the opening credit is a lift descending into a nightclub) is a visual equivalent of punk's thrashy and atonal sounds. The energetic, proto-violent atmosphere is goaded by Cook's constant ridicule of the bands and the audience. The mini-narrative (the music, the clothes, the opening and closing credits, the colloquialisms) are a clear indication of 1970s Britain. Cook's comic interludes and Hill's monologues are terse and caustic. The bands' music is identical in sound and style, their material is standard and formulaic: short, uncomplicated songs. The minimalist aesthetic is evident in the dress sense of the performers: a uniform of drainpipe jeans, multi-coloured mohair sweaters, ripped T-shirts and cropped, spiky hair. There is an undercurrent of menace which adds a frisson to the cut-and-paste, jerky appearance of *Revolver*. While it is a shop window to break bands such as the Lurkers, the Boyfriends and the Autographs, the closing credits of the show are inane faux-punk slogans and graffiti – 'Peter Cook Rules OK', 'Chris Hill Is King Of The Kids', 'Les Ross Flogs Junk Food' – intended to ridicule punk style. In essence, the programme definitively captures the moment when the punk rock of the Sex Pistols morphed into the power pop of Blondie and bands such as XTC, and coincided with Jon Savage's announcement of 'a new style about which to hyper-ventilate, sparked by the success of The Jam – Power Pop'.[7] The bands in Episode 2 all represent 'power pop', and the identification of *Revolver* as 'the punk generation's version of *Ready Steady Go!*'[8] might be legitimately extended to assert that *The Tube* was the next generation's version of *Revolver*.

By Episode 3, Cook is beginning to deliver his sarcastic comments in a nasal slur reminiscent of Johnny Rotten/John Lydon; Les Ross, a Birmingham DJ, prepares hamburgers on a grill in the middle of the dance floor; and audience members dance robotically. Musically, there is a more eclectic mix. Post-punk acts such as Siouxsie and the Banshees, Ian Dury, the Buzzcocks, and the Vibrators stand alongside Bonnie Tyler, the Roy Hill Band, and Sore Throat, who perform

---

[7]   Jon Savage, *England's Dreaming* (London, 1991), p. 481.

[8]   Ibid., p. 484.

the novelty 'Zombie Rock', accompanied by crude, pre-music video images of the undead in a graveyard. The energy and enthusiasm of the audience draws attention to the significant gap in age between it and the presenters (and some of the performers). In a sense, the audience members are the stars of the show. They heckle Cook, and their reaction to the bands is scrutinised, recorded, and interpreted by the cameras. Put simply, there is a cynicism in the air: the performers want to sell; the (teenage) consumer wants to buy:

> This new type was the ultimate psychic match for the times: living in the now, pleasure-seeking, product hungry, embodying the new global society where social inclusion was to be granted through purchasing power. The future would be teenage.[9]

But here we see a post-punk audience that appropriates the meanings promulgated by the show's presenters and the intentions of its creators. Cook, who was 41 when *Revolver* was broadcast, 'wasn't interested in the music'; Hill was 34, and admits he 'should have been 18'.[10] The evident importance of popular music's commercial imperative was not lost on the programme's reviewers, one of whom described it as 'entirely cynical ... no-one even bothers to pretend these days that the pop industry is about anything more than the sound of money singing'.[11] However, despite such misgivings, *Revolver*'s studio audience (and, by implication, the non-studio and non-TV audiences) clearly, and actively, interpret the music as meaningful rather than manipulative.

The night-club conceit is used to convincing effect at the start of Episode 4. Cook introduces the acts (Elvis Costello, Matumbi, the Rezillos, the Motors, Nick Lowe, and 'the support act' Brent Ford and the Nylons, whose stage gimmick was to wear stockings on their heads) with the quip, 'Birmingham – the city that makes lead poisoning the in-thing'. Short, jerky camera angles give the on-screen events a televisual shudder, which intensifies the frenetic dancing of the audience and visually complements the angular music. As in the previous episodes, the performers' dress style and music (the minimalist punk aesthetic of a standard three chord thrash) are notable for their similarity. The contrived spontaneity of the show is enhanced by what is now a standard *Revolver* tactic: the headline band finishes a song as the opening credits roll, presumably to give the sensation of gate-crashing a party in full swing. While this willingness to extemporise contributes to the show's vitality and unpredictability, it also gives it a provisional feel: Cook is unable to steady the ship and the programme drifts from act to act. The approach is almost 'amateurish' and, in a sense, ahead of its time. Thirty years later, the unprofessionalism and postmodernist irony of *Revolver* is standard fare on contemporary British television: in 1978, it alarmed television executives.

---

[9] Jon Savage, *Teenage: The Creation Of Youth* (London, 2008), p. 465.

[10] Hill, personal interview.

[11] Craig Raine, 'Vicious And Company', *The Observer*, 13 August 1978, p. 19.

Throughout the first four episodes, Cook's introductions (in the guise of the middle-aged club manager) express a typical late-1970s insensitivity to gender and race. The majority of the bands are male, white, independent pop/rock acts, and the few black acts – Steel Pulse, Hi Tension, Matumbi – are announced in a casually racist manner. When introducing Steel Pulse, he intones, 'I've met a lot of wonderful coloured people who move and dance … the Drifters and Sammy Davis. Don't boo! You'll be had up under the Race Relations Act'. After Matumbi's performance, he says, 'Thanks! Coffee and cream!' Siouxsie and the Banshees prompt the remark, 'There's nothing wrong with a woman and a group, but when they get together – Jesus!' The sensitivity of playing with the politics of racial identity within the show's setting has been explained by Hill:

> He [Cook] used to say things like, 'They're black! I won't have black people in my club!', and I'd be rucking with him, going, 'This is the band I want!' I had actually persuaded them to have an all-black show with Kandidate, Hi Tension, Heatwave, and it was very cool to have Heatwave 'cos they were just starting out, and the reggae bands Steel Pulse and Matumbi … ATV would hate an all-black show. But at least we managed to get black groups on TV although, when you look at the audience, it didn't make sense, because firstly there are lots of black people dancing, and then there isn't. You think, 'What?!' But Peter, because he's playing the bigoted National Front fucking Herbert, made lots of racialist, but very funny, remarks.[12]

The Cook/manager persona may have been employed as a vehicle for (politically incorrect) humour, but was not untypical of the mainstream entertainment industry's attitudes to gender and race in 1978. Many of the post-punk bands were actively engaged in Rock Against Racism and/or the Anti-Nazi League: the two organisations staged a huge rally in London's Victoria Park in April of that year, which included performances from X-Ray Spex, the Tom Robinson Band, Steel Pulse and The Clash. Significantly, when Steel Pulse made their appearance on *Revolver*, members of the band wore Ku Klux Klan hoods.

Related attitudes to gender are explored in Episode 5. The opening segment shows a scantily-clad woman, in underwear and suspenders, astride Cook's desk; each time the camera returns to the manager's office between acts, she removes another item of clothing. Down on the dance floor, the audience are lying on their backs, gyrating to the theme tune from ATV's long-running, and critically-derided, soap opera *Crossroads* (1964–88). Cook announces the line-up: the Fabulous Poodles, Dire Straits, the Boomtown Rats, The Jam, Heatwave, and funk act Jab Jab. Also promised is a film screening of the Sex Pistols and fugitive Great Train Robber Ronald Biggs performing 'No-one Is Innocent': however, the video is not broadcast and the word 'Censored', in large red letters, fills the screen.

---

[12]   Paul Hamilton, 'My Favourite Earache', in Gordon et al. (eds), *How Very Interesting*, p. 230.

The episode demonstrates the pursuit of controversy and (mock) outrage that *Revolver* actively desired. A rumour that Ronnie Biggs was to arrive on the rooftop of the ATV building in a helicopter was so convincing that Birmingham police came to the studios in the hope of arresting him.[13] The reality of the audience's staged dancing and responses to Cook's insults includes them as partners in the alternative reality of the programme's conceit. But it also represents a genuine, subcultural re-contextualisation, whereby the (artificial) cynicism of *Revolver* is transformed into an (authentic) experience of the music. The programme effectively provides a free space, in which new meanings can be developed and articulated. The signs in the text reflect a period in which uncomfortable political messages (sexist and racist) flowed freely, but the carnival spontaneity of the audience emphasises their rejection of that discourse, aided, no doubt, by the rich musical variety of this episode.

The variety of musical genres in Episode 6 stretches from the Motors, Ian Dury, the Steve Gibbons Band, through Goldie and Suzi Quatro, to US band the Shirts (fronted by a Debbie Harry-like vocalist) and punk poet Patrik Fitzgerald whose performance of 'Bingo Crowd' includes the refrain, 'Bingo crowd, I'd rather wear a shroud'. In a visually uninspiring programme, the bands are accompanied by randomly selected, sepia-tinted archive clips reminiscent of the vintage black-and-white film extracts used on *The Old Grey Whistle Test*. A pantomime horse weaves its way through the dancers, and Hill tells the audience that 'the neighbours are complaining about the noise, and they might take our licence away'.

Episode 7 begins with the stunt motorcyclist Eddie Kidd's attempt to cash in on his celebrity status by releasing a pop single: 'Leave It To The Kid' is piece of clichéd pop/rock music that says much about the opportunistic, and blatantly commercial, tendencies characteristic of British pop music in the late 1970s. Cook introduces him by sardonically stating that he would rather see him 'jump under a bus' than over one. X-Ray Spex and Eddie and the Hot Rods both perform examples of melodic 'power pop'. In fact, much of X-Ray Spex's music (especially their 1978 album *Germ Free Adolescence*) is furiously anti-consumerist, and sits uneasily alongside the marketing of post-punk bands and, indeed, *Revolver* itself. The Roy Hill Band present a Lou Reed-pastiche ('Piccadilly Lights') and the folk-oriented Lindisfarne perform two songs ('Juke Box Gypsy' and 'Kings Cross Blues') patently at odds with the post-punk ethos.

The most revealing contributions are made by two black bands: Merger and C-Gas 5. Merger's reggae performance of 'Soweto' is intercut with newsreel of the South African township near Johannesburg. It is a serious piece of political pop, whose protesting lyrics ('Nico born in the ghetto, My brother died in Soweto') and skilful musicianship are more impressive than many of the fashion-rock bands who appeared in the series. Significantly, the audience too is multicultural (in previous weeks it had been entirely white). Cook introduces the band as 'the totally tropical taste of Merger'. C-Gas 5 perform a conventional three-minute, three-chord, post-

---

[13]   Hill, personal interview.

punk blast, but their presence challenges the common perception that punk, and post-punk, were exclusively white territories. Cross-fertilisation did take place: the Sex Pistols were reggae fans, and much of The Clash's music was reggae-influenced. Savage's assessment of The Clash's 'White Man In Hammersmith Palais' points to the uncomfortable cultural collision and ideological tension between punk and black music in 1978:

> The narrative of 'White Man In Hammersmith Palais' has Joe Strummer attending a reggae all-nighter: not only is he the only white present, but he finds that the cultural baggage he brings to the event is confounded. He has come for 'roots rock rebel', while everybody else has come for entertainment. Here is the perennial problem of the knee-jerk white approach to black culture, which holds that what is, in fact, pop and highly mediated, is 'authentic', the voice of struggle ... But, like all great pop records, the music subverts the song's lyrical message: at the time Strummer realises the limits of his well-intentioned rhetoric, the group's music is their most full, sympathetic fusion of punk and reggae to date, with its dub-like space, the slightly phased hi-hat and the plaintive, melodic-style harmonica.[14]

Revolver explored such attitudes to race and identity, and the very concept of Britishness. The pop culture of the time was far from uniform, and bands on the show were chosen to represent a particular genre of music, but there were notable exceptions, and many musicians fused 'black' and 'white' styles to create hybrid forms of music. TV critics who saw *Revolver* as a cynical marketing tool to sell insubstantial pop bands overlooked its capacity to 'freeze in aspic' the pop culture of 1978, and the social and political relevance of that culture for contemporary events, including the race riots in Notting Hill and Brick Lane.

The final episode is marked by a mood of resigned desperation that runs through its anarchic and fragmented broadcast. The opening 'act' is an unknown, middle-aged, audience member who sings an acapella version of 'I Guess It Doesn't Matter Anymore'; Cook, signalling that the audience are aware of the joke, encourages them to 'Scream! A star is born!' This self-conscious routine sets the template for the whole show: it is knowing, ironic, and the audience members are actively involved in the elaborate conceit. The (genuine) music begins with Whitesnake's performance of 'Lie Down, I Think I Love You'. The audience head bang and pogo, in a hybrid dance that lies somewhere between punk and heavy metal, and the accompanying graphics kaleidoscope into a screen heart, thus telling us that it is a 'love song'.

Hill announces that this is the last show, and introduces the Tourists who, with vocalist Annie Lennox sporting silver stars on her cheeks, perform 'You Wanna Be With Me Tonight'. Again, the camera concentrates on the audience, resplendent in their dog collars, studded jackets and bracelets. Cook's introduction of the

---

[14]   Savage, *Dreaming*, p. 488.

Rich Kids is accompanied by (apparently well-rehearsed) jeers and boos. Their performance of 'Ghosts Of Princes In Towers' is matched by a repetitive use of graphics, in which art director Geoff Pearson uses Peter Blake pop art numbers to illuminate the chorus. Part One of the programme ends with 'End Of Side One' filling the screen; after the commercial break, the Rich Kids return to perform the electro-pop 'Falling In Love/Jet Plane Age'.

Throughout the show, a large-screen image of Cook, in an imitation of George Orwell's Big Brother, looks down menacingly on the performers. When introducing the Only Ones, he remarks, 'And now living proof that there is such a thing as unintelligent life in outer space. Direct from the Crab Nebula – the Only Ones'. They perform 'Another Girl/Another Planet' to a sci-fi graphic. Vocalist Peter Perret's lyrics appear in speech bubbles and the screen is split into a comic-book grid. Hill re-appears to tell the audience that the club is to be closed down by 'the local council, the police, and the Independent Bingo Authority' (a reference to the Independent Broadcasting Authority). He invites them to start a sit-down protest, and they chant 'We Shall Not Be Moved'. Then the Show Biz Kids perform a typically energetic 'It's A Young Man's World'.

The final segment of the show belongs to Cook. In his role as the club manager, he leaves his office for the only time during the series and walks onstage, to be greeted by a torrent of sexual gestures. His response suggests a degree of pre-planning and rehearsal: 'Don't all throw your knickers at once, you load of onanists! Next week, it will be Bingo, with superb prizes.' He introduces the nine-piece, doo-wop revival band, Darts, who perform the final three songs of the series: 'Who's That Knocking On My Door?', 'Bones' and 'I Gotta Go Home'. Finally, Hill, with a member of the camera crew in view, declares, 'We can't do another one, because I don't think the machinery can stand it'.

Revolver is now a largely forgotten footnote in accounts of popular music on British television. However, it deserves to be remembered, for several different reasons: it opens a window on racial and sexual politics Britain in 1978; and it stands as an unsuccessful attempt to manipulate New Wave fashion, which failed because of the active contribution of the audience, who forced their own meanings on to the text that was provided:

> From the perspective of dominant taste, fans appear to be frighteningly out of control, undisciplined and unrepentant … Unimpressed by institutional authority and expertise, the fans assert their own right to form interpretations, to offer evaluations, and to construct cultural canons.[15]

Although the conceit is contrived, the fans' spontaneity 'poaches' any dominant cultural meanings, and re-interprets them for their own purposes: in effect, the audience hijack the show. It is rare in television that the focus is on the crowd, as much as it is on the performers. Four years later, *The Tube*'s impact largely

---

[15]   Jenkins, *Poachers*, p. 18.

rested on its spontaneity and 'unprofessionalism', but in 1978, this approach was considered too anarchic by television executives and, in general, the critical consensus was that the show was an unstructured mess, whose elaborate deceit was either overlooked or condemned as irresponsible:

> A deplorable entertainment threatened for the summer, and tried out last weekend, under the title *Revolver* (ATV) appears to be based on the proposition that it's nice to be able to appeal to your audience's likes, but safer to rely on their loathings. Peter Cook, eyes wavering on some indeterminate point ahead of him as if reading from a dodgy teleprompter, is supposed to be the manager of a dance hall reluctantly turned over to pop and rock music clientele. From an elaborately armoured eyrie, he introduces the numbers with maximum disparagement.[16]

Here, the writer touches on two of the main features of the show: it was unprofessional, and it was unpredictable. But the unpredictability came from the risks that the series was prepared to take, and the unprecedented audience involvement.

Revolver took those risks, and the gaudy, informal images of awkwardly dancing, out-of-control adolescents would resonate through the next 30 years of television pop. The programme failed to conform to the conventions of televised light entertainment in 1978; had it been created post-*The Tube*, it might have fared better. In the event, its postmodernist irony and studied amateurishness made it the right programme in the wrong place at the wrong time.

Historically, *Revolver* also deserves serious consideration because it (almost uniquely) captures the tensions and contradictions of 1970s post-punk culture. Designed with a calculated and stylised sameness – 'an enthusiastic obedience to the rhythm of the iron system'[17] – it was subverted and re-contextualised by its Birmingham audience into a meaningful discourse about their lives. Hill believes *Revolver* might have succeeded, had it captured the initial punk explosion of 1976–77, and had it been made in London with a 'hipper audience'.[18] The implication is that a provincial audience was 'not ready' for the programme whereas, in fact, the programme is that much more interesting because of its audience. John Storey has recognised that 'media professionals ... determine how the "raw" social event [is] encoded in discourse' but, when those codes of discourse are established in the public domain, 'the message is now open'.[19] The members of *Revolver*'s audience took messages and meanings that were not determined by media professionals:

---

[16]   Philip Purser, 'Revolver', *The Sunday Telegraph*, 28 May 1978, p. 13.

[17]   Theodor W. Adorno and Max Horkheimer, *Dialectic Of Enlightenment* (New York, 1944), p. 120.

[18]   Hill, personal interview.

[19]   John Storey, *Cultural Studies And The Study Of Popular Culture* (Edinburgh, 2003), p. 11.

'He/she detotalizes the message within some alternative framework of reference ... what we must call an oppositional code.'[20] Through its failure to realise the strength of these processes, *Revolver* brought about its own failure.

It is significant that post-*Revolver*, Cook (who died in 1995) made no recorded comments about the programme; in Harry Thompson's definitive biography, it warrants only one reference.[21] Cook's reluctance to refer to it and the fact that it was entirely improvised shows how lightly he took the project and how it suffered as a result, and helps to explain why, despite its ambition, it remains a relatively minor entry in the histories of comedy, popular music, and television in Britain:

> Everything he said was off the top of his head. Nothing was scripted at all ... which is a pity, really, because I'm sure if they let him script things, it would be more of a comedy thing than a music show.[22]

---

[20]   Stuart Hall, 'Encoding/Decoding' in Stuart Hall, Dorothy Hobson, Andrew Lowe and Paul Willis (eds), *Culture, Media, Language* (London, 1980), p. 138.

[21]   Harry Thompson, Peter Cook: *A Biography* (London, 1997), p. 357.

[22]   Hamilton, 'My Favourite Earache', p. 228.

Chapter 11

A Sunken Dream: Music And The Gendering Of Nostalgia In *Life On Mars*

Estella Tincknell

My name is Sam Tyler. I had an accident and I woke up in 1973. Am I mad, in a coma, or back in time? Whatever's happened, it's like I've landed on a different planet. Now, maybe if I can work out the reason, I can get back home.

Life on Mars (BBC1, 2006–2007) was an unexpected hit in 2006.[1] It offered an improbable mix of police procedural, fantasy and mystery as it cast its 'new man' police detective hero Sam Tyler (John Simm), as an uncertain time-traveller who is apparently propelled back to 1973 after a hit-and-run accident and forced to live a second life in a world that is socially and culturally alien to him. But it was precisely this generic hybridity and the deft interweaving of elements drawn from the cop show and science fiction that seemed to appeal to audiences. Narratively, *Life On Mars* is dominated by its police procedural structure, including the setting up of a crime to be solved each week as the series progresses. Structurally and discursively, however, it draws on the conventions of the period drama to stage social dilemmas, while at the level of its emotional economy it is saturated with ironic nostalgia for an apparently simpler, if sometimes technologically primitive, past. As the story proceeds, Tyler not only has to come to terms with a world in which the mobile phone is unimaginable and evidence is sent to Scotland Yard for a forensic examination that will take two weeks to be concluded, but also finds himself torn between two sets of social and ethical values which are loosely figured as 'pre' and 'post' feminist. In this way, 'tradition' is positioned against the 'modernity' supposedly represented by Tyler. This is largely articulated in terms of a struggle between competing discourses of masculinity in which Tyler is set against his 1973 boss, the hyper-masculine DCI Gene Hunt (Philip Glenister), a fantasy of omnipotent male power whose 'instinctive' approach to policing and preparedness to bend the rules (or simply ignore them) is repeatedly contrasted with Tyler's 'feminine' conscientiousness and rigorous methods. Importantly, the programme uses a range of vintage pop music tracks from the early 1970s for the

---

[1]   *Life On Mars* ran for just two series (in 2006 and 2007), won a number of awards, and was both a critical and popular success in the UK and abroad. An American version of the show was commissioned and ran for one series (2008–2009). A Spanish version was produced in 2009.

exposition of dramatic tension and as an ironic commentary on Sam's emotions. It is in the skilful balancing of these musical functions that it also speaks to the affective pull of a nostalgia that is itself problematically selective. It is this that I will explore in this chapter.[2]

Wishing Well: Tradition Versus Modernity

Claudia Gorbman has established that on film (and indeed in cinematically styled television drama) the musical score works to stitch together narrative and to provide formal unity, mainly through melodic themes and character leitmotifs.[3] Such themes generally express the affective dimensions to a text by their power to speak to the emotional and the pre-conscious. While traditionally they have been part of a score composed especially for the screen text, the additional use of a 'prefabricated score' of vintage pop music has become increasingly standard in contemporary cinema. As Robb Wright points out, 'today, the musical landscape of a feature film may contain a full score, a soundtrack of radio hits, or different combinations of source music and score, including commissioned music composed to resemble successful pop songs'.[4] Indeed, the rise of the soundtrack movie with its pre-recorded collection of tracks has been a central element in the development of globalised entertainment media since the 1980s, in which various 'platforms' (whether films, games or soundtrack CDs) work to cross-reference and cross-promote each other. There is, for example, a *Life On Mars* soundtrack CD which offers an edited selection of the vintage tracks used in the programme.

This process of cross-promotion is not a simple matter of cynical exploitation, however, since one of the cultural consequences has been the rediscovery and re-imagining both of the score as a component of textual production, and of the pre-recorded music track as an entity that is both discrete and a rich part of the warp and weft of a particular text. It is impossible, for example, to hear Dick Dale's 'Misirlou' without being vividly reminded of *Pulp Fiction* (Quentin Tarantino, 1996) but that does not mean that the song is wholly sutured to the film. Instead, the film text offers a re-articulation of 'Misirlou', even as 'Misirlou' adds new and complex layers of meaning to *Pulp Fiction*. Similarly, *Life On Mars* has quite literally recast both 'Life On Mars', the David Bowie song after which it is named,

---

[2]   *Life On Mars* ended with Tyler back in 2006 but choosing to 'remain' in 1973 by committing suicide so that he can return to his other life which now seems more real. The spin-off series, *Ashes To Ashes* followed on BBC1 in 2008; this featured a female detective, Alex Drake who apparently finds herself in 1981 after a shooting. Drake also encounters Gene Hunt and his squad, who have been re-assigned to the Metropolitan Police.

[3]   Claudia Gorbman, *Unheard Melodies: Narrative Film Music* (London/Bloomington, 1987).

[4]   Robb Wright, 'Score Vs. Song: Art, Commerce And The H Factor In Film And Television Music', in Ian Inglis (ed.), *Popular Music And Film* (London, 2003), p. 9.

and the collection of (sometimes hitherto forgotten) 1970s pop and rock songs that are woven into the programme.

Crucially, it is the use of such pre-recorded music to connote period that is such an essential part of the construction of the past, particularly the 'just remembered past' of the years between 1955 and 1985, when youth-oriented pop music assumed its cultural hegemony.[5] The 'affect' of nostalgia, its emotional and psychological 'pull', has been a powerful component of the success of the soundtrack movie.[6] Now, increasingly, television has begun to borrow those conventions for its own period dramas set in the recent past.[7] Indeed, it is television's privileging of realism as its primary dramatic discourse that invites the use of 'real' recordings to evoke a 'real' moment in the 'real' past. For the television cop show, which has a prior commitment to 'the real' in the form of social realism and the staging of conflicts around law and order, the use of music to connote the past becomes particularly interesting, given the polysemic character of music as a cultural form and the way in which the pre-recorded song may be stitched into (or pull apart from) diegetic meaning.

James Chapman points out that while *Life On Mars* draws on a more cinematic aesthetic than is traditional in British television, including fast-paced action-centred filming, it retains the social issue-driven storylines of popular realism, especially those found in the cop show.[8] The programme was deliberately modelled on the multi-layered narrative structures and high production values found in American 'quality television' such as HBO's *The Sopranos* (1999–2007) and Fox's *House* (2004–), and was produced by Kudos, the company responsible for other glossy British popular television shows such as *Spooks* (BBC1, 2002–) and *Hustle* (BBC1, 2004–). Like these shows, *Life On Mars* sought to integrate 'serious' ideas into popular forms of narrative; but unlike these shows, the programme's hybrid generic status and intriguing mix of cop show social realism and science fiction fantasy adventure helped to turn it into a television 'event', in which its highly knowing referentiality about the 1970s and about the genre were woven into a particularly successful example of the postmodern television text.

Gene Hunt's macho disdain for procedure is, then, a pastiche of the 'maverick' cop's approach, a highly referential restaging of the tropes found in 1970s police

---

[5]   The notion of the 'just remembered past' was developed by Roger Bromley in *Lost Narratives: Popular Fictions, Politics And Recent History* (London: Routledge, 1988).

[6]   I discuss different aspects of the construction of nostalgia in relation to the soundtrack film in Estella Tincknell, 'The Soundtrack Movie, Nostalgia And Consumption', in Ian Conrich and Estella Tincknell (eds), *Film's Musical Moments* (Edinburgh, 2006), pp. 132–45.

[7]   For example, *A Passionate Woman* (BBC, 2010), a mainstream two-part drama set in the 1950s and 1980s, made quite extensive use of vintage 1950s pop music to code period, setting and emotion.

[8]   James Chapman, 'Not Another Bloody Cop Show: *Life On Mars* And British Television Drama', *Film International* 7/2 (2009), pp. 6–19.

shows such as *The Sweeney* (ITV, 1975–78), but here endowed with the status of a refreshing unconventionality. Indeed, while the 'double act' between Hunt and Tyler, which is so central to the staging of competing values and meanings about masculinity that weave through the programme, is richly entertaining, it is also grounded in a binarist model of gendered identity that makes little space for complexity. Furthermore, the character of Hunt became an increasingly celebrated iconic figure within British popular culture as the series progressed, operating inter-textually and meta-textually as a signifier of an apparently authentic 'old style' male power. This intensified when he reappeared in the sequel, *Ashes To Ashes* (BBC1, 2008–10) where his male chauvinism was positioned against the critical attitudes of Alex Drake's (Keeley Hawes) overtly feminist police officer, who encounters him in her own time-slip into 1981.[9] The popularity of the character, and its 'afterlife' beyond the television texts in which he features, thus points to a tacit ambivalence about the 'post-feminist' values present in both *Life On Mars* and *Ashes To Ashes*. Thus, the over-determination of sexual inequality as part of a past that is represented as wholly alien means that inequality is no longer acknowledged as part of the present too.

The opening episode of *Life On Mars* sets up the show's recurrent thematic contrast between 1973 and 2006, 'then' and 'now,' very clearly. Episode 1 of Series 1 begins by establishing a narrative context of contemporary policing that is structured through the 'politically correct' discourses of multiculturalism and gender parity, in which Asian and female police officers work alongside their white male counterparts as colleagues not subordinates. Shortly into the story, a suspect is interviewed in a clean, modern and well-lit room, where he is accompanied by his lawyer, psychiatrist and social worker. This contemporary *mise-en-scene* is filled with hard-edged reflective surfaces: light-flooded windows, television monitors and PC screens, together with sharply angled furniture and shiny metallic desks. This is a style of policing driven by technology and by an emphasis on 'kit' and equipment, coded by the silver-blue filter through which these early scenes are shot. It is also culturally dominated by a psychological approach to crime solving, a highly regulated set of procedures, and by an elaborate consideration of human and civil rights that seem unreflective rather than truly liberating. Indeed, the post-credits opening sequence to the first episode immediately foregrounds this twenty-first-century emphasis on speed and efficiency in its focus on the high-tech

---

[9]   Two books written from the in-character perspective of Hunt have been published: *The Rules Of Modern Policing* (1973) in 2007 and *The Future Of Modern Policing* (1981) in 2008. In 2009, a third book was published by Bantam written from the in-character perspectives of Chris Skelton and Ray Carling, called *The Wit And Wisdom Of Gene Hunt*; an official website was also produced in order to market the third book. Hunt also featured in an ill-advised General Election poster for the Labour Party in April 2010, which warned voters not to go back to the days of Gene Hunt by voting Conservative. Clearly, nobody at Labour Party HQ had properly understood the significance of the over-weaning popularity of his character.

silver wheels of two unmarked police cars hurtling through urban streets and then screeching to a halt, rapidly followed by a chase through the back alleyways of inner-city Manchester.

Our hero, Sam Tyler, is introduced in action in these opening scenes: a Detective Chief Inspector in the Greater Manchester Police Force, he is an officer of impeccable integrity who can work on his feet to catch criminals, but whose underlying disenchantment with his work is also quickly established. It is this alienation that appears to render him vulnerable to the time travel, or delusions of time travel, that his coma induces. The question of whether Sam Tyler really is 'mad, in a coma, or back in time' is partially resolved by the programme's intermittent use of what seems to be the sounds of hospital equipment and the voices of medical staff on the soundtrack when Tyler slides into sleep, unconsciousness, or uncertainty. This appears to confirm that he is indeed in hospital in 2006 and that Gene Hunt and his squad are part of a complex dream induced by the accident. However, the programme cunningly keeps this question relatively open, balancing out the possibility that Tyler is imagining this version of '1973' with its close attention to an unglamorous and singularly un-dreamlike form of realist detail that suggests, conversely, that he really has travelled back in time, since the alien world he encounters is initially so distasteful to him.

The opening credit scenes and the immediate post-credits sequences of Episode 1 are accompanied by a pulsing, ruthlessly 'techno' (and therefore anti-human) styled signature tune (composed by Edmund Butts) with a strong 'hook,' in which a digitalised keyboard melody is counterpointed by electronic chords and 'seventies' style heavily reverberating guitars, alongside a powerful percussive riff. This theme tune thus incorporates elements from both contemporary dance music and the 1970s guitar-led rock that the programme later references within a single musical text, and it is used throughout the diegesis as incidental music, as well as working as a signature tune. However, this composed score, as opposed to the period selection of vintage pop that appears later, is largely employed to counterpoint the police procedural aspects of the story or to accompany the moments at which Sam questions or reflects on his situation. For example, in the tormented hours between waking and sleeping that he regularly experiences while apparently in '1973' a 'test card girl' with her clown doll steps out of the television and into Tyler's consciousness, accompanied by an eerie, keyboard leitmotif that signals her paranormal status.[10] The composed score is thus used to underpin and elaborate on Sam's sense of self as fluid, fragmented and riven. In contrast, the pre-recorded music frequently switches between being diegetically produced, perhaps emanating ambiently from a record player or radio, to playing non-diegetically on the soundtrack, sometimes spilling over between the two or between scenes, sequences and montages. As such, it destabilises the narrative boundaries between

---

[10]   The test card was a vision-standardising image used by BBC to fill the screen in the long hours between midnight and the late afternoon during which television programmes were not shown in the UK.

the exterior 'reality' of the world of the screen and the interior and psychological 'reality' of the characters, in powerful ways.

This central tension in *Life On Mars* about what constitutes the 'real' is not confined to the programme's playfulness with memory, identity and the conscious self, however. It is also a part of its textual ontology. The narrative's expositional problematisation of contemporary culture's excessive attention to procedure, regulations and a lack of what is cast as 'gut feelings' about cases, suspects, crime and, indeed, the social relations between police officers, is established early in the first episode. Here, the present-day Sam curtly dismisses his estranged lover, Maya (Archie Panjabi) from the case on which they are jointly working despite her protests, asking, 'what use are feelings in this room?' The question signals Tyler's own incipient alienation from contemporary policing, a dissatisfaction that will eventually lead him to elect to stay in what the programme represents as a more emotionally authentic historical moment, 1973.

At this point, however, it is Maya who 'follows her feelings' about a suspect whom she rashly pursues, only to be kidnapped by him. Tyler finds her bloodied shirt abandoned at a children's playground. The score at this point consists only of a series of unresolved chords played on an electronic keyboard and barely discernible on the soundtrack, their lingering reverberation a signifier of foreboding rather than of an immediately explicit meaning. However, it is this sequence of events that triggers Tyler's apparent time-slip into '1973' and the first use of the show's titular record track over a sequence of scenes that will set up the story structure and the time travel theme. Tyler's dissatisfaction with the social relations of 2006 leads him into an alternative world in which those relations are reversed.

This lengthy sequence charting his shift into '1973' is undoubtedly a televisual *tour-de-force* in which music and image work superbly together to set up the central enigma, move the narrative forward, underpin character, establish motivation, and, perhaps most importantly, identify period. It begins with Tyler driving back to Greater Manchester Police HQ when, distracted by misery (the emotionality he has suppressed and defied), he narrowly misses a collision with another car. Shocked, he stops in the middle of an urban freeway and clambers out of his car for air, only to be violently thrown to the ground by another vehicle hurtling towards him. It is at this moment that the programme shifts from the composed score to the first use of the pre-recorded title song. The opening bars of David Bowie's 'Life On Mars' are heard, initially quietly, over a close-up of Sam's tear-stained face as he drives along the urban freeway in the present day; then, once he has got out of the car and leans, shaken, on the bonnet, a rapid cut shows the title and artist indicated on the iPod he has left on the front seat.

As Sam is hit by the speeding car, the music stops abruptly, the soundtrack is silent, and the music momentarily fades out, to be replaced by an audio montage indicating Sam's unconscious state. Sirens, voices and whispers swell over a swirling dreamlike series of images of leaves and sky, and what appears to be a fluttering red dress just caught at the corner of the eye. The song re-appears, increasing further in volume to fill the soundtrack as the point of view shifts between Sam's own perspective and a tight close-up on his bewildered eyes. As he regains consciousness and stumbles to his feet, having apparently time-shifted to '1973', and stares at the bleak industrial urban wasteland that has taken the place of the 2006 freeway, the camera circles tipsily around him, and the song completely fills the soundtrack.

The music initially appears to be in some way extra-diegetic in the sense that it is both outside the world of the screen but also expressive of Sam's interior world and his confusion but, as the song diminishes in volume, it becomes clear that it is being diegetically produced: first from the iPod and then emanating from the cassette deck of a Rover P6 which Tyler has apparently just abandoned (in his other life in 1973), and towards which he now staggers, presumably in search of the music's source and an explanation of his predicament. As he silently begins both to realise and to question his arrival in this place, the song's lyrics clearly work to articulate his growing confusion – the world he sees around him is as alien as another planet.

On reaching the Rover, Sam is immediately confronted by an old-style black helmeted 'copper' who has evidently spotted him wandering around the empty wasteland and challenges him, only to spot Tyler's 1973 transfer papers on the Rover's front seat: 'Can you tell me what happened, sir?' As Sam runs in confusion across the empty, rubbish-strewn lot he is next confronted by a gigantic billboard proclaiming the imminent arrival of the very freeway he has just driven along in 2006 – Manchester's 'Highway In The Sky'.[11] Bowie's 'Life On Mars' swells up again, having rapidly shifted back to its extra-diegetic status, and there follows a montage sequence in which Tyler wanders through the artfully retro-styled streets of a drably working-class Manchester, bewildered by what he sees, as everyday life in '1973' carries on around him, and the song plays on the soundtrack in ironic commentary on his confusion. Finally, having spotted his reflection in a car wing mirror, he looks down in horror at the flared trousers, cheap leather jacket, cheesecloth shirt, chest medallion and zip-up ankle boots he is now wearing, and tentatively checks his inside pocket where a warrant card confirms that he really is Sam Tyler, but one who lives in '1973', occupies a lower rank than in 2006, and who has been transferred to Central Manchester from the Hyde branch of the Greater Manchester force. Dazed, he wanders into the Police HQ to confront his fate and the song finishes as his first verbal encounter with Hunt's squad looms.[12]

---

[11]   This was one of a series of historical anachronisms found in the programme that might seem to confirm that the '1973' scenes really are in Tyler's head. The real motorway, the Mancunian Way, was built in 1967, so already six years old by the time of Sam's time shift back to 1973. It also indicates the extent to which the programme constructs the early 1970s in terms of 'tradition' rather than 'modernity', and as a decade in which motorway travel is relatively unknown, despite the UK's first major motorway, the M1, having opened in 1959.

[12]   This building is itself a monument to the worst kind of 1970s architectural brutalism, looming darkly over the characters in 2006 and in 1973, and thus works as an ironic signifier

'Life On Mars' remains the indexical signature tune to Sam's emotional and psychological condition, its cryptically surreal yet intensely suggestive lyrics and soaring melody weaving social comment into a dreamlike series of images in a way that prefigures the television drama's own hybrid combination of British social realism and fantasy. The song re-appears in the final episode of the first series when its lyrics structure Tyler's recurrent oedipal crisis as he witnesses as an adult his own father's desertion of his mother and himself as a child. In this episode, the enigma of Tyler's father's 'true' character is revealed as Sam discovers him to be a gangland mobster rather than the small-time gambler he had remembered. In a climactic scene, the adult Sam spies on his mother and father dancing at a family wedding through a peep-hole in a pavilion wall, and then sees his father walk outside, knowing with hindsight that he is about to leave the family. At this point 'Life On Mars' builds again on the soundtrack, its bleak lyrics expressing Sam's own anguish as he attempts to intervene in his father's actions and to change history. Of course he can't do this: the desire to alter the course of future events is a familiar trope of the time travel narrative, and one that is generally deployed in order to demonstrate the inevitability of the individual's fate. And the lyrics and key changes of the song confirm this, their fatalism and surrealism offering a wry assertion of life's little tragedies and of Tyler's impotence.

'Life On Mars' is therefore used both to code Tyler's emotional alienation from the world in which he finds himself, and to structure the narrative. But it also has another indirect function. If it is indeed Tyler's leitmotif, the music that encapsulates his character, the choice of a David Bowie song whose extra-textual connotations, linked to the performer's androgynous 1970s star persona, adds further layers of meaning to what we know about Tyler, including his 'feminine' or 'new man' qualities when contrasted with the hyper-masculinity of Hunt. These 'feminine' qualities are themselves problematised by the text's valorisation of Hunt's machismo, which is repeatedly presented as both authentic *and* as a stylisation of the self, as the programme positions him in terms of a wittily intertextual self-reflexivity that itself references a different, more macho stomping Bowie song: 'I am the gene genie.'

Later in this first episode, the bombastic early seventies rock of The Who's 'Baba O'Reilly' with its guitar solos and aggressive vocal, is deployed in a key scene to powerfully underline Hunt's character and stylised masculinity, and is also used to establish Tyler's complex relationship with him as he begins his first investigation in '1973', following up a lead to a serial killer. The song begins diegetically, playing in a sound booth in a record shop that Tyler notices and remembers from his childhood, and then shifting to become a non-diegetic soundtrack commentary as Tyler confronts Hunt outside Manchester Police HQ over his approach to the case, and is physically overpowered by the older man. The music continues as Tyler and Annie Cartwright (Liz White), the young WPC who will become his

of the 'progress' heralded by the billboard. Oddly, however, it has considerably improved its lighting by 2006!

confidante and ally, discuss the case and Sam is faced with compromising his modern-day principles in order to secure a conviction. The confident assertiveness of The Who's song thus works to articulate specific meanings about Gene Hunt as a character, to move the narrative forward by implying that this confidence will lead to the killer being arrested, as well as operating to establish deftly the temporal and cultural context for the story – the 'teenage wasteland' of the killer's amoral psychological state. As we discover, the long-haired killer spends his days indoors in a drug-induced haze, leaving only to kidnap a new victim who will first be subjected to his taste in psychedelic heavy rock, before she is murdered.

The programme therefore uses two strands of music on its soundtrack: first, the selection of vintage rock and pop that will both code the period and articulate character emotion; secondly, the composed score that structures the narrative development and points to the fantastical aspects of Sam Tyler's story. The period music is within the world of 1973 even when it is non-diegetic, while the theme tune inhabits a space entirely outside the central diegesis even while it is also sometimes linked to Sam's unconscious. However, the shift between score and compilation soundtrack is by no means consistently deployed. In the first few episodes of Series 1, vintage recordings are frequently used throughout the text to establish period and to code character. For example, a wailing guitar solo from Cream's 'White Room' is heard (appropriately) on the soundtrack in the first episode as Hunt and Tyler start a door-to-door search for the serial killer who keeps his victims imprisoned in a soundproofed room, and appears again as the now arrested culprit is brought into the police station. In later episodes, they are used more sparingly, to introduce and conclude each episode in a way that comments, sometime elliptically, on the events that have just unfolded, or on Sam's frustration with his situation. Nina Simone's 'I Wish I Knew How It Would Feel To Be Free' is used in this way over the closing credits of Episode 5.

However, while the programme's early episodes depend heavily on a particular kind of white rock to structure meanings about character and narrative, this is frequently also a form of ironic commentary, since the distance between the cultural moment of the pre-recorded music in question and the implied position of the viewer invites a 'knowing' and self-reflexive reading of many of its discursive tropes. Hunt's machismo is both reinforced and undercut by the use of 'Baba O'Reilly', and his resistance to the feminine principle is frequently intimated to be a stylisation of the self produced by the anxious defence of male power, rather than an innate or essential quality. As Tyler himself knowingly comments in the final episode of Series 1, Gene Hunt is an 'overweight, over-the-hill, nicotine-stained, borderline alcoholic homophobe, with a superiority complex and an unhealthy obsession with male bonding' to which Hunt responds, equally knowingly, 'you make it sound like a bad thing'.

This process of destabilisation frequently works to undercut or to ironise the performance of masculine heroics through bathos. In the pre-credit sequence to Episode 2, there is a chase from a grimly municipal swimming pool along an equally grim urban canal towpath (as yet unprettified by the heritage regeneration of the 1980s), as the trio of Hunt, Tyler and Chris Skelton (Marshall Andrews) clad in unbecomingly snug swimming trunks and the obligatory chest medallions, puff after and then rugby tackle an escaping suspect, also sporting skimpy seventies Speedos. This sequence is accompanied by the crashing chords and urgent chorus of Wings' 'Live And Let Die', but any claim to macho posturing as the suspect is wrestled to the ground is instantly subverted by Skelton's cry of 'Get off him – he's got a verucca!'

This brief sequence is set in motion by the song's thundering main chord, but it has begun as a story 'hook' as diegetic ambient music emanating from an unseen transistor radio in Tyler's scruffy bedsit, when he wakes from an alcohol-induced sleep and stares at his reflection in a cracked shaving mirror, while getting ready for work. The scene then cuts to the swimming pool, and then to the chase as the music shifts from diegetic to non-diegetic and swells on the soundtrack, becoming increasingly louder as the chase heats up. The comic absurdity of the scene is effectively underlain by the song's own rapid shifts from bombast to pathos, and back again. Without it, the scene would be merely comic. With it, the text's meaning and its delicate balance between seriousness and humour is held together. Crucially, 'Live And Let Die' also concludes the episode, emphatically playing over the closing credits, but first heard in the background of the final scene as Sam returns to the pub where the CID squad are regulars, and decisively joins them in a card game – thus confirming his temporary commitment to his new identity. The music acts as the signifier both of Sam's tentative relationship with seventies machismo and of the serio-comic nature of his adventure. This move between a diegetic and non-diegetic relationship to the text helps to stitch the narrative flow of the scenes neatly together, while also potentially destabilising the show's critical representation of 'old style' masculinity.

Indeed, because *Life On Mars* pastiches the 1970s cop show, rather than purporting to accurately recreate 1970s policing, there are numerous opportunities for music to be used as part of this humorous meta-textuality. In addition to its self-reflexive relationship to *The Sweeney*, which is most visible in the character of Hunt (whose irascible machismo resembles John Thaw's Jack Regan in the original show, and which is implicitly coded in the fast-paced signature tune) the programme plays with other popular cultural references. The pre-credit sequence to Episode 5 connotes the US series *Starsky And Hutch* (ABC-TV, 1975–79) with a red Cortina standing in for the iconic Ford Gran Torino in a comedy chase sequence choreographed to an instrumental that is remarkably similar to the original show's theme tune.

Sweet's 'Ballroom Blitz' opens a similarly urgent pre-credit chase in Episode 3; its trashy, camp version of glam rock an ironic commentary on Tyler's position and on the emergent crisis in industrial relations that the episode references in its plot about a struggling cotton mill and its desperate workers. The series' playfulness about its period music references is frequently touching as well as amusing. 'Marc Bolan' makes a guest appearance in the 'executive suite' of a faux-glamorous nightclub in Episode 4, alongside Manchester City footballer 'Francis

Lee'. As Bowie's 'The Jean Genie' plays (in another knowing reference) on the dance floor, Sam approaches 'Bolan' excitedly, and then remembers the glam rock star's untimely death in a car crash in 1977: 'Be careful when you're driving,' he warns him, 'especially minis.'

The programme therefore lightly foregrounds period in a way that signals the knowledge of hindsight, while also often invoking nostalgia for a lost world of white working-class male solidarity, even while the oppression of sexism and racism is acknowledged. Each episode is constructed around these tensions, in which Sam's contemporary values are set against those of '1973', and between Tyler's quotidian experience of the past and the paradoxical consequences of Britain's transformation into an essentially post-industrial society.

The enormous changes wrought by urban redevelopment are signalled in Tyler's shocked recognition that his 2006 converted loft apartment is located in a building that really was once a working cotton mill employing hundreds of women and men. And in Episode 5, which centres on football rivalry, Tyler arrests a Manchester United football fan whose extremism has led him to commit murder, and delivers a brief sermon on the long term consequences of inciting football gangs to violence (the Hillsborough Stadium disaster in 1989) that only his hindsight vouchsafes. Football's shift into thuggery in the 1970s is then sentimentally contrasted with what appear to be represented as the last days of 'authentic fandom' – local football teams with a local, working-class, mainly white male fan base – marked in the closing moments of the episode, when Tyler is surrounded by a crowd of what are clearly portrayed as working-class men and boys, cheerfully making their way home on foot after the match. Here, the location of the programme in a Manchester that still has the industrial infrastructure and 'authentic' northern working-class culture destroyed by Thatcherism, together with willingly subordinated women who do not question patriarchal authority, is crucial to its specific production of what Fredric Jameson calls 'pastness'.[13] However, it is this desire for the authentic that also renders the programme's specific kind of nostalgia troubling. Having noted that the show effectively pre-empts criticism of its representation of 1970s sexism and homophobia through ironic self-reflexivity, it is useful to return to the music soundtrack and subject this to further critical interrogation.

The Boys Are Back In Town: Recuperating White Masculinity

The use of an already familiar selection of vintage songs to evoke the past is the hallmark of the nostalgia film, a genre which was itself initiated in the very year *Life On Mars* re-visits – 1973 – by the release of Francis Ford Coppola's *American Graffiti*. The strain of wistful longing for an apparently safer, more stable, but irrecoverably lost past that *American Graffiti* powerfully articulates is inflected

---

[13]   Fredric Jameson, *Postmodernism Or, The Cultural Logic Of Late Capitalism* (New York, 1991), pp. 19–20.

anew in *Life On Mars*, which relocates this stability and apparent simplicity into the 'just remembered past' of the 1970s. This is a past whose relative austerity is bolstered by the imagined community of northern working-class life, and, crucially, patriarchal power. Indeed, much of the critical acclaim for the show acknowledged these aspects as part of its appeal.

The range of vintage pre-recorded music used in the series is overwhelmingly British, white, and predominantly rock, rather than pop, or at least the 'rockier' end of pop. It includes selections from popular glam-rock bands such as T. Rex and Sweet, 'heavy' guitar-led rock groups like Deep Purple, Cream, The Who and Free, melodic rock including the music of Wings and Electric Light Orchestra, and the occasional eclectic selection such as John Kongos's 'Tokoloshe Man'. With the exception of the latter, what is missing, very noticeably – and especially so because of the series' gesture to multiculturalism in the form of the dreadlocked African-Caribbean barman, Nelson (Tony Marshall) who presides over Greater Manchester CID's favourite pub – is music composed or performed by black artists or by female artists. The only other black performer included is Nina Simone, whose status is that of a jazz artist rather than a 1970s pop star. Furthermore, there is no recognition of the emergent and almost exclusively working-class Northern Soul scene, whose iconic venue, the Wigan Casino, actually opened in 1973, and which might therefore be expected to figure in such a self-reflexively musical show.

Indeed, 'Tokoloshe Man' is featured only briefly in Episode 8 as a snatched excerpt played over a scene in which the CID squad are watching a series of seized illegal porn movies. The correlation between music produced by a black performer and the explicitly sexualised male body presumably seemed self-evident, but is clearly rendered even more problematic given the privileging of white rock to accompany the show's more conventional action sequences, in which Hunt and Tyler run, jump, leap and tear through public space and the public sphere, accompanied by the output of the kind of long-haired bands whose fan base was, and remains, primarily white, male and middle-class.

US 'teenybopper' stars such as David Cassidy and the Osmonds are, perhaps predictably, entirely absent from the soundtrack, given their association with a devalued and 'inauthentic' feminine culture, despite their dominance of the British pop charts in 1973, but so too are soul recordings by the Detroit Spinners and Hot Chocolate, both of whom had hits in that year. Strong, 'grown-up', female balladeers such as Helen Reddy and Kiki Dee, who also had chart hits in the early 1970s, are also absent. Mike Oldfield's *Tubular Bells*, the biggest selling album of 1973, and a seminal text in the history of 'prog rock' but by no means a conventional piece of guitar-led composition is, perhaps understandably, absent, but so too is reggae (Bob Marley released two albums in 1973). *Life On Mars* offers, then, a selective and very white memorialisation of British pop history in which masculine guitar rock is the privileged site of meaning.

This deployment of musical genres largely dominated by white men connotes very powerfully the programme's valorisation of masculine experience and what might be called a masculine consciousness. Because the narrative events are presented as potential figments of Tyler's unconscious, this may be defended on the grounds that the music is an extension of his imagined version of 1973, assuming that someone of Tyler's age and education has such an impressively extensive collection of early seventies rock. Yet the programme is also anxious to position him as a feminist friendly 'new man', and such a figure might therefore be expected to embrace a more divergent range of musical tastes in this imagined past, including the music of Carole King, Joni Mitchell, or even Suzi Quatro. The absence of women's voices and of more 'feminine' popular music genres such as folk, pop and soul, suggests a deeper, perhaps unconscious, desire to re-inscribe the 1970s not simply as 'pre-feminist' but as non-feminist: a period in which women are culturally silent despite the historical evidence to the contrary and the growth of the women's movement after 1970.[14]

The show's place in the schedules of British television, where it was given a prime-time 9.00 p.m. slot on BBC1, is perhaps indicative of the extent to which the revisionist version of the 1970s it offered re-articulates contemporary common-sense assumptions that gender inequality is a thing of the past, and that the acquisition of women's rights was the consequence of evolutionary gradualism rather than bitter struggle. Furthermore, the programme erases the way in which second wave feminism was initiated by women themselves in order to address such inequalities. Instead, Tyler's sensitive 'new man' persona appears to have been produced entirely independently of women's challenges to patriarchal power, just as the feminisation of the workplace in 2006 is presented as a given rather than something still being contested.

Such cultural conservatism is linked in important ways to the far from 'innocent' choice of 1973 as the year in which Sam Tyler finds himself. *Life On Mars* is part of a larger conjunctural moment of cultural nostalgia marked by comedy films such as *Austin Powers In Goldmember* (Jay Roach, 2002), *Starsky & Hutch* (Todd Phillips, 2004) and *Anchorman: The Legend Of Ron Burgundy* (Adam McKay, 2004), all of which offer a knowing take on 1970s popular culture. In these Hollywood texts, alongside the inevitable compilation score of seventies music, the kitschiest tendencies of the decade are cast as norms, and consumer brands are foregrounded as a form of instant period recognition. In each of these films, too, an apparent longing for an absurdly excessively 1970s machismo is present, even if it is 'tongue in cheek'.

Given the economic recession which dominated the decade, it is perhaps surprising that the 1970s have emerged as the preferred site for these exercises in media retro-nostalgia. Yet the period also enjoys a privileged status within the contemporary culture of the lads' magazine, as a hallowed decade whose sexism and homophobia is both exaggerated and then recast as the stolen inheritance of white masculinity. 1973 has become the somewhat improbable *annus mirabilis*

---

[14]   In contrast, in the US version of the show, Dusty Springfield is featured on the soundtrack.

of such nostalgia.[15] In these representations, '1973' is constructed almost entirely through reference to a reduced and heavily male-dominated form of popular culture: a popular culture of tabloid newspapers, *Carry On* films, 'soft' pornography, *The Sweeney* television series, and Michael Caine movies such as *Get Carter* (Mike Hodges, 1971). 1973 is thus recast as the dying moment of the ascendancy of an old-style 'cool' masculinity: a year in which the heroic dinosaurs of male chauvinism are allowed to bellow their last, before they are driven out by the feminism *Ashes To Ashes* presents as an already established norm of modernity.

Except of course, it wasn't. They didn't. And *Life On Mars* struggles to reconcile an apparently conscious intention to problematise the past with its unconscious desire *for* the past. For example, the 'authentic' *mise-en-scene* of the 1970s offices of the Greater Manchester Police HQ is marked by the iconography of the supine naked female pin-up, an iconography that contrasts graphically with the heroically active male bodies of both Tyler and Hunt. Indeed, while *Life On Mars* in some ways reverses the conventions of televisual heritage spectacle found in the classic serial, or the 'lavish' costume drama, in its emphasis on the drab and the grimy, this focus is also symptomatic of the specific form its nostalgia takes, and its relish in representing 1970s urban working-class life as discursively structured by a brutalised sexism on the one hand and by a comfortably dowdy banality on the other. The programme revels in the downmarket and 'masculine' pleasures of canteen food, mocking Sam's twenty-first century and feminised taste for 'healthy' foreign foods such as olive oil, wine and coriander, while also celebrating Hunt's apparently authentic preference for saturated fats and masculine comfort: a pint, chips cooked in dripping, and beans on toast.

But this is quite as much a *fantasy* of 1973 as the lads' magazine version with its ante-bellum utopia of masculine plenitude. Not only is Gene Hunt a spectacle of hyper-masculinity but, in addition, he is a constellation of the retro-fixated desire for the 'hard man' who is also 'cool' rather than a convincing representation of 1970s policing. His mod-style feathered haircut would be unlikely to be found on the head of a hardened middle-aged copper who would have already been 30 when the teenage subculture first emerged, while his sexism is closer to the contemporary graphic banter of *Loaded* than it is to the casual sexism mixed with back-handed chivalry of the 'real' 1973.[16] Perhaps none of this matters. And yet *Life On Mars* is so pleasurably seductive in its nostalgic evocation of a 'safer' past, I think it does.

---

[15]   *Cemetery Junction* (Ricky Gervais and Stephen Merchant, 2010) is also set in 1973 and deploys a mix of vintage pop on its soundtrack.

[16]   And it is interesting to note that while the script revels in Hunt's colourful linguistic euphemisms and charged disgust for homosexuality and femininity, it rarely ascribes racist attitudes to Hunt – these are loaded onto the secondary characters such as Ray Carling (Dean Andrews).

Conclusion

By polarising 'then' and 'now' through an exaggerated contrast between enlightenment and prejudice, the programme is able to reproduce the very conventions of the cop show that it ostensibly critiques. The main female character, Annie Cartwright, is represented in highly conventionalised 'feminine' terms as supportive, sympathetic, emotionally intelligent and morally responsible, but never as the instigator of action or of events. In other words, she occupies the traditional narrative position of women in the cop show rather than working to overturn the conventions which Tyler's *post-hoc* knowledge should question. This is legitimated by the 'period logic' of the programme, and its exaggerated discursive structure of 'tradition' versus 'modernity'. It is only Tyler's arrival which enables her to recognise and resist her oppression, rather than a feminist coming to consciousness. Other female characters are also presented through the filter of retro-sexism. The only other significant woman in the 1973 squad, Desk Sergeant Phyllis Dobbs (Noreen Kershaw) is a stereotypical battle-axe, and any remaining women appear as mothers, wives, girlfriends and potential girlfriends, their agency limited to supporting (or not) the actions of male protagonists. Even in 'post-feminist' 2006, where active female agency might be expected to figure more visibly, Maya's attempt to intervene in the case she and Tyler are investigating is represented as reckless and foolhardy: she ends up as another victim, initially apparently returned to the conventionalised function (a dead body) of female characters in the police procedural. In all of this, the soundtrack's privileging of masculine voices, musical forms and idioms, works to recuperate any genuinely radical potential the show may promise. Indeed, Sam's desire to return to '1973' confirms this. The affective power of music may therefore occasionally destabilise narrative structure and meaning, but it also disrupts the progressive intentionality of British televisual social realism. *Life On Mars* offers a dream of '1973' in which the modernity represented by feminism is ultimately rejected in favour of a fantasy of stability and hyper-masculine power.

PART IV
Audiences And Territories

Chapter 12

Here, There And Everywhere: Introducing The Beatles

Ian Inglis

The velocity of the Beatles' sudden and spectacular impact in the UK through 1963 was, and is, without precedent in popular music's history. After several years of performing to small, local audiences in the clubs of Merseyside and Hamburg, they had released their first single, 'Love Me Do', in October 1962. It was a minor hit[1] and the group began the new year still relatively unknown, playing out a final engagement at The Star Club in Hamburg, before returning home to Liverpool. By the end of the year, they had, in addition to selling millions of singles and albums, completed four nationwide tours, hosted their own 15-part weekly radio series *Pop Go The Beatles*, approved the monthly publication of *The Beatles Book*, been named as the Variety Club's Show Business Personalities of the Year, given their name to a new form of mass hysteria, contracted to make their US debut on CBS-TV's *The Ed Sullivan Show*, performed to more than 100,000 fans over 16 sell-out nights at London's Astoria Theatre in *The Beatles Christmas Show*, negotiated a three-picture contract with United Artists, and established their own music publishing company, Northern Songs.

It was, by any standards, a tale of dramatic and overwhelming proportions. Contemporary and subsequent explanations for the group's phenomenal achievements have ranged across the managerial strategy of Brian Epstein, the studio skills of George Martin, the songwriting abilities of Lennon-McCartney, the sorry state of popular music at the time, the growth of the teenage market, the complex attractions of 'the Mersey sound', a breakdown in parental and adult authority, and the commercial novelty of a group structure that presented the public with four points of contact in contrast to the singular attraction of the solo singer.

In addition, several accounts have referred to the importance of a small number of television appearances in promoting and consolidating the public identification of the group.[2] All were broadcast towards the end of 1963, at a time when the

---

[1]   'Love Me Do'/'P.S. I Love You' reached Number 17 in the *New Musical Express* singles charts in December 1962.

[2]   Similar claims have been made about the critical importance in the US of the Beatles' first national appearance on CBS-TV's *The Ed Sullivan Show* in February 1964. See Laurel Sercombe, 'Ladies And Gentlemen … The Beatles', in Ian Inglis (ed.), *Performance And Popular Music: History, Place And Time* (Aldershot, 2006), pp. 1–15.

Beatles were poised to repeat their British success on a global scale. Bookended by two historic national television events (the coronation of Queen Elizabeth II in June 1953, and England's victory over Germany in the World Cup Final in July 1966) TV ownership grew from 2.1 million to 13.6 million households in the same period, as television-viewing quickly eclipsed radio-listening and cinema-going as the country's leading leisure-related media activity. Two channels – BBC and ITV (which comprised 13 regional companies) – enjoyed a duopoly of terrestrial broadcasting which, until 1968, was exclusively monochrome.

Yet despite the growth of TV ownership and the impact of rock'n'roll (and, to a lesser extent, skiffle) in the 1950s, the attention given to popular music – by both channels – was, for the most part, intermittent and desultory. Several series had attempted, with varying degrees of success, to reproduce the format of such US shows as ABC-TV's long-running *American Bandstand*. On BBC, these included *Off The Record* (1955–56), *Six-Five Special* (1957–58), *Dig This!* (1959) and *Drumbeat* (1959); ITV had countered with *Cool For Cats* (1956–61), *Oh Boy!* (1958–59), *Boy Meets Girls* (1959–60) and *Wham!* (1960). However, with the exception of the once-weekly, 15-minute *Cool For Cats*, all were abandoned after relatively short runs. By the early 1960s, popular music's place on television in the UK was restricted to two weekly programmes: BBC's *Juke Box Jury* (1959–67) and ITV's *Thank Your Lucky Stars* (1961–66). Both were transmitted in the busy Saturday teatime/early evening schedules, when competition to attract and retain an audience was at its fiercest. *Juke Box Jury* was sandwiched between *Doctor Who*, *The Telegoons* and *Dixon Of Dock Green*; *Thank Your Lucky Stars* was typically surrounded by such popular series as *Cheyenne*, *Holiday Town Parade* and *The Arthur Haynes Show*. The only other occasions on which performers might be seen lay within the limited opportunities offered by children's television, variety shows and news-magazine programmes. It was against this unpromising background that the television career of the Beatles began, and that the historical celebration of the significance of three specific appearances has continued unchallenged.

In chronological sequence, the first of these was the group's debut on ITV's *Sunday Night At The London Palladium* on 13 October 1963. From 1955 to 1967, the programme was transmitted across the country every Sunday night during prime-time viewing hours. The one-hour show – televised live from the theatre affectionately known as 'the home of the stars' in London's West End, and famously concluding with all the performers gathered together on a revolving stage – was regarded as the single most important platform in British popular entertainment, and regularly featured international musicians, dancers and comedians of the calibre of Danny Kaye, Jack Benny, Judy Garland, Maurice Chevalier, Rudolf Nureyev and Bob Hope.[3] Years later, Ringo Starr readily admitted the group's enthusiasm: 'Going on the Palladium was amazing. I always wanted to play there,

---

[3]   See, for example, Patrick Pilton, *Every Night At The London Palladium* (London, 1976); Christopher Woodward, *The London Palladium: The Story Of The Theatre And Its Stars* (Huddersfield, 2009).

to get on that roundabout stage. There was nothing bigger in the world ... and we played *Sunday Night At The London Palladium*, and we were on the roundabout and it was *dynamite*.'[4] Topping the bill (above US singer Brook Benton and British comedian Des O'Connor), the group appeared briefly, and unexpectedly, on stage at the start of the show, returning 45 minutes later to perform 'From Me To You', 'I'll Get You', 'She Loves You' and 'Twist And Shout' to an estimated television audience of more than 15 million viewers. Throughout the day, the theatre had been surrounded by thousands of fans, which had necessitated a strong police presence, and stimulated extensive TV trailers and news updates before and after the event. Many assessments of the aftermath of the show emphasised the significance of the immediate shift in the nature of media coverage:

> The Beatles stopped being simply an interesting pop music story and became hard news...the front page of every newspaper next day had long news stories and large pictures of the hysterical crowd scenes. The stories weren't about how well or how badly the group had played their songs, but simply about the chaos they had caused.[5]

> Whatever actually happened that night, the Beatles were irrefutably front-page headlines the next day for the first of countless times. Now even the man-on-the-street who didn't listen to rock'n'roll was beginning to hear about something called, improbably, unforgettably, 'the Beatles'.[6]

In the week following their Palladium appearance, it was announced that the group had been invited to take part in the forthcoming *Royal Variety Performance*. Although it would become greatly devalued in subsequent decades, the annual fundraising event for the Entertainment Artistes Benevolent Fund – traditionally attended by members of the royal family – was, through the 1950s and 1960s, the most prestigious occasion of the British popular entertainment calendar. After receiving and accepting the invitation, manager Brian Epstein commented: 'I felt it was inevitable that the show business sensation of 1963 should be represented in this show.'[7] The three-hour show took place at London's Prince Of Wales Theatre on Monday 4 November, and was televised in its entirety by ITV the following weekend on Sunday 10 November, to a national audience of 26 million. The Beatles' participation promptly enhanced their personal status in two ways. First, their presence on a bill that included such familiar domestic and foreign stars as Max Bygraves, Charlie Drake, Dickie Henderson, Wilfred Brambell and Harry H. Corbett (Steptoe & Son), Tommy Steele, Harry Secombe, Nadia Nerina, Buddy

[4]   The Beatles, *Anthology* (London, 2000), p. 102.

[5]   Hunter Davies, *The Beatles: The Authorised Biography* (London, 1968), pp. 195–6.

[6]   Peter Brown and Steven Gaines, *The Love You Make: An Insider's Story Of The Beatles* (London, 1983), p. 93.

[7]   Brian Epstein, *A Cellarful Of Noise* (London, 1964), p. 73.

Greco and Marlene Dietrich (with Burt Bacharach) confirmed their dual role of rock'n'roll performers *and* family entertainers. Secondly, the images of Lennon, McCartney, Harrison and Starr chatting informally with the Queen Mother and Princess Margaret after the show gave them a royal seal of approval which effectively undermined many of the negative comments that had been occasionally directed at the group's appearance and music earlier in the year.

Seeking to capture the same positive response to their appearance at the London Palladium, the Beatles presented a near-identical set: 'From Me To You', 'She Loves You', 'Till There Was You' and 'Twist And Shout'. However, the lasting impression of the group's performance, in the televised broadcast and in the press coverage, was the universal delight at Lennon's appeal to the audience: 'For our last number, I'd like to ask your help. Will the people in the cheaper seats clap your hands? The rest of you, if you'll just rattle your jewellery ...'[8] The ecstatic responses in the national daily press and the music press were remarkably similar in tone and content. The editorial comment in the following day's *Daily Mirror* declared:

YEAH! YEAH! YEAH!

You have to be a real sour square not to love the nutty, noisy, happy, handsome Beatles. If they don't sweep your blues away – brother, you're a lost cause. If they don't put a beat in your feet – sister, you're not living. How refreshing to see these rumbustious young Beatles take a middle-aged Royal Variety Performance by the scruff of their necks and have them Beatling like teenagers. Fact is that Beatle People are everywhere. From Wapping to Windsor. Aged seven to seventy. And it's plain to see why...[9]

The review in the *New Musical Express* began:

The Beatles made Royal Variety history for me on Monday at the Prince Of Wales Theatre, London. Teenagers' idols stopped the show for the first time on any of these gala occasions. The storming applause following the Beatles' act was punctuated with cries of 'More!' from a bejewelled and evening-suited adult audience. Right from the start, Princess Margaret had led the applause, and soon the Queen Mother and Lord Snowdon were joining in![10]

---

[8]   Although it is often cited as a spontaneous ad-lib, Lennon had rehearsed and refined the remark in the hours leading up to the show. See, for example, Ray Coleman, *John Lennon* (London, 1984), p. 175; Alistair Taylor, *A Secret History* (London, 2001), p. 89.

[9]   *Daily Mirror*, 5 November 1963, p. 5.

[10]   Andy Gray, 'Beatles Stop The Royal Variety Show', *New Musical Express*, 8 November 1963, p. 10.

Since its introduction in 1959, the rigid structure and formal presentation of *Juke Box Jury* had made it one of the most popular and durable TV programmes – of any kind – in the UK. Under the chairmanship of disc-jockey David Jacobs,[11] and watched by a small studio audience, a panel of four assorted celebrities would listen to and comment on each week's selection of new single releases before delivering its verdict: Hit or Miss. The programme lacked any live music, but was a key promotional vehicle through which to reach a regular audience of around 12 million. Earlier in 1963, Lennon had been one of the four panellists (alongside child actor Bruce Prochnik, TV presenter Katie Boyle, and the Chancellor of the Exchequer's daughter Caroline Maudling) in the edition broadcast on 29 June; Brian Epstein had been a panellist on 26 October. Both programmes were recorded, as normal, at BBC's Television Theatre in London.

However, on 7 December, the programme uniquely featured all four Beatles as the panellists. In order to accommodate the group's other commitments, including a half-hour concert to be televised the same night, it was recorded in the afternoon at Liverpool's Empire Theatre in front of 2,500 fan club members from the North of England. When it was broadcast later in the day, it attracted a TV audience of 23 million, who watched the Beatles give their opinions on ten new records.[12] Few of the group's comments were controversial, as the following extracts demonstrate:

The Chants 'I Could Write A Book'
Lennon: It's gear. Fabulous. Fab. It's it.
McCartney: I talked to the Chants recently about the disc. They said it's powerful. It is.
Starr: I'll buy it.
Harrison: It's great. Enough plugs and they've got a hit.

Elvis Presley 'Kiss Me Quick'
McCartney: What I don't like about Elvis are his songs. I like his voice. This song reminds me of Blackpool on a sunny day.
Starr: Last two years, Elvis has been going down the nick.
Harrison: If he's going back to old tracks, why not release 'My Baby Left Me'? It'd be a Number One.
Lennon: It'll be a hit. I like those hats with 'Kiss Me Quick' on.

---

[11]   In addition to being one of the UK's leading radio and TV presenters, Jacobs was held in high regard by Brian Epstein, who described him as 'very shrewd, full of visual charm, poise and television-warmth. He is an immaculate D.J. and a very nice man. He is also the best-looking disc-jockey'. See Epstein, *Cellarful*, p. 98.
[12]   The programme has gained something of a mythical status, since the BBC has lost or erased all known tapes. Periodic appeals to the public have unearthed reel-to-reel sound recordings, but (to date) no complete visual recordings have been discovered.

The Swinging Blue Jeans 'Hippy Hippy Shake'
Starr: Good, but not as good as the original by Chan Romero.
Harrison: It's a popular song around Liverpool. We used to do it. Could be a hit.
Lennon: The boys nearly made it before. I like Bill Harry's version as well.
McCartney: Doesn't matter about Chan Romero's disc. Nobody remembers. It's
    as good as a new song.

In fact, much of what they said was drowned by the constant screaming of the theatre audience,[13] and the focus of the debate that followed the transmission was about the BBC's wisdom in tampering with the established structure and location of a highly-regarded programme, and the success or failure of the experiment:

> There was considerable consternation about this within the higher echelons of the corporation, executives feeling that the coup it had achieved in presenting the Beatles so exclusively to the nation had somewhat rebounded against them in that the technical shortcomings were obvious and embarrassing.[14]

In all three cases – *Sunday Night At The London Palladium*, *The Royal Variety Performance* and *Juke Box Jury* – television coverage (and other media's reporting of the occasions) was not confined exclusively, or even mainly, to the event itself, but to the surrounding context, the preparations, and the repercussions of what took place.[15] Furthermore, that coverage blurred the boundaries between news and entertainment, so that for tens of millions of viewers, the idiosyncrasies of the Beatles, the quality of their music, and the issues and analyses that their appearances triggered were subsumed under the new, popular and emerging category of 'Beatlemania'. A consensual view quickly developed which unequivocally, and persistently, identified the centrality of these three programmes in helping to determine the Beatles' destiny. Brian Epstein saw them as a sign that the group had successfully broken traditional barriers of age and social class in their audience appeal;[16] the Beatles themselves acknowledged the acceleration in

---

[13]   The programme was described in one review as 'the noisiest, screamingest ever screened'. Alan Smith, 'Backstage With The Beatles', *New Musical Express*, 13 December 1963, p. 3.

[14]   Mark Lewisohn, *The Complete Beatles Chronicle* (London, 1992), p. 133.

[15]   This expansion of TV interest beyond the performance itself has parallels in the coverage of sport: the 'game event' (the action on the field), the 'stadium event' (the complete sequence of events occurring in the stadium) and the 'medium event' (the total telecast) have developed as simultaneous and overlapping dimensions of television presentation. See Brien R. Williams, 'The Structure Of Televised Football', *Journal Of Communication* 27/3 (1977): pp. 133–9.

[16]   Ray Coleman, *Brian Epstein: The Man Who Made The Beatles* (London, 1989), p. 221.

their career that followed each appearance;[17] contemporary Beatles biographers continue to endorse the same beliefs.[18]

However, while there is little doubt that this trio of shows were of enormous significance in presenting the Beatles to British viewers, they provide only a partial insight into the relationship between the group, television, and their respective audiences that was developing at the time. In their inventory of the Beatles' collective and individual TV engagements in the 1960s, Bench and Tedman warn that 'it is easy to overplay particular events in a group's history'.[19] Having enjoyed three consecutive Number One singles ('Please Please Me', 'From Me To You' and 'She Loves You') in the first eight months of the year, the group was hardly unknown at the time of its Palladium appearance, and had gathered extensive experience of television, both regional and national. In fact, their TV debut had been in October 1962. These earlier programmes have often been overlooked, or dismissed as relatively unimportant, but they played a crucial part in shaping public knowledge of, and affection for, the Beatles. As Table 12.1 indicates below, television's role in introducing the Beatles to British viewers began more than a year before the nationwide excitement of *Sunday Night At The London Palladium*.

Table 12.1   The Beatles' UK Television Appearances 1962–63

Date	Programme	TV Station	Songs Performed
17/10/62	*People And Places*	Granada	'Some Other Guy' 'Love Me Do'
02/11/62	*People And Places*	Granada	'Love Me Do' 'A Taste Of Honey'
03/12/62	*Discs A Gogo*	TWW	'Love Me Do'
04/12/62	*Tuesday Rendezvous*	Associated Rediffusion	'Love Me Do' 'P.S. I Love You'
17/12/62	*People And Places*	Granada	'Love Me Do' 'Twist And Shout'
08/01/63	*Roundup*	Scottish Television	'Please Please Me'
16/01/63	*People And Places*	Granada	'Ask Me Why' 'Please Please Me'

(continued)

---

[17]   Beatles, *Anthology*, pp. 102–5.

[18]   See, for example, Philip Norman, *Shout! The True Story Of The Beatles* (London, 1981), pp. 190–92; Tony Barrow, *John, Paul, George, Ringo & Me* (London, 2005), pp. 100–101; Bob Spitz, *The Beatles* (New York, 2006), pp. 426–34; Jonathan Gould, *Can't Buy Me Love: The Beatles, Britain, And America* (New York, 2007), pp. 168–9.

[19]   Jeff Bench and Ray Tedman, *The Beatles On Television* (London, 2008), p. 14.

Date	Programme	TV Station	Songs Performed
19/01/63	*Thank Your Lucky Stars*	ITV	'Please Please Me'
23/02/63	*Thank Your Lucky Stars*	ITV	'Please Please Me'
02/03/63	*ABC At Large*	ABC Television	'Please Please Me' *plus* group interview
09/04/63	*Tuesday Rendezvous*	Associated Rediffusion	'From Me To You' 'Please Please Me'
16/04/63	*The 625 Show*	BBC	'From Me To You' 'Thank You Girl' 'Please Please Me'
16/04/63	*Scene At 6.30*	Granada	'From Me To You'
20/04/63	*Thank Your Lucky Stars*	ITV	'From Me To You'
16/05/63	*Pops And Lenny*	BBC	'From Me To You' 'Please Please Me'
18/05/63	*Thank Your Lucky Stars*	ITV	'From Me To You' 'I Saw Her Standing There'
29/06/63	*Thank Your Lucky Stars*	ITV	'From Me To You' 'I Saw Her Standing There'
14/08/63	*Scene At 6.30*	Granada	'Twist And Shout'
19/08/63	*Scene At 6.30*	Granada	'She Loves You'
22/08/63	*Day By Day*	Southern TV	'She Loves You'
24/08/63	*Thank Your Lucky Stars*	ITV	'She Loves You' 'I'll Get You'
07/09/63	*Big Night Out*	ITV	'From Me To You' 'She Loves You' 'Twist And Shout'
04/10/63	*Ready Steady Go!*	ITV	'Twist And Shout' 'I'll Get You' 'She Loves You'
09/10/63	*The Mersey Sound*	BBC	'Twist and Shout' 'She Loves You' 'Love Me Do' *plus* documentary footage and interviews
13/10/63	*Sunday Night At The London Palladium*	ITV	'From Me To You' 'I'll Get You' 'She Loves You' 'Twist And Shout'
18/10/63	*Scene At 6.30*	Granada	'She Loves You'

Date	Programme	TV Station	Songs Performed
26/10/63	*Thank Your Lucky Stars*	ITV	'All My Loving' 'Money' 'She Loves You'
07/11/63	*This Week*	ITV	Documentary footage and interviews
08/11/63	*Six Ten*	BBC (Northern Ireland)	Group interview
08/11/63	*Ulster News*	Ulster Television	Group interview
10/11/63	*Royal Variety Performance*	ITV	'From Me To You' 'She Loves You' 'Till There Was You' 'Twist And Shout'
12/11/63	*Day By Day*	Southern TV	Group interview
12/11/63	*South Today*	BBC (South)	Group interview
16/11/63	*Move Over, Dad*	Westward Television	Group interview
26/11/63	*East At Six-Ten*	BBC (East)	Group interview
27/11/63	*Late Scene Extra*	Granada	'I Want To Hold Your Hand'
07/12/63	*Juke Box Jury*	BBC	Panel discussion
07/12/63	*It's The Beatles*	BBC	'From Me To You' 'I Saw Her Standing There' 'All My Loving' 'Roll Over Beethoven' 'Boys' 'Till There Was You' 'She Loves You' 'This Boy' 'I Want To Hold Your Hand' 'Money' 'Twist And Shout'
20/12/36	*Scene At 6.30*	Granada	'This Boy'
21/12/63	*Thank Your Lucky Stars*	ITV	'I Want To Hold Your Hand' 'All My Loving' 'Twist And Shout' 'She Loves You'

The table does not include unused footage,[20] repeats,[21] contributions to foreign television,[22] movie newsreel features[23] and incidental TV news coverage. Nevertheless, it is clear that the Beatles enjoyed considerable television exposure throughout the whole of 1963 which, alongside their prolific radio output,[24] effectively alerted local and national audiences to the group and its music.

Even within the space of the 15 months covered by the table, the beginnings of a distinct shift in the nature of the group's appearances are apparent. The extent to which the Beatles' earliest TV bookings were exclusively linked to each new single release was initially demonstrated by the repetitive nature of their performances: in November–December 1962, the first five programmes on which they appeared all featured versions (either live or mimed) of 'Love Me Do'; in the first six months of 1963, 'Please Please Me' and 'From Me To You' were each performed on seven consecutive television appearances; 'She Loves You' was included in nine consecutive programmes between August and October. This lack of variation and the relative absence of any album tracks from the group's TV performances were not surprising. Given the entertainment industry's emphasis on singles sales as a measure of success, television's preference for short, topical contributions from its performers, and Epstein's absolute conviction that 'the way to stardom lay in the charts',[25] the broadcasting template that had evolved on British television was accepted without question as the only legitimate way in which to present pop music. However, towards the end of this period, there was a clear change of emphasis. Of their nine television appearances in November 1963, seven were non-musical, reflecting the changed status of the Beatles themselves as a serious news item worthy of discussion and analysis.

Of course, the broadcasting landscape in the early 1960s was vastly different from that which has evolved in subsequent decades. In addition to the two television channels, there were three national radio networks, all of which were provided

---

[20]   In August 1962, the Beatles were filmed at The Cavern for inclusion in Granada's lunchtime magazine programme, *Know The North*. However, doubts about the quality of the film led to its exclusion from the show. A brief extract of the group's performance of 'Some Other Guy' was included in *Scene At 6.30* in November 1963.

[21]   Segments of the *Ready Steady Go!* edition of 4 October were repeated in the editions broadcast on 8 November and 31 December.

[22]   During its short tour of Sweden in October, the group performed four songs – 'She Loves You', 'Twist And Shout', 'I Saw Her Standing There' and 'Long Tall Sally' – for Sveriges Television's *Drop In* show, broadcast on 3 November; and in Ireland, the Beatles were interviewed on RTE's nightly *In Town* programme on 7 November.

[23]   *The Beatles Come To Town*, filmed by Pathe News on 20 November, was shown in British cinemas in the week beginning 22 December.

[24]   From *Teenagers Turn: Here We Go* (8 March 1962) to *The Beatles Say From Us To You* (26 December 1963), the Beatles made 44 national radio appearances. See Kevin Howlett, *The Beatles At The BBC: The Radio Years 1962–70* (London, 1996).

[25]   Epstein, *Cellarful*, p. 56.

by the BBC: the Light Programme (popular entertainment), the Home Service (news, current affairs and drama) and the Third Programme (classical music).[26] This paucity of choice – the only other option was the European-based Radio Luxembourg[27] – meant that the audiences for radio and television programmes, of all kinds, in Britain were enormous. Ironically, the peripheral role and restricted time allocated to popular music by ITV and BBC meant that those first cohorts of 'baby-boomers' born in the late 1940s, who were familiar with the sounds of rock'n'roll through the jukebox, the cinema, the package tour, and occasional radio airplay, were desperately keen to seek out any examples of its inclusion on television. Thus, the TV appearances of the Beatles were watched by two distinct sets of viewers: a general, passive audience for whom there were no alternatives, and a specific, active and highly-motivated audience of younger pop music fans.[28] And this applied equally to programmes targeted at children (*Tuesday Rendezvous*, *Pops And Lenny*), teenagers (*Thank Your Lucky Stars*, *Ready Steady Go!*) and family audiences (*Big Night Out*, *Sunday Night At The London Palladium*); to performance-based shows (*Discs A Gogo*, *The 625 Show*), news-magazine programmes (*People And Places*, *Scene At 6.30*) and documentaries (*The Mersey Sound*, *This Week*); and to regional and national transmissions (eight of the group's first ten television appearances were local broadcasts).

The significance of television as a vehicle for presenting images of, and information about, popular music has been repeatedly articulated:

> Television has had a direct effect on the musical experience of vast numbers of people – teenagers and children in particular who are more likely to be moved by seeing musical performances on television than through attending a concert or club ... it has also been significant in addressing their parents within the context of the domestic family environment in which most television reception is still embedded.[29]

Yet despite this recognition, there has been relatively little systematic analysis of the mutual benefits that popular music and TV brought to each other in the late 1950s and early 1960s (a crucial period in the development of both mediums) nor of the synergistic outcomes that characterised that association. This has remained

---

[26] Pirate radio stations began to broadcast in 1964; the first BBC local radio stations appeared in 1967; commercial radio was introduced in 1973.

[27] Radio Luxembourg had begun evening transmissions across the continent in the 1930s. It began to concentrate on popular music in 1960, but its reception was notoriously unreliable in the UK.

[28] The significance of the potential economic and commercial power of the adolescent market had first been identified in the late 1950s. See Mark Abrams, *The Teenage Consumer: LPE Paper No 5* (London, 1959).

[29] Keith Negus and John Street, 'Introduction To Music And Television', *Popular Music* 21/3 (2002): pp. 245–6.

true, even when the likely consequences of prolonged exposure to the glamorous alternatives that the small screen introduced have been noted. Bradley's assertion that 'TV came to occupy an unprecedentedly large place in the lives of children and young adults ... the whole world was represented in the living room, and a vast new range of stars and fictional characters became available as objects of identification and desire'[30] remains undeveloped in his discussion of popular music in Britain between 1955–64. Chambers's investigation of pop music's place in postwar popular culture barely mentions the importance of television.[31] Donnelly's study of music in film and television concentrates on its provision of stock, background and incidental sounds, rather than its performative elements.[32] Frith's assessment of the contribution made by television since the 1950s to the organisation and operation of popular music (particularly in its star-making potential) ends with the conclusion that 'TV, for all its influence on rock performance, was never really part of its culture'.[33] This general reluctance to acknowledge TV's fundamental role within the popular music experience has created a 'critical lacuna'[34] in the scholarly study of popular music on television. More specifically, it has discouraged an appreciation of its significance for the Beatles, other than a persistent, but largely untested, claim that these three programmes were momentous occasions in their career.

Despite the euphoric reception and attribution of celebrity status to the group that followed *Sunday Night At The London Palladium*, *The Royal Variety Performance* and *Juke Box Jury*, they were not moments of transition, but moments of completion, in the story of the Beatles. They confirmed, rather than introduced, the Beatles as national figures whose presence had become increasingly acceptable through 1962 and 1963 across a range of television schedules, and who were already widely known. Tony Barrow's sleevenotes for *Please Please Me*, released in March 1963, provide an apt illustration:

> It was during the recording of a Radio Luxembourg programme in the *EMI Friday Spectacular* series that I was finally convinced that the Beatles were about to enjoy the type of top-flight national fame which I had always believed that they deserved. The teen audience didn't know the evening's line-up of artists and groups in advance, and before [presenter] Muriel Young brought on the Beatles, she began to read out their Christian names. She got as far as 'John ... Paul ...'

[30]   Dick Bradley, *Understanding Rock'n'Roll: Popular Music In Britain 1955–1964* (Buckingham, 1992), pp. 96–7.

[31]   Iain Chambers, *Urban Rhythms: Pop Music And Popular Culture* (London, 1985).

[32]   K.J. Donnelly, *The Spectre Of Sound: Music In Film And Television* (London, 2005).

[33]   Simon Frith, 'Look! Hear! The Uneasy Relationship Of Music And Television', *Popular Music* 21/3 (2002): p. 288.

[34]   Norma Coates, 'Filling In Holes: Television Music As A Recuperation Of Popular Music On Television', *Music, Sound And The Moving Image* 1/1 (2007): p. 21.

and the rest of her introduction was buried in a mighty barrage of very genuine applause. I cannot think of more than one other group – British or American – which would be so readily identified and welcomed by the announcement of two Christian names.[35]

The contribution he describes was recorded in front of an audience of around one hundred youngsters at EMI House in London, on 21 January 1963, less than two weeks after the release of 'Please Please Me'.[36] Although the Beatles had by then made just a handful of regional TV appearances (mostly on Granada, the ITV company whose reception area includes Liverpool) and one national appearance (on *Thank Your Lucky Stars*) it was already evident that Epstein's reluctance to turn down any potential booking – a strategy which 'was not planned to capitalize financially, but to gain recognition, exposure and credibility'[37] – was beginning to be successful. The following extracts from the Beatles' engagement diary reveal the demands routinely made of them during this formative period in their career:

16 January 1963
3.00–4.00. Granada TV Centre, Manchester. Rehearsal, Granada TV's *People And Places.*
4.30–5.30. Playhouse Theatre, Manchester. Rehearsal, BBC Light Programme's *Here We Go.*
6.35–7.00. Granada TV Centre. Live television transmission, *People And Places.*
8.45–9.30. Playhouse Theatre. Recording (*Here We Go*, broadcast on 25 January).

2 March 1963
6.15–10.15. City Hall, Sheffield. Two separate shows on nationwide package tour with Helen Shapiro.
11.00–11.50. Didsbury Studio Centre, Manchester. Live television transmission, ABC TV's *ABC At Large.*

9 April 1963
12.30–1.45. Paris Studio, London. Rehearsal and live radio broadcast, BBC Light Programme's *Pop In.*
2.00–6.00. Wembley Studio, London. Rehearsal and live television transmission, Associated-Rediffusion's *Tuesday Rendezvous.*
8.00–10.30. Gaumont Cinema, Kilburn, London. Live concert appearance.

---

[35] Tony Barrow (1963), *Please Please Me* (Parlophone PMC 1202).
[36] Lewisohn, *Chronicle*, p. 97.
[37] Coleman, *Epstein*, p. 153.

However, despite their exhausting timetable, Paul McCartney's comment in September that 'happily, we've spent a lot of this year in front of television cameras'[38] suggests that not only Epstein, but the Beatles themselves, were well aware of the benefits to be gained from their persistent exposure.

The Beatles themselves never lost their enthusiasm for television.[39] Through 1964 and 1965, as BBC and ITV gradually expanded their range of popular music programming in response to the undeniable growth of relevant audiences, they continued to made regular appearances on *Thank Your Lucky Stars*, *Ready Steady Go!* and, from January 1964, BBC's *Top Of The Pops*. In addition, they were frequent guest attractions on a wide range of family-oriented variety shows, returning to *Sunday Night At The London Palladium*, as well as starring on *The Morecambe And Wise Show* (ITV) and *Blackpool Night Out* (ITV). Increasingly, they were also the subject of feature-length television specials or documentaries (ITV's *Around The Beatles* and *The Music of Lennon And McCartney*, BBC's *Follow The Beatles*) that sought to explore and explain the group's unceasing success. Nor did their global status diminish the Beatles' willingness to appear on regional television in the UK, and they participated in editions of Granada's *Scene At 6.30*, Southern TV's *Day By Day*, Tyne Tees Television's *Star Parade*, Scottish Television's *Roundup* and Grampian Television's *Grampian Week*.

It is hardly surprising, therefore, that the screenplay of *A Hard Day's Night* (Richard Lester, 1964) is constructed around the difficulties encountered by the Beatles as they rehearse and star in a live TV show.[40] Briefed by producer Walter Shenson to portray an exaggerated day in the life of the Beatles in 'mock-documentary' style, writer Alun Owen travelled with the group to Ireland in November 1963, in order to watch the four at close quarters, personally and professionally. After observing their crowded and claustrophobic schedule, which included two concerts and three television appearances in two days, he was able to offer a succinct outline of his script:

> They're prisoners of their success. They go from the airport to the hotel to the theatre or stadium or concert hall, back to the hotel, back to the airport. In any city, it's always the same. They travel in a cocoon ... there's the manager, the road manager, a publicity man, the car driver, the guy who carries the equipment. That's all they see.[41]

---

[38]   Chris Hutchins, 'Beatles Are Going On Holiday', *New Musical Express*, 13 September 1963, p. 10.

[39]   This enthusiasm also extended to their viewing habits. In 1963, Lennon and McCartney both listed 'TV' among their hobbies. See 'Lifelines Of The Beatles', *New Musical Express*, 15 February 1963, p. 9.

[40]   See Roy Carr, *Beatles At The Movies: Scenes From A Career* (London, 1996), pp. 28–57; Bob Neaverson, *The Beatles Movies* (London, 1997), pp. 11–30.

[41]   Andrew Yule, *The Man Who 'Framed' The Beatles: A Biography Of Richard Lester* (New York, 1994), p. 6.

After many comic delays and mishaps, the movie's closing scene, in which the group perform four songs ('Tell Me Why', 'If I Fell', 'I Should Have Known Better' and 'She Loves You') to a studio audience, as the finale of a live programme that has also included dancers and a magician, is an astonishingly accurate re-creation of the television variety shows in which they repeatedly appeared in 1963 and 1964. Indeed, as a location in which to depict the daily reality of the Beatles at this time, the choice (by Lester and Owen) of the TV studio could not be more appropriate.

The tendency to focus on individual television programmes as key moments in the group's history would continue throughout the 1960s. In December 1966, Lennon's cameo role as a lavatory attendant in Peter Cook and Dudley Moore's BBC satirical series *Not Only ... But Also* was interpreted as an early sign of his preparation for life after the Beatles.[42] The promotional films made by the group for the release of 'Penny Lane'/'Strawberry Fields Forever' in February 1967, and distributed to TV stations around the world, were regarded as pioneering contributions to the development of music video.[43] The Beatles' participation in the first live global tele-broadcast, *Our World* (transmitted in the UK by BBC in June 1967), allowed them to perform 'All You Need Is Love' to a TV audience of more than 200 million.[44] And in December 1968, their 50-minute television film, *Magical Mystery Tour*, broadcast by BBC on Boxing Day, was unanimously labelled as their first critical failure.[45]

By the time of these appearances, however, the Beatles were arguably the four most famous young men in the world, and treated as objects of 'fascination ... constant, expectant scrutiny ... and stupendous, collective adoration'.[46] Six years earlier, at the start of their television career, they were four aspiring musicians from Liverpool, unfamiliar to all but a few hundred local fans. Television had both initiated and reflected the changes through which they had gone. Just as the dramatic impact of pivotal events in world history were emphatically enhanced by their exposure to global television audiences through the 1960s (the Sharpeville massacre in March 1960, the assassination of President Kennedy in November 1963, the Black Power salute by athletes Tommie Smith and John Carlos at the 1968 Mexico Olympics, Apollo 11's moon landing in July 1969) in a way that would have been impossible a decade earlier, so too many historical explanations of the Beatles' spectacular ascendancy have invariably clustered around key moments

---

[42]   Philip Norman, *John Lennon* (London, 2008), pp. 455–6.

[43]   See, for example, Bill Harry, *Beatlemania: The History Of The Beatles On Film* (London, 1984), p. 138; Neaverson, *Movies*, pp. 120–21.

[44]   See George Martin, *All You Need Is Ears* (New York, 1979), pp. 192–3.

[45]   See, for example, Peter McCabe and Robert D. Schonfeld, *Apple To The Core: The Unmaking Of The Beatles* (London, 1972), pp. 93–4; Tony Bramwell, *Magical Mystery Tours* (New York, 2005), pp. 240–41.

[46]   Norman, *Shout!*, p. 264.

in their career that were broadcast to Britain's new, and rapidly developing, community of TV viewers.

A frequent observation about popular music and television is that there exists an ideological opposition between the two that subverts and problematises the point at which viewing and listening occur; Negus notes that 'for many broadcasters and musicians the domestic setting of television reception has appeared as villain. It is perceived to undermine the rebellious spirit of rock'.[47] While this may be true for many of the self-consciously 'serious' music programmes that were broadcast (to specific audiences) on British TV in the 1970s, epitomised by BBC's *The Old Grey Whistle Test* (1971–87), it was a caveat that did not apply to the early Beatles. A significant portion of the group's popularity was achieved precisely because of its presence on programmes whose routine reproduction (in form and content) of conventional broadcasting styles and approaches helped to ensure that the Beatles themselves were rarely regarded as potential rebels.[48]

In addition, it has been suggested that as their career progressed, the songs of the Beatles became markedly less important in perpetuating their success than the increasingly familiar screen personae with which viewers were commonly acquainted:

> The appearances by the Beatles on both British and American television represent a key moment when the *look* of popular music achieved a new threshold of significance ... Whilst the Beatles' music was the vehicle of their success, its overdetermining significance lessened as their exposure through film and television increased, as their image assumed increased importance in defining their meaning as cultural icon and commodity.[49]

Such an analysis, though not inaccurate, is misleading. The real work of introducing the Beatles to the British public had been accomplished long before their international fame, through the group's willingness to pursue a demanding schedule of appearances that were brief in duration, restricted to regional audiences, and often broadcast in off-peak hours. However, the cumulative impact of the strategy was to ensure that in the 12 months preceding the *Sunday Night At The London Palladium* broadcast, the group's consistent visits to television studios across England, Wales and Scotland had helped to give it a formidable, national

---

[47]   Keith Negus, 'Musicians On Television: Visible, Audible And Ignored', *Journal Of The Royal Musical Association* 131/2 (2006): p. 324.

[48]   Ironically, it was the leading role adopted by the Beatles in the 'intellectualisation' of popular music from the mid-1960s that led directly to shows like *The Old Grey Whistle Test*. See Ian Inglis, 'Men Of Ideas? Popular Music, Anti-Intellectualism And The Beatles', in Ian Inglis (ed.), *The Beatles, Popular Music And Society: A Thousand Voices* (London, 2000), pp. 1–22.

[49]   John Mundy, *Popular Music On Screen* (Manchester, 1999), pp. 190–91.

presence.[50] The fact that so many of the programme tapes were erased shortly after their initial broadcast only serves to emphasise their unremarkable status at the time. In 1963, TV programmes featuring the Beatles were commonplace, and any notions that they might be preserved as important historical documents were considered fanciful. It was the ubiquity, rather than the rarity, of their appearances that introduced large sections of the public to their music, defined their (stereo)typical visual characteristics, and provided the platform upon which the explosion of Beatlemania would be ignited.

---

[50] In addition to its TV and radio appearances, the group also fulfilled around 600 live engagements in 1962–63. See Mark Lewisohn, *The Beatles Live!* (London, 1986), pp. 88–161.

Chapter 13

Granada TV, Johnny Hamp, And *The Blues And Gospel Train:* Masters Of Reality

Mike Brocken

Granada

Granada is the United Kingdom's ITV contractor for the North West of England (and, more recently, the Isle of Man) and the only one of the original four Independent Television Authority (ITA) franchises that has endured into the twenty-first century. In 1954, it was awarded the North of England contract for weekdays; ABC, a fledgling company of the Associated British Picture Corporation (ABPC) served the same area at the weekend. When its transmissions began in May 1956, Granada served an area stretching from Liverpool and Blackpool on the West coast to Kingston-upon-Hull on the East coast, taking in counties such as Lancashire and the West and East Ridings of Yorkshire, and major conurbations such as Manchester, Leeds, Bradford, Sheffield and Doncaster. In 1968, this broadcast region was divided into two area monopolies (Granada and Yorkshire TV) and Granada was given the full weekly franchise for the North West.

Away from television, the company's early development was typical of the entrepreneurial activities associated with cinema growth in the inter-war period. During the 1930s, brothers Cecil and Sidney Bernstein had created a cinema chain in the South of England which they named Granada Theatres Limited, following a visit to the Spanish city by Cecil in 1926. Some 20 years later, at the dawn of commercial television, the Bernsteins decided to bid for a franchise in the new independent television industry: a visible competitor to their own cinema chains.

They selected the North of England for its strong pre-existing sense of regional identity and locality; other possible franchises had included the London area which was not selected because of the quantity and quality of other candidates, and the Midlands franchise which was considered too challenging because of its many disparate regional identities. They also believed that a TV franchise in the North of England would not have any detrimental effects on their own Southern-based cinema chain which continued to trade as normal. In the 18 months between the award of the franchise and the start of transmission, Granada built a brand new TV studio complex in Quay Street, Manchester, on bomb-clearance land close to the River Irwell. This facility – which predated the BBC Television Centre by four years – proved to be revolutionary. While the three other new ITV franchises favoured production offices in London and regional offices in their constituencies,

Granada wanted to be at the epicentre of their adopted area. It was also the first British TV company to use facilities purpose-built for television production. Before this (and for some time afterwards) companies converted former film studios, cinemas or other large buildings. To embellish the scale, studios were eccentrically numbered with even numbers only: 'Studio 10' was not actually part of the Manchester complex at all but was located in London's Chelsea Palace Theatre, which was owned by the Bernsteins and used by Granada for recording comedy and variety shows when performers were unwilling or unable to travel to Manchester.

The political culture of Granada was distinctly more left-of-centre than that of the BBC and some of the more conservative ITV franchises. The Bernsteins were known as 'entrepreneurial socialists' and felt that Granada TV would only succeed if their adopted area recognised an authenticity in the company. The brothers certainly appeared to understand issues of homology at the heart of local broadcasting: there had to be some kind of embodiment of, and by, the people of the North of England in Granada's visual images. In addition, this embodiment had to contrast sharply with the forms of 'one nation' cultural capital preferred by the BBC. They therefore sanctioned hard-hitting documentary series – most famously the multi-award winning *World In Action* (1963–98) and *Seven Up* (1964–) which periodically tracks the experiences and aspirations of children growing up in the post-war era. Gritty dramas such as *A Family At War* (1970–72) were also seen as part of Granada's mandate. The classic soap opera *Coronation Street*, which began a 13-week regional run in December 1960, was very much a part of the legacy of the 'kitchen sink' social realism engendered by such 'Northern' plays as Shelagh Delaney's *A Taste Of Honey* (1958).[1] Granada made important contributions to ABC's *Armchair Theatre* (1956–68) helping to commission writers such as Alun Owen (later screenwriter for *A Hard Day's Night*), Ted Willis and Harold Pinter, and the company initiated a unique experiment in 1968 with the creation of the Stables Theatre Company (under the direction of Gordon McDougall) which employed actors to work in television and theatre on the same contract.

There were key individuals: a young Jeremy Isaacs was involved in the development of a significant portion of its factual programming; future TV executives such as John Birt and Gus MacDonald were fellow producers on *World In Action*; and broadcasters such as Michael Parkinson, Mike Scott, Gay Byrne, Tony Wilson and Brian Trueman gained their early experience at Granada. Although it could be argued that Granada's news and documentary output has in recent years become rather standardised, in the early and mid-1960s its campaigning and critical approach reflected few of the attitudes and interests of its BBC counterparts.

Vertical integration slows down capacity for change, and when an integrated system also draws its recruits largely from a rarefied atmosphere such as at

---

[1]   The play was filmed in 1961 on location in Salford and Blackpool, directed by Tony Richardson.

Oxford and Cambridge universities, the social mores of its recruits are not only re-presented but ratified. Thus, according to Robert Hewison, the post-war BBC displayed 'the greatest potential for producing a homogenous, middlebrow society, and in the middle 1950s seemed to have turned the social solidarity of wartime into a respectful deference for authority and tradition'.[2] While the BBC did, at times, tolerate a modicum of dissent and modest debate, only those who had been socially 'sanctioned' were allowed to contribute to such programmes. Granada, on the other hand, was seen from the outset (especially by its regional public) as somewhat instinctive, less prescriptive and patronising, and far more adventurous and opinionated than its state-controlled (and some of its independent) competitors.

However, it is interesting to note that Granada did not engage wholeheartedly in its own regional pop music programming until the 1970s (under the guidance of TV producers like Mike Mansfield and Muriel Young). Until then the company was largely content to network programmes produced by its ITA partners, such as ABC's *Oh Boy!* (1958–59) and *Boy Meets Girls* (1959–60) and, for the younger audience, Associated Rediffusion's *Five O'Clock Club* (1963–66). This might have been a reflection of the common attitude towards popular music at this time as a transient and ephemeral product for youngsters, but the Granada cinema chain was already renowned in the South of England for promoting popular music, and was immersed in the appeal of all things popular; during the 1950s, an impressive diversity of performers, including Frank Sinatra, Winifred Atwell, Cliff Richard and the Shadows, appeared at Granada cinemas in the Home Counties. It is more likely that Granada's lack of in-house pop music programming in the late 1950s was influenced by its reluctance to compete with the widely-admired *Oh Boy!*, a show whose dynamism and exuberance contrasted sharply with the staid efforts of its competitors, such as BBC's *Six-Five Special*:

> *Oh Boy!* was a brilliant piece of television and could never have been made by the BBC. *Six-Five Special* was pathetic. Boxer Freddie Mills trying to do a comedy routine with a brush in his hand? Dance band singer for the Mums and Dads, Dennis Lotis, trying in vain to appeal to teenagers? It was terrible … patronising in the extreme and it was rightly put to the sword by *Oh Boy!* I don't think the BBC had a clue about rock'n'roll. *Oh Boy!* wiped the floor with *Six-Five Special*.[3]

Such testimonies suggest that, at the very least, a commercial indulgence of popular culture existed within ITV at a time when it was seen as ephemeral and patronised by the BBC.

Granada's probing, thoughtful and perceptive local news service, which sought to develop a cultural fit between broadcasters, news items and the populace of the

---

[2]   Robert Hewison, *In Anger: Culture In The Cold War* (London, 1988), p. 209.

[3]   Mick O'Toole, personal interview, 9 May 2009.

region, was similarly absorbed and attentive. For example, the company showed great interest in the growing music scene in Liverpool and, in August 1962, filmed the Beatles at The Cavern just as Ringo Starr was making his debut with the group (an appearance marked by audience abuse hurled at the new drummer and a black eye for guitarist George Harrison). By its vigilance, Granada (perhaps inadvertently) captured a key moment in popular music history: as the Beatles perform 'Some Other Guy', an irate member of the audience clearly shouts 'We want Pete!'[4] The transmission of this information throughout the region brought to public attention not only the energetic activity and unifying potential of popular music in 'Granada-land', but also the poverty of discourses that surrounded rock'n'roll and its impact on youth in the UK. To those who saw the TV coverage, it was quite evident that something was happening, that this was a 'serious' music, and that it carried with it a profusion of commentaries. The man largely responsible for keeping such a watchful eye on the region's youth culture was producer, director and, later, presenter Johnny Hamp.

Johnny Hamp

The vibrant television career of Johnny Hamp (more than 30 years at Granada, much of that time as Head of Light Entertainment) displays an impressive range of associations, from the early days of the Beatles to the later days of *The Comedians* (1971–85) and *The Wheeltappers And Shunters Social Club* (1974–1977). Hamp trained as a Granada cinema manager in Kingston-on-Thames, before moving to the company's flagship venue at Tooting for Frank Sinatra's 1953 tour. His successful relocation to Tooting was followed by his pioneering promotion of Granada's one night-stand tours, featuring many of the most popular performers of the decade. Retaining responsibilities for film publicity and stage show management, he was in at the beginning of Granada's television activity in 1956, recruiting celebrities for the panel game *My Wildest Dream* (1956–57) and guest stars for the London-based variety showcase *Chelsea At Nine* (1957–60). Granada chairman Sidney Bernstein soon saw Hamp's potential as a producer, and persuaded him to work on programmes such as *Make Up Your Mind* (1956–58), *Spot The Tune* (1956–63) and *Criss Cross Quiz* (1957–67). It was Hamp who sent a Granada TV crew to Liverpool to film the Beatles, and who brought them to Manchester for their first appearance on *People And Places* in October 1962; he continued to co-produce the programme (under its new name of *Scene At 6.30*) from 1963 to 1966.

Between 1963 and 1965, Hamp produced a string of American jazz, blues, gospel, pop, and rock'n'roll-based TV specials: *Sarah Sings And Basie Swings* (1963) with Sarah Vaughan and Count Basie; *I Hear The Blues* (1963) featuring Memphis Slim, Muddy Waters, Sonny Boy Williamson and Willie Dixon; *It's*

---

[4]   Drummer Pete Best had been replaced in the Beatles by Ringo Starr in August 1962.

Little Richard (1964); *The Blues And Gospel Train* (1964) featuring Sister Rosetta Tharpe, Muddy Waters, Sonny Terry and Brownie McGhee, and Cousin Joe Pleasant; and *A Whole Lotta Shakin' Goin' On* (1964) with Jerry Lee Lewis, Gene Vincent, the Animals and the Nashville Teens. Hamp continued his popular culture series with *Woody Allen* (1965), *The Bacharach Sound* (1965) and *The Music Of Lennon And McCartney* (1965).[5]

Hamp's articulatory comprehension of the popularity of such artists in Britain was to eventually mark a significant change in the dissemination and appreciation of disparate musical genres in the UK in the mid-1960s. The inclusion of what might be described as a 'listening component' into programme-making was not a common feature of television schedules at this time. Notwithstanding the popularity of *Thank Your Lucky Stars* (ITV 1961–66) which included the commentaries of trendy young typecasts Janice Nichols and Billy Butler, and *Juke Box Jury* (BBC 1959–67) where celebrity guests offered their verdicts on new releases, there was little or no serious exploration of the ways in which listeners were 'constructing' tunes, rhythms and genres, and were holding in mind different musical validations (while also linking these to anticipate the future). Hamp, however, represented an understanding of the 'Presbyterian' nature of popular culture from the 'bottom up' and, alongside his colleagues, perhaps understood that it was his duty to underwrite Granada's responsibility to acknowledge and represent the authenticities of its public – whether that be through footballers such as Manchester United's George Best or Everton's Alex Young (documentaries were made about both players), or blues musicians such as Sonny Terry and Brownie McGhee (featured in *The Blues And Gospel Train*). The former Liverpool musical agent and manager Joe Flannery recalls:

> Johnny Hamp was just an amazing man to meet – he knew what you were all about without you having to explain yourself. Imagine that in early-sixties Britain! I recall discussing this with Brian [Epstein] and we were both amazed at how different he was from the BBC people at Oxford Road [Manchester]. Hamp was genuinely 'show-business', whereas those at the BBC in Manchester seemed more or less like civil servants in white lab coats. We felt that in Hamp we had a kind of expressway to the business, I suppose ... and that Granada had *our* interests at heart. It was all very exciting.[6]

---

[5]   The fact that none of these were BBC productions challenges the self-publicising aspect of the BBC's historical vision of itself, which at times seems to place the Corporation at the centre of youth activity during the 1960s. But 'nothing could be further from the truth: throughout the entire decade, the "Beeb" was usually playing a game of catch-up with its leaner competitors such as Granada' (O'Toole, personal interview).

[6]   Joe Flannery, personal interview, 21 August 2009.

Blues, Folk And R&B

By 1963 jazz, blues, folk and R&B acolytes had already organised themselves into clubs and societies with their own networks, journals, promoters and even occasional record labels (Esquire, Tempo, Topic) creating events, venues and scenes that allowed them to hear such sounds simultaneously, and to develop a perceived unity. There had been at least three routes into an appreciation of the blues that were seldom taken into account by most British broadcasters at the time. One was via jazz (conceivably how the older enthusiasts discovered the music), another was via skiffle and/or rock'n'roll, and the third was through the burgeoning folk scene which, at that stage, still accommodated blues and gospel music: 'against this musical backcloth a small Fifth Column of Blues fans were growing and pursuing this underground culture. It was like being a member of a secret society'.[7]

These sounds obviously constituted a language, a communication with a structural resonance between the sounds and the receivers. This language was evidently generative and held, for some, a far deeper embodiment than the surface-based syntagma of TV shows such as *Thank Your Lucky Stars*. By 1964, many television producers were attempting to deliver an unambiguous message about popularity and a singular visage of youth culture – a rather flawed idea which overlooked the fact that the pleasures of the musical text involve real, repeatable, ambiguously enjoyable, and individual musical experiences. Listeners and viewers were, in fact, becoming increasingly and actively discriminatory and, in his championing of the blues, Johnny Hamp realised this. He also realised the power of TV: everyone within earshot of a television would hear it and, although people might not listen intently, several would direct their eyes differently towards the same screen, in the same room, at the same time.

Such partially-hidden diachrony can help to explain how *The Blues And Gospel Train* actually came about, and the examination of another particular diachronic strand may broaden this mode of enquiry further. Two years earlier, on 21 October 1962, an event at Manchester's Free Trade Hall played a significant part in the contribution made by blues music to changing identities among young people. While 30 miles along the East Lancashire Road, the Beatles were playing a Sunday night booking at The Cavern to promote 'Love Me Do', the seeds of the UK blues and folk boom were being definitively cultivated in Manchester's rain-soaked centre, as the city hosted the visiting American Folk Blues Festival. It was to be a seminal moment in its own right: the only UK date of a successful European tour which introduced British fans to performers like John Lee Hooker, Willie Dixon and T-Bone Walker. It attracted musicians such as the Macclesfield-born John Mayall, and scouting parties from London that included Mick Jagger, Bill Wyman, Brian Jones and Paul Jones. The tour had been conceived by German

---

[7]   Mike Rowe, *The American Folk Blues Festival: The British Tours 1963–1966 DVD* liner notes (2007).

blues and jazz enthusiasts Horst Lippmann and Fritz Rau, and was promoted by Stockport-based Paddy MacKiernan, under the 'Jazz Unlimited' brand. This was not the first time that blues audiences had been able get close to their heroes; tours by Big Bill Broonzy, Muddy Waters and others had already taken place. But it was perhaps a more memorable occasion that allowed the likes of Memphis Slim, Sonny Terry and Brownie McGhee, Helen Humes, Jump Jackson and 'Shakey' Jake Harris to perform in front of 2,000-plus British fans.

The following year saw a return visit of the tour with an equally impressive line-up, headlined by Muddy Waters, Sonny Boy Williamson, Otis Spann and Memphis Slim. Hamp and Granada TV director Philip Casson approached Sidney Bernstein with the idea of filming a one-off studio special. Hamp later recalled that 'it was a groundbreaking time … we had all sorts of ideas for what we then called "light entertainment". They [the Granada management] were very receptive; we got away with murder, really'.[8] The programme was approved, and *I Hear The Blues* was broadcast by Granada in December 1963. The setting was what might be described as 'down home': a bare, wooden stage, and a studio audience very close to the performers. From the outset, Casson and Hamp wanted to create an appropriate ambience for the music.

The European tours of The American Folk Blues Festival contributed greatly to the profile of blues music across Europe and, for many in the UK, illuminated the social, political and economic plight of African-Americans. Blues music became a catalyst for subsequent investigations and developments. *Blues Unlimited*, founded in May 1963 by Mike Leadbitter and Simon Napier-Bell, recognised the connections clearly: 'we were part of that generation that saw Blacks as oppressed. So there was that kind of moralistic approach to it. We felt that by supporting the blues, we were supporting the Civil Rights movement. There was that romantic side to it'.[9] Rob Bowman has suggested that the tours contributed to a 'transition of public consciousness'.[10] In this sense, Granada also contributed to such a shift by expanding the discourse around the possibilities that consumers of popular music might become communal producers. As the music presented by Hamp's TV 'specials' impacted upon them, those consumers became more interested in particular genres of music, and began to characterise themselves (or were defined by others) as connoisseurs and aficionados who used the music with other like-minded people. This is but a short step away from actually making music.

For a while it almost seemed that every other British teenager was interested in the blues, either by listening, attempting to play, or researching the music. In July 1964, Howlin' Wolf's 'Smokestack Lightning' hovered around the lower reaches of the pop singles charts; John Lee Hooker's 'Dimples' was there for ten

---

[8]   Johnny Hamp, quoted in Neil Henderson, *Destination Manchester* (http://www. modculture.com).

[9]   Mike Broven, quoted in Rob Bowman, *The American Folk Blues Festival 1962–1965 DVD* liner notes (2003).

[10]   Rob Bowman, ibid.

weeks; in September, Jimmy Reed's 'Shame Shame Shame' entered the charts. Chess compilations entered the album charts, Pye's R&B International EPs sold in abundance, in May 1964, Chuck Berry's 'No Particular Place To Go' reached Number Three on the singles charts; and the Rolling Stones' version of Howlin' Wolf's recording of 'Little Red Rooster' (written by Willie Dixon), released in November 1964, topped the singles charts.

By the end of 1964 the Beatles had been long gone from both The Cavern and Liverpool and, for a while, there were probably more R&B bands than 'beat' or rock'n'roll groups in the city. R&B bands such as Almost Blues, The Hideaways and TL's Bluesicians were successful locally, and Cavern deejay Bob Wooler signed several of them to a management deal, despite his own lack of interest in blues:

> I wasn't really a fan of the music; I found it rather dour. But I could see that after the success of the Rolling Stones, there was a surge of interest in Chicago-style blues – so I went along with it, because there was something of a musical hiatus at The Cavern by 1964, and I wanted to keep the place going. It actually attracted a different type of music-lover to The Cavern – they were more 'beatnik' and, at times, it was probably more like the fifties days when The Cavern was a jazz club.[11]

Jim Ireland, who owned the Mardi Gras and Downbeat clubs in Liverpool, and also managed several local R&B groups, confirms that by 1964 he too had noticed that listening practices were changing: R&B and soul music – portable, repeatable and relatively affordable – began to make inroads into live music in Liverpool. Record requests became increasingly important in his clubs, and the cult of personality began to embrace not only the groups, but also the deejays playing the (Motown or early Stax) discs between sets; by 1965, live groups were in direct competition with R&B and soul records.[12] In addition, the weekly music press began to broaden its coverage from previous concerns (*Melody Maker*'s emphasis on jazz, *Disc*'s preference for pop) to cover the mushrooming blues, soul, and R&B scenes, and jazz magazines such as *Jazz News* also began to feature blues-based activities.

Two major blues tours were scheduled for 1964: The American Folk, Blues and Gospel Caravan (in April–May) and The American Folk Blues Festival (in October). The second of these, featuring Howlin' Wolf, Sonny Boy Williamson and Lightnin' Hopkins, was considered the major event, but it was the first that Johnny Hamp felt he could capture for Granada because of its visit to the region. On 7 May 1964, he produced the 40-minute TV special entitled *The Blues And Gospel Train*, broadcast in August. Directed by Casson, and featuring a set designed by Michael Bailey, it presented performances by Muddy Waters, Cousin Joe Pleasant,

---

[11]   Bob Wooler, personal interview, 4 November 1997.
[12]   Jim Ireland, personal interview, 18 October 1998.

Sister Rosetta Tharpe, Sonny Terry and Brownie McGhee, with backing by Otis Spann, Little Willie Smith and Ranson Knowling.

The Blues And Gospel Train: Meaning, Imagery, Locality

The associations between the musical and the visual in the construction of meaning have been well-noted: John Mundy's examination of British popular music cinema of the late 1950s and early 1960s, observes that the 'structural barriers that are part of the British social formation, class, gender, age and economics dissolve with the construction of an imagined community'.[13] The invention of this imagined community via a recognisable discourse of generational politics and a happy ending, is illustrated in two Cliff Richard films of the early 1960s – *The Young Ones* (Sidney J. Furie, 1961) and *Summer Holiday* (Peter Yates, 1963) – both of which convey and verify the singer as an authentic mainstream British entertainer. Cliff's social rite of passage is acted out on screen: his recognition and re-evaluation by the older generations featured in these movies 'officially' certify his membership of British society. In a similar, yet actually inverse, manner *The Blues And Gospel Train* transformed blues music from a little known and 'troublesome' (i.e. 'racialised') area of musical activity into the public consciousness of those watching. In this case, an imagined community was offered as an opposition that could be assimilated – in contrast to the Cliff Richard presentation of society effectively 'shaking hands with itself'.

All of Hamp's popular music 'specials', but particularly his blues programmes, set in motion visible acknowledgements of peripherals and oppositions, and at the same time allowed viewers to recognise and confirm 'idealised' ('racialised') types and sounds. Such programmes are representations of how non-institutional stereotypes, representing strategies of 'otherness', can cut against the conventional narrative values of 'entertainment' in the imagined sense. As a result, *The Blues And Gospel Train* suggested that the received notion that all popular music was pre-digested and interchangeable could be challenged.[14] Thus begins a process whereby stereotypes are acknowledged but then perhaps refuted, and where a specific musical content within a specific context can be acknowledged in its own right: as Brian Longhurst suggests, the linking together of aural and visual images is inextricably entwined with context.[15]

---

[13]   John Mundy, *Popular Music On Screen: From Hollywood Musical To Music Video* (Manchester, 1999), p. 169.

[14]   One might even go so far as to say that such works are precursors to popular music studies as an academic discipline, so significant are they in suggesting to the consumer that there are 'idealised' types of different cultural forms, where core aspects facilitate a discourse of authenticity between consumers.

[15]   Brian Longhurst, *Popular Music And Society* (Cambridge, 2007), pp. 153–8.

In the shows produced by Hamp for Granada, time, space, place (and cost) were manipulated to produce musically and visually-linked moments to cater for a specialised yet emergent music taste culture in the UK. In doing so, established conventions of the British broadcast media – particularly those that positioned its criteria of intelligent and original music above the novel and standardised – were confronted and contested. Indeed, Hamp not only produced visual and aural imagery of immense synchronic significance, but also left a lasting diachronic impression.

The Blues And Gospel Train also employed a subcultural narrative. An intricate *mise-en-scene* of an imagined American South (bales of cotton, broken farm equipment, washtubs of laundry) was openly presented on a real platform at the abandoned Wilbraham Road Station, in the Manchester suburb of Chorlton. The narrative was therefore, synchronically challenging and self-reflexive. Such expressive and 'truthful' imagery can be seen to have worked on a number of levels, turning the locus of the viewers' attention increasingly towards the emotions presented by the performers as the programme proceeded. To turn the station into a scene from the Deep South (with shutters attached to windows and a platform sign bearing the words 'Chorltonville and all stations South') pronounced a somewhat critical stance. If the blues did indeed expose a 'kind of moralistic approach', then for these evangelists the very presence of sacks, crates, 'wanted' posters, and even a few chickens and goats added not only to the effect, but also to the affect of inequality. Bailey's props were not presented on a surface level alone – these visual signifiers were deeply embedded within the text.

To the extent that the programme's goals were to capture the popularity of the blues and to display the inherent dignity of the music (rather than portray the musicians as caricatures) the production team needed to ensure that the sources depicted on set did not slip into tasteless stereotypes. In fact, Casson, Hamp and Bailey avoided cultural and genre stereotypification, and were able to re-present and re-construct forms of the blues that juxtaposed and questioned. They suggested a solidarity alongside the variegated possibilities of the blues, and transmitted both messages to Granada's audience (no mean feat in mid-1960s Britain). Each performer represented quite different genre-based sources: Muddy Waters played his 12/8 electric Chicago blues, Cousin Joe Pleasant displayed his New Orleans-style bordello piano blues; Sister Rosetta Tharpe presented her electrified gospel sound, and Sonny Terry and Brownie McGhee offered their eclectic, softly sung roadhouse folk-blues interlaced with a howling harmonica. The material not only constituted a different code with an unquestionable history of separateness and autonomous musical development (even though, as Philip Tagg suggests, we can trace a process of interrelatedness between this and other 'white' forms of music)[16] but it also displayed its own internal cultural geography and genre-based

---

[16]   Philip Tagg, 'Open Letter: "Black Music", "Afro-American Music" And "European Music"', *Popular Music* 8/3 (1989), pp. 285–98.

'otherness' to the viewers (an 'otherness' that was also recognised by the youth of Manchester that evening).

One performance-related paradigm of immediate authenticity demonstrates this vividly. Cousin Joe Pleasant's routine at the piano (upon which was a chicken in a cage, rather crudely representing his song 'Fried Chicken Blues') is captured by the cameras in great detail and is sincerely implanted into the entire structure of the transmission. Pleasant begins nervously, but as he realises that the young, appreciative audience are in full support of his aesthetic, he moves into his customary blues position at the piano and settles into a thoroughly assured performance. At the end of his own brief set, he assists Sister Rosetta Tharpe from her horse-drawn buggy at the side of the platform and 'cake-walks' her to centre stage. He then leaves the platform by the waiting room door at the rear. However, whether by direction or inspiration (it matters little to the viewer), he soon re-joins Sister Tharpe on the platform/stage where he sits in an old rocking chair and listens to her continuing performance – a wonderful moment of organic unity and relaxed self-confidence, and nothing to do with 'Uncle Tom' typecasting.

As for the audience, they consisted of those lucky few who were invited or able to obtain one of the limited number of tickets for the 'Hallelujah train', as it was titled for the day (the steam locomotive used in the event was an Ivatt Class 2MT 2-6-0 engine, fitted with an 'authentic' cowcatcher and a lamp on top of the smoke box) and those who picked up their more standard tickets from Granada's Quay Street offices. No admission fee was charged, but special tickets were printed for the invited train travellers (largely made up of camera-friendly young local blues and jazz fans known to the director and producer). They were requested to meet at Manchester Central Station (now the GMEX) at 7.30 p.m., and board the train to the old Wilbraham Road Station (where one side of the railway track was converted into a stage for the performers and the facing platform was terraced to seat the audience of enthusiastic blues fans). Some judicious editing makes this work effectively for the cameras, and the young passengers are seen disembarking during Muddy Waters' opening riffs. The movement of the train and the physicality of the surge of young fans attempting to find a remaining place on the bench-terracing create an atmosphere of expectancy and set a scene. Those not arriving by train were asked to make their own way to the disused station with instructions to 'come early!' The dress code on the show tickets specified 'Casual gear essential: Denims, Sweaters'. However, a rather cool and decidedly damp evening also dictated that many duffle-coats were worn, perhaps representing a middle-class, 'student' demographic. The class dimension of blues (and clothing, of course) continues to be of interest to popular music historians, for it does tend to appear that the youthful middle-classes were often the principal audience for such sounds.

South Manchester Reporter columnist James Chapman-Kelly was just 16 at the time, and his recollections of the event are significant:

It was incredible because we loved these blues players in those days. My mates were all mods and the blues were the key to the new scene that was springing up around us – even the Rolling Stones were still playing blues then. People only heard about the concert through word of mouth but there was a huge crowd and it inspired people to go off and make their own music. Not many people know about it. It is like a piece of forgotten history.[17]

This was undoubtedly an issue of cultural capital: how informal knowledge could be passed amongst those in Manchester with an understanding of the language of the music, and of the visual imagery on screen. The programme employed two distinct types of signifiers to support the cultural capital of the occasion in particular ways. The first was the use of visual 'access' signs, erected so that those viewers with a cultural investment in the genre could recognise those entering the station, and endorse the set as a domain of authenticity, activity and participation. This was at least partially accomplished by the titles sequence cutting between young (white) fans 'travelling' to the event on the train and the (black) blues musicians 'travelling' on a well-appointed motor coach. So although the compliant fan/artist dichotomy supported by conventional narratives was indeed presented, it was immediately undercut by race, thus raising issues that would perhaps be recognised as important connotations for the blues devotees watching television at home.

Secondly, 'discovery' signs, which sought to draw pictures for the relatively uninitiated were also utilised in the programme. They included visual encodings of cultural marginalisation (through the material poverty suggested by the set) but these stereotypes were contrasted with the connotations attached to the evidently upward mobility of the performers. Sister Rosetta Tharpe's presence signified her own and also (black) female mobility in a (black and white) male world; her modes of dress and musicianship (the sequin-encrusted coat and her use of a Gibson SG electric guitar) definitively stated that she was not the stereotypical woman to be 'looked at' by men, or the typecast black woman of 'double jeopardy'. Tharpe had already garnered a formidable reputation as a gospel diva par excellence before her arrival in the UK. In true Mancunian fashion, the heavens opened as the show began (apparently prompting her to switch the scheduled song at the last minute to 'Didn't It Rain') and by the time she made her entrance, her appearance was taking on almost regal proportions. However, the ironies associated with such an entrance were not lost on either Sister Tharpe, Casson or the concert-goers, as double meanings connected with African-American *signifyin'* practices were made visible in the 'cake-walk' between her and Pleasant. The implications of this walk/dance remain vast: the cake-walk was a celebratory dance, often performed by nineteenth-century black Americans as an acerbic comment on the dancing proprieties of 'elevated' white society, with a cake sometimes awarded to the

[17]   James Chapman-Kelly, quoted in Gareth Tidman, 'When The Blues Train Rolled Into Chorlton', *South Manchester Reporter*, 9 November 2006.

most 'ridiculous'. The participants here were well aware of the connotations that such displays involved, and were willing to use such symbols as *signifyin'* double utterance evidence to all concerned that they were self-aware, self-reflexive and ironic. Furthermore, Sister Tharpe's performance included a thunderous guitar solo: 'Pretty good for a woman, ain't it?' she quipped, as the song came to an end. Au uncredited review in *R&B Scene* (Manchester's Twisted Wheel Club's in-house monthly magazine) reported 'Her guitar playing was a real *shock* and the audience loved every note'[18] (emphasis added).

This dichotomy was also pursued further by Cousin Joe Pleasant and Sonny Terry and Brownie McGhee who (probably because of the rain) were heavily 'suited and booted' for the occasion. The self-conscious questioning of the 'prop' stereotypes by their 'sophisticated' clothing gave Casson and Hamp a visual opportunity to present the 'real' sounds and images of African-American society alongside the conventional received wisdoms; while not completely invalidating them, they were able to place them in a critical, historical relief. Such clarity of distinctions in (tele)visuals is central when viewers' predispositions towards music and race are illuminated. For example, at the beginning of the programme Muddy Waters was on the 'audience' (rather than the 'performance') platform, playing his Fender Telecaster, and surrounded by a group of happy and excited youngsters, as they exited the incoming train. For a brief moment, the stereotype of the solo black man busking on a station platform is resurrected – but this is not the usual depiction, in which busy passers-by ignore the singer. Quite the reverse: the white youngsters surrounding Muddy are hanging upon his every note or clapping along to the boogie. His hat is not on the ground as a receptacle for spare change but is firmly on his head as, still in his overcoat, he proceeds to utterly engage his audience. On this occasion, the black musician at the railway station is far from 'invisible'.

By being intrinsic to the demands of commercial television (an advertising break in the middle) the programme's musical and visual distinctions culturally resonated as realistic. Far from being 'sidelined' within a commercial context (as might have been the accusation at the time) the advertising made them hyper-realistic in a televisual sense. Unlike the BBC, Granada did not patronise its performers or viewers. *The Blues And Gospel Train* did not feel obliged to include an accompanying 'ethnomusicological' discourse, or an older TV presenter 'getting down with the kids'. This is the 'listening component' discussed earlier; rather than be confronted with imposed and condescending value systems at the heart of the show, we witness presence *as* affect, and are allowed to work things out for ourselves.

This is further confirmed by the 'stage right' performance of Sonny Terry and Brownie McGhee (coded for us by being seated at the far end of the platform, as if waiting for the last train home). Already well known and respected by many British enthusiasts, Terry and McGhee were, by 1964, an integral part of the UK

---

[18]   *R&B Scene*, September 1964, p. 1.

folk and blues scenes. Their celebrated 'Walking Blues' (also known as 'Walk On') was performed here with such delicate precision that it came, in effect, to 'bookend' the entire evening. The song was the physical and sonic encapsulation of an already-known repertoire, for many at Chorlton that evening knew it as the duo's 'signature tune'. And while there was a grand finale in which the assembled musicians performed their version of 'He's Got The Whole World In His Hands' (known to pop fans in the UK through Laurie London's 1957 hit single), it was Sonny Terry and Brownie McGhee's relaxed, distinguished blues that truly signalled the end of the (musical and television) programme.

Therefore, these sounds and images are 'historical' in the purest sense – they reflect a contested discourse, an embattled terrain in which we are asked to consider various blues and gospel sounds not only as representations of 'struggle' but also as 'entertainment'. Interpretations could be constructed by viewers from their own pasts and the present, and through their attitudes towards preconceived ideas concerning music and race. The images and sounds suggest diachronic, rather than definitive, history; in this programme the history of African-American struggle could be viewed as a shifting signifier without *a priori* certainties. When one adds television's need for entertainment, this creates an interesting issue: these stories exist synchronically, for the moment (they are 'entertaining' in their own right). *The Blues And Gospel Train* informs us that in any culture nothing is certain. The images of these African-Americans on the railway platform were not absolutes; they deconstructed and made arbitrary and pragmatic the connections that had previously been made between the 'common sense' of persistent, habitual homilies concerning truth and certainty surrounding race and society. The televised image of Muddy Waters 'alone' on the platform, yet 'surrounded' by young people, still suggests that we are partners with uncertainty. Do the fans acknowledge him as a cultural icon? As an entertainer? Both? The programme therefore endures not only in a practical sense, as a representation of important social and musical conjunctures in a very significant year for the exposure of African-American genres in Britain, but also as a theoretical deconstruction of the myth of origin and truth. The programme is a fact, not a truth. It is for these reasons that *The Blues And Gospel Train* should be regarded as something of a seminal moment, not only in the history of the blues, but also in the history of British commercial television.

But that railway station location also pursued other forms of imagery. Unlike the theatres that The American Folk, Blues and Gospel Caravan visited, and the clubs from which much of this music emanated in the US, the evocative and theatrical *mise-en-scene* of Wilbraham Road Station produced a theatrical, narrative flow that addressed issues at the roots of all blues enquiries, such as migrations and returns, arrivals and farewells. And while it can be asserted that dressing the station simply made for better television, the choice of the train platform as a stage is intensely rooted in webs of blues authenticity: travelling, railroads and rail yards, and the circulatory nature of blues and African-American internal migration. Furthermore, it confirms to the television audience Manchester's affinity with such visual imagery, and denotes how this area of the North of England was, for Granada TV, a place of authenticity in its own right (somewhat run-down, but vibrant). After all, railway stations – occupied or disused – are, curiously, very authentic places. They are what they appear to be – openly transient, openly discursive.

Perhaps also in the wake of the Beeching rail closures of the early 1960s (the demise of Wilbraham Road Station actually preceded those cutbacks), the railway platform location spoke to those disaffected by the severity of political decisions.[19] The blues was not simply an authentic signifier of its place in American society, but came to represent an authenticity within *this* city and *this* region of England, which were also subject to social and cultural stereotyping. The young audience at Wilbraham Road Station may or may not have been the sons and daughters of upper middle-class power-brokers, but their presence was evidence of a discourse concerning sacred cows, moral vacuums and popular prejudices. The location of the programme itself is, therefore, of great historical significance: perceptions of 'authenticity' surround cities and, within them, particular places and spaces can be identified as authentic. In 1964, Manchester possessed a growing authenticity – not only as the 'hidden' part of the adjacent Merseybeat scene, from which groups such as the Dakotas, Herman's Hermits, Freddie and the Dreamers and the Hollies emerged, but also because of the importance of institutions such as the Halle Orchestra's presence at the Free Trade Hall which promoted classical music for all. Such dialogues both complemented and countered the visual communications presented by Granada's own, hugely successful, *Coronation Street* which depicted Salford and Manchester as cities of great working-class authenticity (and poverty).

It had long been believed that the old Chorlton-cum-Hardy Station (now adjacent to the site of a Morrison's supermarket) was used for the show. However, following a screening of *The Blues And Gospel Train* in Manchester in 2008, C.P. Lee confirmed the correct location:

> As always at the Q&A the question arose, 'wasn't the site at the current Morrison's on Wilbraham Road in Chorlton?' No, it wasn't. The venue for the recording was at the disused Wilbraham Road Railway Station, accessed at the end of Atholl Road.[20]

The mistaken identification of the venue probably occurred because of Hamp's invention of the 'Chorltonville' name – intended to convey the idea of a Southern whistle-stop station. The venue's original name was not Chorlton Station, but Alexandra Park Station; it was on the Manchester, Sheffield and Lincolnshire Railway line (later the Grand Central line) from Manchester Central, via Chorlton,

---

[19]   In March 1963, in the first of two reports on the future of rail travel in Britain, Dr Richard Beeching (Chairman of the British Railways Board) recommended that a quarter of the UK's rail network and more than 2,000 local stations should close.

[20]   C.P. Lee (http://www.cplee.co.uk).

to Fairfield and Guide Bridge – once known as the Fallowfield Loop. The station itself was near the junction of Alexandra Road South and Mauldeth Road West (the old Railway House is still there, next to allotments on Alexandra Road). The station was re-named as Wilbraham Road (which was about 250 yards away) in 1923, to avoid possible confusion with the north London suburb of Alexandra Park. The line was closed to passenger traffic in July 1958, but remained open to freight until it finally closed in October 1988; it has since been converted into the Fallowfield Loop cycle track. Such a locality becomes significant in terms of the routes that popular music takes. Not only was the setting important in a televisual sense, but also because of its suggested reality: like the music, the station was obscure (and unlike the music, would remain so).

This contemporary use of TV, therefore, served up self-reflexive images and sounds that reproduced the significance of blues and gospel music as communal, less individualistic, less needful of verbal explanation, and (given Sister Tharpe's performance as a thoroughly committed Christian) less uptight about the body. Analysis of the event was further complicated by the nature of the programme as a televised concert that employed a 'studio' audience comprising real, young Mancunians (even a few children are in evidence). Granada involved itself in the authenticity of word-of-mouth blues culture, by positioning television as a contributor to the already accepted multi- and inter-textuality of blues appreciation in 1964; it increased a sense of its own, and Manchester's, growing authenticity across the region; and it participated in a general debate about regionality, decline and control. Just as Kaplan identifies self-representation and coded signification within music video,[21] such reflexivity can also be detected in independently-produced TV programmes of earlier decades. In *The Blues And Gospel Train*, Johnny Hamp (and Granada) explored cultural stereotypes in the immediacy of a televisual presentation, which (while held together by significant diachrony) was also able to visually address issues surrounding music and its interactions with race, localities, and authenticities.

---

[21]   E. Ann Kaplan, *Rocking Around The Clock: Music Television, Postmodernism And Consumer Culture* (London, 1987).

Chapter 14

A Postman Mans Up: The Changing Musical Identities Of *Postman Pat*

Nicholas Reyland

In the everyday lives of young British children, exposure to television programming scored in the style dubbed 'pop scoring' by Jeff Smith (music 'composed or compiled in one or more popular musical styles') and thereby saturated with semiotic codes derived from Western rock and pop musics, is remarkably high.[1] Recent research has demonstrated that music occurs during more than 80 per cent of the waking lives of three-year-olds and that the main activity facilitating these musical episodes is the audio-viewing of television programmes, advertisements, trails and films targeted at this audience.[2] This chapter explores how young children's television immerses the under-fives in a sea of musically-mediated stories and subtexts which, while manifestly offering a range of educational, moral and developmental instruction, latently contributes to the moulding of individual subjectivities, not least by preparing children to undertake gendered roles as productive consumer-citizens in contemporary British society. Such codes may impede the development of politically progressive worldviews regarding issues of gender, ethnicity and equality; the stereotyping involved may also indoctrinate children into attitudes at odds with the politically correct surface content of many shows. These aspects of children's television are one reason why 'the widely supported idea that children's programmes are a good thing, beneficial to society'[3] deserves scrutiny. The motivations and effects of such television are likely to be considerably more complex.

This analysis focuses on music and other audio-visual content in the four main incarnations of the long-running BBC children's television programme

---

[1]   Jeff Smith, *The Sounds Of Commerce: Marketing Popular Film Music* (New York, 1998), p. 4. Smith further defines pop scoring as being formally accessible to the average audience member, listing recurring stylistic features including the use of song forms and other simple structures, tonal harmony, riffs and hooks, rhythmic inflections such as swing, pentatonic (modal) melodies against tonal harmony, melodic inflections (e.g. blues notes) and distinctive timbres (such as guitars).

[2]   Alexandra Lamont, 'Young Children's Musical Worlds: Musical Engagement In 3.5 Year-Olds', *Journal Of Early Childhood Research* 6/3 (2008), pp. 247–61.

[3]   Jonathan Bignell, *An Introduction To Television Studies, Second Edition* (London, 2008), p. 245.

Postman Pat.[4] It builds on theories of subliminal conditioning in audio-visual contexts (specifically the work of Philip Tagg) to explore the manner in which, over the course of its three major branding reincarnations, changes to *Postman Pat*'s use of music – most markedly apparent in the evolution of its main title sequences – have created a shift in ideological emphasis, albeit perhaps unconsciously and primarily in the service of changing commercial imperatives. *Postman Pat*'s well-known main title theme ends with the line: 'Pat feels he's a really happy man.' In the three decades since its initial appearance, the titles and, more broadly speaking, the entirety of the show's musical content (of which the titles are representative) have contributed to a shift in emphasis away from the suggestiveness of the equivocal statement 'Pat *feels* …' (implying a character of emotional depth, empathy, sensitivity, interiority, even a degree of uncertainty) to a more rigid articulation of the notion 'he's a really happy *man*' – not least through an emphasis on connotations more stereotypically associated with that final word. By 2008, the hero of *Postman Pat* had come to embody an archetype of heroic masculinity far removed from the idling postal worker whose gentle adventures first aired in 1981. Pat has been transformed from a rural postman with an unreliable van and cat for companionship to an all-action, helicopter-flying superhero – and a family man to boot. That process has been articulated, in part, through sound and music, the flagship for which is the main title sequence for each Pat incarnation. The main titles indicate dramatic changes to the show's mode of discourse, which have occurred while the show's basic moral subtexts have remained largely unaltered. The show continues to promote ideas such as teamwork and community, but a dissonance has developed between the intended moral subtexts of the show's stories and their mode of representation. That dissonance is reflected in the symbolic contradiction that develops in its theme tune over the course of its four incarnations.

Decoding Children's Television Music

British children's television programming may be divided into subcategories related to those K.J. Donnelly finds at the root of all television: drama and current affairs.[5] Admittedly, children's 'current affairs' programming (which ranges from *Blue Peter* to the links between shows on the CBeebies channel) contains rather more craft, songs and glove-puppet assistants than the output of the BBC newsroom. The principles, however, are similar: one strand deals in live, studio-based 'reality', the other in works of fiction. Alongside educational (current affairs) content, David Buckingham divides children's drama into two further subcategories: storytelling

---

    [4]   I would like to thank my Keele University colleague Dr Alexandra Lamont for the many stimulating and detailed discussions we have shared concerning *Postman Pat* and children's television.
    [5]   K.J. Donnelly, *The Spectre Of Sound* (London, 2005).

and entertaining (or 'surreal' storytelling). *Postman Pat* falls into the storytelling tradition:

> A line can be traced here from *The Woodentops* through programmes like *Camberwick Green* and *Trumpton* in the 1960s and *Postman Pat* and *Cockleshell Bay* in the 1970s [*sic*] to *Rosie And Jim*, *Tots TV* and *Fireman Sam* in the 1980s and 1990s. Programmes in this tradition are predominantly based in domestic or pastoral settings, representing the idealized communities of 'middle England'. There is often an implicit pedagogy here – with lessons about tolerance and sharing – but moral messages are really laid on thick.[6]

Such messages and pedagogy, explicit or implicit, are what permit the widely supported idea that children's programmes are basically a 'good thing' to prosper.

Unsurprisingly, the range of basic functions performed by music in children's television is also comparable to adult programming. There is a predominance of performances and music-video styled montage, albeit with presenters more likely to burst into song than their grown-up counterparts; there are also more cues in the dramatic underscoring of children's TV. This is partly because contemporary children's programming maintains links to classical Hollywood cartoons and their cueing practices, but also because of the influence of canonic programming for children, such as *Sesame Street* (Children's Television Workshop 1969–2000; Sesame Workshop 2000–). In this benchmark US educational show, at least 71 per cent of all action is accompanied musically.[7] The cues on children's television, in turn, conform to the basic categories of adult television music. As Donnelly observes, the scoring divides between original underscoring (drawing on film practices), reiterated blocks of original music (a process more typical of television) and the use of library or stock music (rare on film), although divisions between categories are often blurred. An original score, in later episodes of a show, can be cut in as regularly reiterated blocks; library or stock music can be used to create the illusion of an original score.[8] Surveying a range of children's programming produced between the 1960s and 2000s suggests, however, a gradual evolution of practice as the market has become both more lucrative (through syndication and spin-off merchandising) and competitive, with production budgets commensurately expanded. Shows with reiterated blocks were once the norm. Programmes such as *Trumpton* (BBC, 1967) *Mr Benn* (BBC, 1971) and *Ivor The Engine* (ITV, 1959–64; BBC, 1976–77) featured charming and often innovatively scored blocks (such

6   David Buckingham, 'Child-Centred Television? *Teletubbies* And The Educational Imperative', in David Buckingham (ed.), *Small Screens: Television For Children* (London, 2004), p. 54.

7   D.E. Wolfe and S. Stambaugh, 'Musical Analysis Of *Sesame Street*: Implications For Music Therapy Practice And Research', *Journal Of Music Therapy* 30/4 (1993), pp. 224–35.

8   Donnelly, *Spectre*, p. 115.

as cues led by Ivor's bassoon 'voice', created by Small Film's house composer Vernon Elliott, or *Mr Benn*'s psychedelic take on Debussy and Stravinsky in the hands of Don Warren), original to the show but reused, in later episodes, as a library of show-specific stock. The initial series of *Postman Pat* followed this practice. More recently, however, the prestige end of children's programming (including *Postman Pat*) has tended to include a mixture of original scoring in every episode alongside stock cues; the function of the stock cues has in turn diversified, with some iterations acting like an intra-textual ident reinforcing brand identity (see the discussion below of *Postman Pat: Special Delivery Service*); similar situations pertain in contemporary programming like *Bob The Builder* (BBC, 1999–) and *In The Night Garden* (BBC, 2007–). Such shows have to work harder and shout louder to make their presence felt in a market overloaded with choice (in comparison to the mere minutes per day of television programming available to UK children as recently as the 1980s): in Britain alone there are dozens of children's channels. Music and sound are weapons in this lucrative battle.

The semiotic content, manifest or latent, of scoring in children's television is rarely subtle. As Donnelly argues, quoting Nicholas Cook, the intertextual confection of television pop scoring's 'styles and genres offer unsurpassed opportunities for communicating complex social or attitudinal messages practically instantaneously'.[9] Cues within television's tessellated form are always more reliant on knee-jerk connotations than, say, the thematic associations or careful structuring of mood permitted by filmic practices. On children's shows, however, the pixels making up the style topical content are distinctly low-res. This makes for some crude examples of musically-mediated ideology, which would seem laughable were it not for the manner in which such music can indelibly stain a young mind.[10] In children's television, such stains mark the impression of musical content with a single-entendre symbolism. In the second season of *Thomas The Tank Engine* (ITV, 1984–92) the arrival of Diesel, a villainous non-steam engine, provides a ludicrously obvious example of the musical creation of an evil-doing 'other'. Diesel's appearances are not scored with the bright Ionian chuffing of the other engines' shared themes, but rather with a subset of reiterated slithering melodies whose reedy synth scoring and chromaticism imply somewhat more exotic climes than the pastoral English haven of Sodor. Intertextually, Diesel's cues play on what Jon Paxman has called a 'religious/mystical metonymy' connecting such scoring clichés to Oriental or Oriental-Semitic traditions and to evocations of the Arabic *Hijaz* mode.[11] Diesel is scored, in other words, as an exotic bogeyman: listen to the US series *24* (Fox, 2001–) and it becomes striking that Diesel's

---

[9]   Nicholas Cook, 'Music And Meaning In The Commercials', *Popular Music* 13/1 (1994), p. 35; quoted in Donnelly, *Spectre*, pp. 127–9.

[10]   Donnelly, ibid., pp. 123–4.

[11]   Jon Paxman, 'Preisner-Kieślowski: The Art Of Synergetic Understatement in *Three Colours: Red*' in Miguel Mera and David Burnand (eds), *European Film Music* (Aldershot, 2006), p. 154.

presence is cued in precisely the same way as that drama's Islamic extremists. The problem of such musical stereotyping is obvious, but representative more generally of television music's rich play on pop scoring's stylistic associations. The astonishing diversity of non-Western musical cultures is reduced, in such instances, to a style topic structuring, by dint of repetition in villainous contexts from children's programming upwards, an automatic connection in the mind of the audio-viewer linking dastardly behaviour to 'other' musics.[12] By extension, cultures associated with such musics become dastardly. Carried to an extreme, in a mind responding in this conditioned manner to a lifetime spent listening to screen music, thanks to the scoring of programmes ranging from *Thomas The Tank Engine* to *24*, all Muslims are terrorists. Just for good measure, Diesel's villainous bodywork is painted black.[13]

Other children's television themes perform gender stereotyping, and it would be naïve to argue that such mediations merely reflect the nature of the societies whose infants they are made to entertain. Such music participates in the construction of society's nature for the very young. *Postman Pat*'s main title and end title sequences, for instance, have been marked by strong changes over the years. Reading the changes in relation to Tagg's polarities of gender in television music's semiotics, Pat's scoring appears to have undergone something of a sex change. As Pat's character has evolved from an idling, somewhat emasculated rural postman (his best friend is Jess the cat, and his symbol of prowess – his van – often breaks down) to an urban, alpha-male superhero, his scoring has changed its costume. Audio and visual changes have pushed Pat away from the nuanced subjectivity presented by the show's original version in 1981, in which markers of masculinity are unthreateningly counterbalanced by feminine voices, and into a harder, faster, more vigorously accented, texturally busier and sound effect-laden realm. As the music's stylistic significations have become more stereotypically masculine, the main title's general audio-visual environment has also changed. As well as signalling Tagg's 'reveille' function, which Donnelly cites as a function for television title sequences alongside being an attraction in and of themselves as a form of a musical performance,[14] *Postman Pat*'s titles now stand proud alongside performances of masculinity in children's programming like *Bob The Builder*'s main title sequence, whose laddish singalong blends the Britpop of Oasis with the

---

[12]   This is scarcely a new phenomenon in audio-visual texts aimed at children. There are reasons other than feline breed, for instance, behind the pentatonic duet of the goldfish- and Lady-taunting Siamese cats in *Lady And The Tramp* (Clyde Geronomi et al., 1955): 'We are Siamese if you please', and racist stereotyping even if you don't please.

[13]   Other black or notably dark-hued engines in *Thomas The Tank Engine*'s realm include, by accident or design, Douglas and Donald (Scottish), Emily (female), and Bert and 'Arry (diesels and distinctly working-class), all of whom contrast sharply with the primary-hued, upper middle-class, public schoolboy personae of Thomas, James, Edward, Gordon and Percy.

[14]   Donnelly, *Spectre*, p. 113.

football terrace chanting delivery of Neil Morrissey, an actor otherwise best known for being one of two *Men Behaving Badly* (ITV, 1992; BBC, 1994–98).[15] Pat and Bob are not superheroes saving the world, of course; they are just decent lads doing their jobs. The shows glamorise everyday clichés of masculine roles as heroic, forming an extension of television's promotion of patriarchal culture every bit as apparent in the lives of their televisual predecessors, such as the firemen, mayors, factory workers, carpenters, Lords and soldiers of Trumptonshire.[16] Early *Postman Pat*, however, partially bucked that trend, offering a version of masculinity more nuanced and politically progressive than his more recent incarnations.

A Postman Scored

The four ages of *Postman Pat* discussed below are referred to as follows: Classic Pat, Neo Pat, New Pat and Nu Pat. These titles refer to the following quartet of periods in the show's production history: its original run as *Postman Pat* (1981), brief flurries of programming along very similar lines but under the title *Postman Pat And His Black And White Cat* (1991–96), a substantial re-imagining of the show under the original title (2004–2007) and its most recent reincarnation as *Postman Pat: Special Delivery Service* (2008–). Throughout these different versions of the show, key aspects of the series pertain, as summarised by Hal Erickson:

> Created for Britain's BBC1 in 1981, *Postman Pat* was a 15-minute children's show utilizing stop-motion animation and set in the mythical Yorkshire village of Greendale. The bushy-haired, needle-nosed titled character was the meticulously polite and endlessly resourceful Pat Clifton, the town's postman. In each episode, Pat's efforts to deliver mail were invariably complicated by unforeseen problems, at which point virtually every citizen in the tightly knit community pulled together to help Pat (or themselves) out. The object of this, of

---

[15]   Stan Hawkins's discussion of encodings of laddish masculinity in Britpop could easily have included *Bob The Builder*'s main title theme alongside his other examples (Oasis, the Manic Street Preachers and Pulp): 'Unsettling Difference: Music And Identity In Britpop', paper given at *Analysing Popular Music In Context Symposium*, University of Liverpool, 16 November 2007.

[16]   Such encodings are apparent even in TV aimed at children as young as one. *In The Night Garden*'s boyishly blue, Tintin-fringed boy-thing Iggle Piggle is permitted to fool around and be naughty after all his friends have gone to bed. Those better-behaved friends include pink-dressed, brown-faced, dreadlock-sporting Upsy Daisy, who prefers collecting flowers, singing, dancing and going to bed as soon as she's tired to boundary-pushing acts of disobedience. In spite of her styling's nod to politically-correct diversity, like so much children's television, that progressiveness is only skin deep. Piggle is clearly marked as the heroic figure that boys should aspire to be and girls celebrate (in the main title sequence, it is literally suggested that dreaming children metamorphose, in their dreams, into Iggle Piggle).

course, was to help the kiddies in the audience hone their own problem-solving and other cognitive skills. The huge and colorful 'supporting cast' included Pat's pet cat, Jess; schoolkids Katy and Tom Pottage, Charlie Pringle, and Lucy Selby; local prelate Rev Timms; farmers Alf Thompson, George Lancaster, and Peter Fogg; auto-shop owner Sam Waldron; handyman Ted Glen; waitress Nisha Bains; Police Constable Selby; and general practitioner Dr. Sylvia Gilbertson. Although Postman Pat was popular the world over under a variety of titles – in Poland it was known as *Listonosz Pat*, in Holland it was *Pieter Post*, and in Iran it was *Pat-e Postchi*, etc. – the series was not widely seen in America until September of 2005, when it was picked up for daily play by the HBO Family channel.[17]

The reading of the show's music advanced here draws on Tagg's theorising of the manner in which style topical clichés in screen scoring encode equally clichéd representations of idealised masculinity and femininity: 'Music – even without words or accompanying visuals – is capable of creating and communicating semantic fields of considerable ideological potential ... manag[ing] to influence our attitudes towards such phenomena as male, female, nature, Native Americans, etc.'[18]

Considering musical characteristics alongside visual and verbal associations, Tagg hypothesised polarities of gender expressed by mainstream scoring practices, as shown in Table 14.1 below:

Table 14.1   Tagg's Hypothesised Dualities Of Male And Female Scoring Clichés

Male	Female	Male	Female	Male	Female
fast	slow	sudden	gradual	active	passive
dynamic	static	upwards	downwards	outwards	inwards
hard	soft	jagged	smooth	sharp	rounded
urban	rural	modern	old times	strong	weak

Postman Pat's main and end titles have metamorphosed to substitute one state of masculinity, in which feminine and masculine character and musical traits

---

[17]   Hal Erickson, 'Postman Pat', *All Movie Guide* (www.fandango.com/postmanpat[an imatedtvseries]_v355895/-summary).

[18]   Philip Tagg, 'Music, Moving Image, Semiotics, And The Democratic Right to Know', paper given at *Music And Manipulation* Conference, Nalen, Stockholm, 18 September 1999); now available in developed form in Philip Tagg and Bob Clarida, *Ten Little Title Tunes: Towards A Musicology Of The Mass Media* (New York and Montreal, 2003).

mingle, for another. It is also possible to suggest how changes to the main titles' other audio-visual content[19] – alongside story details, basic parameters such as pace of cutting and density of sound effects – have participated in Pat's reinvention; see Table 14.2 below:

Table 14.2   *Postman Pat* Main Title Shots And Sound Effects Density

	Classic Pat	**Neo Pat**	**New Pat**	**Nu Pat**
Shots	11	13	33	35
Sound Effects	3	17	18	31

Classic Pat

The original *Postman Pat* main title song was composed by Brian Daly, who also wrote music for 1980s children's series *Bertha* (BBC, 1985). It explores a semiotic richness blending the masculine and feminine scoring stereotypes identified by Tagg. The vocal 'persona'[20] is obviously male, although the singing of Ken Barrie (the narrator for the series and thus the 'voice of Pat') is breathy and restrained, with the precise consonants needed to enunciate clearly for children. There is a suggestion of a Northern English accent and the delivery, swung and slightly bluesy, also has a hint of Louis Armstrong. His performance thereby references various clichés of authenticity and trustworthiness which underline the performance's playful and benign authority.[21] However, the song's 'environment'[22] has an obvious feminine aspect, accentuating the restraint and lack of threat of the persona. The vocal melody is doubled throughout by what sounds like a banjo, its harp-like timbre complementing the acoustic rhythm guitar; a solo flute and wordlessly murmuring female chorus sound alongside the persona's vocals;

---

[19]   In Classic Pat the 11 shots are discrete, but in New Pat there are more subtle camera effects (pans, zooms) which intensify the business of the action. In Neo Pat the sound effects mainly consist of cat meows and various noises connected with the van (doors opening and closing, engine noise, braking noise) while in Nu Pat sound effects also include non-realistic cueing for visual events. Gradually there is a shift, in other words, from fidelity and realism to greater degrees of fantasy (or, in Buckingham's terms, 'surreal storytelling').

[20]   Allan Moore, 'The Persona-Environment Relationship In Recorded Song', *Music Theory Online* 11/4 (2005).

[21]   Authenticity may also be ascribed to the song by way of the alternation of bars of 4/4 and 3/4 as discussed below; see Moore's discussion of John Lennon's 'Working-Class Hero' (1970) in 'Authenticity As Authentication', *Popular Music* 21/2 (2002), pp. 209–23. In turn, a later development of the theme song (also discussed below) may tempt one to revoke any such authentication.

[22]   Moore, 'The Persona-Environment'.

McCartney-like bass guitar lines wander around the song's chords, forming harp-like arpeggios; the other elements of the rhythm section are notably hushed (acoustic strumming, a gentle shuffle beat on bass drum, brushed snare and hi-hat). This stack of 'musemes'[23] connotes notions of the angelic feminine and also a safe pastoral h(e)aven: Greendale as a kind of Eden, with Pat an angelic presence, part paternal, part maternal.

The song is a pop ballad tinged with folk influences. Most obviously, this connotes the show's rural setting. More subtly, its broadest stylistic connotations – alongside its timbres, smooth lilt, unrushed progress and evocations of the pastoral and past – suggest stereotypes of femininity, as do further lyrical, melodic and musical characteristics evoking passivity, isolation and weakness. After a two-bar instrumental pick up in 4/4, in which melody is passed from acoustic guitar to an ornate flurry of flute, the vocal begins. Doubt begins to be suggested when the persona sings about Jess the cat. The 4/4 established at the start of the song, and reinforced by the first bar of vocal ('Postman Pat, Postman Pat ...'), moves (perhaps in an echo of folk song practices) through a bar of 3/4 to accommodate the feline tagline ('Postman Pat and his black-and-white cat'). This is an iconic musical moment and the song's most original hook; it is also peculiar. The major key and tonic chord of the opening two iterations of the show's title – already pushing into minor territory through the melody's ascent to scale degree $\hat{6}$ on each 'Pat' – slip to vi on 'cat' as, modally and metrically, the song is immediately diverted into uncertainty and even melancholy then amplified, by omission, in the persona-less bar of 4/4 and unchallenged vi that follows. This moment contrasts the crowded syllables in the first bar with its precise opposite, musical and textual space, as cramped rhythmic velocity cedes to a reflective void.

Pat is not, of course, a tragic character, and so, while the opening of the song suggests complexities, the music quickly moves to signify the likelihood of a positive denouement, in an example of musical problem-solving mirroring the show's typical 'the mail must get through' plotlines. By the time Pat 'picks up the postbags in his van', major mode, tonic and 4/4 metre have all been firmly reinstated via tonality's (or at least Heinrich Schenker's) favourite contrapuntal-harmonic pincer movement: IV-ii-V and eventually I in the harmony, with a melodic pattern embellishing (initially via a rising $\hat{4}$-$\hat{5}$-$\hat{6}$) a $\hat{3}$-$\hat{2}$-$\hat{1}$ descending line sinking to the security of the tonic. Like many other theme tunes connoting aspects of a male protagonist,[24] obstacles are overcome, suggesting that the show's hero will do the same in the ensuing episode. Pat's overcoming is quite gentle though: an erosion of boundaries rather than a show of force. This permits, as the song continues, a lingering sense of equivocation.

---

[23]   See the analysis of Abba's 'Fernando' in Philip Tagg, *Fernando The Flute: Analysis Of Musical Meaning In An Abba Mega-Hit* (Liverpool, 1991).

[24]   See, for example, Philip Tagg, *Kojak. 50 Seconds Of Television Music: Towards The Analysis Of Affect In Popular Music* (New York and Montreal, 2000).

After reiterating Pat and Jess's identities, the song offers its qualified assertion of the protagonist's mental state over a repeat of the tonic centring progression: 'All the birds are singing and the day is just beginning, Pat feels he's a really happy man' (female voices here mark the only significant musical change, providing a mimesis of sorts for 'singing'). Not Pat *is* a really happy man, note, or Pat *knows* he's a really happy man: Pat *feels* this – it is an intuition. It would be ludicrous to imply that Pat's song signifies a character given to moments of existential brooding, but there is none of the cocksure certainty here of, say, *Bob The Builder*'s 'Can we fix it? Yes we can!' With Pat, the song suggests, the answer to the same question would be 'maybe … if I get around to it'. Throughout Classic Pat's run, Pat spends a good deal of time daydreaming, idling, and not really performing his job. For instance, he stops to lean on a dry-stone wall and admire the hard work of farmers to the sound of Daly's 'Looking at life through a farmer's eyes', thereby engaging in a show of empathy underscored by that delightful song; elsewhere, he stops for a nap on a sunny day, presumably just because he can. Classic Pat would not cut the mustard in Bob's hard-driven team, yet the lessons he offers – not regarding a heroic transcendence of odds but rather the need to be sympathetic to the feelings and lives of other people – feel at least equally valuable. Such values – intuition, empathy, kindness – are stereotypically inscribed as feminine domains by screen music practices, yet it is towards such notions that Pat's original main title leans. His qualities, his theme song suggests, include being in touch with his feminine side.

Classic Pat's main title also hints that his community values him for precisely these qualities. As the song explains in its middle eight, not only does everybody know Pat's bright red van, but 'all his friends will smile as he waves to greet them' – a warm embrace of community, amplified by the environment of the song when wordless backing vocals surround the solo persona. Doubt does return a final time, but as part of a gesture extending the subtext of the song to the audio-viewer, as the focus shifts from third-person 'Pat' to second-person 'you'. Over a lengthy sojourn on vi, the persona informs the audience (with a $\hat{3}$-$\hat{2}$-$\hat{1}$ descent in vi) that 'maybe … you can never be sure'. A IV-ii-V preparation, accompanying the phrase 'there'll be knock … ring … letters through your door', then expels concerns, not least through the timely arrival of this main title's three sound effects as Pat, finally, delivers the mail (to 'you'). Musical tension, teased out by the silences and rising vocal contour around 'knock' and 'ring', is further defused by the chuckle of the persona. By shifting the pronoun from he to you, the song extends Pat's subjectivity and experiences to the audience. The verse returns and the female chorus swells affirmatively behind the persona, the flute offering a bird-like countermelody, as the song protests twice more (too much?) that 'Pat feels he's a really happy man'. Slowing down to half-speed for a third and final statement of the 'Pat feels he's a really happy …' refrain then provides room for harp-like broken chords on the acoustic guitar, and more spaciousness and musing. As a final flourish on the flute mirrors the song's introduction, the word 'man', scale degree $\hat{1}$ and chord I reunite to close the song with a smiling admission of success.

Visually, the main title is a partial illustration of the song's lyrical content containing subtler features worth exploring. First, it connects musical signifiers of the feminine and pastoral to the visual, right from the rising flute flourish, which calls attention to the sun dominating the upper left quadrant of the opening image, before the camera pans right as Pat's van moves silently into view. Attention is thereby gently shifted from a focus on the pastoral environment – fields, trees, hedges, dry stone walls, hills, mountains in the distance – to the character who explores it, as revealed in the next shot (which cuts to a close-up of Pat in his van). Classic Pat is unambiguously a rural man. This is not where a male protagonist should be, as Tagg's findings demonstrated: women belong in the countryside, not men. Classic Pat, however, is presented as a man at home with the flora and fauna. The visuals reinforce this: Pat is (feline aside) alone in his environment. One hears talk of his community but, crucially, one does not see them.

The other striking characteristic of the visuals in Classic Pat's main title suggests a connection between the rhythm of the montage and its gendered musical significations. The very long shot of the post box, as Pat collects mail, is typical of the sequence. The camera focuses on the box long before Pat's van arrives. He then ambles out, retrieves the letters, stops for a bit of a look around, gets back in, backs up the van and drives off. The camera stays put throughout the entire sequence of events for a bathetic 25 seconds. Elsewhere, the camera pauses (like Pat's tendency to idle in admiration of nature) on flora, against which writer John Cunliffe's credit appears; another long pause accompanies a credit for Ivor Wood, designer and director of the show; as the van passes through a village, it lingers as composer Brian Daly gets a credit too (his name appearing in a smaller font size). Overall, just 10 cuts occur in the sequence, and only three sound effects. Visually and stylistically, as with the lyrics and music, the main title evokes Classic Pat's realm and character. It speaks of gentleness, empathy, emotions, community and kindness.

Neo Pat

The 1990s remake of *Postman Pat* was, in many respects, an attempt directly to replicate the look and success of the original series, albeit on a higher budget that did not, oddly, extend to new music (the show is devoid of underscoring, thus unable to replicate the already sparse block scoring of Classic Pat). The audio track is dominated instead by a plethora of prominent sound effects, a decision which impacts on the main title sequence.

While similar to Classic Pat, the most obvious musical development in Neo Pat's main titles is the re-recording of the song, which is much more cleanly mixed. Other elements have changed subtly too, reorienting the song's significations of gender in the direction of a more stereotypical display of masculinity. The percussion is more prominent (sleigh bells on the off-beats, for instance); the chordal filler's texture has been reinforced through the addition of low synthesised strings occupying a masculine register akin to Barrie's, hinting at weight and profundity; the female backing vocals are less prominent and the flute also recedes in the mix, both being somewhat masked by the string pad. The flute's hitherto prominent closing figure is also obscured by the most prominent addition to the main title's audio content: sound effects, and in this case Pat's van horn, beeped in time to the music and on the tonic pitch. 'Man', scale degree $\hat{1}$, chord I and 'horn' thus combine at the song's now less gentle moment of triumph. Engine and van noises, in fact, dominate the opening titles, creating an exhaust cloud of signs far removed from Classic Pat's pastoral utopia. The rattling combustion engine, whining brakes and horn, alongside the reinforcement of drums and lower timbres, combined with the paring back of female vocals and flute, dress Neo Pat's title in more masculine garb. The persona is even partially obscured by the engine noise, most notably at the end as the moments of feeling, thoughtful pauses and harp-like chords are revved into submission.

The visual track also changes to signify a more active form of agency, in terms of both its story content and mode of discursive presentation. One no longer has time to admire the landscape as Pat's van races immediately (and noisily) into view along with the main title (and then the subtitle 'and his black and white cat'). Pat thus appears to be more dynamic. He is also less isolated: the titles pedantically show the people waving to Pat; he is also seen knocking, ringing and posting letters to 'you'. A sense of a man in a (more urban) community is one result, the hamlet-like dwellings of Classic Pat now replaced by intimations of a larger village or small town. Pat also appears to be more proficient at doing his job, thanks to the sequence's editing. That 25-second epic of mail collection is pared back via ellipses (making time for the pedantic shots). Neo Pat is a man who gets the job done, and more quickly than Classic Pat. The number of cuts is higher in this sequence, and the camera is more active (with pans) and the audio more cramped: here the song must compete with 17 discrete sound effects (more than five times as many as Classic Pat). Visually and sonically, Neo Pat begins to suggest the more dynamic, faster, harder, urban, impetuous, modern, active and strong hero revealed in New and Nu Pat.

New Pat

Technical developments in animation in the decade since Neo Pat meant that New Pat's animation was slicker yet more banal than its predecessors. While its style evokes the stop animation of Classic and Neo Pat, the show's increased reliance on digital effects lacks visual depth and (for the nostalgic) charm. The music is also much denser within each episode, straining, as in other puppet shows, to compensate for the still limited range of facial expressions, body movement and ability of the puppets visually to signify emotion.[25] The changing of the artistic guard is marked in the credits: the show is now 'based on' and 'upon' the original series. The music credit, moreover, is removed completely from the main title

---

[25]   See Donnelly, *Spectre*, 120.

sequence. Daly gets an end title mention for the main title song, but it is Simon Woodgate of Echobass Studios who receives the most prominent music credit. Ken Barrie remains as vocalist and voice of Pat (although he and Carole Boyd, the latter prominent in Neo Pat's episodes, have been augmented by further voice artists, including those better placed to provide ethnic authenticity in the more diverse environment of twenty-first-century Greendale). On the surface, this is therefore a more politically correct show: the railway is run by Nisha and Ajay Baines, female characters are more prominent, and Pat is seen interacting with all adults as equals. New Pat's music and the look of the titles, however, make Pat himself feel more of a cliché, and rather less like the 'new man' intimated by Classic Pat's music.

The new arrangement of the theme (presumably by Woodgate) is less nuanced than Daly's. The individuality of instrumental lines gets lost in an accompaniment shackled to the articulation of the main melodic line. The track is rhythmically busier and more densely scored, thereby accruing extra loudness. The kit is more prominent, the kick drum being precisely that – a kick, not a muffled whump. Bell sounds are louder and the side drum is brushed more aggressively; the second verse adds cowbells and other metallic percussion to reinforce its clanking beat; tuned percussion add a counter melody (perhaps suggesting New Pat's multi-ethnic dimension). The tuned percussion (perhaps a synthesised marimba) is also interesting for suggesting mechanisation and industry. This could be heard as an extension of Pat's van, reinforcing the presence of that masculine symbol alongside the prominent vehicular sound effects. More subtly, it evokes a shift from a character associated with the rural 'past' to an industrialised urban 'present'. Other elements blend with the percussion and signifiers of the urban to stress New Pat's more heroic male credentials.

Barrie's voice is multi-tracked from the start, strengthening the persona's line in a manner that makes it sound more laddish and rather like the delivery of *Bob The Builder*'s title song (Woodgate, notably, has also worked on that BBC show). Multi-tracked female voices double the persona's utterances, adding heft to the vocal line. They stress, as the song begins, the name 'Postman Pat', but the image being stressed on screen is not Pat but a *Postman Pat* logo, complete with embedded ™ sign: it is only ten seconds later that it becomes clear this is a song about a postman, not a brand. (It is both, of course, and always has been, but now this is thematicised within the action of the titles itself – a trait carried to product-placing extremes in Nu Pat.) The vocal reinforcement permits them to compete against the many other instruments. The strings occupy a more trebly register, working against the flute, guitar and some of the vocals. The blandness of the track is not solely an issue of the reliance on synthesised sounds, although the flute has been replaced with a notably crude digital approximation: it is also an issue of arrangement. A diversity of 18 loud sound effects, not merely those of the van and delivery, also vie for one's aural attention. Jess meows, the birds tweet, the van blots out the music some of the time; at other times, music itself becomes a non-realistic sound effect, as when a glockenspiel sound points the moment Pat tips his hat to handyman Ted, evincing the beginnings of a move from realist storytelling to surreal storytelling continued in Nu Pat's repositioning of Pat as a far from realistic superhero.

The end of the sequence contains the payoff for New Pat's reinforced audio-visual masculinity: an image of the newly urban Pat, framed against his cottage with his wife, son, and Jess re-imagined as a family pet. So this is why Pat feels so happy: he is a heterosexual family man, complete with a wife and child, and a cat who is the icing on the familial cake, rather than the emotional support structure of a lonely idler (notably Jess jumps into the boy's arms, not Pat's). Compared to the earlier incarnations of the main title, it almost feels as if the shot has been added to dissuade one from speculating about Pat's sexuality in light of the more nuanced significations of Classic Pat. Pat is now a family man, driving a daringly noisy van and moving beyond reproach as a basic male stereotype/role model. The pace and activity of the montage's 33 shots, making it three times more active than the original title sequence, in turn ramps up the evocations of strength, pace, activity and dynamism. This discursive clarification of Pat's masculinity goes hand in hand with the more patronising nature of the action leading up to the shot of his family: every single nuance of the song is now spelled-out. All the birds are singing, and so birds are *seen* singing; Pat really does pick up postbags in his van; animated Pat chuckles when Barrie chuckles. The simple has been rendered simplistic, if not boneheaded – a distinction one may wish to reserve for Nu Pat.

Nu Pat

For its most recent incarnation, *Postman Pat*'s main title arrangement was recomposed as an evocation of joy, magic and daring do, transporting the show from realistic storytelling into a realm of surreal fantasy and virtually superheroism. Full of Fairy Godmother's wand sounds and other non-realistic sonic additions (as when Pat performs an impossible, superheroic flying dive – in slow motion – to save Jess from some catastrophe), the mix suggests higher levels of energy and, indeed, testosterone: this is postman as superman. Nu Pat no longer only drives his van: he rides a motorcycle, drives a *bigger* van and, in the show's most preposterous addition, flies a helicopter. The 'village' of Greendale sports a massive rail terminal and heliport, presumably to support his postal endeavours (no wonder the Royal Mail is going bankrupt). Tagg's analysis of scoring clichés suggested that, in the world of screen music semiotics, heroic men are never sad (in direct contradiction, amongst other things, of the fact that more men commit suicide than women). The Pat laughing at the end of Nu Pat's title sequence cackles maniacally in front of an adoring crowd, having just airdropped presents to the children (including his own son, depicted here receiving – in a moment of blatant product-placement – a toy model of his father driving Classic Pat's old van). Perhaps the steroids permitting Nu Pat to perform his heroic deeds have driven him slightly mad. How else to explain his changed relationship to the rural environment he so fought to preserve back in 1981 (the show's lessons usually revolving around upholding the Country

Code)? In Nu Pat, he rides his motorbike (Jess in the sidecar) through a hedge, punching an enormous hole in it. The mail must get through: screw the livestock. Nu Pat even has a catch phrase. At the end of each episode, he raises two thumbs aloft and hails his own achievements with a hearty 'Mission accomplished'. He'd certainly get an interview with Bob.

Nu Pat's clichés of masculine heroism are also channelled into the rearrangement of the song and the style of montage. The synthesised drums are thumped, moving from Classic Pat's shuffle into a hard rock style. Indeed, the entire track begins with the rock cliché of a drum fill, followed by a whoosh effect signifying the flight of Pat's helicopter, which sweeps into view above the sprawl of Nu Pat's Greendale. Every sound has digital clarity and an edge which creates a rattling noisiness to the mix, but the biggest musical change of all – also symbolic of the shift from nuanced mixed gendering to outright masculinity – is the handling of that moment of metrical doubt when Jess is first mentioned. Lamentably, the track follows the 3/4 with a bar of 5/4, not 4/4, in effect rendering the pair as a clunkily accented succession of 4/4 bars.[26] Doubt is thus stomped out. The flute has also been disciplined. The initial gesture is present, but not so prominent in the mix and curtly shortened; it is henceforth buried mid-texture. While the flute's symbolising of a feminine voice is there but never again prominent, however, actual female voices have been literally erased. All three previous versions of the theme had a chorus of females supplementing Barrie's performance; here one hears only the persona's masculine presence. Nu Pat, it would seem, needs music that is all man – a sentiment reinforced by the use of sound effects and cuts. 35 shots are seen (more than three times as many as Classic Pat), although the titles last no longer (still around 45 seconds). There is also much busier camerawork (this continues into the show itself, which now features *24*-style split-screen effects when Pat, like Jack Bauer on a CTU mission, takes urgent calls on his Special Delivery hotline). There are also 31 sound effects, ten times as many as Classic Pat, adding to a bulldozing audio-visual density (dozens of characters now vie for one's attention, where once only Pat and Jess wandered the landscape).

This process extends to the end titles too. Classic and Neo Pat's end title sequences were perfunctory but charming instrumental renditions of the main title song, with Pat/Barrie humming along. New Pat's end titles, however, featured an entirely new song, presumably by Woodgate: an up-tempo singalong, complete with call-and-response, enquiring of the audience 'Postman, Postman Pat, can you tell what's in his van?' (Clue: it has four legs.) The vocal chorus is mixed, but many other aspects of the song are in keeping with the clichéd masculinity of New Pat. The beat is almost twice as fast as the main title tune and the music has a fuller-throttled rock-style drum track (no brushes here, anticipating Nu Pat). The most striking timbral addition, however, is to the chordal filler layer: brass chords replace the main title's strings. Pat is thereby seen and heard in New Pat's end

---

[26] In doing so, one site for ascriptions of authenticity is also erased as another is erected. See footnote 21.

titles surrounded by drums and brass, like a military hero on parade. There is no room for doubt and interiority here: the only moment of harmonic uncertainty (on the first 'what's in the van' question) is a ii chord swiftly transformed into a II (V of V), as the song powers away from minor modality to solve that question with the arrival of a perfect cadence. The song is leadenly mixed, with no moments of textural respite, and the surface speed of the music is very fast.

Nu Pat goes further still: while Woodgate is credited with 'Music and Songs', title music is credited to Karl Twigg. Presumably this should read 'End Title music' – the regretful omission of any mention of Daly in *Postman Pat: Special Delivery Service* renders this information ambiguous.[27] But that omission also reads symbolically: just as the creator of the show's familiar title song has been airbrushed from its credits, so too have the nuances of Pat's character that his song and arrangement once articulated. Classic Pat's combination of masculine and feminine character traits have been steamrolled in a rush to conformity. Twigg, partnered with Mark Topham, is best known for his work at PWL; they co-wrote and produced hit records for Steps, Five and Westlife. Pat's musical realm has metamorphosed from folk-tinged pop pastoralism to mainstream, child-marketed pop. For *Postman Pat: Special Delivery Service*, Twigg provides the end title song of the same name. But the 'Special Delivery Service' theme is heard throughout the show, marking the commercial territory of the programme with its spinning logo (at scene transitions) always seen alongside the opening of its musical ident, and foreshadowing its eventual annunciation over the end title credits, which finish searing the show's rebranded identity into the audio-viewer's consciousness. Fast and upbeat, the song's style is reminiscent – of all things – of the Lightning Seeds in its combination of rock styling, electronica and pop sensibilities. That makes it, in a sense, atypical Britpop: the Lightning Seeds offered a more sensitive, poppier approach and were fronted by an (immensely talented) singer-songwriter (Ian Broudie) with a 'weaker' voice and image. Yet the band also has laddish credentials as impeccable as *Bob The Builder*'s singer: they are most famous for 'Football's Coming Home', the English fans' anthem at the 1996 European Soccer Championships.

A Postman Scorned

It is unsurprising that *Postman Pat*'s main title and end title sequences have evolved significantly over its 30-year period, while remaining synced to the screen music conventions of the scoring practices of adult television. Those changes, in part, reflect broader trends in televisual aesthetics, and primarily the move, over the past ten to 15 years, into a more frenetic mode of discourse or 'intensified

---

[27] Could it be that the metrical changes to the Nu Pat title theme were intended to circumnavigate copyright issues and thus permit authorship to be reassigned?

continuity':[28] a world of whip pans, lens glare, blue filters and jump cuts, usually accompanied by a whoosh or bang of sound. Sometimes modern television, its individual channels vying with myriad digital alternatives, feels designed merely to stimulate the orientation response, keeping audio-viewers locked into a 'what was that?' startle effect and thereby distracting one from the temptation of the remote control (not to mention the web or mobile phone). Modern *Postman Pat* competes in a similarly crowded, noisy, multimedia marketplace. It must shout, loud and often, to thrive.[29] The changing sound of *Postman Pat*'s title sequences, however, also tell a more subtle story.

As Buckingham notes, 'Spotting the intertextual references and symbolic associations, or alternatively "hunting the stereotypes"' in children's television 'are easy games to play, but they tell us very little about how children themselves interpret and relate to what they watch': such responses 'tell us much more about ourselves than they do about the intended audience'.[30] Children, in fact, have significant difficulties 'chunking' narrative information into coherent stories up to the ages of four or five[31] and prove even more resilient to a story's moral subtexts. What sticks, then, in young children's minds, in response to their ever-rising exposure to television? Where once Pat was characterised, by music, sounds and images, as a man one might now deem 'Metrosexual' – a nuanced balance of stereotypically feminine and masculine qualities – he has been gradually turned, not least through his scoring, into a blunter, more stereotypical superman. Nu Pat exists, it seems, noisily to fight his ground against not just Bob The Builder and Fireman Sam but Ben 10, the Power Rangers, and a plethora of other characters aimed (as programmes, websites and lucrative toy franchises) at the junior male marketplace. In doing so, there has been a simplification of the manner in which *Postman Pat* contributes to a moulding of audience consciousness regarding, particularly, the gendering of roles, thoughts, emotions and actions deemed fit for men and women in contemporary Western societies. While the effect of such mouldings will depend on an individual's viewing experience[32] and may be

---

[28]   David Bordwell, *The Way Hollywood Tells It: Story and Style in Modern Movies* (Los Angeles, 2006).

[29]   While Bordwell does not venture to suggest how such changes might be linked to broader currents in society, in a thoughtful review John Orr outlines possible routes for consideration of intensified continuity's links to 'a growing anxiety – the addled fragmentation of cultures in the so-called information age with its various forms of dysfunctional communication'. See John Orr, 'Feature Review: *Figures Traced In Light: On Cinematic Staging* by David Bordwell. *The Way Hollywood Tells It: Story and Style in Modern Movies* by David Bordwell', *Senses Of Cinema* 42 (2007).

[30]   Buckingham, *Small Screens*, p. 58.

[31]   Barry Gunter and Jill McAleer, *Children And Television, Second Edition* (London, 1997), p. 41.

[32]   See Bernadette Casey, Neil Casey, Ben Calvert, Liam French and Justin Lewis, 'Children And Television', in *Television Studies: The Key Concepts, Second Edition*

partially offset by parental guidance, experience of the show's music will clearly help condition young children's musical thoughts to respond, unthinkingly, to the 'correctness' of the scoring clichés that view certain characteristics and traits as more appropriately manly role models.

The emergent irony of *Postman Pat*'s changing identity is therefore as obvious as it is problematic. In terms of the show's action and characters, Nu and New Pat strain to be politically correct. Classic Pat's lone female professional (a doctor) holds not a candle to the range of diversity glimpsed in the more recent series. Its hero, however, has moved in the other direction and gradually become a cliché of masculinity, thanks in significant part to his scoring and the expectations raised by the main title sequences. The show's stories remain in step with progressive liberal politics, as one would expect from the BBC through the age of New Labour, but its hero – ultimately answering (like that government) to more brutal commercial imperatives – is now (like that government?) a less progressive role model than earlier incarnations. That paradox is reflected, decisively, in the shift in the main title sequence's 'persona-environment relationship' over the four incarnations. To borrow Allan Moore's terms, where once the song's environment provided 'support, amplification and explanation of the persona's situation', it has moved into a relationship of 'contradiction'.[33] Following Moore's analogy of body language, the persona's lyrics and melody (just about) continue to say one thing about the range of masculinities open to men in the early twenty-first century, but, rather like a politician saying one thing while his body language reveals that he is lying, Pat's environment forcibly asserts a more conservative and even reactionary agenda. One day – I feel you can probably be sure – that dissonance will have palpable consequences in the everyday thoughts of Pat's fans.

(London, 2008), pp. 30–33.
[33]   Moore, 'Persona-Environment', p. 27.

Bibliography

Abrams, Mark, *The Teenage Consumer: LPE Paper No 5* (London: London Press Exchange, 1959)

Abrams, Philip, 'Radio And Television', in Denys Thompson (ed.), *Discrimination And Popular Culture* (Harmondsworth: Penguin, 1964): 50–73

Addison, Roy, 'Elkan Allan', *The Independent*, 29 June 2006

Adorno, Theodor and Max Horkheimer, *Dialectic Of Enlightenment* (New York: Social Studies Association, 1944)

Adorno, Theodor, 'On Popular Music', in Richard Leppert (ed.), *Adorno On Music* (Berkeley CA: University of California Press 2002): 437–69

Allsopp, Kenneth, 'Pop Goes Young Woodley', in Richard Mabey (ed.), *Class: A Symposium* (London: Anthony Blond, 1967): 127–43

Aslama, Minna and Mervi Pantti, 'Talking Alone: Reality TV, Emotions And Authenticity', *European Journal Of Cultural Studies*, 9/2 (2006): 167–84

Bannister, Matthew, *White Boys, White Noise: Masculinities And 1980s Indie Guitar Rock* (Aldershot: Ashgate, 2006)

Barnard, Stephen, *On The Radio: Music Radio In Britain* (Milton Keynes: Open University Press, 1989)

Barrow, Tony, *John, Paul, George, Ringo and Me* (London: Sevenoaks, 2005)

Barrow, Tony, *Please Please Me* sleevenotes. (Parlophone PMC 1202, 1963)

Barthes, Roland, *Image–Music–Text* (London: Routledge, 1977)

Barthes, Roland, *Mythologies* (London: Cape, 1972)

Baxendale, John, 'You And I – All Of Us Ordinary People: Renegotiating "Britishness" In Wartime', in Nick Hayes and Jeff Hill (eds), *Millions Like Us? British Culture In The Second World War* (Liverpool: Liverpool University Press, 1999): 295–322

Bayley, Stephen, *Labour Camp: The Failure Of Style Over Substance* (London: Batsford, 1998)

Beatles, *Anthology* (London: Cassell, 2000)

Bell, Duncan, 'Mythscapes: Memory, Mythology And National Identity', *British Journal Of Sociology* 54/1 (2003): 63–81

Bell, Erin and Ann Gray, 'History On Television: Charisma, Narrative And Knowledge', *European Journal Of Cultural Studies* 10/1 (2007): 113–33

Bell, Erin, 'Televising History: The Past(s) On the Small Screen', *European Journal Of Cultural Studies* 10/5 (2007): 5–12

Bench, Jeff and Ray Tedman, *The Beatles On Television* (London: Reynolds & Hearn, 2008)

Bennett, Andy, 'Heritage Rock: Rock Music, Re-presentation And Heritage Discourse', *Poetics*, 37/5–6 (2009): 474–89

Bennett, Andy, *Cultures Of Popular Music* (Buckingham: Open University Press, 2001)

Bignell, Jonathan, *An Introduction To Television Studies, Second Edition* (London: Routledge, 2008)

Black, Cilla, *Through The Years: My Life In Pictures* (London: Headline, 1993)

Black, Jeremy, *Using History* (London: Hodder Arnold, 2005)

Booker, Christopher, *The Neophiliacs: A Study Of The Revolution In English Life In The Fifties And Sixties* (London: Collins, 1970)

Bordwell, David, *The Way Hollywood Tells It: Story And Style In Modern Movies* (Berkeley, Los Angeles: University of California Press, 2006)

Bourdieu, Pierre, *Distinction: A Social Critique Of The Judgement Of Taste* (London: Routledge, 1984)

Bowman, Rob, *The American Folk Blues Festival 1962–1965 DVD* liner notes (Reelin' In The Years Productions, 2003)

Boym, Svetlana, *The Future Of Nostalgia* (New York: Basic Books, 2008)

Bradley, Dick, *Understanding Rock'n'Roll: Popular Music In Britain 1955–1964* (Buckingham: Open University Press, 1992)

Bramwell, Tony, *Magical Mystery Tours* (New York: Thomas Dunne, 2005)

Brent Toplin, Robert (ed.), *Ken Burns's The Civil War: Historians Respond* (Oxford: Oxford University Press, 1996)

Breward, Christopher, David Gilbert and Jenny Lister (eds), *Swinging Sixties: Fashion In London And Beyond 1955–1970* (London: V&A Publications, 2006)

'Brinsley Schwarz', *Shindig* 2/11 (2009): 52

Bromley, Roger, *Lost Narratives: Popular Fictions, Politics and Recent History* (London: Routledge, 1988)

Brown, Mick, 'UK Report: Sex Pistols And Beyond', *Rolling Stone*, 27 January 1977

Brown, Peter and Steven Gaines, *The Love You Make: An Insider's Story Of The Beatles* (London: Macmillan, 1983)

Brunsdon, Charlotte, *Screen Tastes: Soap Opera To Satellite Dishes* (London: Routledge, 1997)

Bruss, Elizabeth, 'Eye For I: Making And Unmaking Autobiography In Film', in James Olney (ed.), *Autobiography: Essays Theoretical And Critical* (Princeton: Princeton University Press, 1980): 296–320

Buckingham, David, 'Child-Centred Television? *Teletubbies* And The Educational Imperative', in David Buckingham (ed.), *Small Screens: Television For Children* (London: Leicester University Press, 2002): 38–60

Burchill, Julie and Tony Parsons, *The Boy Looked At Johnny: The Obituary Of Rock And Roll* (London: Pluto, 1978)

Burns, Ken, 'Four O'Clock In The Morning Courage', in Robert Brent Toplin (ed.), *Ken Burns's The Civil War: Historians Respond* (Oxford: Oxford University Press, 1996): 153–84

Cannadine, David (ed.), *History And The Media* (London: Palgrave, 2004)

Carr, Roy, *Beatles At The Movies: Scenes From A Career* (London: UFO, 1996)

Casey, Bernadette, Neil Casey, Ben Calvert, Liam French and Justin Lewis, 'Children And Television' in *Television Studies: The Key Concepts, Second Edition* (London: Routledge, 2008): 30–33

Catterall, Peter (ed.), *The Making Of Channel 4* (London: Frank Cass, 1999)

Chambers, Iain, *Urban Rhythms: Pop Music And Popular Culture* (London: Macmillan, 1985)

Chapman, James, 'Not Another Bloody Cop Show: *Life On Mars* And British Television Drama', *Film International* 7/2 (2009): 6–19

Cloonan, Martin, *Banned! Censorship Of Popular Music In Britain 1967–1992* (Aldershot: Ashgate, 1996)

Coates, Norma, 'Filling In Holes: Television Music As A Recuperation Of Popular Music On Television', *Music, Sound And The Moving Image* 1/1 (2007): 21–25

Cohn, Nik, *Awopbopaloobop Alopbamboom* (London: Weidenfeld & Nicholson, 1969)

Coleman, Ray, *Brian Epstein: The Man Who Made The Beatles* (London: Viking, 1989)

Coleman, Ray, *John Lennon* (London: Sidgwick & Jackson, 1984)

Conrich, Ian and Estella Tincknell (eds), *Film's Musical Moments* (Edinburgh: Edinburgh University Press, 2006)

Cook, Nicholas, 'Music And Meaning In The Commercials', *Popular Music* 13/1 (1994): 27–40

Cooke, Lez, *British Television Drama: A History* (London: BFI, 2003)

Corner, John 'Epilogue: Sense And Perspective', *European Journal Of Cultural Studies* 10/1 (2007): 135–40

Corner, John, 'Documentary In A Post-Documentary Culture? A Note On Forms And Their Functions' (www.lboro.ac.uk/research/changing.media/John%20Corner%20paper.htm)

Corner, John, 'Performing The Real: Documentary Diversions', *Television and New Media*, 3/3 (2002): 255–69

Corner, John, 'Sounds Real: Music And Documentary', *Popular Music* 21/3 (2002): 357–66

Couldry, Nick, *Media Rituals: A Critical Approach*, (London: Routledge, 2003)

Davies, Hunter, *The Beatles: The Authorised Biography* (London: William Heinemann, 1968)

Davies, Russell T., 'First Ladies Of Rock', *The Observer Review*, 16 June 2002: 9

Denisoff, R. Serge and William D. Romanowski, 'MTV Becomes Pastiche: Some People Just Don't Get It!', *Popular Music And Society* 14/1 (1990): 47–61

DeNora, Tia, *Music In Everyday Life* (Cambridge: Cambridge University Press, 2000)

Dickinson, Kay, *Off Key: When Film And Music Won't Work Together* (Oxford: Oxford University Press, 2008)

Dickinson, Kay (ed.), *Movie Music: The Film Reader* (London: Routledge, 2003)

Donnelly, K. J., *The Spectre Of Sound* (London: BFI, 2005)

Dovey, Jon, *Freakshow: First Person Media And Factual Television* (London: Pluto Press, 2000)

Duffett, Mark, 'Imagined Memories: Webcasting As A "Live" Technology And The Case Of Little Big Gig', *Information, Communication and Society* 6/3 (2003): 307–25

Edgerton Gary R., *Ken Burns's America* (New York: Palgrave, 2001)

Edgerton, Gary R., 'Mystic Chords Of Memory: The Cultural Voice Of Ken Burns', in Gary R. Edgerton, Michael T. Marsden and Jack Nachbar (eds), *In The Eye Of The Beholder: Critical Perspectives In Popular Film And Television* (Bowling Green, Ohio: Bowling Green State University Popular Press, 1997): 11–26

Egan, Suzanne, 'Encounters In Camera: Autobiography As Interaction', *Modern Fiction Studies* 40/3 (1994): 593–618

Epstein, Brian, *A Cellarful Of Noise* (London: Souvenir Press, 1964)

Erickson, Hal, 'Postman Pat', *All Movie Guide* (www.fandango.com/postmanpat[animatedtvseries]-_v355895/summary)

Feuer, Jane, 'HBO And The Concept Of Quality TV', in Jane McCabe and Kim Akass, *Quality TV: Contemporary American Television And Beyond* (London: I. B. Tauris, 2007): 145–57

Fiddy, Dick, *Missing, Believed Wiped: Searching For The Lost Treasures Of British Television* (London: BFI, 2001)

Fisher, Neil, 'Orchestral Manoeuvres', *The Times: Features*, 15 June 2007: 21

Flett, Kathryn, 'Nights With The Laydeez', *The Observer*, 10 March 2002

Flew, Terry, *Understanding Global Media* (London: Palgrave, 2007)

Freud, Sigmund, *Totem And Taboo* (London: Routledge, 2001)

Frith, Simon, 'Music And Identity' in *Taking Popular Music Seriously, Selected Essays* (Aldershot: Ashgate, 2007): 293–312

Frith, Simon, 'Look! Hear! The Uneasy Relationship Of Music And Television', *Popular Music* 21/3 (2002): 277–90

Frith, Simon, *Performing Rites: On The Value Of Popular Music.* (Oxford: Oxford University Press, 1996)

Frith, Simon, Andrew Goodwin and Lawrence Grossberg (eds), *Sound And Vision: The Music Video Reader* (New York: Routledge, 1993)

Gilbert, Pamela K. (ed.), *Imagined Londons* (Albany: State University of New York Press, 2002): 137–58

Gittins, Ian, *Top Of The Pops: Mishaps, Miming And Music* (London: BBC Books, 2007)

Glynn, Prudence, 'The Medium Is A Missed Opportunity', *The Times*, 20 February 1968.

Gorbman, Claudia, *Unheard Melodies: Narrative Film Music* (London/Bloomington: BFI/Indiana University Press, 1987)

Gorton, Kristyn, 'There's No Place Like Home: Emotional Exposure, Excess And Empathy On TV', *Critical Studies In Television* 3/1 (2008): 3–15

Gorton, Kristyn, 'A Sentimental Journey: Television, Meaning And Emotion', *Journal Of British Cinema And Television* 3 (2006): 72–81

Gould, Jonathan, *Can't Buy Me Love: The Beatles, Britain, And America* (New York: Harmony Books, 2007)

Gould, Tony, 'Rock Political', *New Society*, 9 June 1977: 513–14

Gracyk, Theodor, *I Wanna Be Me: Rock Music And The Politics Of Identity* (Philadelphia: Temple University Press, 2001)

Gray, Andy, 'Beatles Stop The Royal Variety Show', *New Musical Express*, 8 November 1963: 10

Green, Jonathon, *All Dressed Up: The Sixties And The Counterculture* (New York: Random House, 1968)

Greig, Charlotte, *Will You Still Love Me Tomorrow* (London: Virago, 1989)

Grindstaff, Laura, *The Money Shot: Trash, Class, And The Making Of TV Talk Shows* (Chicago: University of Chicago Press, 2002)

Grove, Valerie, 'Celebrity Culture Is Killing The Serious Biography', *The Times*, 5 September 2008

Gunter, Barry and McAleer, Jill, *Children And Television, Second Edition* (London: Routledge, 1997)

Hall, Stuart, 'Technics Of The Medium', in John Corner and Sylvia Harvey (eds), *Television Times: A Reader* (London: Arnold, 1996): 3–10

Hall, Stuart, 'Encoding/Decoding', in Stuart Hall, Dorothy Hobson, Andrew Lowe and Paul Willis (eds), *Culture, Media, Language* (London: Routledge 1980): 128–38

Hall, Stuart and Paddy Whannel, *The Popular Arts* (London: Hutchinson, 1964)

Hamilton, Paul, 'My Favourite Earache', in Peter Gordon, Dan Kieran and Paul Hamilton (eds), *How Very Interesting: Peter Cook, His Universe, And All That Surrounds It* (London: Snowbooks, 2006): 226–33

Hamilton, Paul, 'Revolter', in Peter Gordon, Dan Kieran and Paul Hamilton (eds), *How Very Interesting: Peter Cook, His Universe, And All That Surrounds It* (London: Snowbooks, 2006): 215–25

Harris, Bob. *The Whispering Years* (London: BBC, 2001)

Harry, Bill, *Beatlemania: The History Of The Beatles On Film* (London: Virgin, 1984)

Hawkins, Stan, 'Unsettling Difference: Music And Identity In Britpop', *Analysing Popular Music In Context Symposium*, University of Liverpool, 16 November 2007

Hayes, David (2006), 'Take Those Old Records Off The Shelf: Youth And Music Consumption In The Postmodern Age', *Popular Music And Society*, 29/1 (2006): 51–68

Hayes, Nick and Jeff Hill (eds), *Millions Like Us? British Culture In The Second World War* (Liverpool: Liverpool University Press, 1999).

Henderson, Neil, *Destination Manchester* (http://www.modculture.com)

Hepworth, David, 'The Difficult Business Of Putting Music On The TV: A Conversation With The BBC's Mark Cooper', *The Word*, 16 May 2008

Hesmondhalgh, David and Sarah Baker, 'Creative Work And Emotional Labour In The Television Industry', *Theory, Culture And Society*, 25/7–8 (2008): 97–118

Hewison, Robert, *In Anger: Culture In The Cold War 1945–60* (London: Methuen, 1988)

Hill, John, 'Television And Pop: The Case Of The 1950s', in John Corner (ed.), *Popular Television In Britain: Studies In Cultural History* (London: BFI, 1991): 90–107

Hills, Matt, *Fan Cultures* (London: Routledge, 2002)

Hochschild, Arlie Russell, *The Managed Heart: Commercialization Of Human Feeling* (Berkeley: University of California Press, 1983)

Holmes, Sue and Sean Redmond (eds), *Framing Celebrity: New Directions In Celebrity Culture*, (London: Routledge, 2006)

Homan, Shane (ed), *Access All Eras: Tribute Bands And Global Pop Culture* (Buckingham: Open University Press, 2006)

Howlett, Kevin, *The Beatles At The BBC: The Radio Years 1962–70* (London: BBC Books, 1996)

Hulanicki, Barbara, *From A To Biba* (London: Hutchinson, 1983)

Hutcheon, Linda, *The Politics Of Postmodernism, Second Edition* (London: Routledge, 2002)

Hutchins, Chris, 'Beatles Are Going On Holiday', *New Musical Express*, 13 September 1963: 10

Inglis, Ian, 'Popular Music History On Screen: The Pop/Rock Biopic', *Popular Music History* 2/1 (2007): 77–93

Inglis, Ian (ed.), *Popular Music And Film* (London: Wallflower, 2003)

Inglis, Ian, 'Men Of Ideas? Popular Music, Anti-Intellectualism And The Beatles', in Ian Inglis (ed.), *The Beatles, Popular Music And Society: A Thousand Voices* (London: Macmillan, 2000), 1–22

'The Insider: BBC4', *Music Week*, 13 August 2005: 16

James, Alex, *Bit Of A Blur* (London: Little Brown and Company 2007)

Jameson, Fredric, 'Postmodernism And Consumer Society', in Hal Foster (ed.), *The Anti-Aesthetic* (New York: New Press, 1999): 111–25

Jameson, Fredric, *Postmodernism or, The Cultural Logic Of Late Capitalism* (New York: Verso, 1991)

Jancovich, Mark and James Lyons (eds), *Quality Popular Television: Cult TV, The Industry And Fans* (London: BFI, 2003)

Jenkins, Henry, *Textual Poachers: Television And Participatory Culture* (London: Routledge, 1992)

Kaplan, E. Ann, 'Feminism(s)/Postmodernism(s): MTV And Alternate Women's Videos And Performance Art', *Women And Performance: A Journal Of Feminist Theory* 6/1 (1993): 55–76

Kaplan, E. Ann, *Rocking Around The Clock: Music Television, Postmodernism, And Consumer Culture* (London: Routledge, 1987)

Klein, Bethany, *As Heard On TV: Popular Music In Advertising* (Aldershot: Ashgate, 2009)

Lamont, Alexandra, 'Young Children's Musical Worlds: Musical Engagement In 3.5 Year-Olds', *Journal Of Early Childhood Research* 6/3 (2008): 247–61

Landsberg, Alison, *Prosthetic Memory* (New York: Columbia University Press, 2004)

Landsberg, Alison, 'Prosthetic Memory: The Ethics And Politics Of Memory In An Age Of Mass Culture', in Paul Grainge (ed.), *Memory And Popular Film* (Manchester: Manchester University Press, 2003): 144–61

Landsberg, Alison, 'Prosthetic Memory: *Total Recall* And *Blade Runner*', in Mike Featherstone and Roger Burrows (eds), *Cyberspace, Cyberbodies, Cyberpunk* (London: Sage, 1999): 175–90

Lane, Jim, *The Autobiographical Documentary In America* (Madison: University of Wisconsin Press, 2002)

Lannin, Steve and Matthew Caley (eds), *Pop Fiction: The Song In Cinema* (Bristol: Intellect, 2005)

Lanning, Dave, 'Ready Steady Goes Live!', *TV Times*, 25 March 1965: 4–5

Lanning, Dave, 'Stand by By For Takeoff: Ready Steady Go!', *TV Times*, 2 August 1963: 32

Lasch, Christopher, *The Culture Of Narcissism: American Life In An Age Of Diminishing Expectations* (New York: Norton, 1978)

Latouche, Serge, *The Westernization Of The World* (Cambridge: Polity, 1996)

Leitch, Michael, *Great Songs Of World War II* (London: Wise Publications, 1985)

Levy, Shawn, *Ready, Steady, Go! Swinging London And The Invention Of Cool* (London: Fourth Estate, 2002)

Lewis, G. H., 'Who Do You Love? The Dimensions Of Musical Taste' in James Lull (ed.), *Popular Music And Communication* (London: Sage, 1992): 134–51

Lewis, Lisa A. (ed.), *The Adoring Audience: Fan Culture And Popular Media*, (London: Routledge, 1992)

Lewisohn, Mark, *The Complete Beatles Chronicle* (London: Pyramid, 1992)

Lewisohn, Mark, *The Beatles Live* (London: Pavilion, 1986)

'Lifelines Of The Beatles', *New Musical Express*, 15 February 1963: 9

Littler, Jo, 'Making Fame Ordinary: Intimacy, Reflexivity, And "Keeping It Real"', *Mediactive* 2 (2004): 8–25

Longhurst, Brian, *Popular Music And Society, Second Edition* (Cambridge: Polity, 2007)

Look, Hugh, 'The Author As Star', *Publishing Research Quarterly* 15/3 (1999): 12–29

Lowy, Adrienne, *DustyCillaSandieLulu As Seen on TV: A Study Of Interrelations Between Pop Music, Television And Fashion* (PhD Thesis, University of Liverpool, 2008).

Lulu, *I Don't Want To Fight* (London: Time Warner, 2002)

Lyneham, Chris, 'The People's War', *Socialist Review* 176, June 1994

Mabey, Richard, *The Pop Process* (London: Hutchinson, 1969)

McCabe, Jane and Kim Akass (eds), *Quality TV: Contemporary American Television And Beyond* (London: I. B. Tauris, 2007)

McCabe, Peter and Robert D. Schonfeld, *Apple To The Core: The Unmaking Of The Beatles* (London: Sphere, 1972)

McCarthy, Jim and Steve Parkhouse, *The Sex Pistols: A Graphic Novel* (London: Omnibus Press, 2008)

MacDonald, Ian, *Revolution In The Head: The Beatles' Records And The Sixties* (London: Fourth Estate, 1994)

McGuigan, Jim, *Rethinking Cultural Policy* (Maidenhead: Open University Press, 2004)

McPhail, Thomas L., *Global Communication* (Chichester: Wiley-Blackwell, 2010)

Maland, Charles J., '1978: Movies And Changing Times', in Lester D. Friedman (ed.), *American Cinema Of The 1970s: Themes And Variations* (Oxford: Berg, 2007): 205–27

Marcus, Greil, *Like A Rolling Stone: Bob Dylan At The Crossroads* (London: Faber, 2005)

Marshall, P. David, *Celebrity And Power: Fame In Contemporary Culture* (Minnesota: University of Minnesota Press, 1997)

Martin, George, *All You Need Is Ears* (New York: St Martin's Press, 1979)

Matlock, Glen, *I Was a Teenage Sex Pistol* (London: Virgin Books, 1996)

Mazlish, Bruce, 'The Tragic Farce Of Marx, Hegel, And Engels: A Note', *History and Theory* 11/3 (1972): 335–37

Melly, George, *Revolt Into Style* (London: Allen Lane, 1970)

Menkes, Suzy, 'Fashion Extra', *The Times*, 31 January 1967

Mestrovic, Stjepan G., *Postemotional Society* (London: Sage, 1997)

Middleton, Richard, *Studying Popular Music* (Milton Keynes: Open University Press, 1990)

Monroe, Alexei, 'Bread And (Rock) Circuses: Sites Of Sonic Conflict In London', in Pamela K. Gilbert (ed.), *Imagined Londons* (Albany: State University of New York Press, 2002): 137–58

Moore, Allan, 'The Persona-Environment Relationship In Recorded Song', *Music Theory Online* 11/4 (2005)

Moore, Allan, 'Authenticity as Authentication', *Popular Music* 21/2 (2002): 209–23

Morley, Paul, 'Showing Off', *Observer Music Monthly* 74, November 2009: pp. 48–49

Mundy, John, 'Singing Detected: *Blackpool* And The Strange Case Of The Missing Television Musical Dramas', in *Journal Of British Cinema And Television* 3/1 (2006): 59–71

Mundy, John, *Popular Music On Screen* (Manchester: Manchester University Press, 1999)

Nadel, Ira, B. 'Narrative And The Popularity Of Biography', *Mosaic* 20/4 (1987): 131–41

Neaverson, Bob, *The Beatles Movies* (London: Cassell, 1997)

Negra, Diane, 'The Feminisation Of Crisis Celebrity', *The Guardian*, 9 July 2008

Negus, Keith, 'Musicians On Television: Visible, Audible And Ignored', *Journal Of The Royal Musical Association* 131/2 (2006): 310–30

Negus, Keith and John Street, 'Introduction To Music And Television', *Popular Music* 21/3 (2002): 245–8

Neville, Katy, 'The Post Cool School', *The Face*, February 1984

Nichols, Bill, 'The Voice Of Documentary', *Film Quarterly* 36/3 (1983): 17–30

Norman, Philip, *John Lennon* (London: Harper Collins, 2008)

Norman, Philip, *Shout! The True Story Of The Beatles* (London: Hamish Hamilton, 1981)

O'Brien, Lucy, *She Bop II: The Definitive History Of Women In Rock, Pop And Soul* (London: Continuum, 2002)

O'Hagan, Sean, 'Guerillas In Our Midst', *The Observer*, 20 February 2000

Orr, John, 'Feature Review: *Figures Traced In Light: On Cinematic Staging* by David Bordwell; *The Way Hollywood Tells It: Story And Style In Modern Movies* by David Bordwell', *Senses Of Cinema* 42 (2007)

Palmer, Tony (ed.), *All You Need Is Love: The Story of Popular Music* (New York: Grossman, 1976)

Paxman, Jon, 'Preisner-Kieślowski: The Art Of Synergetic Understatement In *Three Colours: Red*', in Miguel Mera and David Burnand (eds), *European Film Music* (Aldershot: Ashgate, 2006): 145–62

Pilton, Patrick, *Every Night At The London Palladium* (London: Robson Books, 1976)

Purser, Philip, 'Revolver', *The Sunday Telegraph*, 28 May 1978: 13

Raine, Craig, 'Vicious And Company', *The Observer*, 13 August 1978: 19

Rawsthorn, Alice, 'Tomorrow's Girl', *The Guardian*, 19 June 2004

Reid, Jane, 'Triumph Of R&B', in Robert H. Hill (ed.), *The Year Book 1965: A Record Of The Events, Developments And Personalities Of 1964* (London: The Grolier Society, 1965): 200–204

Renov, Michael, *The Subject Of Documentary* (Minneapolis: University of Minnesota Press, 2004)

Reynolds, Simon, *Rip It Up And Start Again* (London: Faber, 2005)

Reynolds, Simon, *Blissed Out: The Raptures of Rock.* (London: Serpent's Tail, 1990).

Richards, Jeffrey, *Films And British National Identity: From Dickens To Dad's Army* (Manchester: Manchester University Press, 1997)

Roberts, Graham and Philip M. Taylor (eds), *The Historian, Television And Television History* (Luton: Luton University Press, 2001)

Rose, Cynthia, 'Worn Out: Career Chic', in Tony Stewart (ed.), *Cool Cats: 25 Years Of Rock'n'Roll Style* (London: Eel Pie Publishing, 1981): 66–67

Rose, Sonja O. *Which People's War: National Identity And Citizenship In Wartime Britain, 1939–1945* (Oxford: Oxford University Press, 2004)

Rowe, Mike, *The American Folk-Blues Festival: The British Tours 1963–1966 DVD* liner notes (Reelin' In The Years Productions, 2007).

Sabin, Roger, (ed.), *Punk Rock: So What?* (London: Routledge, 1999)

Samuel, Raphael, *Island Stories: Unravelling Britain* (London: Verso, 1999)

Sandbrook, Dominic, *White Heat: A History Of Britain In The Swinging Sixties* (London: Abacus, 2006)

Savage, Jon, *Teenage: The Creation Of Youth* (London: Chatto and Windus, 2007)

Savage, Jon, *England's Dreaming* (London: Faber, 1991)

'Schlock Jollies', *New Musical Express*, 10 April 1976

Schmutz, Vaughn (2005) 'Retrospective Cultural Consecration In Popular Music', *American Behavioral Scientist*, 48/11 (2005): 1510–23

Sercombe, Laurel, 'Ladies And Gentlemen … The Beatles', in Ian Inglis (ed.), *Performance And Popular Music: History, Place And Time* (Aldershot: Ashgate, 2006), 1–15

Shaw, Sandie, *The World At My Feet: A Personal Adventure* (London: Harper Collins, 1991)

Shepherd, John, *Music As Social Text* (Cambridge: Polity Press, 1991)

Shuker, Roy, *Understanding Popular Music, Second Edition* (London: Routledge, 2001)

Silverton, Pete, 'Pistols, Clash, etc.: What Did You Do On The Punk Tour, Daddy?', *Sounds*, 18 December 1976

Simpson, Mark, *Saint Morrissey* (London: SAF Publishing, 2004)

Smith, Alan, 'Backstage With The Beatles', *New Musical Express*, 13 December 1963: 3

Smith, Anthony, 'Set In The Silver Sea: English National Identity And European Integration', *Workshop: National Identity And Euroscepticism. A Comparison Between France And The United Kingdom.* (Oxford: Centre for the Study of Democratic Government European Research Group, 2005)

Smith, Jeff, *The Sounds Of Commerce: Marketing Popular Film Music* (New York: Columbia University Press, 1998)

Sobchak, Vivian (ed.), *The Persistence Of History: Cinema, Television And The Modern Event* (London: Routledge, 1996)

Southall, Brian, *The Sex Pistols: 90 Days At EMI* (London: Omnibus Press, 2007)

Spitz, Bob, *The Beatles* (New York: Little, Brown and Company, 2006)

Stanbridge, Alan, 'Burns, Baby, Burns: Jazz History As A Contested Cultural Site', *The Source: Challenging Jazz Criticism* 1/04 (2004): 82–99

Steele, Valerie, *Fifty Years Of Fashion: New Look To Now* (New York: Yale University Press, 1997)

Stefani, Gino, 'Sémiotique En Musicologie', *Versus* 5 (1973): 20–42

Steward, Sue and Sheryl Garratt, *Signed, Sealed And Delivered: True Life Stories Of Women In Pop* (London: Pluto, 1984)

Storey, John, *Cultural Studies And The Study Of Popular Culture* (Edinburgh: Edinburgh University Press, 2003)

Strachan, Robert, 'Where Do I Begin The Story? Collective Memory, Biographical Authority And The Rock Biography', *Popular Music History* 3/1 (2008): 65–80

Strachan, Robert, 'Micro-independent Record Labels In The UK: Discourse, DIY Cultural Production And The Music Industry', *European Journal Of Cultural Studies* 10/2 (2007): 245–66

Strausbaugh, John, *Rock Till You Drop* (London: Verso, 2002)

Strongman, Phil, *Pretty Vacant: A History Of Punk* (London: Orion, 2007)

Tagg, Philip and Bob Clarida, *Ten Little Title Tunes: Towards A Musicology Of The Mass Media* (New York and Montreal: Mass Media Music Scholars Press, 2003)

Tagg, Philip, *Kojak. 50 Seconds Of Television Music: Towards The Analysis Of Affect In Popular Music* (New York and Montreal: Mass Media Music Scholars Press, 2000)

Tagg, Philip, *Fernando The Flute: Analysis Of Musical Meaning In An Abba Mega-Hit* (Liverpool: Institute of Popular Music, 1991)

Tagg, Philip, 'Open Letter: "Black Music", "Afro-American Music" And "European Music"', *Popular Music* 8/3 (1989): 285–98

Tarasti, Eero, 'On Music And Myth', in Derek B. Scott (ed.), *Music, Culture And Society. A Reader* (Oxford: Oxford University Press, 2000), 46–47

Taylor, Alistair, *A Secret History* (London: John Blake, 2001)

Television Show Book (London: Purnell, 1964)

Thompson, Harry, *Peter Cook: A Biography* (London: Hodder & Stoughton, 1997)

Thussu, Daya Kishan, *International Communication: Continuity And Change* (London: Arnold, 2000)

Tidman, Gareth, 'When The Blues Train Rolled Into Chorlton', *South Manchester Reporter*, 9 November 2006

Tincknell, Estella. 'The Soundtrack Movie, Nostalgia And Consumption', in Ian Conrich and Estella Tincknell (eds), *Film's Musical Moments* (Edinburgh: Edinburgh University Press, 2006): 132–45

Valentine, Penny and Vicki Wickham, *Dancing With Demons: The Authorised Biography Of Dusty Springfield* (London: Hodder & Stoughton, 2000)

Wall, Tim, *Studying Popular Music Culture* (London: Arnold, 2003)

Wheatley, Helen (ed.), *Re-viewing Television History: Critical Issues In Television Historiography* (London: I. B. Tauris, 2007)

Whiteley, Sheila, Andy Bennett and Stan Hawkins (eds), *Music, Space And Place: Popular Music And Cultural Identity.* (Aldershot: Ashgate, 2004)

Wikstrom, Patrik, *The Music Industry* (Cambridge: Polity, 2009)

Williams, Brien R., 'The Structure Of Televised Football', *Journal Of Communication* 27/3 (1977): 133–39

Williams, Pat, 'Getting Together', *The Observer*, 5 January 1964

Williams, Pat, 'Mixing The Colours', *The Observer*, 12 January 1964

Williams, Richard, 'The Birth Of Cool', *The Guardian*, 13 February 2006

Williamson, Dugald (1989) 'Television Documentary', in John Tulloch and Graeme Turner (eds), *Australian Television: Programs, Pleasures And Politics* (Sydney: Allen & Unwin, 1989): 88–102

Wiseman-Trowse, Nathan, *Performing Class In British Popular Music* (London: Palgrave, 2008)

Wolfe, D. E. and S. Stambaugh, 'Musical Analysis Of *Sesame Street*: Implications For Music Therapy Practice And Research', *Journal Of Music Therapy* 30/4 (1993): 224–35

Woodward, Christopher, *The London Palladium: The Story Of The Theatre And Its Stars* (Huddersfield: Jeremy Mills, 2009)

Wright, Robb, 'Score vs. Song: Art, Commerce And The H Factor In Film And Television Music', in Ian Inglis (ed.), *Popular Music And Film* (London: Wallflower, 2003): 8–21

Yule, Andrew, *The Man Who 'Framed' The Beatles: A Biography Of Richard Lester* (New York: Donald I. Fine, 1994)

Index

ABC At Large 191
Abicair, Shirley 1
'Addicted To Love' 114
Adventures Of Barry McKenzie, The 151
Adverts 64
Albarn, Damon 117, 118
Aldred, Michael 74, 79
Alice In Wonderland 151
All You Need Is Love 14
'All You Need Is Love' 193
Allan, Elkan 72–3, 76, 78, 80
Almost Blues 204
'Always Something There To Remind Me'
     76
Ambrose 130
American Bandstand 73, 180
American Folk, Blues And Gospel Caravan
     204
American Folk Blues Festival 202–3, 204
American Graffiti 171–2
Amy Winehouse: What Really Happened
     27, 31–2, 34
Anchorman: The Legend Of Ron Burgundy
     173
Andrews, Marshall 170
Animals 201
'Another Girl/Another Planet' 157
Anthology 15
'Anyone Who Had A Heart' 77, 78
Apostrophe (') 52
Apple A Day, An 151
Appleton, Michael 57–60, 63, 64, 67
Arctic Monkeys 119
Area Code 615 61
Armchair Theatre 198
Armstrong, Louis 17–18, 220
Around The Beatles 192
Arthur Haynes Show, The 180
'As Long As You're Happy Baby' 76
Ashes To Ashes 164, 174
Askey, Arthur 134
Astley, Rick 108

Atwell, Winifred 199
Austin Powers In Goldmember 173
Autographs 152

'Baba O'Reilly' 168
Babyshambles 32–3
Bacharach Sound, The 201
Bailey, Michael 204
'Ballroom Blitz' 170
Band, The 64
'Band Who Wouldn't Die, The' 145–6
Barrie, Ken 220, 226
Baseball 15
Basie, Count 200
Be Here Now 118
Beach Boys 42
Beatles 6, 42, 45, 55, 56, 73, 76, 111,
     179–95, 200
Beatles Book, The 179
Beatles Christmas Show, The 179
Beckham, Victoria 31, 35–7, 38, 39
Bed Sitting Room, The 151
Bedazzled 151
Bee Gees 96
Beggars Banquet 43
Being Brian Harvey 27
Being Mick 27, 38
Being Victoria Beckham 27, 35–7
Bennett, Alan 150
Benson, Ivy 130
Benton, Brook 181
Bernstein, Cecil 197
Bernstein, Sydney 197, 200, 203
Berry, Chuck 203
Bertha 220
Best, George 201
Beyond The Fringe 150
Biba 82–3
Big Night Out 189
Biggs, Ronnie 154–5
'Bingo Crowd' 155
Birt, John 198

Birthday Party 110
Black, Cilla 4, 71–84
Black Moses 61
'Blackout Stroll' 131
Blackpool Night Out 192
Blade Runner 91
'Blue Monday' 60
Blue Peter 214
'Blue Skies Are Round The Corner' 131
'Blueberry Hill' 140
Blues, The 15
Blues And Gospel Train, The 6, 197–212
Blues Unlimited 203
Blur 116, 117
Bob The Builder 216, 217, 222, 228
'Bones' 157
Boomtown Rats 151, 152, 154
Bowie, David 162, 168, 171
Boy Meets Girls 180, 199
Boyd, Carole 225
Boyfriends 152
Bragg, Billy 109
Brand, Russell 96
Bridge Over The River Kwai, The 133
Briggs, Anne 18, 24
Brill Building 59–60
Brinsley Schwarz 63
Britain's Got Talent 7
Britannia 3, 11–26
    Blues Britannia 11
    Classic Britannia 11, 13
    Comics Britannia 11
    Dance Britannia 11
    Folk Britannia 11, 16, 18–19, 24
    Heavy Metal Britannia 11
    Jazz Britannia 11, 12–13, 17, 19–20, 21, 22
    Pop Britannia 11, 19, 22
    Prog Rock Britannia 11, 17
    Soul Britannia 11, 17, 18, 24
    Synth Britannia 11, 13
Britpop 4, 6, 105–19, 217, 228
Britpop Now 117
Broonzy, Big Bill 203
Brothers In Arms 43, 114
Broudie, Ian 228
Brown, Arthur 105
Buckingham, Lindsey 49–50

Buddha Of Suburbia, The 96
Burns, Ken 17–18, 23
Bush, Kate 150
Butler, Billy 201
Buzzcocks 152
Byrne, Gay 198

Caine, Michael 174
Carry On 174
Carthy, Martin 18
Cassidy, David 172
Casson, Philip 203, 204, 208, 209
C86 114
C-Gas 5 155–6
Chants 183
Chapman, Michael 64
Charlie's Bus 111
Chart Show, The 114–15
Chelsea At Nine 200
Cheyenne 180
Chills 108
Christian, Terry 117
Cilla 84
Civil War, The 15
Civilisation 57
Clark, Dave 83–4
Clash 64, 107, 149, 154, 156
Classic Albums 3, 41–53
Clive Anderson Show, The 96
Cobain, Kurt 51–2
'Colonel Bogey' 133
Cole, Lloyd 108
Collins, Phil 45, 48–9
Colour Me Pop 13, 57
Comedians, The 200
'Coming In On A Wing And A Prayer' 131
'Concise British Alphabet, A' 20
Conquistadors 14
Cook, Paul 94
Cook, Peter 5, 149–59, 193
Cooke, Sam 114
Cool For Cats 180
Cool, Rickie 150
Cornwell, Charlotte 142
Coronation Street 198, 211
Costello, Elvis 153
Cotton, Billy 1, 130
Covington, Julie 142

Cream 169, 172
Creation Records 118
Creem 58
Criss Cross Quiz 200
Crossroads 154
Cult, The 112
Culture Club 107
Cunliffe, John 223
Cymande 19

Dad's Army 4–5, 123–36
Dakotas 211
Dale, Dick 162
Daly, Brian 220, 223, 225, 228
Dann, Trevor 64–7
Dark Side Of The Moon 43–4, 45
Darts 157
Data-Run 111
Davies, Ray 118
Davies, Russell T. 141
Day By Day 192
Dee, Kiki 172
Deep Purple 172
DEF II 66, 115
Denny, Sandy 19
'Der Fuehrer's Face' 133
Derek And Clive 151
Desert Island Discs 118
'Destroy The Heart' 115
Detroit Spinners 172
'Dickie Davies Eyes' 115
'Didn't It Rain' 208
Dig This! 180
'Dimples' 203
Dinosaur Junior 108
Dire Straits 154
Disco 2 57–8, 59
Discs A Gogo 73, 189
Disraeli Gears 43
Dixon Of Dock Green 180
Dixon, Willie 200, 202, 204
Doctor Who 141, 180
Doherty, Pete 31, 32–4, 39
Donegan, Lonnie 55
Don't Look Back 27–8
Doors, The 41
Dowie, John 150
Driscoll, Julie 152

Drumbeat 180
Dunn, Clive 124
Duran Duran 107, 114
Dury, Ian 152
Dusty 84

Earsay 113
East 17 34
Echo and the Bunnymen 108
Echobelly 116
Ed Sullivan Show, The 55, 179
Eddie and the Hot Rods 155
Elastica 116
Electric Light Orchestra 172
Ellen, Mark 66, 111
Ellington, Duke 1, 17–18
Elliott, Vernon 216
Elton John: Me, Myself And I 27, 37–8
Epstein, Brian 76, 78, 179, 181, 183, 184, 188
Eric Sykes Shows A Few Of Our Favourite Things 151
Evans, Chris 117

Fab 208 58
Fabulous Poodles 154
Face Value 45, 48–9
Factory Records 111, 112, 116
Fall, The 110
'Falling In Love/Jet Plane Age' 157
Fame Academy 28
Family 57
Family At War, A 198
Fanny 60
Ferguson, Nicholas 76, 78–9
Fielder-Civil, Blake 31–2, 34
Filth And The Fury, The 98, 103
'Fire' 105
Fitzgerald, Patrik 155
Five 228
Five O'Clock Club 199
Flame 140, 141
Flanagan, Bud 132, 134, 135
Fleetwood Mac 49–50
Fleetwood, Mick 49
Focus 62
Follow The Beatles 192
'Football's Coming Home' 117, 228

Ford, Brent 153
Fordyce, Keith 74
Formby, George 134
Forsyte Saga, The 57
Fortunes 57
Frankie Goes To Hollywood 113
Freddie and the Dreamers 211
Free 172
French and Saunders 113
Fripp, Robert 57
'From Me To You' 181, 182, 185, 188

Gabriel, Peter 114
Gallagher, Noel 116, 118
Garrick, Michael 22
Gas 64
Gaye, Marvin 114
Gene 116
Genesis 43
Geri 36
Germ Free Adolescence 155
Get Carter 174
Get Fresh 109
'Ghosts Of Princes In Towers' 157
Gibbons, Steve 155
Gimme Shelter 28, 61
'Girls & Boys' 117
'Glad To Be Gay' 150
Glenister, Philip 161
Goddess In The Doorway 38
Godspell 138
Going Live 109
Goldie 155
'Good Behaviour' 145
Good, Jack 56
Good Old Days, The 134
Goodies 95, 101
Goodnight Sweetheart 136
Graceland 49
Graham, Davey 19
Grampian Week 192
Granada 6, 197–212
Granada Reports 110
Grease 138
Great Rock'n'Roll Swindle, The 89, 97, 102, 103
Grohl, Dave 51–2
Grundy, Bill 4, 85–104

Guildford Stranglers 116

Half Man Half Biscuit 115
Hall, Henry 130
Halliwell, Geri 35, 36, 119
Hamp, Johnny 6, 197–212
'Hand In Glove' 111
'Hang Out Your Washing On The Siegfried Line' 132
'Happy Hour' 114
Hard Day's Night, A 192, 198
Harriott, Joe 19
Harris, Bob 55, 61–2, 63–5, 67
Harris, 'Shakey' Jake 203
Harty, Russell 96
Harvey, Brian 31, 34, 39
Hawes, Keeley 164
Hayes, Isaac 60, 61
Head 61
Heatwave 154
'Heaven Knows I'm Miserable Now' 110–111
Hepworth, David 66
'Here's Looking At You' 1
Herman's Hermits 211
'He's Got The Whole World In His Hands' 210
Here We Go 191
Hideaways 204
Hill, Chris 151, 152, 153, 154, 155, 158
Hill, Harry 96
Hill, Roy 152, 155
'Hippy Hippy Shake' 184
History Of Britain 14
Hi-Tension 152, 154
Holiday Town Parade 180
Holland, Dave 22
Holland, Jools 65, 67
Hollies 211
Honeybus 57
Hooker, John Lee 202, 203
Hooligans And Thugs: Soccer's Most Violent Fan Fights 98
Hopkins, Lightnin' 204
Hot Chocolate 172
Hotel California 44, 45
House 163
House Of Love 115

Housemartins 114
Hulanicki, Barbara 82–3
Hullablaoo 78
Human League 107
Humes, Helen 203
Hustle 163

'I Could Write A Book' 183
'I Gotta Go Home' 157
'I Haven't Said Thanks For That Lovely
    Weekend' 131
I Hear The Blues 200
I Love The 1970s 15
'I Only Want To Be With You' 75
'I Should Have Known Better' 193
'I Wish I Knew How It Would Feel To Be
    Free' 169
'If I Fell' 193
'I'll Get You' 181
I'm A Celebrity, Get Me Out Of Here 99
'I'm Free' 115
'I'm Going To Get Lit Up' 130
'In My Cans' 146
In Search Of Myths And Heroes 14
'In The Air Tonight' 45, 48
In The Night Garden 216
Indie 105–19
Isaacs, Jeremy 198
It Ain't Half Hot, Mum 134–5
'It's A Young Man's World' 157
It's Little Richard 200–201
Ivor The Engine 215–16

Jab Jab 154
Jackson Five 60
Jackson, Jack 1
Jackson, Jump 203
Jacobs, David 74, 183
Jagger, Mick 28, 31, 38
Jam, The 64, 116, 154
James, Alex 106, 116, 117
Jansch, Bert 24
Jazz 15
Jazz News 204
Jazz 625 13
'Jean Genie, The' 171
Jesus And Mary Chain 108
Jesus Christ Superstar 138

John, Elton 31, 37–8, 60
John Lydon's Megabugs 99
Jones, Grace 96
Jones, Steve 85–6, 89–90, 94–5, 97–8, 101,
    102, 103, 104
Jones-Davies, Sue 148
Joshua Tree, The 44
Joy Division 108, 112
Joyce, Mike 106
Jubilee 88–9, 102
'Jubilee' 145
'Juke Box Gypsy' 155
Juke Box Jury 74, 84, 180, 183–5, 190, 201

Kandidate 152
Kerr, Patrick 79
Kershaw, Noreen 175
Kidd, Eddie 155
Kinch, Soweto 19
King, B. B. 64
King, Carole 173
'Kings Cross Blues' 155
Kinks 116
'Kiss Me Goodnight Sergeant Major' 133
'Kiss Me Quick' 183
Knowling, Ranson 204
Kongos, John 172
Krautrock 13

*Ladies And Gentlemen: The Fabulous
    Stains* 98
Ladybirds 60
Lamarr, Mark 117
Late Night Line Up 57, 61, 66
Late Show, The 57, 66, 115
Later...With Jools Holland 32, 57, 58, 60,
    66, 67, 84, 118
Lavender, Ian 129
Le Mesurier, John, 123–4
'Leave A Little Love' 77
'Leave It To The Kid' 155
Led Zeppelin 1, 45, 61, 62
Lennox, Annie 156
Lenska, Rula 142
Lewis, Jerry Lee 201
Lewis, Leona 1
'Lie Down, I Think I Love You' 156
Life On Mars 5–6, 161–75

'Life On Mars' 162–3, 166–8
Lightning Seeds 117, 228
'Lili Marlene' 133
Lindisfarne 155
Lindsay-Hogg, Michael 79
Lippmann, Horst 203
Little Dog Laughed, The 135
Little Ladies 137–48
'Little Red Rooster' 204
Live Aid 1
'Live And Let Die' 170
Lodger 116
'Long Live Love' 77
'Loose Change' 145
'Love Me Do' 179, 188, 202
'Love Of My Life' 51
'Love Of The Loved' 76
Lowe, Arthur 123–4
Lowe, Nick 153
'Lowlands Away' 18
L7 117
Lulu 4, 71–84
Lulu's Back In Town 84
Lurkers 152
Lush 116

MacDonald, Gus 198
McGee, Alan 118
McGhee, Brownie 201, 203, 204, 206,
    209–10
McGowan, Cathy 71, 73, 74, 76, 77, 79,
    80, 81–3, 84
Mackay, Andy 139, 140, 148
McKay, Helen 1
MacKiernan, Paddy 203
McLaren, Malcolm 88–9, 95, 97, 99
McLaughlin, John 22
McVie, Christine 49–50
McVie, John 50
Magical Mystery Tour 193
Make Up Your Mind 200
Mamas and Papas 60
Mame 138
Manfred Mann 57
Mansfield, Mike 199
Mantovani 130
Marion 116
Marley, Bob 172

Marr, Johnny 106, 111
Marshall, Tony 172
Martin, George 179
Matlock, Glen 85, 89, 94, 101
Matthew, Brian 74
Matthews, Sheila 1
Matumbi 153, 154
May, Brian 51
Meat Is Murder 110
Melody Maker 59, 106, 204
Men Behaving Badly 218
Menswear 116
Mercury, Freddie 51
Merger 155
Mermaid Frolics, The 151
Mersey Sound, The 189
Miami 7 137
Mighty Lemon Drops 108
Mighty Wah, The 112, 114
Miller, Jonathan 150
Minipops 113
Minogue, Kylie 108
'Misirlou' 162
Mission, The 112
Mitchell, Joni 173
Mojo 45
Monitor 13
Monkees 56
Monte Carlo Or Bust 151
Moondog Matinee 65
Moore, Dudley 150, 151, 193
Morecambe And Wise Show, The 192
Morrison, Van 55, 63
Morrissey 106, 109–11, 118
Morrissey, Neil 217
Most, Mickie 149
Motors 153, 155
Mott the Hoople 62
Mr Benn 215–16
MTV 1, 113–14
Music Of Lennon And McCartney, The
    192, 201
Music While You Work 130
'My Baby Just Cares For Me' 114
My Bloody Valentine 108
My Wildest Dream 200

Nashville Teens 201

Network 7 115
'Never Gonna Give You Up' 108
Never Mind The Bollocks Here's The Sex Pistols 102
Nevermind 51–2
New Musical Express 114, 106, 147–8
New Nightmare 91
New Order 60, 115
New Pop 107, 108–9, 110
New York Dolls 63–4
Nichols, Janice 201
Nicks, Stevie 49–50
Night At The Opera, A 44, 51
Nightingale, Annie 64
1940s House 14
Nirvana 51–2, 117
No Direction Home 15
'No Particular Place To Go' 203
'No-one Is Innocent' 154
Not Only...But Also 150, 193
'Not Such An Innocent Girl' 35
Novoselic, Krist 51–2
Number 73 109

Oasis 116, 117, 118, 217
Ocean Colour Scene 116, 118
O'Connor, Des 181
Off The Record 180
Oh Boy! 28, 56, 180, 199
'OK' 145, 146
Old Grey Whistle Test, The 3–4, 13, 55–67, 109, 111, 149, 150, 152, 155, 194
Oldfield, Mike 172
On A Clear Day You Can See Forever 138
100 Greatest Albums 15
One Life 34
Only Ones 157
Orange Juice 108
Orton, Beth 24
Osmonds 172
Our World 193
Over-nite Sensation 52
Owen, Alun 192, 198
Oxford Road Show, The 66, 112
O-Zone, The 66

Page, Jimmy 1
Palmer, Robert 114

'Panic' 106, 111
Panjabi, Archie 166
Parkinson, Michael 198
Pearson, Johnny 60
Pebble Mill At One 109
Peel, John 110
Pennies From Heaven 144, 145
'Penny Lane' 193
People And Places 189, 191, 200
People Like Us 60
Perry, Jimmy 124, 134
Pet Shop Boys 58
Pet Sounds 42–3, 44, 45
'Piccadilly Lights' 155
Pink Floyd 62
Pinter, Harold 198
Plastic Ono Band 41
Pleasant, Cousin Joe 201, 204, 206, 207
'Please Don't Ask' 48
'Please Please Me' 185, 188, 191
Pleasure At Her Majesty's 151
Police 64
Pop Go The Beatles 179
Pop Idol 28
Pop In 191
Pops And Lenny 189
Postcard Records 108, 112, 116
Postman Pat 6, 213–30
Potter, Dennis 139, 144
'Praise The Lord And Pass The Ammunition' 133
Pratt, Andy 61
Prefab Sprout 108
Presley, Elvis 55, 183
Private Eye 151
'Promised Land' 64
Public Image Ltd 64, 98
Pulp 116
Pulp Fiction 162
Punch Review, The 99

Quant, Mary 82
Quatro, Suzie 155, 173
Queen 51, 62, 87
Queer As Folk 141

Radcliffe, Mark 118
R&B Scene 209

Rau, Fritz 203
Ready Steady Go! 4, 28, 56, 58, 60, 71–84, 117, 149, 189, 192
Real Dad's Army, The 136
Red White And Bluegrass 64
Reddy Helen 172
Reed, Jimmy 203
'Reet Petite' 114
'Relax' 113
REM 108
Revolver 5, 58, 149–59
Rezillos 153
Rialto 116
Rich Kids 150, 157
Richard And Judy 99
Richard, Cliff 105, 199, 205
Rio 44, 45
Rise And Rise Of Michael Rimmer, The 151
'Riverboat Song, The' 118
'Road, The' 146–7
Robinson, Tom 150, 154
Rock And Roll Hall Of Fame 42
Rock And Roll Years, The 15, 64–5
Rock Follies 5, 137–48
Rock Goes To College 65
'Rocket Man' 38
'Rockin' Robin' 60
Rodgers, Clodagh 57
'Roll Out The Barrel' 130
'Rollercoaster' 146
Rolling Stone 42, 45, 58, 89
Rolling Stones 94, 101, 204
Ross, Jonathan 96
Ross, Les 152
Rotten, Johnny 85, 94, 97–9, 102–3, 104
Rough Trade Records 110
Roundup 192
Rourke, Andy 106
Roxy Music 62, 139
Royal Variety Performance 181–2, 184–5, 190
'Rule Britannia' 126
'Rules And Regulations' 115
Rumours 43–4, 49–50
'Run Rabbit Run' 135
Russell Harty Show, The 96
Rutles, The 5

Sandie Shaw Supplement, The 84
Sarah Sings And Basie Swings 200
Saturday Superstore 109
Scene At 6.30 73, 189, 192, 200
Schuman, Howard 139, 140, 141–2, 144, 148
Scott, Mike 198
Secret Policeman's Ball, The 151
Sensational Alex Harvey Band 62
Sesame Street 215
Seven Ages Of Rock, The 15
Seven Up 198
Sex Pistols 4, 64, 85–104, 149, 154, 156
Sgt Pepper's Lonely Hearts Club Band 42–3, 57
'Shadowplay' 112
'Shame Shame Shame' 203
Shaw, Sandie 4, 71–84, 111
'She Loves You' 181, 182, 185, 188, 193
Shine A Light 28
Shirts 155
'Shout' 77
Show Biz Kids 157
Simm, John 161
Simon, Rosemary 76
Simone, Nina 114, 169, 172
Sinatra, Frank, 199, 200
Singleton, Gay 79
Siouxsie Sue 86, 152
Sisters of Mercy 112
Six-Five Special 56, 73, 180, 199
625 Show, The 189
'Sledgehammer' 114
Sleeper 116
Slim, Memphis 200, 203
Small Faces 57
Smash Hits 106
Smith, Willie 204
Smiths 4, 105–119
Smiths, The: The Complete Picture 110
'Smokestack Lightning' 203
Snow White And The Seven Dwarfs 129
So It Goes 58, 112, 150
'Soft As Your Face' 115
Soft Machine 20
'Some Other Guy' 200
Something Else 66
Sopranos, The 163

Sore Throat 152–3
Sounds 102, 106
Soup Dragons 115
South Bank Show, The 115
Spandau Ballet 114
Spann, Otis 203, 204
Sparks 62
Spice Girls 35–6, 119
Spice World 119
Spooks 163
Spot The Tune 200
Springfields 72, 75, 76, 82
Springfield, Dusty 4, 71–84
'Stairway' 146–7
Star Parade 192
Stardust 140, 141
Starsky And Hutch (TV Series) 170
Starsky & Hutch (Movie) 173
Steel Pulse 150, 154
Steps 228
Stock-Aitken-Waterman 108
'Stone Fox Chase' 61
Stone Roses 115
Strange Days 91
Stranglers 152
'Strawberry Fields Forever' 193
Street-Porter, Janet 115
'Sugar Mountain' 146
Summer Holiday 205
Sunday Night At The London Palladium
    180–81, 184–5, 189, 190, 192, 194
Supersonic 58
Sweeney, The 164, 170
Sweet 170, 172
Swinging Blue Jeans 184
Synchronicity 44

Talking Heads 64
Tamla Motown 76
Taste Of Honey, A 198
Taupin, Bernie 60
Telegoons, The 180
Television Personalities 86, 96
'Tell Me Why' 193
Terry, Sonny 201, 203, 204, 206, 209–10
TFI Friday 117
Thank Your Lucky Stars 74, 84, 180, 189,
    191, 192, 201, 202

Tharpe, Sister Rosetta 201, 204, 206, 207,
    208–9
That Was The Week That Was 78
That's Entertainment 138
'There'll Always Be An England' 132
'This Charming Man' 109, 110, 111
This Is Spinal Tap 5
This Week 189
Thomas The Tank Engine 216–17
'Till There Was You' 182
Time Out 61
'Tiny Dancer' 60–61
Tippet, Keith 22
TL's Bluesicians 204
Today 4, 85–104
'Tokoloshe Man' 172
Tommy 138
Top Of The Pops 28, 55, 56, 58, 59, 60, 62,
    64, 66, 67, 74, 84, 104–7, 109–111,
    112, 114, 115, 117, 118, 119, 150,
    192
Topham, Mark 228
Total Recall 91
TOTP2 55, 105–6, 107
Tourists 156
Tracey, Stan 20
'Trampled Underfoot' 61
T. Rex 172
'True Faith' 115
Trueman, Brian 198
Trumpton 215
Tube, The 65, 84, 110, 111, 112–13, 114,
    117, 149, 150, 152, 157–8
Tubular Bells 61, 172
Tuesday Rendezvous 189, 191
Tutti Frutti 137
Twenty Five Years Of Rock 64
24 216–17, 227
Twigg, Karl 228
Twiggy 83
'Twist And Shout' 181, 182
Two Tone Records 112, 116
Tyler, Bonnie 152

Under Milk Wood 20
'Underneath The Arches' 134
U2 65–6

Variety 1
Vaughan, Sarah 200
Vibrators 152
Vicious, Sid 97
Victoria's Secrets 35
Vig, Butch 52
Vincent, Gene 201

Walker, T-Bone 202
'Walking Blues' 209
Warren, Don 216
'Waterfall' 115
Waters, Muddy 200, 201, 203, 204, 206,
        207, 209, 210
'We Don't Talk Anymore' 105
'We'll Gather Lilacs' 130
'We'll Meet Again' 130
Welling, Bob 96
Wedding Present 108
'Weekends' 114
Wellins, Bobby 20
Went The Day Well 128
Westbrook, Mike 22
Westlife 228
We've Got A Fuzzbox And We're Going
        To Use It 115
Wham! 180
'What Difference Does It Make' 106
Wheeltappers And Shunters Social Club,
        The 200
'Where's Bill Grundy Now' 86
White, Liz 168
'White Man In Hammersmith Palais' 156
White Room 118
'White Room' 169
Whitesnake 156
Who, The 168, 169, 172
'Who Do You Think You Are Kidding, Mr
        Hitler?' 134, 135
Who The Fuck Is Pete Doherty? 27, 32–4
Who Put The Bomp 58
'Whole Lotta Love' 1
Whole Lotta Shakin' Goin' On, A 201
Who's Next 43–4, 45

'Who's That Knocking On My Door?' 157
Wickham, Vicki 76, 77, 82
'Wild Children' 55
Williams, Richard 59, 60–61, 66
Williamson, Sonny Boy 200, 203, 204
Wilson, Jackie 114
Wilson, Tony 100, 111, 198
Willis, Bobby 76,
Willis, Ted 198
Winehouse, Amy 31–2, 34, 39
Wings 170, 172
'Wish Me Luck As You Wave Me
        Goodbye' 131
Wogan 109
Wolf, Howlin' 203, 204
Wood, Ivor 223
Woodgate, Simon 225
Woody Allen 201
Word, The 117–18
World In Action 28, 198
Worst Jobs In History, The 14
Wright, Steve 106
Wrong Box, The 151
Wyatt, Robert 20

X Factor, The 1, 7, 15, 28, 119
X-Ray Spex 154, 155
XTC 64, 150

Yates, Paula 65
Yes 43
'You Don't Have To Say You Love Me' 77
'You Wanna Be With Me Tonight' 156
'You're My World' 77
Young, Alex 201
Young, Muriel 199
Young Ones, The 205
YouTube 95, 119

Zappa, Dweezil 52
Zappa, Frank 52
'Zombie Rock' 153
Zoo Records 112, 116